The Art
of the
Illuminated Manuscript

Other books by David M. Robb:

Art in the Western World (with J. J. Garrison)
The Harper History of Painting

The Art
of the
Illuminated Manuscript

David M. Robb

THE PHILADELPHIA ART ALLIANCE

© 1973 by A. S. Barnes and Co., Inc.

Associated University Presses, Inc.
Cranbury, New Jersey 08512

Library of Congress Cataloging in Publication Data
Robb, David Metheny, 1903–

The art of the illuminated manuscript.
Bibliography: p.

1. Illumination of books and manuscripts—History.
I. Title.
ND2900.R63   091   78-37830
ISBN 0-87982-001-2

Printed in the United States of America

to

J. H. R.

Contents

List of Illustrations

Where not otherwise indicated, copyright in photographs belongs to the museum or library in which the book is located, by whose courtesy the reproduction is allowed.

Monochrome

Color

Preface

In writing this book, I have hoped to fill in some measure the long-standing need for a reasonably comprehensive descriptive and interpretive discussion, in English, of the illuminated manuscript as an art form. The bibliography of monographs on individual manuscripts, and of discussions of groups of manuscripts as parts of period studies, is extensive, as may be inferred from the selective listing given below. But much scholarship has changed many opinions since the most recent attempt to present an evaluation, such as the present one, of the illuminated manuscript as one of the distinctive efforts by man to record and glorify the thoughts that are the expression of one of his uniquely human capacities. This scholarship has been taken into account as far as possible.

The conception underlying the structure and content of this book is that of an interpretive essay, one that might accompany an exhibition in which any illuminated manuscript desired could be shown. There will probably be general agreement on the selection from the earlier periods; from the later periods of the Middle Ages a choice is not so easily made and, of necessity, books admired by many readers may not be found here. Nevertheless, those which have been chosen are known to the author, and have been decided upon for their effectiveness in illustrating certain points in the discussion. Books of the non-European artistic traditions, such as Oriental and Persian examples of illuminated manuscripts, have been excluded as beyond my province.

Friendly advice and encouragement in pursuing the researches involved in the writing of this book have come from many people. Philip Hofer, of the Houghton Library of Harvard College, provided many insights into the qualities of fine books that were of great value. Dorothy Miner, Keeper of Books of the Walters Art Gallery in Baltimore, has been a continuing and unfailing friend in giving advice and help that often brought new life into flagging inspiration. Rudolf Hirsch, associate director of the University of Pennsylvania Libraries, gave generously of his time and unique understanding of the problems of the book in mediaeval and Renaissance times; his kind yet firm criticism allowed errors in fact and judgment to be corrected before doing irreparable injury. It need not be said that such errors as may be found are those of the author and his alone. Some measure of the aid received from my mentors and friends, Charles Rufus Morey and Erwin Panofsky, is provided by the citations of their writings; impossible to measure but invaluable were the new understanding and perception gained from discussion with them and suggestions resulting therefrom, all of which have entered into the shaping of this book.

Without the cordial assistance and help provided by librarians and custodians of fine books in many places, the author's most hopeful intentions could not have been realized. Citation of the ownership of the books

from which miniatures have been illustrated must
suffice to acknowledge many of these favors, but particular thanks must go to the late Anselmo, Cardinal
Albareda, Prefect of the Biblioteca Apostolica of the
Vatican, and to the late Jean Porcher, conservateur en
chef of the department of manuscripts of the Bibliothèque Nationale in Paris for the privileges extended
by them. W. O. Hassall of the Bodleian Library of
Oxford University has been most helpful, as have the
authorities of the British Museum in London and the
John Pierpont Morgan Library in New York.

Aid of a most tangible kind in supporting the researches involved in the writing and illustration of this
book was provided by grants from the John Simon
Guggenheim Foundation and the American Philosophical Society of Philadelphia, and the award of Fulbright
Research Fellowships by the Committee on the International Exchange of Persons. These are gratefully
acknowledged.

I am indebted to Martha R. Spiegel for compiling
the indices of the text and the listing of manuscripts
cited in it. To the staff of the Associated University
Presses, and particularly to Mathilde E Finch, I extend
my thanks for the care with which the original type-
script was prepared for printing.

A comprehensive bibliography for each of the manuscripts discussed would have been disproportionately
large, but the references given have been selected to
provide recent citations of other sources. Abbreviations
of the most frequently cited titles follow.

AB—*Art Bulletin*
ABI—Weitzmann, K. *Ancient Book Illumination*
AM—Boeckler, A. *Abendländische Miniaturen*
BM—Meiss, M. *Painting in the Time of Jean de
    Berry; The Boucicaut Master.*

BP—Grabar, A. *Byzantine Painting*
CR—Hubert, J., Porcher, J. and Volbach, W. F.
    The Carolingian Renaissance
ECA—Morey, C. R. *Early Christian Art*
"ECM"—Morey, C. R. "Notes on East Christian
    Miniatures."
EDA—Hubert, J., Porcher, J. and Volbach, W. F.
    Europe in the Dark Ages
EMP—Grabar, A. and Nordenfalk, C. *Early Me-
    dieval Painting*
ENP—Panofsky, E. *Early Netherlandish Painting*
14th cent.—Meiss, M. *French Painting in the Time
    of Jean de Berry; The Late XIVth Century and
    the Patronage of the Duke*
GLP—Thompson, E. M. *An Introduction to Greek
    and Latin Palaeography*
IAECP—Henry, F. *Irish Art in the Early Christian
    Period*
IAVI—Henry, F. *Irish Art during the Viking Inva-
    sions*
IBMAR—Miner, D. *Illuminated Books of the Mid-
    dle Ages and Renaissance*
IRC—Weitzmann, K. *Illustrations in Roll and
    Codex*
MA—Morey, C. R. *Mediaeval Art*
MFM—Porcher, J. *Medieval French Miniatures*
MRA—Swarzenski, H. *Monuments of Romanesque
    Art*
PiBMA—Rickert, M. *Painting in Britain; The Mid-
    dle Ages*
RP—Grabar, A. and Nordenfalk, C. *Romanesque
    Painting*
SFRMP—*Bulletin de la Société française de repro-
    ductions de manuscrits à peintures*
SIM—Wattenbach, W. *Das Schriftwesen im Mittel-
    alter*

David M. Robb
6 November, 1971

Introduction

The books known as illuminated manuscripts, written and decorated or embellished by hand, have a threefold place in the story of man: in the history of books, the history of art, and the history of ideas. In the first category, they make up a body of material antedating and partly overlapping the beginnings of printing and so provide an essential background to the understanding of that means of recording and disseminating knowledge so fundamental in the modern world. In the history of art, illuminated manuscripts are important for two reasons. They are source material for the history of design and ornament for more than a millennium, and as the largest single category of painting during the Middle Ages, they provide works of pictorial art more nearly in original condition, unaffected by physical change or the restorer's hand, than any others of the time. And finally, as documents in the history of ideas, illuminated manuscripts illustrate, whether in paintings or drawings, the evolution of human knowledge, reflecting in their ever-changing forms and decoration the movements and reorientations of thought that underlie the kaleidoscopic patterns of succeeding generations of cultural evolution.

Pertinent to this last point is the fact that today, the illuminated manuscript is almost solely a historical phenomenon. The modern book, printed on a press and illustrated with reproductions of photographs or mechanically created copies of paintings or drawings is undeniably the lineal descendant of the illuminated manuscript. But the concept underlying this symbol of the post-mediaeval world is very different from that implicit in the handwritten and decorated volume of the Middle Ages. The very term *illumination,* defined in part by Webster as "rendering illustrious or causing to be resplendent," indicates that the spirit underlying this art is very different from the motivation of modern book illustration or decoration. For the written word is the direct manifestation of man's uniquely human ability to record and transmit thought—the gift that most of all distinguishes him from other animal life. And the inspiration to decorate and make more beautiful such symbols is the expression of the awe which this supernatural, even divine power once evoked. Illumination, the "causing of words to be resplendent," can be a creative process only when the written word is held in such high regard—whether simply because it exists or whether it is thought to be divinely inspired —that its form is appropriately made more illustrious. Such was the case in the world of classic antiquity, to some extent, but even more in the Middle Ages, periods when the very uniqueness of every book gave it value beyond anything conceivable today. This idea is not invalidated by the fact that many undecorated books were made in those times; the concept of the embellished word can exist only when the word itself has more than literal meaning and significance.

Two distinctive types of book were known in the ancient world—the *rotulus* or scroll, and the *codex* or flat-leaved book. It is almost certain that the rotulus came into use before the codex, at least it was the form employed in Egypt for copies of the *Book of the Dead* written as early as the fourth millennium B.C. Egyptian scrolls were written on papyrus, material made from the stems of marsh plants or reeds (*cyperus papyrus*) grown along the shores of the Nile.[1] This vegetable substance, comparable in some characteristics to paper, was best employed in scroll form, for it was comparatively fragile and little resistant to folding. But it could be rolled in considerable lengths (as much as 150 feet, although the normal full length seems not to have been much more than 30)[2] on spindles which were turned from hand to hand, exposing the text written in vertical columns. Although the rotulus was only sparingly employed after the fourth century A.D.,[3] a number of terms derived from it are still in use. Since it was turned on spindles while being read, it was known as a *volumen,* from the Latin *volvere* meaning "to turn," whence *volume* as a synonym for book. The opening or unfolding of a scroll was described by the verb *explicare;* the end of the text was indicated by *liber explicit,* a term which appears at the conclusion of many chapters or sections of books in codex form. A scroll was usually labeled on a strip of material attached to one of the spindles, called a *titulus* or title. A brief indication of the contents might also appear; it was called the *index.*[4]

The *codex,* made up of flat leaves or pieces fastened together on one edge or margin, was a book form known quite early in hinged wooden or clay tablets, the inner surfaces of which were coated with wax to receive writing by a sharp instrument or *stylus.*[5] Writing in the first century A.D., Seneca (*De brevitate vitae* 13) speaks of such a gathering of writing tablets as a *caudex,* a term used for pieces of wood split from a tree trunk. Coming into general use with the advent of parchment as a writing material, the earliest examples are small books, used for diaries, notations of accounts and the like. Literary codices were still comparatively rare in the second and third centuries A.D.[6] But the gradual supersession of papyrus by parchment as a writing material by the fourth century A.D. (at least outside Egypt) led to the almost complete replacement of the rotulus by the codex, and this has been the case from that time on in the Occident, with the exception of occasional formal or official documents, diplomas and the like.

It is not without significance in this connection that the codex was preferred for Christian texts from earliest times, even in the case of Greek manuscripts for which the Hebraic tradition of the scroll might have been considered a determining factor. Practical elements contributed to this as well. Only one side (recto) of a scroll could be written upon. A few scrolls with writing on the other side (verso) are known,[7] but usually only when the original text had been discarded and the scroll was being reused. Greater facility in storing codices was also in their favor, as well as in indexing and the finding of specific passages in the text. Problems of editing and correcting were also more easily solved when it was a question of changing or replacing a single sheet rather than cutting and splicing a roll. This appears to have been a particularly important consideration when the authenticity of a text was in question.[8]

Codices of papyrus are not unknown,[9] but for the reasons given above, parchment was the material preferred for this book form. Made from animal skins like calf, sheep, or goat, this substance, by its toughness and flexibility, was particularly well suited for use in leaved books. Denser and less absorbent than papyrus, it had very considerable advantages for the illuminator as well as the scribe, not least of which was greater ease in making corrections. The animal skins were cleaned, dried, smoothed, and polished, producing parchment that varied in character and quality depending on the kind of skin and the care taken in processing it.[10] The earliest parchment known in Latin manuscripts is rather dark, brittle, and harsh in texture. But as production processes were developed in the fourth century, the material improved in quality, becoming lighter in color, more uniform in thickness and texture, and more flexible. During the sixth and seventh centuries, increasing demands were often met with less well-produced parchment, mottled in color, rough in texture, and often rather ragged, but in subsequent periods, the quality is generally higher. Some late mediaeval and Renaissance manuscripts are written on an exquisitely thin and uniformly white parchment called uterine vellum, supposedly made from the skins of unborn, but more likely, of very young, animals, or, possibly, of rabbit skins. Certain regional differences in parchment may also be noted, though of a very general character. Italian and Spanish parchments tend to be somewhat lighter in color and thinner than French and German, which are usually darker and heavier. Much English parchment has a velvety surface texture. Vellum is a term often used as a synonym for parchment, but more accurately designates the lighter and more delicate types made from younger animals.[11]

Pliny the Younger records a tradition[12] that parchment was first developed as a writing material by Eumenes II of Pergamum (197–158 B.C.) when the Ptolemaic rulers of Egypt refused to send him papyrus for fear it would be used for books to create a greater library than the one at Alexandria. Although it is certain that animal skins were used for writing material earlier than that time, the term *pergamena* referring to parchment appears as early as the fourth century A.D.,[13] which association identifies the city in Asia Minor with the material. In addition to fragments that can be dated around the beginning of the first century A.D.,[14] there is literary testimony to its use at that time. In the *Epistle to Timothy* (II:4, 13), Paul writes explicitly: "bring with thee ... the books, but especially the parchments." Martial writes in the *Epigrammata* (i.2; xiv. 184, 186, 190, 192) of the works of Homer, Vergil, and others *in membranis* (a word also meaning parchment in Latin), a reference in the first century A.D. Although, as remarked above, parchment began to replace papyrus as writing material even before the fourth century A.D., its use for documents does not seem to have begun for some time thereafter, although this may be a question of survival. Among the oldest surviving official parchments is the foundation charter in 670 of the monastery at Bruyère-le-Château. The most ancient Italian document on parchment, in the Archivio di Stato in Milan, is dated 716.

Documentary parchment is usually smoothed only on the flesh side, since but one surface is written on. Codex parchment, however, is finished on both sides, that from which the hair has been scraped being usually somewhat darker and rougher than the other. Differences could be minimized by arranging the sheets with hair side to hair side and flesh side facing flesh side. De luxe volumes are generally noteworthy for the uniformity of the parchment leaves in color, texture, and thickness, while more utilitarian books may show considerable variety in these respects. It is not uncommon to find holes in the parchment, left by encysted larvae of the burrowing warble fly. Another factor affecting the substance of codex parchment was the occasional practice of erasing the text of old or outmoded books and reusing the sheets. Books made of such reemployed parchment are called *codices rescripti* or palimpsests; the practice was most frequent when new parchment was scarce and costly, e.g., in the seventh and eighth centuries A.D.

In making a book, parchment sheets were folded to the desired size and assembled in groups or gatherings. A gathering of four sheets doubled to make eight leaves or sixteen pages is the most common; it is called a quaternion. Two sheets thus folded form a binion, three sheets a ternion, five sheets a quinion, and so on. There was no uniform practice with regard to gathering patterns, even in specific scriptoria or writing establishments, but it is often possible to distinguish the hands of individual scribes and the styles of different illuminators by determining the separate gatherings of a manuscript. This can be done, of course, only if the quires have not been separated for rebinding or other reason, as has happened, for instance, with the Book of Kells. In the later commercial production of manuscripts, scribes and illuminators were paid by gatherings for their work, the individual unit being called a *pecia*.[15] It was also by gatherings that a codex was indexed at times. The usual practice now designates the leaves as *folios,* the right page of an opening being the *recto,* the left the *verso.* Thus a given sheet will be numbered *247 recto* or simply *247,* but its reverse side must always be designated *247 verso* or, abbreviated, 247vo or 247v. When the separate gatherings of a codex were completed, each one was sewed individually through the folded edges, and then assembled and provided with a cover, often elaborately decorated if it was a particularly important or costly volume.

The decoration or embellishment of the text pages in a manuscript is generally called *illumination.* At its simplest, this may be nothing more than an enlarged capital letter at the beginning of a chapter or section of the text. Often the heading or initial line of such a textual unit may be written in red to distinguish it from the black or brown of the other lines. Such a red line is called a *rubric,* from the Latin *rubrica* meaning sanguine or red chalk,[16] the material from which red ink or paint was made. The term rubric is also used for the marginal indications of the responses in a liturgical manuscript, and in the directions for the conduct of a service in similar texts, for these too were frequently written in red. The practice of executing the text of certain luxury volumes in gold or silver may also be termed illumination, particularly when on parchment dyed purple or some other dark color (cf. Fig. 8). The concept of illumination implicit in this discussion is also realized in a highly original form in the elaboration of initial letters to the scale of full-page designs, a practice which can be seen in one of its most original manifestations in Celtic manuscripts of the eighth and ninth centuries like the Book of Kells (Fig. 49).

The term illumination also is used for the illustration of texts by figured compositions or designs which are called *miniatures.* This term, somewhat misleading in modern times since it is also applied to small portraits painted on ivory or gold and the like, seems to have been used but rarely in the Middle Ages in the sense it has in this discussion, although it has a perfectly acceptable Latin etymology. Du Cange[17] defines it with the phrase *minigraphia scriptura cum minio ficta,* the word *minium* meaning orange lead,[18] which was also used as the pigment for rubrics. However, the term *miniature* is so widely used as meaning the illustration of manuscripts, that the possible confusion with the type of small portrait referred to above is not a sufficient reason to give it up.

Miniatures in mediaeval manuscripts were executed with the techniques common to mediaeval painting in general.[19] A number of handbooks or technical treatises used in the Middle Ages are known, and these, along with the evidence supplied by unfinished or broken-down miniatures, are helpful indications of the procedures followed. Usually the text was written first, with spaces reserved for illuminated miniatures and initials. Frequently the scribe indicated the subject to be painted on the space it was to occupy,[20] or gave some clue to it in a marginal note.[21] Simple outline sketches sometimes served the same purpose.[22]

There were many and various practices in the use of models or patterns for composing miniatures. Most frequently, it would appear, the illuminator was given an example, which he followed as faithfully as possible or adapted to his own style. One of the most noteworthy instances of this was the copying or adaptation of the drawings in the Utrecht Psalter (Utrecht: University Library, Script. eccl. 484. Fig. 61, Plate VII) in three later manuscripts (London, B.M., ms. Harley 603, Fig. 91), (Cambridge, Trinity College Library, ms. R 17 1, Fig. 115), (Paris, B.N. ms. lat. 8846, Fig. 117). Cases are also known, particularly in later times, where patterns were reproduced more or less mechanically by tracing or pouncing, in which tiny holes

punctured along the outlines of the model provided guide lines for the copy.[23]

Considerable variety is also found in the actual methods of applying the pigments of miniatures to the parchment folio. In Byzantine illumination until about the eleventh century, they were usually painted directly on the parchment, without a preliminary ground. In cases where such manuscripts have been used a great deal, like the Cosmas Indicopleustes in the Vatican Library,[24] or the Sermons of Gregory of Nazianzus (Fig. 18) in the Bibliothèque Nationale of Paris, the thick pigments have flaked or worn off so much that some compositions are almost unintelligible. Later Byzantine practice, especially in de luxe volumes like the Menologion of Basil II (Fig. 25), also in the Vatican Library (Ms. gr. 1613), was usually more sound, the surfaces to be painted being prepared, or "grounded," to receive the pigments, with more stable results. The early Byzantine illuminators seem to have preferred pigments, largely of mineral origin, that were opaque, and applied them very thickly, a fact chiefly responsible for the frequent deterioration of the painted surfaces. Painting directly on the parchment is also found in early mediaeval illumination in western Europe, e.g., the Gelasian Sacramentary (Fig. 37) in the Vatican (Ms. Reg. lat. 316), but the pigments used (probably of vegetable origin) are much thinner, and lie on the painted surface more like watercolors than the heavy Byzantine impastos. It is not uncommon, however, for such pigments to penetrate the parchment to stain the opposite side; a case in point is a Celtic manuscript in the Vatican Library (Ms. Barb. lat. 570, f.79^{r-v}).[25] On the Continent, it was usual by Carolingian times to prepare the surface to be painted with a priming coat or ground, and more opaque colors also come into more general use, although no comprehensive generalization can be made on this score. When a ground was used, the procedure was not unlike that described in mediaeval handbooks for painting in tempera on panels.[26] For the ground, which is opaque as a rule, various colors may be used in one and the same miniature.[27] Many manuscripts are decorated with line drawings, which are equally termed miniatures. In the Utrecht Psalter, for example (Fig. 61, Plate VII), the illustrations were executed in brownish ink, while some of the subsequent copies used linear patterns of various colors.[28]

The use of gold and silver in manuscript illumination

also appears quite early in miniatures as well as for the text. There are gold highlights in the trees portrayed in the Vatican Vergil, for instance (Fig. 3), and it was also used in the diamond-shaped decorative accents in the borders. Byzantine illuminators used gold for appropriate details at a very early date (Fig. 6), but it is not much found in western Europe until the ninth century. Even then, it is restricted for the most part to nimbi and ornamental details, applied with a thin adhesive to the parchment and taking its texture from the base. It consequently has a matte surface, an example in point being the miniature on f.1 of Charles the Bald's Bible in the library of San Paolo fuori le Mura in Rome.[29] The gold backgrounds of mid-Byzantine miniatures like those of Basil II's Menologion (Fig. 25) were often burnished, but this practice does not appear generally in western European illumination until the later twelfth century, and then after Byzantine precedent.[30] Silver was sometimes used in much the same way, but unless particular precautions were taken to prevent oxydizing, the inevitable darkening of the metal was a disadvantage. Another limiting factor in the use of silver in illumination can be seen in many Celtic and English manuscripts where it has combined with its adhesive support and become corrosive, eating away the parchment underneath.[31] It can, however, remain stable when the oxydizing has been prevented; an example can be seen in the early thirteenth-century Berthold Missal (Fig. 120).[32]

A miniature of Ezra rewriting the sacred texts on f.5a of the Codex Amiatinus in the Laurentian Library of Florence (Fig. 42, Plate IV) gives an idea of the equipment used by a scribe in Early Christian times, and, presumably, when the manuscript itself was made toward the end of the seventh century. He is seated in front of a tall cabinet, on whose shelves are a number of codices. He writes with a large pen in another supported on his knees. On a low table in front of him is a bowl containing unidentifiable objects but possibly including a sponge to dampen the parchment; beside the table, on the floor, are an open codex, an inkwell, and, nearby, a pair of compasses. A little more elaborate is the scriptorium in a miniature representing St. Mark in a tenth-century Byzantine Gospel-book, also in the Laurenziana:[33] there is a knife to sharpen pens, a large metal blade for erasing, a lectern, and additional parchment folios and bottles of ink or color in the cabinet under the writing desk. Illustrations like these[34]

are vivid complements to the formulas for preparing and applying gold and colors given in the practical handbooks that have been preserved. For even the most detailed and specific of these, like the *De arte illuminandi*,[35] an Italian treatise of the late fourteenth century, assume knowledge of the proper tools and give no account of what they are.[36]

Relatively little is known of the circumstances of manuscript production in late antiquity, but it can be assumed to have been the work of professional scribes and illustrators. An example in point is the almanac called the Chronograph of the Year 354,[37] known today through copies made in the sixteenth (Vienna, NB, ms. 3416) and seventeenth centuries (Vatican, Bibl. Apost., ms. Barb. lat. 2154) of ninth-century copies of the original. This latter was made by Furius Dionysius Filocalus, a professional calligrapher known otherwise as the epigrapher who assisted Pope Damasus (366–384) in creating a monumental style of inscriptions for the tombs of the saints. During the early Middle Ages, Byzantine book production presumably continued to be in professional hands to some extent, but in Western Europe, it was almost entirely an activity of the Church,[38] and the scriptoria were almost without exception in monasteries and cathedral centers. C. R. Morey has pointed out[39] that at least three books were necessary to conduct religious services—a psalter, a Gospel book, and a sacramentary in which scriptural passages read in the Mass were gathered—and that only in ecclesiastical libraries were they available either for use in the service or for copying. Not until the closing years of the thirteenth century does the secular illuminator appear on the scene, and the decoration of manuscripts becomes almost entirely professional.

Yet, for all the impersonal anonymity of their creation, the manuscripts of the Middle Ages occasionally contain clues to the feelings of their creators. The *explicit,* or colophon as it is also called at the end of a manuscript of the *Dialogues of Pope Gregory* (Milan, Amb. ms. B. 159),[40] contains the information that it was written during the abbacy of a certain Anastasius, who is believed to have been in the north Italian monastery at Bobbio around the middle of the eighth century. The scribe, George by name, then requests the reader to be indulgent of any errors he may have made and to pray forgiveness for his sins, and concludes: "As the sailor longs for a safe haven at the end of his voyage, so does the writer for the last word!" Even more poignant are the closing lines, written by Prior Petrus, of a manuscript of the Beatus Commentary on the Apocalypse (London, B.M., ms. Add. 11, 695) executed between 1091 and 1109 at the monastery of Santo Domingo de Silos in Spain:[41] "A man who knows not how to write may think this no great feat. But only try to do it yourself and you will learn how arduous is the writer's task. It dims your eyes, makes your back ache, and knits your chest and belly together—it is a terrible ordeal for the whole body. So, gentle reader, turn these pages carefully and keep your finger far from the text. For just as hail plays havoc with the fruits of spring, so a careless reader is a bane to books and writing."

Prior Petrus contributed to the illumination of the Silos Beatus as well as composing its colophon, but the majority of early *expliciti*[42] refer only to the scribe. Among the earliest, if not, indeed, actually the first, known names of mediaeval illuminators is that of Adelricus, a monk in the northern French monastery of Corvey. He identifies himself in an inscription on the frame of a rack with the masks of the *dramatis personae*[43] at the beginning of one of the plays of Terence —the *Andria*—in a manuscript in the Vatican Biblioteca Apostolica (Ms. lat. 3868, f.3). The scribe, Hrodgarius, is also identified, in the colophon on f.92, and the manuscript dates from the abbacy of Adelardus at Corvey, between 822 and 826. Not until the middle of the thirteenth century are illuminators mentioned with anything like the frequency of earlier references to scribes, a point of some interest in its implication of the relative importance of words and pictures in the mediaeval book. Impressive and striking as the embellishment of the word may be, it is the significance of the word that its decoration is intended to emphasize and make clear.

NOTES

1. E. M. Thompson, *An Introduction to Greek and Latin Palaeography* (London: Oxford University Press, 1912), pp. 21–27. (Hereafter cited as *GLP.*)

2. *GLP,* p. 46.

3. For official documents, diplomas, etc., cf. W. Wattenbach, *Das Schriftwesen im Mittelalter,* 4 Auflage (Graz: Akademische Druck-u. Verlagsanstalt, 1958 reprint), pp. 150–74. (Hereafter cited as *SIM.*)

4. *GLP,* pp. 44–53.

5. *GLP,* pp. 13–20.

6. On the early history of the codex, see C. H. Roberts, "The Codex," *Proceedings of the British Academy,* 40 (1954):169–204.

7. Cf. Roberts, pp. 185–87, 194.

8. *Ibid.,* pp. 200–201.

9. *Ibid.,* pp. 182 ff.

10. *GLP,* pp. 28–34. Cf. also D. V. Thompson, *The Materials of Medieval Painting* (London: Allen & Unwin, 1936), pp. 24–30, and Virginia Wylie Egbert, *The Medieval Artist at Work* (Princeton: Princeton University Press, 1967).

11. *GLP,* p. 29.

12. *Nat. Hist.* 13:11 (21).

13. *GLP,* p. 28.

14. Roberts, p. 173, n. 1.

15. *SIM,* p. 185.

16. *SIM,* pp. 244–51, 344–48.

17. D. DuCange, *Glossarium medie et infimae latinitatis* (Paris: Firmin Didot, 1845), 4:413.

18. D. V. Thompson, *Materials of Medieval Painting,* pp. 100–102. H. Roosen-Runge, *Farbgebung und Technik frühmittelalterliche Buchmalerei,* 2 vols. (Munich-Berlin: Deutscher Kunstverl. 4. Kunstwissenshaftliche Studien, Bd. 38, 1967), 1:62–64.

19. Cf. in addition to citations in n. 18, D. V. Thompson, Jr., and G. H. Hamilton, *De Arte Illuminandi* (New Haven: Yale University Press, 1933). G. H. Hawthorne and C. S. Smith, *On Divers Arts; the Treatise of Theophilus* (Chicago: University of Chicago Press, 1963).

20. A. Grabar and C. Nordenfalk, *Early Medieval Painting,* (New York: Skira. 1957), pp. 92–93. Cf. also *SIM,* p. 372.

21. E.g., Vatican Bibl. Apost. Ms. lat. 1122, a collection of treatises by Iohannis de Ienzenstein, archbishop of Prague between 1397 and 1410, with numerous marginal instructions.

22. Cf. the Bible of Jean de Sy, Paris, BN, Ms. fr. 15397 in H. Martin, *La miniature française du XIIIe au XVe siècle* (Paris-Brussels: van Oest, 1923), figs. lix–lxiv.

23. H. Lehmann-Haupt, with S. A. Ives, *An English Thirteenth Century Breviary* (New York: H. P. Kraus, 1942). D. J. A. Ross, "Methods of Book-Production in a XIVth Century French Miscellany," *Scriptorium* 6 (1952):63–75.

24. C. Stornaiolo, *Le miniature della Topografia Cristiana di Cosma Indicopleuste; codice Vaticano greco 699* (Milan, 1908).

25. Cf. G. L. Micheli, *L'enluminure du haut Moyen-age et les influences irlandaises* (Brussels: Editions de la Connaissance, 1939), pp. 28–29, pls. 66, 75. An exhaustive analysis of Celtic illuminating techniques by Heinz Roosen-Runge appears in *Evangeliorum Quattuor Codex Lindisfarnensis,* 2 vols. (Olten-Lausanne: Urs Graf, 1956–60).

26. Cf. n. 19.

27. Cf. D. Miner, "A Late Reichenau Evangeliary in the Walters Gallery Library," *AB* 18 (1936):168–85.

28. Cf. a compendium of canon law in the Biblioteca Capitolare of Vercelli, Ms. CLXV, in J. Hubert, J. Porcher, and W. F. Volbach, *Europe in the Dark Ages* (London: Thames & Hudson, 1969), figs. 156–61; a Life of St. Cuthbert, Oxford, Ms. Univ. Coll. 165

in *English Romanesque Illumination* (Oxford: Bodleian, 1951), pl. 6 a–b; a glossed Jeremiah's Lament by Gislebertus of Auxerre, Baltimore, Walters Ms. 30 in D. Miner, *Illuminated Books of the Middle Ages and Renaissance* (Baltimore: Walters Art Gallery, 1949), fig. 28.

29. Cf. *CR,* fig. 130.

30. W. Oakeshott, *The Artists of the Winchester Bible* (London: Faber & Faber, 1945); Roosen-Runge, *Farbg. u. Tech.* 1: 130–31.

31. *EMP,* p. 181.

32. H. Swarzenski, *The Berthold Missal* (New York: Morgan Library, 1943), frontispiece.

33. Ms. Med. Palat. 244; D. Formaggio and C. Basso, *La Miniatura* (Novara: Istituto Geografico de Agostini, 1960), pl. 2.

34. Cf. also A. Grabar and C. Nordenfalk, *Romanesque Painting* (New York: Skira, 1958), p. 204.

35. Naples, BN, Ms. xii. E. 27; cf. n. 19.

36. *SIM,* pp. 219–32.

37. J. Strzygowski, *Die Kalendarbilder des Chronographen vom Jahre 354,* Jahrb. d. Kais. Deutschen Archälog. (Berlin: Instituts, Erganzungsheft i, 1888). C. Nordenfalk, *Der Kalendar vom Jahre 354 und die lateinische Buchmalerei des 4. Jahrh.* D. Levi, "Allegories of the Months in Classical Art," *AB* 23 (1941), pp. 251–91. H. Stern, *Le Calendrier de 354: étude sur son texte et sur ses illustrations,* vol. 55. (Paris: Institut français d'archéologie de Beyrouth, Bibliothèque archéologique et historique, 1953.

38. Cf. Roberts, "The Codex," p. 204.

39. C. R. Morey, *Mediaeval Art* (New York: Norton, 1942), p. 195.

40. E. H. Zimmerman, *Vorkarolingische Miniaturen,* 5 vols. (Berlin: Deutsche Vereins für Kunstwissenschaft, Hiersemann, 1916–18).

41. *EMP,* p. 168.

42. *SIM,* pp. 278–93, 491–534.

43. L. W. Jones and C. R. Morey, *The Miniatures of the Manuscripts of Terence,* 2 vols. (Princeton: Princeton University Press, 1930–31).

The Art
of the
Illuminated Manuscript

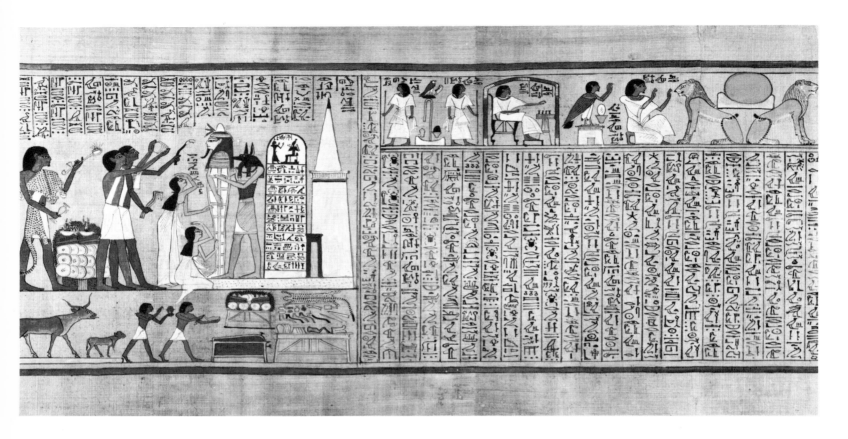

Fig. 1 a-b.
London, British Museum, Pap. 9901, sections 3, 5. The
Book of the Dead of Hunefer, Judgment Scenes.

I

Origins and Early Forms of Manuscript Illumination

One of the earliest known types of book illustration is seen in the scrolls or rotuli of papyrus with the text of the Book of the Dead[1] that were placed in Egyptian tombs to serve the spirits of the dead as guides on their journey to judgment in the underworld. Although the text of the Book of the Dead is known as early as the Vth Dynasty, illustrated papyrus examples like that of Hunefer (Fig. 1) in the British Museum in London (Pap. 9901) began to appear in the XVIIIth Dynasty, around 1400 B.C. The earliest examples have the text written in vertical columns of linear hieroglyphs, reading from right to left. The illustrations are arranged in a frieze at the top for some passages but the text columns are occasionally interrupted by large scenes. These portray the various judgments to be passed upon the soul at indicated points on its passage through the underworld. A little later, in the XXIst Dynasty, the vertical hieroglyphic script columns change to horizontal lines,[2] the so-called hieratic type, and the illustrations are placed at the top of the scroll.

Three elements must be taken into account in evaluating the Book of the Dead as an example of book illustration—the text, the vignettes or illustrations, and its physical qualities of form and material. It hardly needs to be pointed out that the hieroglyphic script originated in pictorial images which were subsequently conventionalized into more stylized forms. From the outset, then, pictorial imagery was a factor in the visual character of the overall scheme. When the vignettes took their place with the text, they were only an augmentation of ideas pictorially stated from the beginning. In a word, there is fundamental consistency and harmony between text and illustration in the Egyptian Book of the Dead. The form of the book was also a factor in establishing the relationship between text and illustration. A scroll or rotulus, its physical form was determined by the papyrus of which it was made. As mentioned above, the nature of papyrus is such that it lends itself particularly well to making long strips attached to spindles at the ends, the book being read by turning the scroll—from left to right in Egyptian examples—to expose the successive columns of hieroglyphs and their illustrations. Both the continuous friezes and the occasional inserted illustrations of the Hunefer scroll are thus in direct relationship to the pertinent text.

The Book of the Dead was not the only text illustrated by the Egyptians, though many more of them are known than any other. The case was quite different in the classical world, so far as can be determined from existent material and the conclusions drawn from it. Recent studies,[3] though not without some debatable or controversial conclusions, present reasonable hypotheses. The evidence is scant, since early classical texts of all sorts were presumably written on papyrus scrolls, and the dry, warm climate that favored their preservation in Egypt did not exist in classical lands. Nonetheless, some facts seem to be established beyond reasonable doubt.

It is highly probable, for example, that technical and scientific books must have been illustrated from very early times.[4] A treatise on flowers or herbs, for example, could hardly be used without pictures. Mathematical, anatomical, and engineering manuals, as well as astronomical texts, also required illustration, some of which are known today through later copies. Weitzmann has argued, moreover, by ingenious reconstruction from other media such as decorated vases and relief carvings, the probability that literary texts—epic, dramatic, poetic, and the like—must also have been illustrated at times, whether the book was a scroll or codex. In a dramatic text, illustrations would have the same function as in technical treatises, providing the reader with a chart, so to speak, of the figures in a given scene.

But other Greek literary texts were also illustrated, as can be seen in a fragment of a second-century A.D. scroll (Fig. 2) in the Bibliothèque Nationale in Paris (Cod. suppl. gr. 1294). The text has not been identified, but it is that of a romance. It is written in horizontal lines arranged in columns, of which portions of three are shown in the illustration. Drawings of people interrupt the text, placed at the points where their actions are discussed. Such being the relationship, it follows that the illustrations are subordinate to the text, a point borne out by their rather sketchy style. The figures have heavy outlines filled in with patches of gray-blue and pink, all painted directly on the papyrus, without indication of setting or background, and unframed.

The papyrus fragment in Paris was probably part of a scroll, the total length of which cannot even be guessed. Weitzmann has suggested[5] that a fully illustrated *Iliad* might have had as many as seven hundred and twenty illustrations; this number was arrived at from his analysis of subjects on decorated bowls and tablets and their distribution through the epic. It can be assumed that each of the twenty-four books of the poem would be a separate scroll. His reconstruction of the appearance of part of such a scroll,[6] supported by evidence including the Paris papyrus fragment and others, assumes columns of text, written in horizontal lines of such length that a section of text with illustration exposed at a given time would be in width approximately four-fifths of its height. Even in the tattered papyrus fragment, it can be seen that such a unit of text and illustration has a format not unlike that of a single page in the other basic type of book—the codex.

The early history of the codex, or flat-leaved book with hinged pages, has been touched on above. It is more than coincidental that it began to come into use by the late first century A.D. at a time when papyrus, the major material of writing in the ancient Mediterranean world, was being gradually replaced by animal membranes like parchment and vellum. By their very nature, such materials lent themselves better to the arrangement of hinged leaves or folios that is a codex than to the scroll form, although parchment rotuli are not unknown in later times.[7] In any event, whatever the contributive reasons, the codex appears almost completely to have superseded the rotulus as the principal

Fig. 2.
Paris, Bibliothèque Nationale, Cod. suppl. gr. 1294. Fragment of an Illustrated Romance.

book form in the Western world by the fourth century A.D.

It is also certain from literary evidence that such books were illustrated in quite early times. Martial writes in the *Epigrams,* toward the end of the first century A.D.,[8] of a parchment copy of Vergil's works (*Vergilius in membranis*) that he admired for its compactness (*Quam brevis immensum cepit membrana Maronem*), and also states that a portrait of the author was its frontispiece (*Ipsius et vultus prima tabella gerit*). No illustrated codices of such early date have survived, but the character of this miniature can be imagined from later copies of similar works. One of these is the portrait of Terence (Fig. 57) painted by Adelricus on f.2 of the manuscript in the Vatican Library (Vat. lat. 3868), referred to earlier. Weitzmann proposes[9] that a portrait like the one in the Vatican Terence—a bust in a circular border resembling a medallion but set in a square frame on a pedestal—may have been an elaboration of the author likenesses found in great numbers in categorical treatises like a late Byzantine medical manuscript in the Ambrosian Library at Milan (Cod. E 37 *sup*), in which more than sixty famous physicians are portrayed in medallion busts inserted in narrow text columns. However this may have been, there can be no doubt that scribes and illustrators were confronted by a compositional problem in the codex page or folio, with its fixed proportions, different from that posed by the relatively limitless lateral extension possible in the rotulus form. Although the solutions reached undoubtedly owed something to traditions established in the illustrating of papyrus rotuli, it is clear that a different conception of the relationship of words and pictures came into being with the illustrated codex.

The oldest known illustrated manuscripts—all fragments of codices—are five in number. They are the *Itala* of Quedlinburg (Berlin, Deutsche Staatsbibliothek, Ms. Theol. lat. fol. 485), the Vatican Vergil (Bibl. Apost., Ms. lat. 3225), the Ambrosian Iliad (Milan, Bibl. Ambrosiana, Cod. F 205 inf.), another Vergil in the Vatican Library known as the *Codex Romanus* (Ms. lat. 3867), and the so-called *Agrimensoria* in the Landesbibliothek at Wolfenbüttel in Germany (Cod. 36.23. Aug. fol.). Although there are differences of opinion about the dating of these manuscripts, it is generally agreed that none are earlier than the latter part of the fourth century for the first (the *Itala* frag-

ment), and that the *Agrimensoria* is the latest, from the early sixth century. The Vatican Vergil and the Ambrosian Iliad are thought to be from the first half of the fifth century, and the *Codex Romanus* a little later in the same period. The *Itala* fragment text is of a portion of the Old Testament, but the others are classical and secular, as their names indicate, the *Agrimensoria* being a compilation of treatises on land surveying.

The *Itala* of Quedlinburg[10] consists of five folios once part of a codex that probably contained the four Books of the Kings in the Old Testament. The text is in the Itala version that was in general use before the revision known as the Vulgate, and the folios were found in the Saxon town of Quedlinburg. Unfortunately, the circumstances of the preservation of this oldest extant example of Old Testament illustration were also responsible for its damaged condition, the parchment sheets having been used in the seventeenth century to bind other volumes. It is still possible to make out the general scheme and some of the details. The illustrations on f.2 (Fig. 3) are for 1 Samuel 15:12–33, the account of the slaying of the Amalekites and their king Agag by Saul. The several episodes are shown in panels with red-banded frames, each appearing as if seen through the pane of a window in a landscape setting, the four scenes filling the greater part of the folio, which is almost square. Where the pigment has flaked or been rubbed off, the preliminary drawings of the compositions can be seen, and also written instructions to the artist as to what should be represented. Thus, in the lower right panel where Samuel is slaying Agag, the instruction reads: "make the city here, and outside, to the right, show the prophet slaying king Agag." Gradations of tone in the ground planes leading to the bands of color that portray the atmospheric changes in hue of the sky can still be discerned. Thus, although it may seem from the instructions to the artist that he was to invent the scenes, i.e., that he was not working from a model, it is clear, nonetheless, that he was working in a well-established and familiar tradition, for these same characteristics of style are found in the illustrations of the Vatican Vergil, a manuscript often thought to be a product of the same atelier that produced the Quedlinburg *Itala,* but at a slightly later date.

The Vatican Vergil (Bibl. Apost. Ms. lat. 3225)[11] consists of seventy-five parchment folios with text in rustic capitals of parts of the *Georgics* and the *Aeneid,* about one-fifth of the original. There are fifty illustra-

Fig. 3.
Berlin, Deutsche Staatsbibliothek, Ms. Theol. lat. fol.
485. The Itala of Quedlinburg, f.2. The Story of Saul,
Samuel and Agag.

tions in all. The first, now placed between the second and third books of the *Georgics,* consists of six scenes framed in bands like those in the Quedlinburg *Itala.* Six of the others are full page while the other forty-three are on text pages, and vary in size from half to two-thirds the composed area of the folios, which, like those of the *Itala* fragment, are almost square. All the illustrations have borders, a narrow black band inside a wider red one, the latter decorated at intervals with small gold lozenges. At least three different artists were involved in the enterprise, but all individual stylistic idioms are couched in a consistent atelier style.

The Old Gardener of Corycus (Fig. 4) on f.7v illustrates verses 125 ff. of the Fourth Georgic, in which Vergil describes the skill in raising bees of an old farmer he had once encountered near Tarentum in southern Italy. The farmer is seated at the left, directing the work of two slaves and conversing with a third person at the right. Trees, left and right, frame the scene, which includes a small tile-roofed building in the middle distance of a landscape of field and trees. The colors are predominantly blues, reds, and violets, painted rather thickly in a scheme not unlike that of the Quedlinburg *Itala,* but differing from the illustrations in that manuscript in that there is no preliminary drawing visible where the pigments have flaked off. Different too is the use of gold to brighten metal objects, underline drapery folds, and represent highlights in foliage, garlands, and the like. In the Gardener illustration, it is particularly striking as a detail of the roof of the building. Notable also is the treatment of the sky, the colors of which modulate from pink at the horizon to blue at the zenith.

J. de Wit[12] has pointed out that the illustration is not

Fig. 4.
Vatican, Biblioteca Apostolica, Ms. lat. 3225, f.7v. The
Vatican Vergil, The Old Gardener of Corycus.

an exact translation of the text, since many details given there are omitted and others (the slaves, for example) have been added. He considers the composition an adaptation of an established genre type and cites a comparable theme in a mosaic from Carthage.[13] The point is significant, suggesting as it does that even in this early period, manuscript illustrations were akin, artistically and iconographically, to contemporary paintings, which could be excerpted or adapted to use as illustrations of texts with which they had no immediate relationship. The isolation of the illustration from the script by the heavy border also indicates a conception of each as an independent entity. Pertinent too is the omission from the rustic capital script of the text of any punctuation in the usual sense, save for breathing marks; the text was clearly conceived as an aural rather than visual value.

In itself, the Old Gardener illustration, like all those in the Vatican Vergil, exemplifies the illusionism of antique pictorial style in a late phase. The scale of the figures, the simple perspective scheme, and the graduated color of the sky create a measure of reality in the ensemble. But by placing the figures in full frontality in a plane parallel to the picture surface and isolated from each other, the artist betrayed the need he felt for clarity of detail, observing all with equal intentness and portraying them as independent forms. Also to be noted is the upward tilting of the ground plane to a high horizon line, which tends to flatten the frontally portrayed figures even more, for all the occasional modeling effects of light, shade, and color.

The illustrations of the *Iliad* in the Ambrosian Library[14] at Milan (Ms. F. 205. inf.), once part of a sumptuous codex, number fifty-eight in all, on fifty-two folios. They were cut from the book at some time and mounted separately, hence the original arrangement and distribution is unknown. Three of the twenty-four books of the *Iliad* are not represented at all, and the distribution of subjects among the other twenty-one is irregular. Estimates of the extent of the original illustration range from two hundred and forty to seven hundred and twenty, the last suggested by Weitzmann.[15] Like the illustrations of the Vatican Vergil, those of the Ambrosian Iliad are framed in colored bands—red and blue—and the color scheme in general is comparable in the two books. Red predominates in the Iliad, with blue, green, purple, and white in measure, different hues often being used to distinguish the nimbi of the various gods. A brilliant yellow is used in the Iliad instead of gold, however, and although the pigments are applied in much the same way in both books, with color being laid on color, and although the patterns of light and shade are quite similar in the two, the Iliad illustrations were painted over preliminary drawings.

There are also some stylistic differences between the illustrations in the Ambrosian Iliad and those of the Vatican Vergil. Picture 25 in the Iliad sequence is of two scenes from Book Six of the poem (Fig. 5). On the left are Hecuba and three Trojan women, with Hector, Paris, and Helen on the right. In proportion and movement, the figures are like those of the Vergil illustrations, but the Iliad artist has not hesitated to make them overlap each other, and to turn from the frontal poses seen there, achieving thereby a somewhat more natural realism. The figures are also larger in scale and are not so closely related to the setting as they are in the Vergil scenes. They appear, as it were, downstage, with the background features (buildings in this case) assembled in dense patterns behind them, creating a quite different effect from that resulting from the uptilted ground plane of the Gardener illustration. These and other characteristics of the Ambrosian Iliad illustrations, particularly the figure style, suggest that for all their approximate contemporaneity with those of the Vatican Vergil—the first half of the fifth century —the Iliad pictures represent another aspect of late antique style than those of the Latin epic. It is generally agreed that it is Greek, and specifically Alexandrian, with the probability—almost a certainty, as Weitzmann[16] points out—that a pictorial tradition of long standing is implied in the synoptic assemblage and combination of themes appearing in the Iliad illustrations.

In both the Vatican Vergil and the Ambrosian Iliad, the illustrations are interspersed in the text. Both manuscripts differ in this respect from the *Codex Romanus* (Vatican, Bibl. Apost. Ms. lat. 3867),[17] whose nineteen miniatures are placed singly, or possibly in pairs in some instances,[18] at the beginning or end of the books they illustrate. The text of the *Eclogues, Georgics,* and *Aeneid* is almost complete on three hundred and nine folios of fine parchment of fairly considerable size, the sheets being approximately thirteen inches square. In this sheet format, the *Codex Romanus* has something in common with both the Quedlinburg *Itala* and the Vatican Vergil; the Ambrosian Iliad illustrations having been cut from the folios, the original format and proportion cannot be determined. In the *Codex Romanus,* the first seven illustrations—of the Georgics—are less than full-page

Fig. 5.
Milan, Biblioteca Ambrosiana, Ms. F. 205. inf., Picture
25. The Ambrosian Iliad, Hecuba and Three Trojan
Women: Hector, Paris and Helen.

size and have text either above or below, but the remaining twelve occupy the full folio. Except for the first one, at the beginning of the Eclogues,[19] all the illustrations have borders, bands of red and gold for the most part, but those of six Aeneid illustrations are of gold alone. Gold is occasionally used for costume ornaments and the like, but not for highlights. The color gamut is somewhat more extended than in the Vatican Vergil pictures, pinks and lavenders being added to the blues, reds, and greens of the other book. The pigments are laid on rather heavily, for the most part, and there is considerable variation in the use of underpaint. In some cases, all the painted area has been so prepared, while in others only the figures were laid in in advance.

The Shepherds Tending Their Flocks (Fig. 6, Plate I) on f. 44v of the *Codex Romanus* is an illustration of the Third Georgic.[20] One shepherd plays the flute as his companion listens, passing the time as their dog sits before them, one horse gambols about while the other nurses a foal, and their sheep and goats graze. The color is rather restrained. The background is painted in var-

iegated tans, which are also used for some of the animals and the shepherds' tunics, while the flesh tones are pink, with white highlights on cheeks, shoulders, hands, and the like. These accenting highlights are about all that remains of the illusionistic devices that still give some three-dimensionality to the forms in the Vatican Vergil illustrations. Instead of modeling light and shade, the figures are outlined with heavy contours, the heads turned into full profiles, and the bodies flattened into tinted planes. Pictorial space has disappeared. There is no horizon, no gradation of color to suggest atmospheric space, and the various shapes seem to have been distributed with no more compositional intention than to fill the enclosed area as fully as possible. Most significant of all in this "crystallizing" of antique illusionism, as Morey[21] has so aptly termed it, is the linear character of the representational formulae. Although the illustration is obviously painted in pigment with a brush, the artist has conceived his forms like a draftsman rather than a painter.

It is generally accepted that the *Codex Romanus* dates

from the latter half of the fifth century, but there is less agreement about its place of origin. An inscription in the book indicates that it was in the Saint-Denis abbey library, near Paris, in the thirteenth and fourteenth centuries; this, along with the style of the illustrations, has led some scholars to ascribe it to a provincial atelier, possibly in southern Gaul. But the quality of the rustic capital script would suggest a major metropolitan center, whether Rome or elsewhere in the Empire. It is significant, in any event, that the trend marked in its illustration, from a painter's style to the more linear manner of the draftsman, is even more pronounced in the latest example of late antique book illustration mentioned above—the *Agrimensoria* in the Landesbibliothek at Wolfenbüttel (Cod. 36. 23. Aug. fol.).[22] This technical treatise on surveying is illustrated with a number of schematic representations of cities[23] rather heavily painted in shapes with pronounced contours, not unlike those of the *Codex Romanus* illustrations. But an author portrait on f. 67v[24] of the manuscript is a pen drawing, in pure line with a minimum of shading, and but the slightest intimation of bulk in the human figure or of enveloping spatial depth. Since this book is generally held to date from the sixth century, the course indicated by its illustrations in relationship to the earlier works is important, revealing as it does a continuing tendency toward the denaturalizing and dematerializing of form.

In addition to the few examples just discussed of actual examples of late classical book illustration, copies of such books made in the later Middle Ages provide some further evidence about it, both stylistic and iconographic. Two such late antique works have already been mentioned, the Chronograph of 354 and the Comedies of Terence. It is easy to understand why the former was reproduced in later times, for it contains, among other things, a list of the Church festivals, a table to determine the date of Easter in a given year, a martyrology, and an illustrated astrological monthly almanac, all useful in insuring the accuracy of records. The figures representing the months of the year in the calendar, and the verses describing the activities appropriate to them, are significant for the traditions of calendar illustration in the later Middle Ages, both in painting and sculpture.[25] Valued for similar reasons were astronomical treatises like that of the late fourth-century Hellenistic poet, Aratus of Soloi.[26] Also very popular was the *Psychomachia* of Prudentius (348–c. 410), one of the

earliest specifically Christian literary texts, describing the conflict between the Vices and the Virtues.[27] Illustrated copies of all of these were made during the later Middle Ages, those of the Carolingian period in the ninth century frequently being faithful, if simplified, stylistic adaptations of original models from late antiquity.

Book illustration in the eastern Mediterranean world until the end of the sixth century is somewhat more amply represented than in the Latin west. Historical and organizational reasons may account for this in part at least. Politically, the Eastern empire was less turbulent than the Western. The establishment of quasi-monastic centers in the East Christian world, with libraries for the study and production of books, also appears to antedate the earliest such institution in the West, Cassiodorus' *Vivarium* founded sometime after 540. However, for all this, a clear and consistent impression of Eastern Mediterranean book illustration during the period in question is not easy to attain. Contributing to this difficulty, among other things, were the considerable number of production centers and their wide diffusion through the Near East. Constantinople, Antioch, Alexandria, and Pergamum are known to have been outstanding among them, and many lesser cities too, yet only a small number of extant books can be identified with them. The iconoclastic vandalism of the eighth century and the decline in power of the Byzantine empire, the depredations of the Crusaders, and the sacking of Constantinople by the Turks in 1453 took a devastating toll, to say nothing of the continuous neglect of cultural treasures until well into modern times. The history of the renowned libraries of Alexandria dating back to the third century B.C. furnishes an instance. As early as 48–47 B.C., much was destroyed there by Julius Caesar. Other parts suffered the same fate c. A.D. 390, and the Mohammedan conquest of the city in 642 brought an effective end to one of the greatest libraries of the ancient world. In view of these circumstances, the importance of the few remaining volumes is all the greater.

The tradition of Alexandrian book illustration, probably reflected in the Ambrosian Iliad pictures, is known directly only through the badly damaged remnants of two books, the Golenisheff Chronicle,[28] an illustrated Greek papyrus in the Museum of Fine Arts in Moscow, and the Cotton Genesis[29] in the British Museum (Ms. Cott. Otho B. vi) of the late fourth and fifth centuries

Plate I. Vatican, Biblioteca Apostolica, Ms. lat. 3867, f. 44v.
The *Codex Romanus,* Shepherds Tending their Flocks.

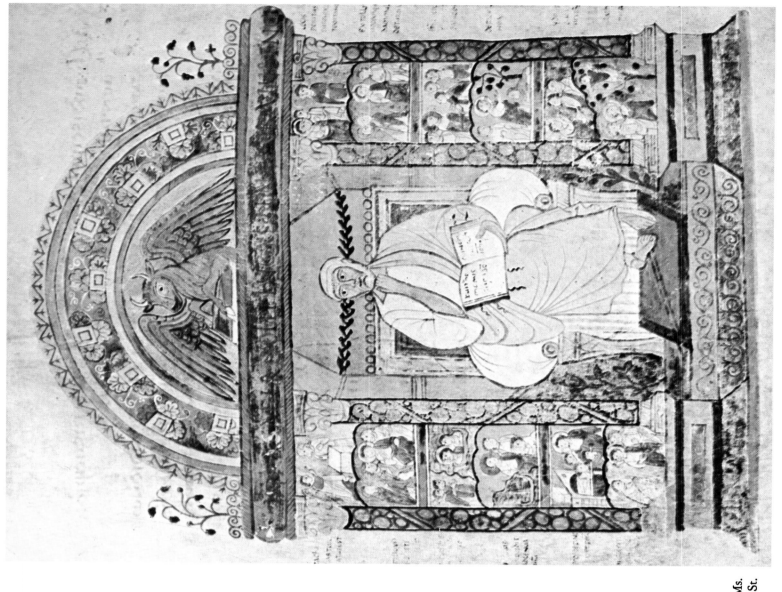

Plate II. Rossano, Archiepiscopal Treasury, The Rossano Gospels, f. 121. St. Mark. (Photo author)

Plate III. Cambridge, Corpus Christi College Library, Ms. 286, f. 129v. The Gospel Book of St. Augustine, St. Luke.

respectively. Some idea of style can be obtained from the fragments of the Golenisheff papyrus, a world chronicle to the year A.D. 392, and enough of iconography from the Cotton manuscript to establish it as probably the immediate model of the Genesis scenes in the narthex mosaics of San Marco in Venice.[30]

Indirect evidence of the nature of Alexandrian illustration can be found in later works copying Alexandrian models. The Paris Psalter (B.N. Ms. grec 139) and the Joshua Roll (Vatican, Bibl. Apost. Ms. Palat. gr. 431) will be considered elsewhere. The illustrations in another Vatican manuscript (Bibl. Apost., Ms. gr. 699) are believed to be ninth-century copies, made in all probability in Constantinople, of an Alexandrian original of the sixth century, the *Christian Topography of Cosmas Indicopleustes*.[31] This account by an Alexandrian monk of his travels to find the sources of the Nile was compiled to provide a Christian substitute based on the Bible for current Hellenistic concepts of the nature of the universe. Although the figure style of the illustrations is Constantinopolitan, the composition of the pages with many unframed author figures and occasional narrative scenes inserted in the text harks back to Alexandrian prototypes. The Evangelists,[32] for example, are shown standing,[33] as in earlier papyrus scrolls, and iconographic details such as the nude Jonah[34] on f.69 bespeak a similar origin.

There are more certain grounds for the judgment of Constantinopolitan style at the beginning of the sixth century in the illustrations of the assemblage of botanical, zoological, and medical treatises known as the Dioscurides Codex in the National Library of Vienna (Cod. Vindob. Med. gr. I).[35] This copy of the texts compiled in the first century by a certain Dioscurides of Anazarbos, a physician and pharmacologist from Cilicia, was made for Anicia Juliana, daughter of a powerful Roman family domiciled in Constantinople, about the year 512. This information is given in an acrostic inscription on the frame of a picture on f.6[36] showing Anicia Juliana receiving the book from a nude putto. She is seated and attended by two female figures labeled (in Greek) Magnanimity and Wisdom, while a third person kneels before her, inscribed Gratitude of the Arts. The illustration refers to Juliana's generosity in paying for the construction of a church in Constantinople in 512, providing a certain date for the volume. The Dioscurides treatise was the standard text on medicinal plants and the like in the Middle Ages,

and is known in numerous other copies.[37]

The Vienna Dioscurides contains some four hundred and twenty folios, and about four hundred and fifty illustrations of plants, birds, and animals. The majority of these are placed singly at the pertinent passages in the text[38] in the established classical tradition of scientific illustration, but on f.483v, twenty-four birds discussed in the following twelve folios have been portrayed in a single frame divided into small panels,[39] like the Quedlinburg *Itala* compositions (Fig. 3) and the first illustration of the Vatican Vergil. The pictorial decoration of the book also includes seven full-page illustrations preceding the text, a peacock on f.1, seven physicians of classic antiquity on f.2, seven pharmacologists,[40] also of historical fame, on f.3v, two compositions showing Dioscurides at work[41] on ff.4v-5v, the dedication picture already mentioned on f.6v, and an ornamental title page on f.7.

Dioscurides is seated on the left in the illustration on f.4v (Fig. 7), gesturing toward a female figure on the right, identified by the Greek incription (*Heuresis*) above her head as a personification of Discovery. In her outstretched right hand she holds a mandrake root (also inscribed but in a later hand) shaped like a human body, while a dog that has just pulled it from the ground lies dead at her feet, its life lost, according to ancient superstition, from hearing the cry of the extracted herb. For the figure of Dioscurides, the artist has adapted one from the group of pharmacologists[42] shown on f.3v, which was presumably itself adapted from an older model in which the author appeared alone as a textual insert. But the addition of the personification of Discovery posed a problem in composition to augment the design to the larger scale of a full page, somewhat like that discussed in connection with the author portrait in the Terence manuscript. A background has been added, a building set against hills under a sky painted in graduated colors, and the whole is framed in a border of bands of lozenges in various colors. In all these respects, the Dioscurides illustrator continues the same tradition of pictorial illusionism, ultimately of Alexandrian origin, that lies behind the style of the Vatican Vergil illustrations (Fig. 4). The mode of representing the figures can be traced to the same source, for they are constructed in patterns of modeling light and shade, and still retain something of the articulate gracefulness of their antique prototypes.

Far-reaching generalization about Constantinopolitan

Fig. 7.
Vienna, Nationalbibliothek, Cod. Med. gr. 1, f.4v. The
Dioscurides Codex, Dioscurides discovers the mandrake
root.

style in the early sixth century on the basis of the single example of the Vienna Dioscurides would be unwarranted, but there can be little doubt that the treatise was produced in a cosmopolitan and eclectic milieu. The figures and setting in the Discovery illustration apparently derive from Alexandrian practice. The border, on the other hand, of bands of lozenges modulating in color from dark at the edges to lighter hues along the center line, is most closely paralleled in the fourth- and fifth-century mosaic floors in the Near Eastern city of Antioch.[43] In Antioch, too, was discovered a mosaic of birds in a reticulated pattern,[44] the closest analogy as yet to the frontispiece of Book III in the Vienna Dioscurides. The interest attaching to this is the greater, since Antioch, or some major Near Eastern center, seems the most likely place of origin of the so-called "purple manuscripts."

There are three illustrated purple manuscripts of major importance, the Vienna Genesis (NB, Cod. theol. graec. 31), the Rossano Gospels (Rossano Calabro, Archiepiscopal Treasury), and the fragment of a Gospel-book from Sinope in Asia Minor (Paris, B.N., Ms. suppl. gr. 1286). They are so designated from the color, varying from purple to reddish-brown, of the parchment folios on which the text is written in gold or silver Greek uncials and the illustrations are painted. It is usually assumed that they were executed for royal patrons, since purple was traditionally a regal color, and while this is not necessarily the case,[45] there can be little doubt that they were luxury volumes, made or intended for royal or aristocratic patrons. The use of silver for the text of the Vienna Genesis, silver with gold rubrics in the Rossano book, and gold throughout for the Sinope fragment would be enough in itself to establish this point. It is generally agreed that all three date from the sixth century, and although there are different opinions about the exact and relative chronology, the Vienna Genesis is usually thought to be the earliest and the Sinope fragment the latest of the three. Such evidence as can be adduced points to their origin in the Near East in general and possibly Antioch specifically, although this last is assumed from the historical importance of the city rather than objective indications. The same date and provenance are suggested for a number of single purple sheets, unillustrated but with gold or silver text in various libraries and museums.[46]

The twenty-four folios of the Vienna Genesis[47] vary in size from 30.4–32.6 cm. (c. 12–12⅞″) in height by 24.5–26.5 cm. (c. 9⅝–10⅜″) in width. The text,

in silver Greek uncials, is in the upper part of each page, the number of lines varying from thirteen to seventeen, and the illustrations are at the bottom. The text is the Septuagint version, i.e., that compiled, according to tradition, by seventy Jewish scholars in Alexandria in the third century B.C. It begins with the Fall of Man (Gen. 3:4) and ends with the Death of Jacob (Gen. 50:1–4), but there are at least seven lacunae where considerable portions of text and presumably accompanying illustrations are missing. Through the first sixteen folios, the text referring to the illustration below is complete, but the last eight apparently had a continuous text, and it is consequently not always complete for the illustration on any given page. In the earlier folios, the text length is often adjusted to the area available for the script, and is syncopated and condensed to some extent. It is clear, in any event, that there was close collaboration between the scribes— two, for the preserved portion of the manuscript—and the illustrators.

Scholarly opinion differs as to the number of artists involved, though it is agreed that there were more than one. F. Wickhoff[48] has identified seven. C. R. Morey[49] sees six, while Gerstinger and P. Buberl[50] have both seen eight different hands, although they do not agree about individual attributions. There are some differences in the relationship of text to illustration. The first six have the illustrations enclosed in framing lines. The next twenty-six are not separated from the text by any such limits and usually represent several episodes arranged in frieze-like continuity on two levels, one above the other. The last sixteen, all on folios written, it should be noted, by the second scribe, do not have frames but there are painted backgrounds in all.

The illustration on p. 14 (the manuscript is paginated rather than foliated) is for Genesis 24:22–31 (Fig. 8). It is of the frieze type, with Rebekah receiving gifts from Abraham's servant after watering his camels in the upper register, where, on the left, is a semi-nude female figure personifying the spring. Below, on the left, a woman talks with Abraham's servant (although the text—v. 29—says that Rebekah's brother Laban did so) and on the right Rebekah tells "them of her mother's house these things" (v. 28). All the forms are painted in thick, opaque pigments that have been laid directly on the purple parchment, a technique not unlike that used in the Vatican Vergil illustrations. However, unlike them, the Vienna Genesis scenes in this group, the most numerous, do not have back-

Fig. 8.
Vienna, Nationalbibliothek, Cod. theol. gr. 31, p. 14. The
Vienna Genesis, Rebekah welcoming Eliezir.

grounds, although there are details of the setting like the trees and hill above right, the rocky spring, and the house of Rebekah's mother.

The lively colors, the brisk movements of the short and stocky figures, and the eyes glancing sideways from heads shown for the most part in three-quarter view, are all stylistic inheritances from the antique past. To these can be added the semi-nude female personification of the spring, and the abbreviated perspective of the landscape and the architectural details. All of these point to a model in late classical style and, more specifically, one from Alexandria, where there is good reason to believe there were illustrated versions of the Septuagint text at a quite early date.[51] Whether the prototype was a scroll with single scenes in the column texts, which the Vienna Genesis artists assembled in the double-register friezes, as Weitzmann holds, or, as Morey believes,[52] the model was a rotulus with continuous illustration and excerpted text, is a matter of opinion. For the former point of view, the ease with which the episodes on a given level in the double-register illustrations can be separated into compositions fitting a single, narrow, text column[53] is persuasive. On the other hand, as Morey points out, in more than a few of these double-level compositions, notably that of Jacob crossing the brook Jabbok and wrestling with the Man of God,[54] the composition moves from left to right above but turns back on itself below to accommodate the unbroken sequence of the assumed rotulus model to the codex folio format. In any event, it is clear that in this, one of the oldest known cycles of Old Testament book illustration, there is a significant aspect of the transformation of classical pictorial conceptions to the purposes of the early Christian Church.

Like the Vienna Genesis, the Gospel-book known as the Codex Rossanensis in the Archiepiscopal Treasury of the cathedral at Rossano in Calabria is a volume of purple-leaved parchment with the text in silver Greek uncials (the opening lines of two chapters are in gold).[55] It is also similar in format to the Vienna Genesis, being rather wide in proportion to height—30.7 x 26.0 cm. (c. 12 x 10¼"). The text, of Matthew and of Mark through chapters 14, is preceded by eight folios, some illustrated, others with painted decoration, with scenes from the life of Christ, a title page to the canons of the Gospels, and a part of the text of Eusebius' letter to Carpianus. On f.121, at the beginning of Mark's Gospel, is a portrait of the Evangelist (Fig. 9, Plate II).

He is seated as he writes the text of his Gospel on a long, opened scroll, attended by an unidentified female figure.

As the earliest extant illustrated manuscript of the Gospel Text, the importance of the Rossano volume is very great, showing as it does that by the time of its execution, about the middle of the sixth century, a tradition for such illustration had begun to take shape. Especially noteworthy are the appearance of the Evangelist portrait, and the assumed presence originally of the canon tables, suggested by the existing title page and the fragment of Eusebius' letter to Carpianus.[56] The Rossano St. Mark is the only author portrait still in the volume; its conceptual parallel with the Dioscurides portrait in the Vienna medical treatise (Fig. 7) is a significant indication of the continuing tradition of antique types, as Morey has pointed out.[57] Such portraits of the Evangelists and the decorated canon-tables, presumably also once part of the Rossano Gospels, are found in almost all decorated Gospel-books throughout the Middle Ages.

Although it is possible to assume an earlier prototype for the individual episodes in the New Testament illustrations preceding the text of the Rossano Gospels,[58] the themes portrayed and the manner of their interpretation mark a significant consolidation of the theological content of Christian art. Selected from the events preceding, and through, Holy Week in a sequence that has been established by Morey,[59] the choice was made for liturgical rather than narrative or chronological reasons. The order is that of the readings for Holy Week in the Greek Church, and, more specifically, as found in the liturgy of Antioch.[60]

The Parable of the Good Samaritan (Fig. 10) is now on f.7v of the Rossano Gospels.[61] At the left is the city of Jerusalem. In the center, the Samaritan attends the victim with the aid of a winged figure, and, at the right, leads the mule carrying the wounded man and gives money to the innkeeper. The illustration is of Luke 10:33–35, but the Samaritan is identified as the Saviour by His cruciform nimbus. The same device gives typological rather than narrative meaning to the bridegroom in the illustration of the Parable of the Wise and Foolish Virgins on f.2v.[62] Beneath the New Testament scene at the top of the folio, four half-length figures, all nimbed, are inscribed as Old Testament prophets, David (twice), Micah, and Sirach. Their uplifted hands point to the fulfillment of their prohecies, written in gold

Fig. 10.
Rossano, Archiepiscopal Treasury, The Rossano Gospels,
f.7v. The Parable of the Good Samaritan. (Photo Girau-
don)

uncials on the scrolls unrolled below them. It is quite
probable that the typological illustrations in the Rossano Gospels are derived from an earlier book cycle,[63]
but two full-page compositions on f.8r-v of Christ before Pilate and Christ Presented to the People were
certainly taken from monumental mural designs, as
Loerke has conclusively demonstrated.[64]

A number of stylistic features, particularly in the
figures, are shared by the illustrations of the Rossano
Gospels with those of the Vienna Genesis. The bodies
are short and stocky, and there are the same sideways-
peering glances of the eyes in heads viewed in three-
quarters. But there are no frames for the narrative
scenes, as there are in some of the Vienna Genesis
illustrations, except for semi-circular arches enclosing
the two trial scenes on f.8r,v, and these refer, as Loerke
points out, to the semi-domed recesses of the presumed
mural prototypes.[65] Moreover, the landscape features

that occasionally appear are treated more symbolically
than in the Vienna volume, without foreshortening and
with little or no indication of perspective depth. It has
been plausibly suggested that such differences are owing
in part at least to stylistic distinctions in the prototypes.
As has been noted, there is good reason to believe that
the Vienna Genesis compositions hark back to models
related to the Septuagint tradition of illustration presumably established in late antiquity, which had a
strong infusion of Alexandrian illusionism. Since no
such venerable tradition could have existed for Gospel
illustration, its episodes are more likely cast in the mold
of current, i.e., Early Christian, style of the region in
which the illustrations and their prototypes were made.
So, for example Christ is portrayed with a beard, Asiatic
rather than Hellenistic in mode, and the background of
the Mark portrait (Fig. 9, Plate II) has its closest
analogue in a late second-century mosaic found in

Antioch.[66] Loerke's argument for the origin of the two trial scene compositions in the decoration of the church of Hagia Sophia erected by the Empress Eudocia in Jerusalem before her death in 460 provides an acceptable hypothesis for both date and provenance of the models used for the gospel narratives.[67]

There are significant differences between the illustrations of the two manuscripts in the use of color. In the Vienna Genesis, they are painted directly on the purple parchment, or the occasional painted backgrounds, in hues seldom varying from frank and simple primary harmonies, both appropriate to and effective in the vestigial illusionism of Alexandrian naturalistic setting. In the Codex Rossanensis, compensation for the waning naturalism of figures and setting is found in the more subtle and decorative harmonies of their forms, the bluish-whites of lighter garments, and the roses, brownish-reds, and violets of darker ones, merging into the purple of the parchment. At the same time, the abstract arabesques of gold in the nimbi and the Saviour's robe strike a resonant note to which the original gleam of silver in the text effectively responded.

The third purple manuscript with illustrations is the *Codex Sinopensis* in the Bibliothèque Nationale in Paris (Ms. suppl. gr. 1286).[68] The text of its forty-three folios[69] comprises the greater part of Matthew's Gospel, from 7:7–22 to chapter 24:3–12. It is written in gold uncials on folios measuring 30.0 x 25.0 cm. (11⅞ x 9¾"). There are five illustrations of episodes referred to in the text, accompanied like those of the Rossanensis by prophet figures holding scrolls inscribed with passages relevant to the New Testament themes. There are but two prophets instead of four, however, and they flank the gospel illustrations instead of appearing below them. Also different in the Sinope manuscript is the placement of the illustrations at the bottom of the folio, below the text, and at the beginning or end of the passages they illustrate, instead of being gathered together at the beginning of the book. In this characteristic, the Sinope book is closer to the Vienna Genesis than to the Rossano Gospels, in which the illustrations are a separate unit instead of being distributed through the text.[70]

The illustration on f.15 of the Sinope fragment (Fig. 11) is of the Second Miracle of the Loaves and Fishes (Matt. 15:32–39). To the left is David, the quotation on his scroll from Ps. 144:15, "Happy is the people that is in such a case"; Moses, on the right side, presents Deut. 12:18, "But thou must eat them

before the Lord thy God in the place which the Lord thy God shall choose. . . ." Unlike their counterparts in the Rossano book, the Sinope prophets do not gesture vigorously toward the consummation of their prophecies, but quietly raise their hands. This, together with their placement at the sides, in the folio margins rather

Fig. 11.
Paris, Bibliothèque Nationale, Ms. suppl. gr. 1286, f.15. The Sinope Gospel fragment, The second Miracle of the Loaves and Fishes.

than in direct relationship to the text, tends to give the pictorial element in the ensemble an identity of its own, equality with, rather than subordination to, the text.

There is greater emphasis on symbological content in the Sinope illustrations than in those of the Rossano codex, and this too is partly a consequence of differences in style. The painting technique is much the same in both, the colored shapes lying directly on the purple parchment. Some similar conventions are also found in both, e.g., the symbol of Jerusalem in the Miracle of the Dried Fig Tree on f.30v[71] and that on f.7v of the Rossano illustration of the Good Samaritan (Fig. 10). But for all the renunciation of much naturalism in the Rossano scenes, a ground line on which the figures move is consistently retained, while it is entirely dispensed with in the Sinope miniatures. Within the silhouetted forms of the Rossano compositions something yet remains of modeling shadow, replaced in the Sinope narratives by heavy black lines for the contours. And although there are occasional heads in three-quarter view in the Sinope illustrations and the eyes peer sideways from them, the bodies are uniformly frontal and flattened in the picture plane. Even a detail of environment pertinent to the theme, like the patch of green representing the hillside setting on the right side of the Miracle of the Loaves, seems to hover over the parchment instead of lying on it.

In his study of the Sinope fragment, Grabar reached the conclusion that it originated in the eastern extremes of the Byzantine world, probably Syria or Mesopotamia, and that it is presumably to be dated in the sixth century. It can thus be grouped with the Vienna Genesis and the Rossano Gospels, for the three manuscripts share many common physical and technical characteristics, such stylistic differences as those pointed out being explained by prototypes of varying origin and character, and, to some extent, of date, though these cannot be very great. It is generally believed, however, that all three must have been made in a cosmopolitan and probably urban center, possibly Antioch, though there is only speculative evidence for such a specific conclusion.

Quite different in these respects is the case of the Rabula Gospels in the Laurentian Library in Florence (Cod. plut. 1, 56).[72] A colophon states that the Syriac text was written by the calligrapher Rabula at the monastery of St. John at Zagba in northern Mesopotamia, who finished it in 586. In addition to the Syriac gospel text, the book contains a gathering of fourteen folios of full-page illustrations and other decorations at the beginning of the text. Although this gathering is an insertion, i.e., it is not physically part of the text portion, there is no reason to dissociate it from the text and the colophon. On the fourteen folios of this inserted gathering, there are twenty-eight compositions: six full-page illustrations of New Testament subjects; one with portraits of Ammonius and Eusebius, who had contributed to the organization of the Canons of Concordance; two decorated text pages, with Eusebius' letter to Carpianus and the prologue to the canon tables; and nineteen full-page designs of architectural arcades enclosing the

canon tables between columns and with representations of Old Testament prophets and incidents in the life of Christ in the margins. With its certain date of 586, the Rabula Gospel-book is an important monument in the history of early mediaeval art, for some of the subjects portrayed in it, and, specifically, for its canon tables, the earliest complete example of the concordance of the four Gospels.[73]

It is now generally accepted that the assembling of the four Gospel texts in a single book had come about by the first half of the second century A.D., posing the problem of unity of tradition and doctrine based on four comparable yet dissimilar sources. An initial effort to resolve this was the *Diatesseron* of Tatian, a Syrian apologist writing in the late second century, in which all four texts were combined in one. This idea was adopted by the Church in Syria and continued in use there until the fifth century, even though it was realized that its somewhat contrived unity sacrificed the weight of multiplicity of testimony. In the third century, the Alexandrian scholar Ammonius attempted to remedy this with an edition of parallel texts with Matthew's as the norm, even though this involved omission of many passages from the other three Gospels. What proved to be the final organization was made by Eusebius (+339/40), bishop of Caesarea in Palestine. The Gospel texts were divided into numbered sections and the numbers then arranged in parallel columns, the basis of what came to be known as the Canons of Concordance, called the Canon Tables for convenience. Initially there were ten of these, the first with passages common to all four Gospels, the next three with parallels found in three, the next five of those in two, and a final one with readings found only in one.

The diffusion of the canon tables from Eusebius' scriptorium in Palestine appears to have been wide and rapid. No extant examples can be dated before the sixth century, but there are both Greek and Latin examples by that date. The Rossano Gospels must once have had them, for this text contains parts of Eusebius's Letter to Carpianus[74] and of the prologue to the tables in which their use is explained.[75] The number of canon tables varies considerably, depending on the division of the text; in Greek examples there may be as few as seven or as many as ten. The Syriac text of the Rabula Gospels has more sections than the standard Greek division, hence the somewhat large number of nineteen canon tables .

It is reasonable to assume that author portraits were a part of Gospel-book illustration from a very early

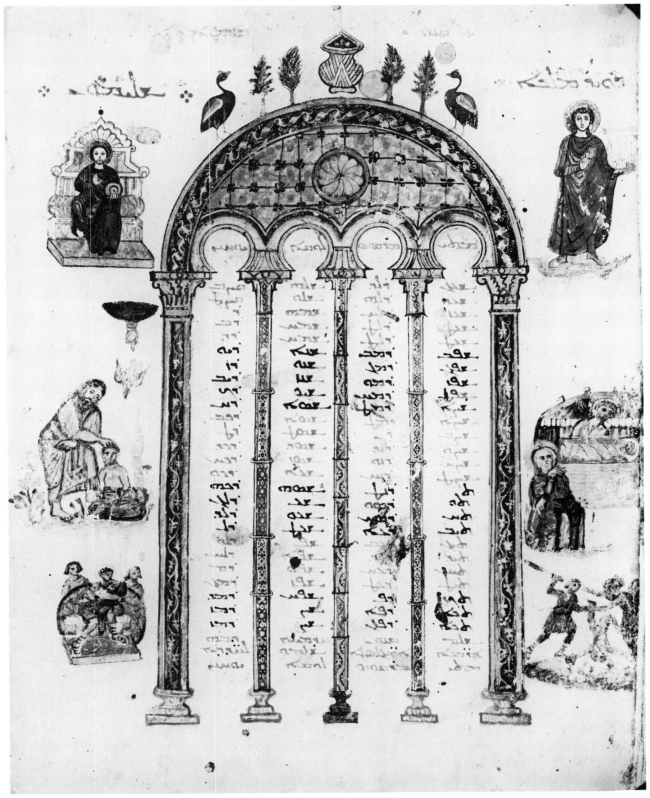

Fig. 12.
Florence, Biblioteca Laurenziana, Cod. Plut. 1, 56, f.4v.
The Rabula Gospels, Canon Table I, 3. (Photo Pineider)

time, following classic example, and Morey suggests[76] that ornamented canon tables were the second element to be added to the text. It goes without saying that the decorative arcades in which the canon tables are usually arranged do not make them any easier to use, and there are instances of the numbers being simply arranged in columns with no frames. But it was typical of the changing concept of the value of the written word in early Christian times that such embellishment should have been considered appropriate. Nor is it surprising, in view of the origin of the canon tables in the Eastern Christian world, that the form of its decorative organization should be of that region, Syria and Palestine, to be specific, where a ready parallel can be found in the columnar arcades of the sarcophagus type associated with the area.[77] Nor should the available ornamental repertory of classic forms seen through Near Eastern eyes in the Antioch mosaics be overlooked. The association of this type of ornament with the canon tables is well illustrated in the decorative peacocks and coloristically flattened rinceaux of the Vatican sixth-century example referred to above, even though its Western origin is unquestionable.

All of these features can be seen in the third section of Canon I on f.4v of the Rabula Gospels (Fig. 12). The four columns of concordant references list the parallel passages in the four Gospels named in the arches above. The flattened forms of the framing and dividing column shafts and the Corinthianesque capitals are decorated in a delicate harmony of rose and blue, which extends into the lunette and its archivolt above. All this is more than slightly reminiscent of the Antiochene mosaic pavements of the second century, as are also the urn, foliage, and birds at the top. The horseshoe-shaped inner arches also have antecedents in the earlier sarcophagi of this Asiatic region, referred to above.

Another distinctive feature of the Rabula canon tables is the appearance of scenes and figures in the margins. On f.4v, Solomon is seated above on the left, balanced by David standing on the right. Below them is the Baptism of Christ, left, and the Nativity, right. The Massacre of the Innocents is divided on the lowest level, Herod enthroned on the left and a soldier slaying an infant on the right. The style of the figures in these marginal vignettes suggests the probability that they were based on models not unlike those that served the illustrators of the Rossano Gospels. The figures have the same stocky forms and lively movement, the bodies

sometimes in three-quarters poses but with frontal heads and sideways-peering glances. Indications of setting are minimal, though occasionally, as in the Nativity, there is a slight indication of spatial depth.

The Old Testament personages are included in the canon table decoration for the same symbological reasons that explain the presence of somewhat similar figures accompanying the gospel scenes of the Rossano and Sinope Gospels (Figs. 11, 12), although there are no specific textual excerpts to accompany them. Such figures appear on many of the canon table folios in the Rabula Gospels, testifying the realization of their Old Testament prophecies in the incidents described in the Gospels. There are also author portraits, comparable in purpose to that of St. Mark in the Rossano book (Fig. 9, Plate II). The likenesses of Ammonius and Eusebius appear on f.2, and those of the four Evangelists on ff.9v–10. The former and Mark and Luke are standing, while Matthew and John are seated, a distinction indicating different sources for their models. As A. M. Friend has shown,[78] the standing author portrait type harks back to Alexandrian prototypes, the seated to Antiochene examples. Whether the marginal narrative scenes are drawn from an earlier cycle and condensed or divided to fit the limited available space on the folio,[79] or composed in a special cycle with such placement in mind,[80] they were apparently a Syrian notion.[81] Too much emphasis should not be placed on the fact that Rabula's book was written in a monastery, for the purple manuscripts may also have been, but it is to be noted that in later Byzantine practice, marginal illustration of this type is more usual in books intended for monastic use and is but rarely found in the later counterparts of the luxurious purple manuscripts.

There are twenty-eight subjects from the life of Christ in the Rabula Gospel illustrations, the most extensive cycle in early manuscript decoration, distributed through the canon tables, as has been noted, and in full-page compositions on f.13r–v. Of these, twelve are among the twenty described by a sixth-century writer, Choricius, in his account of the Sergius church at Gaza in Palestine,[82] among them the Crucifixion, represented on f.13 of the Rabula manuscript (Fig. 13), on the upper level. Below are the Two Holy Women at the Tomb and Christ's appearance to them (Matt. 28:1–10). The Crucifixion, the earliest instance of the theme in manuscript illustration, shows a considerable narrative enrichment of earlier versions like the one on the wooden doors of Santa Sabina at Rome[83] of c. 425, adding the soldiers casting lots for the robe, Longinus piercing Christ's right side and Stephaton raising the sponge to His lips in the center, and on the left the Virgin with St. John, and the Holy Women to the right. In the Resurrection below, the Sepulchre appears in a simplified version of the rotunda with peristylar colonnade and conical roof, described by sixth-century travelers as the building destroyed by Chosroes II in 614 when the Persians raided Jerusalem.[84]

All of this is much as described by Choricius in the same scenes in the Sergius church at Gaza, and it might seem that the Rabula Crucifixion is like the trial scenes in the Rossano Gospels in being reduced from a monumental prototype. But if so, it was seen through the eyes of a Greek artist who shared the propensities of the Rossano illustrators. Against the spatial limitations of the hills of Calvary and the garden setting of the Resurrection scenes, the figures move in the same simplified classic rhythm noted in those of the Rossanensis illustrations; a specific instance is the Christ confronting

Fig. 13.
Florence, Biblioteca Laurenziana, Cod. Plut. 1, 56, f.13.
The Rabula Gospels, Scenes from the Passion of Our Lord.
(Photo Pineider)

the two Marys. There are the same brisk gestures, rounded heads with peering eyes, the same color harmony of rose, blue-gray, and violet. The Eastern background of the artist is also indicated in the long tunic or colobium worn by the crucified Saviour and the red and blue overlapping chevrons making up the border. Yet the prototype followed must have been Greek rather than Asiatic, for the Syrian artist has misspelled the uncial inscription of Longinus as ΛΟΓΙΝΟC in copying his model.

Yet for all the iconographic ties between the three purple manuscripts and the Rabula Gospels, and the stylistic qualities that connote a Syrian origin for all, the attitude of the Rabula artist toward the assumed Greek model is different from that in the other three books. The backgrounds of the Crucifixion and Resurrection scenes on f.13 (Fig. 13) and of Christ's Ascension on f.13v[85] contain much more pronounced traces of the atmospheric landscape backgrounds of classic antiquity than anything comparable in the purple books, and the more compact groups inhabiting them are made up of figures outlined by heavy contours that tend to establish them as separate units rather than parts of integrated groups. The greater abstraction resulting from this directly anticipates the Byzantine style of following periods.

For all the sparse representation of manuscript illustration from the end of the fourth to the late sixth century, the successive modifications of style seen in it are significant. The Vatican Vergil (Fig. 4) and the Milan Iliad (Fig. 5) illustrations still preserve something of late classical realism. Form is rendered in impressionistic color and modeling light and dark, in shapes that occasionally retain something of classic grace and rhythm. There are also some reminiscences of the perspective space of late antiquity, and at least a suggestion of atmospheric modification of form and color. The later Vergil manuscript (Fig. 6, Plate I), the *Codex Romanus,* is illustrated in a style more of drawing than of painting. The forms of its illustrations consist of simplified outlines with little modeling, the figures are frontal and almost without grace or rhythm, and there is only minimal suggestion of space, whether created by perspective or atmospheric illusion. A similar process of denaturalization can be observed in the Eastern manuscripts. In the Vienna Dioscurides (Fig. 7), a measure of antique illusionism remains in figures and settings and their relationship to each other, and the accuracy of detail in the technical illustrations is noteworthy. Insofar as the illustrations of the Vienna Genesis (Fig. 8) are the work of artists grounded in the Alexandrian version of antique illusionism, they, too, reveal the persistence of spatial definition in the settings and in narrative relationships, but in others, these concerns are not so evident. They are even less so in the Rossano (Fig. 9, Plate II, and Fig. 10) and Sinope (Fig. 11) illustrations, while the Rabula compositions (Figs. 12, 13) omit nearly all reference to the antique realistic canon save for occasional wispy streaks of color betokening the atmospheric space of a relatively naturalistic model.

In the Eastern manuscripts, the dematerializing of form might be thought to express Oriental distaste for the representation of things, which is at least implied in the forbidding of images in the Second Commandment. But a compensating imperative led to the development, very early in the process, of a conception of the book page as a homogeneous unit involving both script and illustration, in the formal organization of which color could play an important part. Thus, from a naturalistic point of view measuring perfection by approximation to objective accuracy, the successive changes in style might be considered symptoms of deterioration and decadence. But when the increased potential that these same changes provide for heightened decorative and abstract power is recognized, they become positive and constructive phenomena. Reducing the material naturalism of the forms makes them the more effective statements of transcendental concepts, as far as their content is concerned. From a formal point of view, it allows a decorative integration of script and illustration, since both lie flat on the folio plane. In the purple manuscripts, the gold and silver letters of the text work with the colors of the painted scenes in a coherent design unlike in principle the result of the careful distinction between script and illustration that isolates them from each other in the earlier and still classical volumes.

Seen in historical perspective, it is clear that the successive changes in pictorial and illustrative style just discussed were part of a necessary, indeed, an inevitable process. As a result, the artistic style and modes created in antiquity to give expression to a worldly and material outlook were transformed in order to meet the quite different needs of giving visual form to the spiritual content of Christianity, to illuminate rather than illustrate the words in which that content is defined. Such was the implicit ideal of the scribes and artists who created the manuscripts of the Middle Ages.

NOTES

1. E. H. Naville, *Das Aegyptische Todtenbuch der XVIII–XX Dynastie*, 3 vols. (Berlin: A. Asher, 1886). K. Sethe, *Die Totenliteratur der alten Ägypter. Die Geschichte einer Sitte* (Sitzungsber. Preuss. Akad. Phil.-hist. Kl.) (Berlin, 1931), pp. 520 ff. T. G. Allen, *The Egyptian Book of the Dead. Documents in the Oriental Institute Museum* (Chicago: Oriental Institute, 1960). K. Weitzmann, *Illustrations in Roll and Codex,* 2nd ed. (Princeton: Princeton University Press, 1970), chap. 1.

2. *IRC,* fig. 47.

3. Erich Bethe, *Buch und Bild im Altertum* (Leipzig: Harrassowitz, 1945). Weitzmann, *IRC, passim. Idem, Ancient Book Illustration* (Cambridge, Mass.: Harvard University Press, 1959).

4. *ABI,* pp. 5–30.

5. *ABI,* p. 37.

6. *IRC,* pp. 78, 80, 82; *ABI,* p. 36.

7. Cf. below chaps. 2 and 5.

8. 14:186.

9. *ABI,* pp. 116–127 and figs. 124–127.

10. H. Degering and A. Boeckler, *Die Quedlinburger Italafragmente* (Berlin: Cassiodor-Gesellschaft. 1, 1932).

11. *Fragmenta et picturae Vergiliana Codicis Vatic. lat. 3225* (Codices e Vaticanis selecti, vol. 1) (Rome, 1930).

12. *Die Miniaturen des Vergilius Vaticanus* (Amsterdam: Swets & Zeitlinger, 1959), p. 31.

13. J. de Wit, "Vergilius Vaticanus und nordafrikanische Mosaiken," *Mnemosyne,* 1933/34, pp. 217 ff.

14. R. Bianchi-Bandinelli, *Hellenistic-Byzantine Miniatures of the Iliad (Ilias Ambrosiana)* (Olten: Urs Graf, 1955).

15. *ABI,* p. 37.

16. *IRC, passim* especially pp. 41 ff.

17. *Picturae Ornamentata complura scripturae specimina Cod. Vat. lat. 3867* (Codices e Vaticanis selecti, vol. ii) (Rome, 1902).

18. Cf. D. H. Wright, *AB* 43 (1961):249.

19. *ABI,* fig. 98.

20. For a reproduction in color, cf. *EMP,* p. 96.

21. "The Sources of Mediaeval Style," *AB* 7 (1924):11; cf. also A. Riegl, *Die spätrömische Kunst-industrie* (Vienna, 1901).

22. A. von Heinemann, *Die Handschriften der Hzgl. Bibliothek zu Wolfenbüttel,* vol. 6, no. 2403, pp. 124.

23. C. Thulin, *Die Handschriften des corpus Agrimensorum Romanorum,* i, *facs.* i (Berlin: Teubner, 1913), p. 157, figs. 113–14.

24. H. Swarzenski, "The Xanten Purple Leaf and the Carolingian Renaissance," *AB* 22 (1940), fig. 6.

25. J. C. Webster, *The Labors of the Months in Antique and Mediaeval Art* (Princeton: Princeton University Press, 1938).

26. *ABI,* pp. 24–26.

27. R. Stettiner, *Die illustrierten Prudentiushandschriften* (Text, Berlin, 1895; Plates, Berlin, 1905). H. Woodruff, "The Illustrated Manuscripts of Prudentius," *Art Studies* 7 (1929):33 ff.

28. A. Bauer and J. Strzygowski, *Eine Alexandrinische Weltchronik* (Denkschriften der K. Akademie d. Wissenschaften, Phil.-hist. kl., LI, Abh. 2) (Vienna, 1906), pp. 169 ff.

29. W. R. Lethaby, "The Painted Book of Genesis in the British Museum," *Archaeological Journal* 69 (1912):88 ff; 70 (1913):162 ff.

30. J. J. Tikkanen, *Die Genesismosaiken von S. Marco in Venedig und ihr Verhältnis zu den Miniaturen der Cottonbibel* (Acta Societatis Scientiarum Fennicae, xvii) (Helsinki, 1889).

31. Cf. Introd., n. 24.

32. *IRC,* fig. 98.

33. A. M. Friend, Jr., "The Portraits of the Evangelists in Greek and Latin Manuscripts," *Art Studies* 5 (1927):115–47; 7 (1929):3–29.

34. C. R. Morey "Notes on East Christian Miniatures," *AB* 11 (1929):27.

35. A. von Premerstein, K. Wessely, and J. Mantuani, *Dioscurides Codex Aniciae Julianae picturis illustratus, nunc Vindob. Med. gr. I* (Codices Graeci et Latini photogr. depicti, vol. x, facsimile) (Leipzig, 1906).

36. C. R. Morey, *Early Christian Art,* 3rd ed. (Princeton: Princeton University Press, 1953), fig. 116.

37. E.g. Naples, BN, Ms. già Vienn. gr. 1 of the sixth century; N. Y., Morgan Library, Ms. 652 of the tenth century; Mt. Athos, Lavra Cod. Omega 75, eleventh or twenfth century.

38. *ABI,* fig. 12.

39. *ABI,* fig. 18.

40. *ABI,* fig. 131.

41. *ECA,* figs. 114–15.

42. *ABI,* p. 126.

43. D. Levi, *Antioch Mosaic Pavements* (Princeton: Princeton University Press, 1947).

44. C. R. Morey, *The Mosaics of Antioch* (London, New York, and Toronto: Longmans, Green, 1938), p. 42, pl. xxii.

45. Cf. A. Grabar, *Byzantine Painting* (New York: Skira, 1953), p. 160, who points out that the royal privilege was a signature in red ink.

46. Cf. *ECA,* p. 215, n. 220; a purple sheet with silver Greek uncials in the Morgan Library is believed to be from Antioch and of the sixth century.

47. H. Gerstinger, *Die Wiener Genesis* (Farbenlichtdruckfacsimile) (Vienna: Dr. B. Filser, 1931). E. Wellesz, *The Vienna Genesis* (New York: Yoseloff, 1960).

48. W. von Hartel and F. Wickhoff, "Die Wiener Genesis," *Beilage z. xv u. xvi B. d. Jahrb. d. Kunsthist. Sammlungen d. A. H. Kaiserhauses* (Vienna, 1895).

49. "ECM", pp. 11–16.

50. "Das Problem der Wiener Genesis," *Jahrb. der Kunsthist. Sammlungen in Wien,* N.F. x (1936), pp. 9–58; "Der Wiener Dioskurides und die Wiener Genesis," *Beschreibendes Verzeichnis der illum. H'dschriften in Österreich,* N.F., bd.4: Die illum. H'dschriften u. Inkunabeln der N.B. in Wien, IV Teil, Die byzantinischen Handschriften I, 1937.

51. K. Weitzmann, "Die Illustrationen d. Septuaginta," *Münchener Jahrb.* d. bild. Kunst, 3rd ser. 3/4 (1952/1953).

52. *ECA,* pp. 75–76.

53. *IRC*, pp. 90, 92.

54. "ECM", fig. 16.

55. A. Muñoz, *Il codice purpureo di Rossano ed il frammento Sinopense* (Rome: Danesi, 1907). W. F. Volbach, *Early Christian Art* (London: Thames & Hudson, 1961), pls. 238–41.

56. C. Nordenfalk, *Die spätantiken Kanontafeln* (Göteborg, 1938). *Idem,* "An Illustrated Diatesseron," *AB* 50 (1968):119–40.

57. *ECA*, p. 108.

58. *IRC*, p. 94.

59. *ECA*, p. 111.

60. A. Baumstark, "Bild und Liturgie in antiochenischen Evangelienbuchschmuck des 6. Jahrhunderts," *Ehrengabe deutscher Wissenschaft, Johann Georg Herzog von Sachsen gewidmet,* ed. E. Fessler (Freiburg i/B, 1920), pp. 233 ff.

61. It was probably originally f.lv at the beginning of the sequence; cf. *ECA*, p. 111. The manuscript was rebound sometime before the seventeenth or eighteenth century and it was presumably moved then; cf. W. Loerke, "The Miniatures of the Trial in the Rossano Gospels," *AB* 42 (1961):175.

62. *BP*, p. 163.

63. *IRC*, pp. 93–94.

64. *AB* 42 (1961):171–95, figs. 1, 9.

65. For a hypothetical reconstruction of the "Christ or Barabbas" mural, cf. Loerke, fig. 11.

66. *ECA*, p. 108 and fig. 23.

67. "Miniatures of the Trial . . . ," pp. 188–92.

68. H. Omont, *Miniatures des plus anciens manuscrits grecs de la Bibliothèque Nationale* (Paris: H. Champion, 1929). A. Grabar, *Les peintures de l'évangéliaire de Sinope, B.N. suppl. gr. 1286,* color facsimile (Paris: Bibliothèque Nationale, 1948).

69. A single sheet of text only from the manuscript is in the museum at Mariupol in Russia, just north of the Sea of Azov; cf. H. Omont, "Un nouveau feuillet du 'Codex Sinopensis' de l'évangile de Saint Matthieu," *Journal des Savants* (1901), pp. 260–62.

70. *IRC*, pp. 93–94.

71. Cf. Grabar, n. 68.

72. *The Rabbula Gospels,* ed. and commented by C. Cecchelli, G. Furlani and M. Salmi (Olten: Urs Graf, 1959).

73. Cf. Nordenfalk, n. 56.

74. Cf. the earlier reference to this point in the discussion of the Rossano Gospels.

75. Other Greek examples of the late sixth or early seventh centuries are in Vienna (NB, Cod. gr. 847) and London (BM, Add. Ms. 5111). Early Latin examples include Vatican Bibl. Apost. Ms. lat 3806, of which two folios are preserved (cf. *EMP,* p. 99), London, BM, Harley Ms. 1775, and a purple Gospel-book with silver uncial text in the Biblioteca Queriniana of Brescia, all cited by Nordenfalk.

76. *ECA*, p. 111.

77. *ECA*, pp. 22 ff, 131 ff.

78. Cf. Friend, n. 33, ii, figs. 7–8.

79. *IRC*, pp. 116 ff.

80. Nordenfalk, *Die spätantiken Kanontafeln,* p. 247.

81. A sixth-century Syriac Gospel-book (Paris, BN Ms. syr. 33) also illustrates the idea. Cf. *ECA*, fig. 124.

82. *Choricii Gazaei orationes,* etc., ed. J. F. Boissonade (Paris, 1846), pp. 91 ff.

83. *ECA*, fig. 149.

84. *ECA*, p. 121.

85. A reproduction in color is in *BP*, p. 164.

2

Byzantine Manuscript Illumination

There is little immediate evidence of the nature of manuscript illumination in Constantinople, the capital of the Eastern or Byzantine Empire, from the middle of the sixth until the middle of the ninth century. This is a direct consequence of the unsettled political and cultural circumstances of the time. Even before the death of Justinian in 565, Byzantium was beset by the Persians, and the rise of the Moslem Empire in the early seventh century posed a continuing threat for many years thereafter. Under the successive Heraclian, Isaurian, and Amorian dynasties, the power of the Byzantine throne was able to maintain itself but little more, and not until the accession of Basil the Macedonian in 867 did it become possible for a generally creative atmosphere to develop. Only during the reign of Leo the Isaurian (717–741) was there a suggestion of the power and glory of earlier times. His promulgation in 726 of the *Ecloga,* a Greek revision and modernizing of the Latin legal code drawn up by Justinian and other elements of the military and agricultural institutions of the day, was a major achievement and contribution to the cultural systematization of the mediaeval world.

But no less significant was the Decree against Images pronounced by Leo in the same year, forbidding their worship and use in churches. In so doing, Leo hoped to reform the superstitious abuses that had grown in popular usage, practices stimulated by belief amounting to fetishism in the miraculous and supernatural powers ascribed to icons of Christ, the Virgin, and the saints. His purpose was no more than to cleanse and purify the practices of Christianity by purging the accretions of popular superstition and lingering paganism and returning to the ethic and morality of the early Church Fathers. But the ensuing controversy between those who sought to destroy all images (iconoclasts) and those wishing to retain them (iconodules) raged until the Empress Theodora finally restored the images in 843. For all the reasonableness of Leo's original intention, the destruction of images was widespread during the reigns of his successors, whose support of iconoclasm was a major factor in bringing about the separation of Western and Eastern Churches.

The Iconoclastic Controversy in the Eastern Church was an expression in its way of the opposition to representational images that was one of the principles of Mohammedanism and many other Oriental beliefs. It is not without significance that the eighth- and early ninth-century Byzantine iconoclasts came largely from Anatolia, where contact with the strict monotheism of Islam was direct and general. But the Arab invasions of northern Africa and the westward diffusion of Moslem beliefs resulting therefrom were of even more consequence. As already noted, Alexandria, a center of Hellenistic ideas, played a key role in the initial formation of Christian pictorial style in the fifth and sixth centuries. The conquest of the city in 642 and the final and complete destruction of its libraries, along with the scattering of its artists, were factors as important as Byzantine iconoclasm in affecting the development of Byzantine art.

Two manuscripts, the Paris Psalter (B. N. Ms. grec 139)[1] and the Rotulus of Joshua (Vatican, Bibl. Apost. Ms. Palat. gr. 431),[2] and mural paintings in the Roman church of Santa Maria Antiqua and in the church of Santa Maria Foris Portas at Castelseprio, a small, sub-Alpine town in northern Italy some sixteen miles north of Milan, are the pertinent works. Scholarly discussion of these monuments is extensive, and often polemic.[3] Such agreement as there is accepts the stylistic community of the group, but no more, most controversial of all being the question of the date.

Of the fourteen miniatures in the Paris Psalter, eight of the life of David illustrate the Psalms, the other six referring to the associated canticles. The text is of the tenth century, but there is clear evidence that the miniatures are insertions. Their folios have been cut down to the dimensions of the text sheets, the ornamental borders are in a different style from those of the text folios,[4] and the gold of the miniature pages is different in color and texture from that found in the text portions. It is clear from these considerations that whatever may be concluded about the date and provenance of the miniatures must be based on their style.

A number of different hands have been identified in the fourteen miniatures, of which the most distinguished is seen in the miniature on f.1v of David as Harper (Fig. 14). He is seated in the center, a female figure behind him identified as Melody by a vertical label in Greek uncials. To the right, behind a stele encircled by a knotted ribbon, is another feminine figure, who is unidentified but probably represents Echo. A reclining masculine figure in the right foreground is inscribed as the hill of Bethlehem, although the pertinent symbol of the walled city is in the upper left corner. The well-proportioned figures are built up in patterns of modeling chiaroscuro and have considerable plasticity. Comparable patterns of light and shade create a sense of perspective depth, amplified by the illusionistic treatment of the foliage, and by such details as the triangular dark accents representing the depths of the eye sockets. Also to be noted is the portrayal of the male personification in the right foreground with dark flesh, the feminine ones being much lighter, continuing a well-established convention of

Hellenistic art. The entire composition, in fact, invites comparison with the idyllic landscapes of late antiquity, like those from Pompeii or the Odyssey Landscapes found in a Roman house on the Esquiline in Rome.[6] The style of these mural paintings derives ultimately from Alexandrian practice, and the same is true of the Paris Psalter miniature, particularly in details such as the foliage of the tree, the beribboned column or stele,[7] and the figure of Melody.

Also by the Harper miniature artist is the one on f.419v of the Crossing of the Red Sea by the Children of Israel (Fig. 15).[8] The composition is in two registers. Above, the Israelites move through the desert guided by the pillar of fire (Exod. 13:31–32). Below, Pharaoh and his army are engulfed by the Red Sea. The seated figure in the upper left is identified by the inscription as a personification of the desert, looking up at a half-length personification, also inscribed, of Night. In the lower right angle is a half-length semi-nude female figure with an oar, labeled the Red Sea; she turns away from a male form inscribed Bythos, the abyss of the sea. What was said of the figure style in the Harper miniature is equally pertinent here. Especially to be noted are the strongly accented highlights modeling the nude personifications in the lower register. Equally notable are the beautifully classic rhythm and contrapposto of the nimbed Moses and the figure behind him in the upper register. Both turn to three-quarter view, apparently to look down on the drowning Egyptians below.

For all its distinction, the motive of Moses turning back to gaze on Pharaoh and his army is neither an accurate illustration of the text (Exod. 14:26–29) nor an invention of the artist, but the result of adapting a model of different character to immediate requirements. It was pointed out in discussing the Vienna Genesis that a tradition of Old Testament illustration can be assumed to have been established in Alexandria, the locus of the Septuagint version, by the second century at the latest. Something of the character of its illustration can be inferred from the lifeless, though presumably faithful, copies of much later date, like a twelfth-century Octateuch, the first eight books of the Old Testament, in the Vatican Library[9] (Ms. gr. 746). On f.192v, the Crossing of the Red Sea is portrayed (Fig. 16) much as it is in the Paris Psalter, but with the difference that the Egyptians are being swallowed up as they follow the Israelites, instead of seeming to pass below them, and Moses follows God's command

Plate V. Dublin, Trinity College Library, Ms. 57 (A. IV. 5), f. 192v. The Book of Durrow, Cross Page of St. John's Gospel.

Plate IV. Florence, Biblioteca Laurenziana, Ms. Amiatinus 1, f. 5. The Amiatinus Codex, Ezra rewriting the Sacred Books.

Plate VI. London, British Museum, Ms. Cotton Nero D. IV,
f. 25v. The Lindisfarne Gospels, St. Matthew.

Fig. 14.
Paris, Bibliothèque Nationale, Ms. gr. 139, f.1v .The Paris
Psalter, David as Harper.

Fig. 15.
Paris, Bibliothèque Nationale, Ms. gr. 139, f.419v. The
Paris Psalter, Crossing of the Red Sea.

"Stretch out thine hand over the sea" instead of pointing down at Pharaoh.

From the general similarity of details in the two versions of the Red Sea crossing, it would seem that their respective artists worked from a common or at least similar models. It is reasonable to assume also that that model was probably a long, continuous frieze or strip, painted or drawn on a scroll or rotulus. From its unbroken sequence, the Paris Psalter artist took the appropriate details of the subject and fitted them to the rectangular format of the codex full page by placing one section above the other, following the procedure adopted by the Vienna Genesis artist (Fig. 8) confronted by a similar problem, but introducing another element in the page design by enclosing the narrative scene in an elaborate border. The Octateuch painter, with a different organizational problem, could retain the narrative sequence of the rotulus prototype in his laterally extended arrangement. It was doubtless in adapting a model to differing compositional circumstances that the male personification in the Harper miniature was moved from the place he should occupy on the hill of Bethlehem, behind the psalmist and his inspiring muse.

Proof that scrolls with continuous frieze-like narrative illustrations were in use in the early Middle Ages is found in the Joshua Rotulus. What remains of it today was separated into fifteen sheets or membranes in 1902. Before its dismemberment, the scroll was about thirty-two feet long by one foot in height. It was not complete even then, since the sequence now begins with Joshua sending two spies to Jericho (Josh. 2:1 ff) and ends with the execution of the five Amorite kings (10:26), something less than half of the book. The text is written along the bottom edge of the scroll for the most part, in a tenth-century Greek minuscule hand. There is clear evidence, however, that it was not originally executed along with the illustrations. It is written in darker ink (also used to re-ink some of the label inscription of the figures) in areas unused by the illustrator for the most part, but occasionally invading the pictorial area as it does in the scene of Joshua and the Captain of the Lord's Host (Fig. 17) illustrating Joshua 5:13–15. The illustrations are not painted but executed in line and wash of brown ink with some details like robes and helmets colored blue or violet; there is some difference of opinion as to whether or not these colored washes were original or added when the labeling inscriptions were re-inked.

The stylistic affinity of the Joshua Rotulus drawings with the miniatures of the Paris Psalter has never been seriously disputed. The illusionistic landscape backgrounds of both contain the same elements of hills, buildings, and trees. Both are punctuated with figures personifying places, mountains, streams, and so on (like the crowned seated female beside the tree in Fig. 17, personifying the city of Jericho in the tradition established by Eutychides, c. 400 B.C., in his Tyche of Antioch), and the filleted stele that partially conceals Echo in the Harper miniature (Fig. 14) has many counterparts in the Rotulus illustrations. Although the hand of a copyist is betrayed by occasionally clumsy articulation of arms and legs, and the coarsening of contours like that of the prostrate Joshua, he was a copyist well grounded in the tradition of late antique Alexandrian illusionism and comprehending its conventions.

As the outstanding extant example of the illustrated scroll book, the importance of the Joshua Rotulus can hardly be exaggerated. That its illustration is in an iconographic tradition of long standing is clear from often-mentioned parallels between its scenes and those in the nave clerestory mosaics of Santa Maria Maggiore at Rome.[10] Similar but later parallels may also be found in the illustrated Greek Octateuchs of the eleventh and twelfth centuries.[11] The precise relationship of the Rotulus scenes to these parallels is controversial,[12] centering around disagreement about its date. Internal evidence is not conclusive. The tenth-century script, as noted, cannot be associated with the illustrations, for it is in a different ink and in a different hand from those seen in the inscribed labels in the drawings. The vertical disposition of these labels is a usage unknown before A.D. 600.[13] Beyond this slender evidence, only stylistic comparisons can be invoked to determine a chronological position for the Rotulus.

There are some stylistic parallels to the Paris Psalter

Fig. 16.
Vatican, Biblioteca Apostolica, Ms. gr. 746, f.192v. Books of the Octateuch, Crossing of the Red Sea.

Fig. 17.
Vatican, Biblioteca Apostolica, Ms. Palat. gr. 431, sheet 4.
The Joshua Roll, Joshua and the Captain of the Lord's
Host.

and Joshua Roll illustrations in other media than manuscript illumination. Some have been observed in a series of decorated silver plates found in Cyprus,[14] which can be dated by official stamps as no later than the early seventh century. Others have been pointed out in the fragmentary frescoes in the Roman church of Santa Maria Antiqua,[15] and in the church of Santa Maria Foris Portas at Castelseprio, near Milan in northern Italy.[16] With due allowance being made for inherent differences between monumental mural designs executed by artists of considerable distinction and individuality, metal work in repoussé, and miniatures copied more or less faithfully or adapted from other compositions, all of these works reflect the style most aptly characterized as the Alexandrian aspect of late antique, Hellenistic illusionism.

Historical circumstance, the Moslem conquest of Alexandria in 642, explains the outcropping of Alexandrian style in both the Italian churches and the manuscript illustrations (generally accepted as having been produced in or for Constantinople), and also provides a reasonable basis for dating them. They were the work of Greek artists fleeing Alexandria before the invaders

and finding opportunities to exercise their talents in other areas of the Mediterranean Christian world, or of local artists who were influenced by them. Myrtilla Avery's careful study of the Santa Maria Antiqua frescoes in question associates the "Alexandrian" work there with Pope John VII (705–707), who was a Greek. Bognetti has assembled impressive evidence of the presence of Greek ecclesiastics in northern Italy in the late seventh and early eighth centuries,[17] supported by Tselos.[18] If, as is reasonable to assume, the Alexandrian illuminators of the Paris Psalter and the Joshua Roll executed those works in Constantinople,[19] the Decree against Images could mark a terminal date for their activities there in 726. Efforts to dissociate the manuscript illuminations from the early eighth century[20] by considering them products of a tenth-century classic "Renaissance" rest on the idea that the Joshua Rotulus was an unprecedented and unparalleled invention of the later period. Many of the arguments upon which this conclusion is based are ingenious, but they are themselves assumptions more often than not.

The restoration of the images in 843 prepared the way for the resumption of artistic activity in Constanti-

Fig. 18.
Paris, Bibliothèque Nationale, Ms. gr. 510, f.438v. Sermons of Gregory of Nazianzus, The Vision of Ezekiel.

nople, and it attained full flood in the reign of Basil I (867–886), founder of the Macedonian regime. His interest in the artistic embellishment of his capital is attested by contemporary accounts of new churches built at his command, and the restoration of older ones defaced during the Iconoclastic Controversy. That he also encouraged manuscript illuminators is proven by the illustration of a book made for him between 880 and 886, a copy of the compilation of sermons known as the Homilies of Gregory of Nazianzus,[21] now in the Bibliothèque Nationale in Paris (Ms. grec 510). The content of the volume defines the spirit of a time in which such religious treatises attained a popularity comparable to that of the Bible itself, an esteem also attested by the considerable number of known copies of the text of these sermons by the late fourth-century bishop of Constantinople (389 ?).

Basil I's copy of Gregory's sermons contains forty-six full-page miniatures in two distinct categories of style and composition. One of these, largely of Old Testament subjects, is seen in the illustration on f.438v of the Vision of Ezekiel (Fig. 18) (Ezek. 37:1–10). A rocky and mountainous landscape is framed by four trumpet-shaped forms in the angles of a blue rectangular field with borders of gold. In the upper left, Ezekiel, blessed by the hand of God, stands near the base of a mountain at the opening of the valley. Below, right, he appears again, his attention directed to the dry bones by an angel. There are many reminiscences of the Alexandrianism of the Paris Psalter in the Gregory miniature, such as the picturesque landscape, and the angel's head which can be compared quite directly, in reverse, with that of Moses in the Paris Psalter Crossing of the Red Sea (Fig. 15).[22]

Such similarities have sometimes been interpreted to suggest that the Paris Psalter artist was copying the style, if not actually the compositions, of the Gregory manuscript. But the draperies of the Gregory figures are drier and more angular, are less effectively modeled, and, for all the not-unsuccessful articulation of the bodies in the antique manner, are beginning to reveal the attenuation of proportion found in the early phase of mid-Byzantine style that the late ninth-century date would suggest. Further indication that the Gregory miniatures postdate those of the Psalter is found in the differences between the two manuscripts in treating similar ornamental motives in the borders.[23] All these considerations lend weight to the probability that Basil I's illuminators were acquainted with Alexandrian

style, either through examples in the Constantinopolitan libraries or through a new influx of artists and manuscripts from that part of the Mediterranean world.

There is some reason to believe, in fact, that the miniatures of the Paris Psalter itself were themselves the model for certain of those in the Gregory manuscript.[24] The grounds for this opinion are found, however, in miniatures of the second type among the Gregory illustrations, exemplified by the story of Julian the Apostate (Fig. 19) on f.409v. In the upper register, Julian and his army move to attack a walled city, possibly Ctesiphon. In the middle, St. Basil and a group of his followers implore divine vengeance on the impious ruler who had sought to return the empire to paganism. Their prayers are granted below as an Alexandrian St. Mercurius slays Julian with a touch of his lance, in a landscape indicated by two sloping green planes outlined against a blue sky. Here, as in the majority of the Gregory subjects for which there was no Alexandrian tradition, i.e., themes not found in the Septuagint or capable of adaptation from them, the compositions are of figures isolated or massed in inarticulate groups, in settings of symbolic architecture or two-dimensional landscapes with neutral backgrounds without implication of time or space. These are the characteristics of the so-called Neo-Attic aspect of early Byzantine art, based on antique usage as was the Alexandrian, but native to the region of Constantinople and thus assured of continuation after the Alexandrian inspiration, already declining in the Gregory miniatures, was exhausted.[25]

The full-page miniatures of the Paris Gregory manuscript are typical in their opulence of works executed for such patrons as the emperor. By contrast, the illustration of another ninth-century manuscript of the same text in the Ambrosian Library at Milan (Cod. E 49–50) consists of vignettes in the margins of the text pages. Those on p. 597 are drawn from a variety of sources. The medallions in the left margin represent Moses, Abraham, and Joseph, and that in the upper right is of John the Baptist. Two scenes at the top are of the Anointing of Saul and of David, and below are Elisha and Elijah on Mount Carmel. The narrative subjects are from the Books of Kings and were selected as commentaries on the text rather than as illustrations in the usual sense; the medallion busts also refer to allusions in the text. In this respect, the Milan Gregory vignettes play the same role as the pictorial commentaries in the margins of the Rabula Gospel canon tables

Fig. 19.
Paris, Bibliothèque Nationale, Ms. gr. 510, f.409v. Sermons of Gregory of Nazianzus, The Story of Julian the Apostate.

Fig. 20.
Milan, Biblioteca Ambrosiana, Ms. E. 49–50, p. 597. Sermons of Gregory of Nazianzus, Portraits and Scenes from the Book of Kings.

(Fig. 12). The theological content of associations such as these suggests the probability that both books were intended for use in a monastic rather than a secular environment.

This is also true of a considerable group of illustrated psalters in which marginal commentary—textual and pictorial—is found, often referred to as "monastic" rather than "aristocratic" psalters.[27] Among early examples, in the ninth century, are the Chloudoff Psalter in the Historical Museum of Moscow, and Ms. grec. 20 in the Bibliothèque Nationale in Paris. The illustration on f.4 of the Parisian manuscript (Fig. 21) of Psalm 95 (The Magnificat) shows the Building of the Temple in Jerusalem. Unlike the more formal compositions of the "aristocratic" group,[28] the marginal vignettes of the "monastic" psalters are full of lively anecdote. The colors range from soft rose through reddish-brown and yellow to purple, reminiscent of the Rossano-Sinope scheme, as are also the stocky, animated figures. The combination of narrative and typological content in

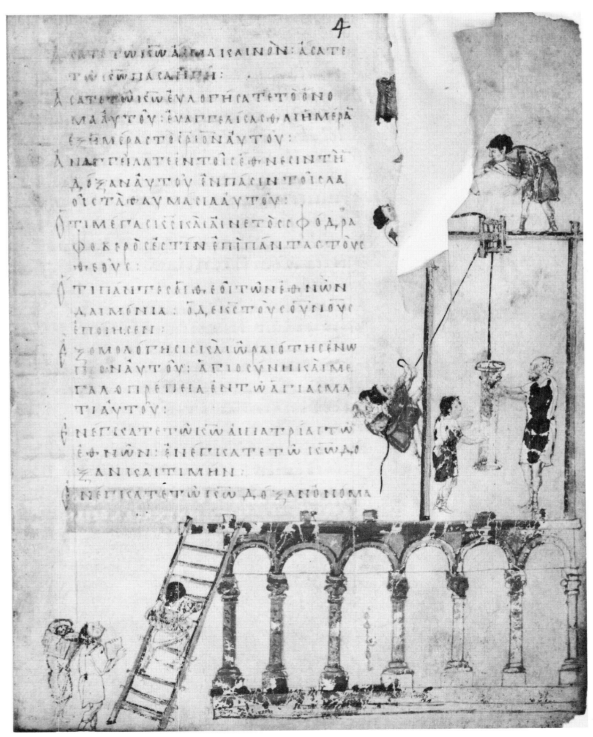

Fig. 21.
Paris, Bibliothèque Nationale, Ms. gr. 20, f.24. Psalter,
Illustrations of Ps. 95, 1, The Building of the Temple.

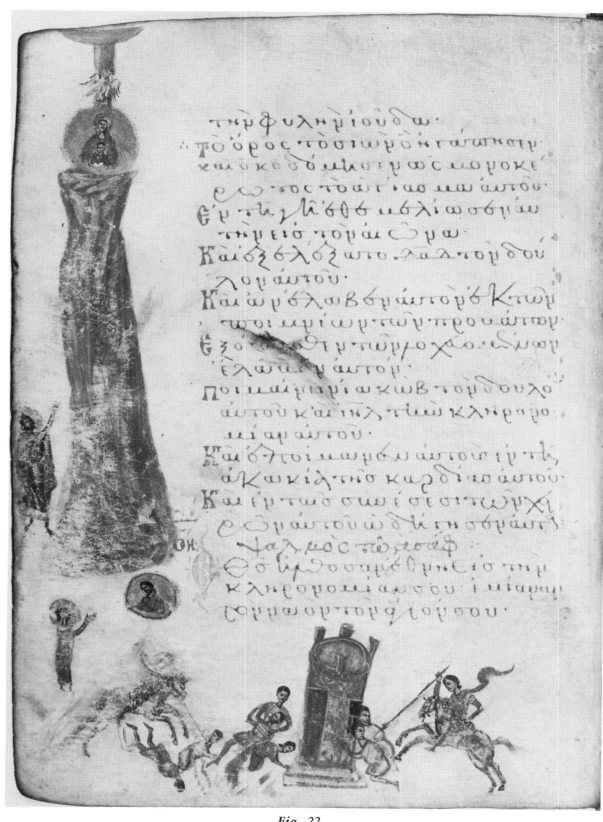

την φυλην ιουδα·
το ορος: το σιων ον ηγαπησ[εν]
και ωκοδομησ ως μονοκε
ρω·τος το αγιασμα αυτου·
εν τη · γη · εθεμελιωσεν αυ
την εις τον αιωνα·
Και εξελεξατο δαδ τον δου
λον αυτου·
Και ανελαβεν αυτον εκ των
ποιμνιων των προβατων·
εξοπισω των τυπ τοκχου ελαβεν
ελαβεν αυτον·
Ποιμαινειν ιακωβ τον δουλο
αυτου· και ιηλ την κληρο
μιαν αυτου·
Και εποιμανεν αυτους εν τη
ακακια της καρδιας αυτου·
Και εν τους συνεσεσιν τ ων χει
ρων αυτου ωδηγησεν αυτ[ους]
ψαλμος τω ασαφ
Ο θς ηλθοσαν εθνη εις την
κληρονομιαν αυτου·εμιαναν
τον ναον τον αγιον σου·

Fig. 22.
Baltimore, Walters Art Gallery, Ms. 733, f.43v. Psalter,
Illustrations of Ps. 78, 69–70; 80, 1–3.

the marginal psalter illustrations was popular for some time. It is found, for instance, in a late eleventh-century example in the Walters Art Gallery in Baltimore (Ms. 733). Psalms 78:69–70 and 79:1–3 in the King James version are illustrated on f.43v (Fig. 22). On the left, the Psalmist prays to the Virgin and Child shown in a medallion on a steep hill, the sanctuary built like high palaces of the text; below, he prays to the Almighty, also shown as a medallion bust. In the lower margin, the vignette illustrates Ps. 79, ". . . thy holy temple have they defiled . . . the dead bodies of thy servants have they given to be meat unto the fowls of the heaven. . . ." Icon-like bust figures like those in the illustration on f.43v appear in many others in the Walters Byzantine Psalter, stressing the value of images in Christian worship. For they continued to be venerated in monasteries even during the Iconoclastic Controversy, and once they could again be created, there are constant references, in monastically inspired books like the marginal psalters, to the wicked as destroyers of images.

By the middle of the tenth century, in the reign of Constantine VII Porphyrogenitus (912–959), the "Macedonian Renaissance" was well under way. In Constantinople, manuscript illumination provides important examples in which the traditional eclecticism of the capital is apparent, and also the ultimate and classic statement of the style. This is defined in part by two examples of mid-tenth-century illumination (Figs. 23, 24), both from Gospel-books and both portraits of St. Mark. It will be recalled that such author portraits were among the first pictorial additions to the Gospel text (Fig. 9, Plate II). A. M. Friend has established the distinction between the principal types in Greek examples, standing and seated figures, on geographic grounds,[29] the former originating in Alexandrian usage, the latter in Near-Eastern Neo-Attic practice. The St. Mark in the Mount Athos manuscript (Stauronikita, Ms. 43, f.11) (Fig. 23) shows the Evangelist seated as he is in the Rossano version, and in this it exemplifies the Neo-Attic group. But the background of a garden wall and other architectural elements set against the gold sky is carried over from the illusionistic settings of Alexandrian origin. By contrast, the St. Mark in the Vienna Gospel-book (Cod., theol. gr. 240, f.97v) is standing as in Alexandrian usage (Fig. 24) against a background that appears at first glance to be neutral gold but actually has a setting of architectural forms tooled in the gold.

In both examples, the figures are reasonably well modeled and substantial, reflecting antique prototypes so faithfully that they have been equated with those of the Paris Psalter and the Joshua Rotulus. But the tightening of the impressionistic style that gives life and vitality to the forms in those earlier works, a phenomenon already noted in the miniatures of Basil I's Gregory (Figs. 18, 19), is even more apparent here. In like fashion, the subordination of realistic setting to the abstract gold background betokens an expressive concern with transcendental content also manifest in the forward thrusting head of the Vienna evangelist. Comparable though it is in some ways to the Ezekiel in the upper register of the Gregory miniature (Fig. 18), the expressive character of the Vienna Saint Mark is quite different, a difference resulting from the modified movement of the figure and its spaceless gold environment, for all the tooled architectural details.

By the beginning of the eleventh century, the progressive transformation of style seen in the modifications of the late antique manner that took place in the ninth and early tenth centuries attains to the full and mature Byzantine synthesis. This is seen in the four hundred and thirty miniatures of the Menologium of Basil II (976–1025) in the Vatican Biblioteca Apostolica (Ms. gr. 1613) and in the mid-eleventh-century fragment of the same text in the Walters Art Gallery in Baltimore (Ms. 521).[30] The Menologium content is a synaxary, a compilation of short readings of the lives of the saints included in the liturgy of their feast days in the church calendar. Neither the Vatican nor Walters text is complete; the former has the readings from September through February, the latter for January. Eight different artists contributed to the Vatican manuscript, each signing a number of miniatures, yet the style is remarkably uniform throughout; there is no significant distinction, save that of slightly later date, to be observed between its scenes and those in the Walters book. The minor differences that do appear are not to be accounted for as those of different hands but probably from using different models. This consistency of style is a product of the process of decorative schematizing and reduction to formula of the style evolved in the late ninth and early tenth centuries.

On page three of the Vatican Menologium, the reading for the feast of St. Michael on September 1 is illustrated (Fig. 25). The appearance of the Angel of God to Joshua is at the left; on the right is the burial of St.

Simeon Stylites, whose feast fell on the same day. As in the portrayal of the same incident in the Joshua Rotulus (Fig. 17), a symbol of the city of Jericho appears in the background but the personification has been omitted. To the right, behind the burial, a sharply peaked hill recalls the mountainous Alexandrian backgrounds of the illustrated scroll, but similarities cease with this. Instead of the neutral parchment on which the Rotulus forms are drawn directly, there is the ground of neutral gold, which becomes increasingly the Byzantine convention for a spiritual rather than material ambient. The

sketchy outlines conveying the impression of flickering light and shade on the Rotulus figures and providing the contours of trees and buildings with an atmospheric envelope have disappeared. Edges are sharp and precise; the figures are frontal or in profile and lack the rhythm of pose and movement that informs their Rotulus counterparts with a sense of actuality. Weitzmann's discerning analysis of the minute stylistic variations in the miniatures[31] makes it clear that classical prototypes are referred to throughout the entire series, particularly in the proportions of the figures and the

occasional modeling of the faces. But these are themselves only elements of an overall process of conventionalization that soon crystallized in formula. When the artists of the slightly later Menologium in the Walters Gallery (Ms. 521) treated similar subjects, they did it with even less individuality and variety of manner, an instance of the traditionalism that Byzantine illumination shared with other forms of Byzantine usage, liturgical, literary, and pictorial, as practiced in mosaic in particular.

Another element in the eclectic synthesis of style in early eleventh-century Constantinopolitan illumination is seen in the Canon Tables (Fig. 26) on f.8 of a Greek gospel book in the Bibliothèque Nationale in Paris (Ms. grec 64). As in the sixth-century Canon Tables of the Rabula Gospels (Fig. 12), the columns separating the references are surmounted by an arch that supports vases, flowers and animals, also as in the Syrian manuscript. But the spandrels above the arch are squared up by a lozenge border, and the sketchy outlines of the Rabula forms are replaced by precise contours that are typically Byzantine. A new note is also struck in the pattern filling the lunette of the arch and the angle spandrels, an unaccented all-over design instead of the centralized symmetry of the Rabula miniature. And instead of the Corinthianesque capitals, still retaining something of antique proportion seen in the Syriac example, those of the Byzantine design are spread and flattened into a form more resembling a palmette. The influence of Islamic style is clear in such details as these, and although the color scheme is the typically Constantinopolitan harmony of blue and gold, the general effect is more like that of the decorative architecture and minutely scaled metal-work and enamels of Iranian origin.

In manuscript illumination of the eleventh and twelfth centuries in Constantinople, the earlier dualism of aristocratic and monastic categories generally continues. This is not so much because a given manuscript may have been executed in a monastic scriptorium (there is some reason to believe that many of the so-called court volumes were made in monasteries) as because of the character of its illustration. An example of the court style is the copy of the Homilies of St. John Chrysostom in the Bibliothèque Nationale in Paris (Ms. Coislin 79). The book itself is being presented to Nicephoros III Botaniates (1078–1081) in the miniature on f.2v (Fig. 27); he is flanked by the archangel Michael on his left and St. John Chrysostom,

from whom he receives the codex, on his right. The small kneeling figure at the archangel's feet may be the copyist. The three principals appear against a neutral gold background framed by a border of small rosettes, a motive also used for the costumes of the emperor and the archangel and the podium on which the ruler stands. This all-over pattern, contrasted by the sober black of the saint's robe, is again of Iranian origin. It is not only the pattern that suggests this, but the reduced scale of the rosette motives, which makes them fitting adjuncts to the disproportionately small hands and feet of the figures. Another contrast is seen between the severely planar bodies and the faces, subtly modeled in delicate gradations of tones and highlights. All these elements of style contribute to a monumental, hieratically expressive ensemble in which the ascetic emaciation of earlier forms (cf. Fig. 24) gives way to an impressively impersonal calm, to which the sonorous harmony of blue and gold also makes an effective contribution.

The second category of eleventh-century style of illumination in Constantinople, the monastic, is abundantly represented in small gospel books like Mss. 115 and 74 in the Bibliothèque Nationale in Paris, and Ms. Plut. 6, 23 in the Florentine Biblioteca Laurenziana (Figs. 28, 29).[32] All are luxury volumes and can be associated in some respects with the courtly tradition of patronage. The book in the Laurenziana, for example, has a series of author portraits in which the Alexandrian tradition of architectural settings and gold backgrounds observed in Stauronikita 43 (Fig. 23) is continued, though in eleventh-century style. Moreover, the Gospel headings like that of St. Matthew on f.5 (Fig. 28) are decorated with the same type of minutely scaled all-over patterns with ornamental birds and flowers, betokening Oriental influence, as noted in the discussion of Paris Ms. grec 64 (Fig. 26). All the miniatures are heavily painted in thick pigments, which have flaked off in some places, as is so often the case with earlier Byzantine miniatures (cf. Figs. 18, 19), an interesting commentary on the soundness of Byzantine illuminating technique. The eighth-century *Compositiones ad tingenda musiva* in the Biblioteca Capitolare at Lucca (Ms. 490),[33] a manual based on current Byzantine practice, gives careful instructions on the preparation of parchment for illumination but touches only lightly on how to make gold and color adhere to it.

It is not in such decorative features as these, however, that the monastic idiom is seen in these eleventh-century

Fig. 23.
Mount Athos, Stauronikita Library, Ms. 43, f.11. Gospels, St. Mark.

Byzantine gospel-books. On f.5 of the one in Florence (Fig. 28), there is a bust of Christ in the top of the letter *rho,* with which the first verse begins, and the Evangelist Matthew is leaning against the vertical stroke of the letter as he sits at his writing desk below. His figure thus repeats the theme of the full-length miniature facing it on f.4v, but, unlike the larger version, it is painted directly on the parchment, without any background. Near the bottom of the right-hand margin of the same folio, a group of figures, also painted directly on the vellum, represents the genealogy of Christ (Matt. 1:1–16), a marginal commentary following the tradition of the monastic psalters of the tenth and eleventh centuries.

But even more individual are the numerous illustrations interspersed in the text of the Constantinopolitan eleventh-century gospel-books. The two on f.8 (Fig. 29) are of the third chapter of Matthew in which John

the Baptist preaches of Christ's coming and baptizes Him. Narrative sequence is stressed in the miniatures, which are composed of frieze-like strips occupying the full width of the text column, as in the Vienna Genesis (Fig. 8) and the Rossano Gospels (Fig. 10). In their narrative role, these miniatures understandably have a quality quite different from the immobile and hierarchic solemnity of their "aristocratic" congeners. For all their diminutive size (the Laurentian book measures only 200 x 165 mm., a little less than 8 x 6.5"), the gestures are lively, the poses and movements expressive. The drawing is hardly impressionistic, but has none of the severe stylization of the court manner. The spirited rhythm of movements and contours is accented by the sharp red, which dominates the color scheme of browns, grays, and blacks, for the most part, with occasional touches of grayish-blue. And instead of the neutral gold backgrounds of the "artistocratic" miniatures, the parchment of the folio provides a place without time or space for the fragmentary shapes of the landscape in which the Baptist's story unfolds. In the illustrated Octateuchs (Fig. 16), which are another characteristic expression of mid-Byzantine monastic sentiment, there is the same feeling for garrulous narrative embodied in forms of

similar character. The only noteworthy difference in the Octateuch illustrations is the more prominent role of landscape in these late derivatives of the Alexandrian tradition of Old Testament pictorial interpretation, but even this is simplified and conventionalized into two-dimensional pattern.

The illustrated Octateuchs and Gospel-books are of the period identified with the Comnenian dynasty in Byzantine history (1057–1185). Much illumination was produced then, the greater part of it in traditional forms of both text and illustration. An occasional new note is struck, however, as in two manuscripts of sermons, called the Homilies of the Virgin, by the monk Jacobus of Kokkinibaphos, dating from mid-twelfth century.[34] One is in the Vatican Library (Ms. gr. 1162), the other, copied from it, is in the Bibliothèque Nationale in Paris (Ms. grec 1208). The Fall of Man (Fig. 30) is on f.47 of the example in Paris. Against a gold background, sinuous lines accented by red and blue trees create the setting of a hilly Paradise. In the upper left corner, Eve is tempted by the serpent, and then is joined by Adam in the upper right in eating the forbidden fruit. Below, in the center, a blue-robed angel accuses them of their sin, and expels them from the

Fig. 25.
Vatican, Biblioteca Apostolica, Ms. gr. 1613, p. 3. The
Menologium of Basil II, Joshua and the Captain of the
Lord's Host; Burial of St. Simeon Stylites.

Fig. 24.
Vienna, Nationalbibliothek, Cod. theol. gr. 240, f.97v.
Gospels, St. Mark.

Fig. 26.
Paris, Bibliothèque Nationale, Ms. gr. 64, f.8. Gospels, Canon Table.

Fig. 28.
Florence, Biblioteca Laurenziana, Ms. Plut. 6, 23, f.5. Gospels, Matthew *incipit. (Photo Pineider)*

Fig. 27.
Paris, Bibliothèque Nationale, Ms. Coislin 79, f.2v. Hom-
ilies of St. John Chrysostom. St. John Chrysostom, Nice-
phoros Botaniates and the Archangel Michael.

Fig. 29.
Florence, Biblioteca Laurenziana, Ms. Plut. 6, 23, f.8.
Gospels, St. John Preaching and Baptizing Christ. (Photo
Pineider)

Fig. 30.
Paris, Bibliothèque Nationale, Ms. gr. 1208, f.47. Homilies of the monk Jacobus, The Fall of Man.

Garden in the lower right angle. Between these two scenes, a partially concealed nude figure holds a red cornucopia, from which flow the Four Rivers of Paradise in curling blue jets with white highlights. This reminiscence of antique symbolism has a stylistic echo in the conventionalized modeling of the nude figures, but the whole is transformed to Byzantine rather than classic effect in the rhythmic rather than axially symmetrical composition. Characteristic of mid-Byzantine style specifically is the multiplication of accents into all-over pattern and the consequent diminution of scale.

Constantinople fell to the Western armies of the Fourth Crusade in 1204, and the interim period before the accession of the Palaeologan dynasty was one of little artistic activity. The ensuing final phase of Byzantine art, ending with the conquest of the city by the Turks in 1453, is notable more for its monumental frescoes and mosaics than for manuscript illumination. Nonetheless, so distinguished a volume as the Rockefeller McCormick New Testament (Library of the University of Chicago, Codex 2400)[35] could be produced in the latter half of the thirteenth century, prob-

ably in the imperial scriptorium. Its illustration is both sumptuous (many of the miniatures are on purple folios) and lavish; it contains one of the most extensive cycles of New Testament illustration in Byzantine illumination, with eighty-two text miniatures preserved of a one-time total estimated at something over a hundred. Unhappily, many of the miniatures have flaked badly; that on f.37v (Fig. 31) of the Healing of the Man from Capernaum (Mark 1:23–27) is one of the better preserved. The unburnished gold background sets off the

Fig. 31.
Chicago, University of Chicago Library, Cod. 2400, f.37v. The Rockefeller-McCormick Gospels, Healing of the Man of Capernaum.

blue, purple-red, and white of the robes where the pigments have not disappeared, to reveal the preliminary drawing of red lines. The hieratic schematizing of Comnenian mid-Byzantine style is somewhat softened, possibly the influence of Macedonian models. Moreover, there is an obvious interest in greater naturalism of

form and the third dimension, accountable for, in part, perhaps, by Occidental ideas introduced during the Latin government of Constantinople in the early thirteenth century.

By the closing years of the fourteenth century, the semi-naturalism of Palaeologan style had become firmly established in Byzantine illumination. The double author portrait in the manuscript of the writings of Emperor John VI Cantacuzene in the Bibliothèque Nationale (Ms. grec 1242, f.123v),[36] executed between 1347 and 1354, presents an extraordinary contrast between the sharply individualized heads and the inexpressive silhouettes of the bodies. The landscape of the Transfiguration on f.92v of the same manuscript seeks, on the other hand, to convert spatial depth into pattern in the manner already taken over and transformed to new purpose in the western Italo-Byzantine style of Siena. The Baptism of Christ (Fig. 32) on f.61v of a Gospel-book in the Walters Art Gallery in Baltimore (Ms. 531) has many of the same characteristics, if on a less monumental scale. Against the gold background, the Byzantine landscape formula of hill and slope is repeated in browns and russet-reds, accented by the Baptist's darker robe and the blue-gray of the angel's with its arbitrary highlights. The sombre flesh tones of hands and faces, and the nude figure of the Saviour accord well with this sere and mournful harmony of color.

Byzantine manuscript illumination is historically important for a number of reasons. From an iconographic point of view, the earliest extant cycles of illustration for Biblical and theological texts, cycles that established patterns for the whole mediaeval period, were Byzantine. It is in Byzantine illumination that the potential of decorative pattern for expressive purposes, particularly in terms of color, is first effectively realized, drawing upon the Oriental component of its cultural tradition in this to make its book art an outstanding expression of the transcendental content of Christian faith. Yet this is combined and harmonized with a lively sense of organic beauty inherited from the classic past, a sense of which the Byzantine tradition was almost the sole conservator during the Early Middle Ages and which it was to transmit to the Occident when the capacity to understand it was finally to develop there. The significance of this Byzantine contribution to the art of the illuminated book can hardly be overstated. Taking its point of departure in the dematerialized and often ugly

Fig. 32.
Baltimore, Walters Art Gallery, Ms. 531, f.61v. Gospels.
The Baptism of Christ.

forms to which classic style had been reduced in the late years of imperial Rome, it created patterns with a new grace and decorative rhythm particularly appropriate to the ornamentation of the manuscript folio. A specific instance in point is the uniquely Oriental contribution to the decorative arrangement of the elements of the Biblical text—the Eusebian canon tables. In them, the verbal substance of the Scriptures is subjected to a process of decorative organization and clarification in order that its meaning may be better understood and more readily grasped. This is the essence of manuscript illumination as an expressive art.

NOTES

1. Cf. Omont, chap. 1, n. 68. H. Buchtal, *The Miniatures of the Paris Psalter; A Study in Middle Byzantine Painting* (London: Warburg Institute, 1938).

2. *Il Rotulo di Giosuè: Codices e Vaticanis selecti V* (Rome: Vatican, 1905). K. Weitzmann, *The Joshua Roll: A Work of the Macedonian Renaissance* (Princeton: Princeton University Press, 1948).

3. Cf. C. R. Morey, "Castelseprio and the Byzantine 'Renaissance,'" *AB* 24 (1952):173–201, for a brief summary.

4. M. Alison Frantz, "Byzantine Illuminated Ornament," *AB* 16 (1934):73–75.

5. "ECM," pp. 28–32.

6. G. Gassiot-Talabot, *Roman and Paleochristian Painting* (New York: Funk & Wagnalls, 1969).

7. *ECA*, p. 173.

8. A good color reproduction is in *BP*, p. 169.

9. Cf. Weitzmann, *The Joshua Roll, passim*.

10. A. S. Keck, "Observations on the Iconography of Joshua," *AB* 32 (1950):267–74.

11. Cf. n. 9.

12. D. Tselos, "The Joshua Roll; Original or Copy?", *AB* 32 (1950):275–90.

13. *ECA*, p. 70.

14. *ECA*, p. 97; cf. Volbach, *Early Christian Art*, pls. 249–51.

15. M. Avery, "The Alexandrian Style at Santa Maria Antiqua," *AB* 7 (1925):131 ff. Cf. *EDA*, figs. 122, 129, 131–33.

16. G. P. Bognetti, A. De Capitani d'Arzago and G. Chierici, *Santa Maria di Castelseprio* (Milan: Fondazione Treccani, 1948). K. Weitzmann, *The Fresco Cycle of Santa Maria di Castelseprio* (Princeton: Princeton University Press, 1951). Morey, n. 3.

17. Bognetti, pp. 201 ff.

18. D. Tselos, "A Greco-Italian School of Illuminators and Painters," *AB* 38 (1956):1–30.

19. "ECM", p. 35.

20. Cf. Weitzmann, *The Joshua Roll, passim.*

21. Cf. Omont, chap. 1, n. 68; Buchtal, n. 1; K. Weitzmann, *Die Byzantinischen Buchmalerei des 9. und 10. Jahrhunderts* (Berlin: Mann, 1935).

22. Cf. C. R. Morey, "The 'Byzantine Renaissance," *Speculum* 14 (1939):139–59, fig. 3.

23. Cf. Frantz, n. 4.

24. *ECA*, pp. 194–95.

25. Many of the Paris Psalter compositions were also adapted in the early tenth-century miniatures of the Leo Bible in the Vatican Biblioteca Apostolica (Ms. Reg. gr. 1), *Collezione paleografica Vaticana, I; Le miniature della Bibbia cod. Vat. Regin. gr. 1, e del Salterio cod. Vat. Palat. gr. 381.* C. Mango, "The Date of Cod. Vat. Reg. Gr. 1 and the 'Macedonian Renaissance,'" *Acta ad Archaeologiam et Artium Historiam Pertinentia,* Institutum Romanum Norvegiae 4 (1969):121–26. (Rome: "L'Erma" di Bretschneider). Cf. Morey, "ECM", p. 35 ff.; "Castelseprio", p. 187; Buchtal, chap. 2, n. 1.

26. Cf. Weitzmann, *Byz. Buchm.*, p. 81; Grabar, A., *Les miniatures du Gregoire de Nazianze de l'Ambrosienne* (Paris: Van Oest, 1926).

27. J. J. Tikkanen, *Die Psalterillustrationen im Mittelalter,* Acta Societatis Scientiarum Fennicae 21, n. 5 (Helsingfors, 1903).

28. *IRC*, p. 131.

29. Cf. n. 33, chap. 2.

30. *Il menologio di Basilio II,* Codices e Vaticanis selecti, vol. 8 (Turin, 1907).

31. *IRC*, pp. 199–205.

32. H. Omont, *Évangiles avec peintures byzantines du XIe siècle,* 2 vols. (Paris: Berthaud, 1908).

33. John M. Burnam, *A Classic Technology edited from Codex Lucensis 490* (Boston: R. G. Badger, 1920). H. Hedfors (ed. and trans.), *Compositiones ad tingenda musiva . . .* (Uppsala, 1932).

34. C. Stornajolo, *Miniature delle omilie di Giacomo Monaco,* Codices e Vaticani selecti, serie minor, vol. 1 (Rome, 1910). H. Omont, "Miniatures des homiliés sur la Vierge du moine Jacques," *Bulletin de la Société française de reproduction de manuscrits à peintures* 11 (1927).

35. E. J. Goodspeed, D. W. Riddle and H. R. Willoughby, *The Rockefeller-McCormick New Testament* (Chicago: University of Chicago Press, 1932).

36. Reproduced in color in *BP*, p. 184.

3
Occidental Manuscript Illumination of the Early Middle Ages

Manuscript illumination in Western Europe from the beginning of the seventh century until Charlemagne's time differs in many respects from that of the Christian Orient, but in none more significantly than that it had little if any of the public character of Byzantine work. From the outset, fine books were made for royal and aristocratic patrons as well as the Church in the Eastern Empire, continuing in a way the tradition of public art of classic antiquity. In the west, on the other hand, the art of the book was nurtured almost solely in the monastic and cathedral centers like Canterbury and York, to mention only two. This was a direct consequence of the political disruption of Western Europe following the collapse of the Latin empire, the result of the successive invasions of non-Mediterranean peoples from the north and east, beginning with Alaric's sack of Rome in 410. Not until Charlemagne's attempt to recreate the glory of the ancient empire toward the end of the eighth century did the arts—including manuscript illumination—begin to enjoy in Western Europe a measure of royal and secular patronage comparable to that in the Byzantine east.

From a historical point of view, the importance of manuscript illumination in the arts that served the Church during this period is very great. Outside Italy, very little monumental painting and sculpture of the time still exists,[1] a fact explained in part, undoubtedly, by the depredations of time and destruction, but also because what building was being done at the time offered but little scope for such ornamentation. For books, however, there was constant need and demand, for they were essential to the function of every church. As C. R. Morey has pointed out,[2] at least three books were required for religious services—a psalter, a Gospel-book, and a sacramentary in which Scripture readings used in the Mass were gathered. However little the need may have been for painting and sculpture to decorate the church building, books were indispensable in the proper conduct of the rites celebrated within its walls.

It was not only for their practical or utilitarian value, however, that the sacred and liturgical texts were held in such high regard. The concept of the "holy book" is a fundamental tenet of the Judaeo-Christian civilization, for both its form[3] and its content.[4] Moreover, waning literacy brought with it the feeling that the book was something meaningful or sacred in its own right. As the ability to read for information and enlightenment declined, the written word became more and more an object of devotion, none the less because its literal meaning may not have been grasped. As such, its decoration became illumination rather than illustration, which had been its traditional role in classic antiquity and the Mediterranean areas of early Christianity. This is not to say that there was no precedent in late classical times for the idea of textual embellishment apart from illustration. The Vergil *Codex Augusteus* of the late fourth century (Vat. Bibl. Apost. Ms. lat. 3526 & Berlin, DSB, lat. fol. 416)[5] begins each page with an enlarged capital letter, detached from the text column and extended down the margins, sometimes even when such initial letters are in the middle of a sentence. The broadened hastae or verticals are often decorated with colored patterns of triangles, shaded stripes, or zigzags. But the Augustan Vergil is unique among manuscripts of its period, and although the practice of enlarging initial letters of chapters reappears in the later sixth century in a volume of the writings of Orosius[6] in the Laurentian Library in Florence (Ms. Plut. 65, 1), it is comparatively rare until well into the seventh century.

Viewed broadly, pre-Carolingian manuscript illumination in the Occident falls into three distinctive yet related categories. The first in time, so far as can be determined, is a group of books in whose miniatures the stylistic dominant is a Latin Early Christian strain; they either originated in or are associated with widely separated centers ranging from Italy, Gaul, and Spain to the British Isles. The general locus of the second group is continental. It is made up of books illuminated in the so-called barbarian style, variously termed Merovingian, Visigothic, and the like, depending on an indicated or assumed place of origin. The third group includes manuscripts illuminated in Celtic monasteries or in foundations established by or related to them on the Continent.

For all the stylistic differences between them, all three groups have in common the fact that they are outgrowths and direct expressions of the expansion of Christianity from Italy through the northern regions of Europe. Christ's Pentecostal admonition to the apostles, ". . . ye shall be witnesses unto me . . . unto the uttermost parts of the earth" (Acts 1:8), was taken quite literally, with the result that Christianity had been established by the fifth century in Ireland and Gaul. Bede records in the *Ecclesiastical History of the English* (i. 13) that in 431 "Palladius is ordained by Pope Celestine, and is sent as their first bishop to the Irish believers in Christ." He was succeeded within a

year by Saint Patrick, whose activities on behalf of the Church have made him legendary. Sidonius, Bishop of Clermont in France in 469, was equally noted for his devout faith. By the middle of the sixth century, affiliates or foundations of the Celtic monasteries had been established in many parts of the British Isles and on the Continent.[7] They are among the centers where a considerable number of pre-Carolingian books were produced.

Some idea of the way in which elements of style and iconography were transmitted from one region to another, influencing and stimulating local developments, can be gained from the traditional history of the Cambridge Gospels[8] in the library of Corpus Christi College in Cambridge (Ms. 286). It is also called the Gospel Book of St. Augustine, for it is believed to be one of the "many codices" that were sent, according to Bede, by Pope Gregory the Great in 596 to aid the saint in his mission to bring Christianity to the English. There are two miniatures, a portrait of St. Luke (Fig. 33, Plate III) on f.129v, with scenes from his gospel in panels between the paired columns flanking his throne,[9] and, of f.125, a full-page miniature of episodes in the Passion of Our Lord[10] in the twelve panels of a trellis-like frame, a scheme comparable to that of the Quedlinburg *Itala* illustrations (Fig. 3).

Many characteristics of the Luke miniature suggest that it is a late sixth-century example of Latin Early Christian style. The rounded head and close-cropped hair can be found in many Roman catacomb paintings of the period,[11] and the drapery formula of simple curves, as well as the bands of various colors that are the backgrounds of the lateral scenes, seem to represent a later phase of the style seen in the late fifth-century illustrations of the *Codex Romanus* (Fig. 6, Plate I). The architecture of flattened capitals and arabesqued pilasters, along with the simplified coffer-and-rosette pattern of the archivolt, is a later version of the type seen in the Chronograph of 354.[12]

Figures much like those in the Cambridge Gospels miniatures in their heavy proportions and bullet-shaped heads are found in a series of illustrations in a manuscript of purple text leaves in the Staatsbibliothek at Munich (Ms. Clm. 23631). They are insertions in a book that once belonged to Hatto, abbot of the monastery at Reichenau between 806 and 823, but there seems to be no reason to associate the making of the miniatures with the text.[13] The Massacre of the Innocents (Fig. 34) is on what is now f.24v. The stylistic

Fig. 34.
Munich, Bayerischestaatsbibliothek, Ms. Clm. 23631,
f.24v. Codex Purpureus, *The Massacre of the Innocents.*

characteristics noted above, which relate it to the Cambridge Gospel miniatures, are also found in an ivory diptych carved with New Testament scenes,[14] which dates from the last half of the fifth century and is thought to have originated in northern Italy or southern Gaul. An iconographic peculiarity is also common to the miniature and the ivory plaque, the slaying of the infants in the Massacre by dashing them on the ground instead of piercing them with a sword or spear. This specific motive appears to have its origin in a liturgical rubric, "in allisione infantum," of the Feast of the Innocents in the Gallican, i.e., south French version of the Order of the Mass, and nowhere else.[15] Another iconographic similarity between the inserted miniatures of the Munich *Codex Purpureus* and the Cambridge Gospel scenes is the portrayal of Peter as beardless although he is usually shown bearded. This too is a usage identifiable with the north Italian-southern Gallic milieu as early as the fifth century, for it appears in the Kranenburg ivory diptych of that date in the Metropolitan Museum in New York.[16] Still further support for a date not later than the early seventh century for the *Codex Purpureus* miniatures is their unusual cross-shaped pattern; the closest analogue is in the figured cross-reliquaries that became popular in the sixth century but were not much used before then.[17]

Also dating from the seventh century, but of much more problematic provenance, are the nineteen full-page miniatures of the Ashburnham Pentateuch in the Bibliothèque Nationale in Paris (Ms. n.a. lat. 2334);[18] they illustrate the Old Testament narrative from the Creation through the exodus of the Children of Israel from Egypt. The story of Jacob and Esau (Gen. 27–28) appears on f.25 (Fig. 35). The folios are of some size (37.5 x 33.0 cm: 14 9/16 x 12 9/16″) and the format is almost square, reminiscent of late fourth- and early fifth-century Latin manuscripts like the two Vergil books in the Vatican (Figs. 4 and 6, Plate I) and the Quedlinburg *Itala* (Fig. 3). The color is lively, the backgrounds of the scenes in different hues, as in the Cambridge Gospels miniatures (Fig. 33, Plate III), which distinguish them from each other as the rather casually treated narrative sequences do not. The story begins in the upper left, where Isaac sends Esau to prepare the venison, continues through the middle register in which Rebekah assists Jacob in deceiving his father and being blessed by him as Esau returns with his offering to the right. Below, Isaac sends Jacob away, and the Vision of the Ladder ascending to heaven ends the nar-

rative in the lower right corner (Gen. 28:11–22). The narrative is as brisk as the coloring, with numerous genre details. In this respect, the Ashburnham miniature surpasses even the Vienna Genesis narratives (Fig. 8), although the frieze-like arrangement is comparable in both. But the architectural settings are more elaborate and suggest a model in which such elements were more functional. The text provides no clue to provenance, either. That of the Scripture itself is the Vulgate version, but the marginal labels and the inscriptions identifying the scenes in the miniature are in the Old Latin recension.

Some details of the Ashburnham Pentateuch miniatures like the parti-colored backgrounds and the spiral-topped angel wings are found in later Spanish illumination like the illustrated Beatus Commentaries on the Apocalypse (cf. Fig. 99, Plate XVI), leading to the speculation that it may be the work of an Iberian scriptorium. Studies of the flora and fauna[19] have suggested a north African source as a possibility, and other hypotheses have sought to establish a connection with the Near East.[20] But to whatever locale they may ultimately be assigned, it cannot be doubted that the miniatures of the Ashburnham Pentateuch, like those of the Cambridge Gospels, are to be linked directly with the style of late Latin antiquity of which they are the last phase. In all probability, the model was a well-illustrated Old Testament of the kind the later illuminators of the eighth and ninth centuries turned to, in part at least, in the scriptoria of northern and western Europe.[21]

But only in part. In the second broad category of pre-Carolingian books, the so-called barbarian manuscripts, there is but little of the representational narrative seen in the volumes just discussed. Instead, the guiding principle is decoration rather than portrayal, glorification rather than illustration. On f.144 of a Lectionary (Fig. 36) in the Bibliothèque Nationale in Paris (Ms. lat. 9427), the initial T of the word *tempore* (Luke 2:1) has been so enlarged that the vertical staff or *hasta* fills the height of the page forming a decorative margin on the left side. Its base is a pair of scrolls and the cross-bar consists of two intersecting arcs that form a fish, supported by two birds whose tails touch the central *hasta* at the level of the first line of cursive script. The line in red rubrics at the top of the folio is further ornamented with an enlarged letter C, of Caesar, whose upper and lower curves are also stylized fish. The broadened *hasta* of the T is filled with a pattern of tendrils and rosettes. The color scheme is simple—the decorative motives of red and green on a yellow ground filling the major outlines.

The script of the Lectionary is the calligraphic minuscule identified with the scriptorium at Luxeuil,[22] in the Vosges Mountains in eastern France, in a monastery founded in 590 by the Celtic missionary Columbanus from Iona in Ireland. The earliest dated example of this script is in a manuscript of St. Augustine's Homilies on the Epistle of St. John in the Morgan Library in New York (Ms. 334), written and deco-

rated at Luxeuil in 669, according to the colophon. The Bibliothèque Nationale Lectionary is not precisely dated, but is thought to be of the late seventh century. In enlarging the initial letter on the folio, the Luxeuil illuminator might seem to have been continuing the practice of the fourth-century Roman decorator of the *Vergilius Augusteus,* but there is no precedent in late antique book ornament, either Western or Eastern, for the zoomorphs of which it is built. So far as can be determined, this idea of the decorated initial seems to

Fig. 35.
Paris, Bibliothèque Nationale, Ms. n.a. lat. 2334, f.25. The
Ashburnham Pentateuch, The Story of Jacob and Esau.

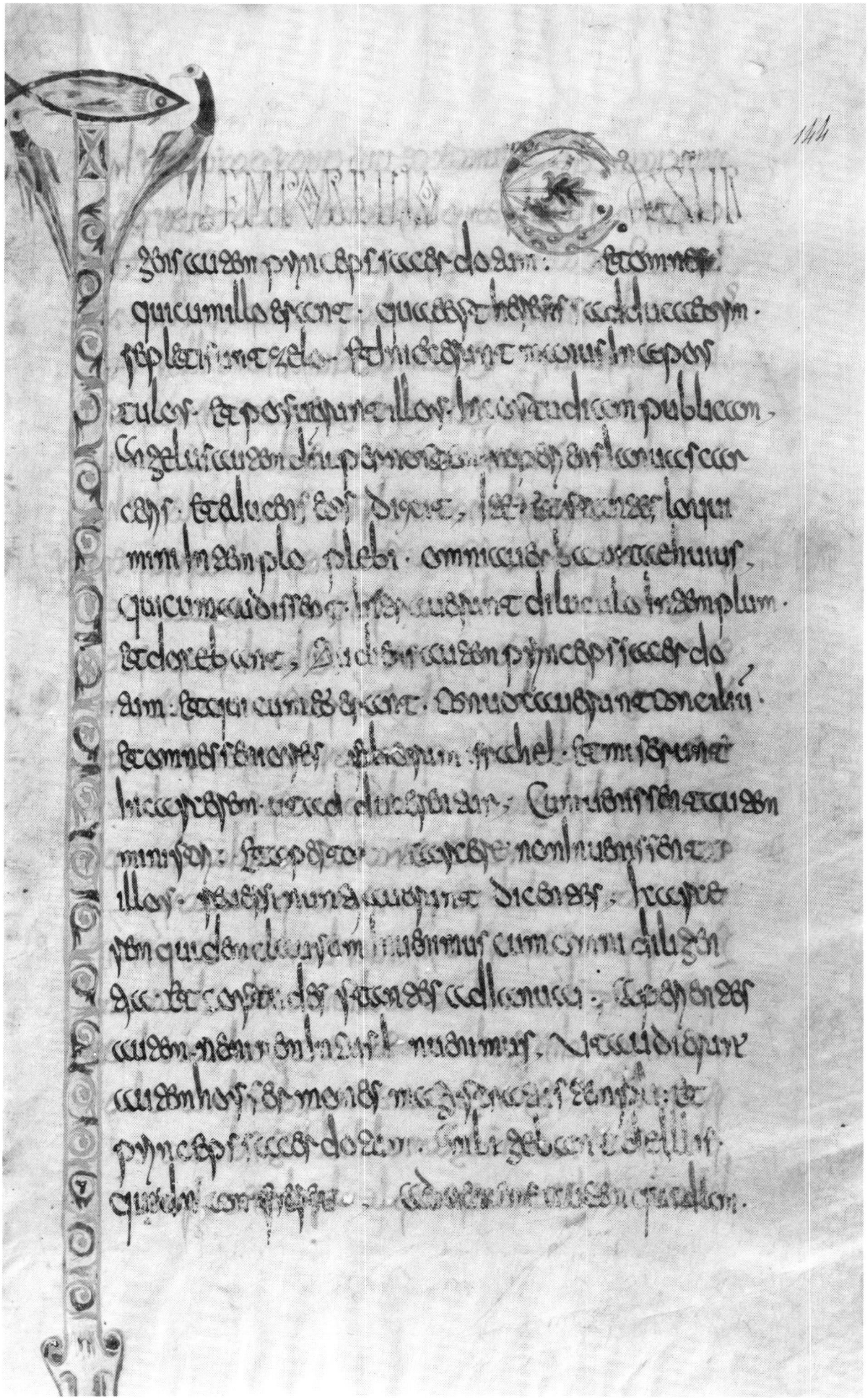

Fig. 36.
Paris, Bibliothèque Nationale, Ms. lat. 9427, f.144. Lectionary from Luxeuil, Luke incipit.

have originated in the Celtic monastic foundations like Luxeuil and Bobbio in northern Italy, where Columbanus was in the last years of the sixth century,[23] though influenced, no doubt, by elements brought from the Near East. For the characteristic forms of this aspect of pre-Carolingian book decoration are also those of the decorative metal and enamel work of the period,[24] however different the treatment might be in the other media. As such, they are seen to be expressions of the barbarian, i.e., non-Mediterranean culture of the nomadic tribes that wandered westward from their Slavic and Scythian places of origin, borrowing from the arts of the peoples they overran.

Once established, the concept of the decorative transformation of the word as seen in the Luxeuil Lectionary developed rapidly. The Gelasian Sacramentary in the Vatican Library (Ms. Reg. lat. 316), is not specifically dated but is probably from about 750. Its provenance is also not certain, but Saint-Denis and Chelles, both near Paris, have been suggested. It seems probable, in any case, that it was produced in some monastery in northeastern France affiliated with the very important foundation established by monks from Luxeuil at Corbie about 660.

The decoration of the Gelasian Sacramentary begins on f.3v (Fig. 37a) with a full-page composition of a cross framed by a semicircular arch. From its arms hang the Greek letters Alpha and Omega, and birds are pendant from these. Birds also appear in the medallions, which serve as capitals of the columns. Their bases are paired animals, and the archivolt above is ornamented with stylized fish and a human head at the crown. Medallions on the cross itself contain rosettes, small crosses, and animals, with the Agnus Dei on the larger decorated one at the intersection of the arms. On f.4, facing this design, is another equally elaborate cross (Fig. 37b) beside the opening invocation of the text, just before the *incipit*. The zoomorphic motives of f.3v appear here as well—birds and animals around the cross, and fish in the pendant Alpha and Omega and the "n" of "In" at the top right. To the colors of orange-red, yellow, and green described in the Luxeuil Lectionary, blue has been added.[25]

Ornamented arches appear in the earlier Luxeuil Lectionary also, on f.32v. The decoration is not so elaborate, and the arches do not frame a cross, but enclose the opening words of the commemorative office of Sts. Julian and Basilissa. They also have a different shape, that of a horseshoe instead of being semicircular,

a profile identified with Near Eastern usage, and more particularly Armenian and Syrian, as in the Rabula Gospels (Fig. 12), a point to support the suggestion that at least some elements in the decorative repertory of this pre-Carolingian style probably came from the Orient.[26] There are other framing arches in the Gelasian Sacramentary[27] on ff.131v and 172v, also semicircular, but the Oriental implications of the enriched decorative repertory of birds, rosettes, griffins, and palmettes are difficult to overlook.[28]

Judging from existing examples, the majority of pre-Carolingian illuminated manuscripts produced on the Continent were of liturgical texts—missals, lectionaries, sacramentaries, and commentaries—rather than scriptural compilations—Bibles, psalters, gospel-books, and the like. Explanations of this fact are varied. A possible reason is the matter of survival, books used in the conduct of services having less chance than others used for study and contemplation. Nordenfalk believes, however, that in the continental monasteries, there was more concern with theological matters than with the missionary interests of their Celtic counterparts, and that an almost superstitious awe of the Word of God inhibited scribes and decorators alike in selecting texts.[29] It has also been suggested that in an age of declining Latinity and waning capacity to understand the Scriptures themselves, there was greater need for dogmatic and interpretive texts. However this may have been, it is doubtless more than coincidence that in the decoration of the dogmatic and liturgical texts which constitute the better part, numerically speaking, of these pre-Carolingian Merovingian books, the human form rarely appears until a relatively late date. The Gelasian Sacramentary in the Vatican Library is one of the most richly decorated; a human motif is found but once in its three cross pages, on f.3v (Fig. 37) at the crown of the arch.

In these circumstances, the decoration of the Gellone Sacramentary[30] in the Bibliothèque Nationale in Paris (Ms. lat. 12048) is of more than usual interest. The text is of the Gelasian rite, though somewhat modified to accord with the Gregorian usage that ultimately supplanted it. The manuscript appears to have been in the Provençal monastery at Gellone soon after it was founded in 804, but it was probably written and decorated in some north French scriptorium; Flavigny, near Dijon, and Meaux, a little to the east of Paris, have both been suggested. There are two hundred and seventy-five folios in the book, and it is richly decorated with a

Fig. 37.
Vatican, Biblioteca Apostolica, Ms. Reg. lat. 316, ff.3v–4.
The Gelasian Sacramentary, Cross Page and incipit of the
Vigil of the Nativity.

developed initial for each rubric (Figs. 38, 39), and several larger compositions of nearly full-page size, including the Crucifixion (Fig. 40) on f.143v.[31] The name of the scribe—David—appears on ff.99 and 254v,[32] and internal evidence suggests a date in the second half of the eighth century.[33]

Some idea of the imaginative resourcefulness of the Gellone Sacramentary decorators can be obtained from two initials on f.99v (Fig. 38). Both are D's, abbreviations of the invocatory *Dominus* with which each prayer begins, the curvilinear parts of the letters being circles enclosing various motives. But the bird supporting the circle in the upper one is not an ornithological abstraction, like the comparable motives in the Gelasian Sacramentary (Fig. 37), but is recognizable as a duck despite the pattern of colors suggesting a textile design on its body.[34] And the fish that is the appendage of the circle in the lower D is attached to it by a human hand holding a spear, an idea that anticipates the drolleries

that enliven the pages of later Gothic manuscripts (Figs. 151, 152).

Elsewhere, the imagery of the decorated initial refers directly to the text (Fig. 39). The initial D of *Dominus* on f.76v begins the Office of the Invention of the True Cross. Within the circle, Christ's cross in red is flanked by two green ones for the thieves. The nails are also red and green, and the Alpha and Omega attached to the arms of the central cross are red. The appendage to the circle that makes a letter D of the whole is a cluster of leaves and branches. Before it, a figure, half bending and half kneeling, holds a tool with a hooked head representing a mattock, with which he is digging—a direct reference to the legendary discovery of the buried relics of the Tree of Life in the time of Constantine the Great.

One of the most impressive miniatures in the Gellone Sacramentary is the Crucifixion (Fig. 40) on f.143v. It is at the beginning of the Canon of the Mass, the most solemn part of the office of the consecration of the Host. The Latin text begins with the words *Te igitur, clementissime Pater.* The initial T has been made into the Cross by extending the lower member above the cross-bar, an example followed for this text by many later illuminators. The rigid figure of the Saviour is fastened to it with a nail in each hand and foot, from the wounds of which streams blood, as it does also from the lance wound in His right side. His semi-nude body is clothed in a robe falling from the waist to just above the knees. Two descending angels touch the cross on either side. The color scheme is simple—white rosettes on the blue cross, white for Christ's robe and yellow for the angels', and red in the cross-pattern of the nimbus, in the H and R of the inscription at the top of the cross, and in the blood of the wounds.

The simplified contours and arbitrary proportions of the figures in the Gellone Sacramentary miniatures are clear evidence that, whatever their model may have been, it was not in the stylistic tradition of the Cambridge Gospels (Fig. 33) or the Ashburnham Pentateuch (Fig. 35). Equally foreign to the lingering naturalism of that tradition are the stylized formulae of anatomy and drapery. Again, as in the birds and

animals of the Gelasian Sacramentary (Fig. 37), it is the Christian East of Syria and Armenia that is suggested by a detail like Christ's robe falling from His waist nearly to the knees. Though not as long as the colobium that covers Him from neck to ankles in the Rabula Gospels Crucifixion (Fig. 13), it is closer to that iconographic tradition (also reflected in Orientalizing Roman frescoes of the seventh and eighth centuries)[35] than the simple loincloth more usual in Occidental treatment of the theme.[36]

In discussing East Christian and Byzantine illumination, I pointed out that the denaturalized forms of their miniatures can be variously evaluated. From one point of view, such denaturalization is a mark of decadence, for the forms lack any of the beauty of which some sense had been inherited from the antique past. But conversely, in the same process, a new concept of beauty developed, creating a harmony of text and illustration, of script and decoration, that is all the more distinctive precisely because there is no concern for the effects of form and space upon which the illusionism of late antique style depends for its beauty. In their own way, the pre-Carolingian manuscript illuminators on the Continent also achieved a decorative harmony of text and

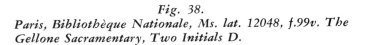

Fig. 38.
Paris, Bibliothèque Nationale, Ms. lat. 12048, f.99v. The Gellone Sacramentary, Two Initials D.

Fig. 39.
Paris, Bibliothèque Nationale, Ms. lat. 12048, f.76v. The Gellone Sacramentary, Initial D of the Office of the Invention of the True Cross.

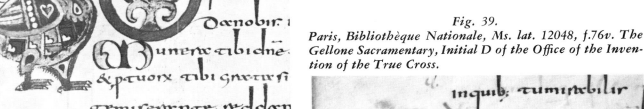

Fig. 40.
Paris, Bibliothèque Nationale, Ms. lat. 12048, f.143v. The Gellone Sacramentary, Te Igitur *with the Crucifixion.*

decoration. The ornamented letters lie as flat on the Luxeuil Lectionary folio (Fig. 36) as the calligraphic minuscules of the script, for they are conceived in the same essentially linear terms, for all the vivacity of the color scheme. This is equally true of the arcaded cross and its facing folio of zoomorphic letters in the Gelasian Sacramentary (Fig. 37), and even the relatively greater realism of the natural forms in the Gellone Sacramentary initials (Fig. 38) is the result of the way the contour lines have been composed. This characteristic is, indeed, the distinctive and individual quality of all the "barbarian" arts of pre-Carolingian Continental Europe —the metal and enamel decorative fibulae and other accessories of costume, the carved stone slabs, and the decorated pages of manuscripts. Common to all are the linear patterns that define forms and unify them in two-dimensional designs.[37]

As mentioned above, the human form appears late in the history of pre-Carolingian manuscript decoration on the Continent. When it does, as in the Gellone Sacramentary, parts of the body—hands or arms or legs— are more likely to be used than the entire figure, although this is not unknown. But it is interesting to observe that, for the most part, the human form was regarded as a source of individual motives to be combined with birds or beasts or fish, rather than as an organic entity. Thus on f.42v of the Gellone Sacramentary,[38] the evangelists Luke and John are portrayed with human bodies but surmounted by the ox and eagle heads of their traditional symbols. Nothing could be more characteristic of the propensity of these pre-Carolingian artists to visualize their ideas in zoomorphic forms and define them with a vocabulary of line.

When an artist of such disposition and temperament was concerned primarily with abstract decorative problems in designing arcaded cross pages and initial letters, his imagination could range freely. Confronted by a traditionally representational theme like the Crucifixion (Fig. 40), the expressive resources of his linear vocabulary were less adequate. Even more than in the Gellone Sacramentary is this apparent in the miniatures of the Gundohinus Gospels in the Bibliothèque de la Ville of Autun (Ms. 3) in Burgundy. One of the few surviving Gospel-books among pre-Carolingian continental manuscripts, it is named from the scribe who wrote it in 754, according to the *explicit* on f.186,[39] in an unidentified monastery that may have been Fleury, now known as Saint-Benoît-sur-Loire. Its miniatures are those usually found in a Gospel-book, canon-tables on ff.6v–12, followed by a full-page design on f.12v of Christ Enthroned, with the evangelist symbols in medallions in the angles of the page,[40] and, at the end of the book, on ff.186v–188, portraits of the Four Evangelists. On f.186v, Matthew stands under an arch, with his winged-man symbol in the lunette above (Fig. 41). The diagonally striped column shafts rest on simple, stepped bases, and are surmounted by equally elementary capitals of plain slabs. The archivolt is decorated with a vine. The nimbed figure stands full face, holding a book in his left hand and pointing to it with his right. The head, with its staring eyes and sharply tapered chin, resembles that of the Saviour in the Gellone Crucifixion (Fig. 40), and the rounded head with cap-like hair of the symbol above is also like those of the angels in the Gellone miniature.

It is not difficult to recreate the general type of the

Fig. 41.
Autun, Bibliothèque municipale, Ms. 3, f.186v. The
Gundohinus Gospels, St. Matthew.

model that the Gundohinus artist was attempting to copy—an Evangelist portrait of the kind already established in both Latin and Eastern traditions that presumably retained something of the quality noted in the Cambridge Gospels St. Luke (Fig. 33, Plate III). But it is clear that his painstaking efforts to reproduce the representational formulae of the prototype were not enlightened by any understanding of what they meant. The Evangelist's robe is a meaningless pattern of lines over his right shoulder, and the spiral flutings of the column shafts have been reduced to a stereotyped repetition of diagonal bands. Only in the vine on the archivolt does his feeling for linear rhythm find a congenial and inspiring motive. In these respects, the Gundohinus Gospel-book drawings are a classic illustration of what resulted from the collision between the lingering traces of Greco-Roman art transmitted by Christianity to the non-Mediterranean peoples of northern Europe, and their own barbarian modes. As C. R. Morey has so aptly phrased it, "The first effect . . . was to neutralize the good points of both; the classic naturalism became grotesque; the barbarian ornament coarse."[41]

Elsewhere in northern Europe, models in the Early Christian version of late antique style evoked a somewhat different response from that of the pre-Carolingian continental illuminators. This can be stated with some certainty, since there is clear evidence of the nature of the models in some instances, and nearly conclusive circumstantial indication of their relationship to copies. It will be recalled that the so-called Gospel-book of St. Augustine in Cambridge, with its portrait of St. Luke (Fig. 33, Plate III), is traditionally believed to have been one of those sent by Gregory the Great to the missionary saint shortly after the monastery at Canterbury was established in 596.[42] From Canterbury, Benedict Biscop (628?–690) went in 674 to found the Benedictine monastery of St. Peter's at Wearmouth in Northumbria, and an affiliate, St. Paul's, at nearby Jarrow in 682. In the contemporary chronicle written by the Venerable Bede (673–735) of Jarrow, it is stated (*Eccles. Hist.*, Bk. iv. chap. 18) that Biscop made no less than five journeys to Rome to buy books for the two monasteries, bringing back at least part of the collection assembled at the study center called Vivarium by the sixth-century diplomat and scholar Cassiodorus.[43] One of these, a Bible called the *Codex Grandior,* was copied three times at the order of Ceolfrid, Bede's mentor and successor to Biscop as abbot of Jarrow-

Wearmouth. Ceolfrid took one of the copies to Rome as a present to Pope Gregory II in 715. Toward the end of the ninth century, it came to the monastery of San Salvatore on Monte Amiato near Siena, from which it was acquired in the 18th century by the Biblioteca Laurenziana in Florence, where it is Ms. Amiatino 1.[44]

The *Codex Amiatinus* is a massive volume of 1030 folios (50.5 x 34 cm: 21.5 x 13.25″) of fine white parchment. It contains all of the Old and New Testaments except the apocryphal book of Baruch, and the text is important in its own right as one of the earliest integral examples of the Vulgate version of the Scriptures. Preceding it in the book is a gathering of eight illuminated folios. An arched frame on f.2 encloses the dedicatory inscription, changed from the original wording that it was the gift of Ceolfrid, abbot of St. Peter's, by Peter the Langobard of San Salvatore to his own account, a pious fraud now revealed by the different color of ink in the modified lines.[45] Folios 2v–3 show the plan of the Temple of Jerusalem, and on ff.4–4v are the prologue and index of the Bible in yellow script on purple parchment. A full-page miniature on f.5 is of Ezra the scribe (Fig. 42, Plate IV), writing the Sacred Books from memory[46] in 458 B.C., while the rectos of ff.6–8 have diagrams of cognate passages in both Testaments. On f.796v, at the beginning of the New Testament, is a full-page miniature of Christ in Majesty (Fig. 43).[47]

Some scholars have suggested that the illuminated gathering at the beginning of the *Codex Amiatinus* may have been taken from another book, possibly from Cassiodorus' library, and inserted in the copy made for Ceolfrid. However, the uncial script of its titles and inscriptions is the same as in the rest of the volume, and the parchment of the illuminated folios is also consistent with that of the text portion. It is therefore generally agreed that the two figured miniatures were executed at Jarrow-Wearmouth between 690, when Ceolfrid succeeded Benedict Biscop as abbot, and 715, when he died at Langres on the way to Rome. Moreover, as Nordenfalk has pointed out,[48] the Amiatinus author portrait follows the Cassiodorus model so faithfully that even the cast shadow of the ink bottle in the lower right corner has been reproduced. Boeckler suggests[49] that the Cassiodorus prototype may have been executed shortly after 540. The elements of its illusionistic and spatial design transmitted by the Amiatinus artist bear this out, such as the foreshortened bench,

Fig. 43.
Florence, Biblioteca Laurenziana, Ms. Amiatinus 1, f.796v.
The Amiatinus Codex, Christ in Majesty. (Photo Pineider)

stool, and writing table, and the careful shading of the left and upper edges of the recessed bookcase panels and the highlighting of the lower and right bevels. There is also a well-observed distinction in intensity of light between the foreground and background on the floor, and the wall behind the bookcase. Only in the flatness of the figure, especially the face, is the artist's lack of comprehension apparent, whether he were

English, continental,[50] or Northumbrian-trained in Italy.[51] The harsh drapery patterns, staring eyes, and unmodeled flesh surfaces bespeak a conceptual parallel with the later figure style of pre-Carolingian continental illumination (Figs. 40, 41), if due allowance be made for the different techniques employed. In the Merovingian books, the miniatures are executed in relatively thin washes. The Codex Amiatinus author portrait was

Fig. 44.
Stockholm, Royal Library, Ms. A, 135, f.150v. Codex
Aureus, *St. John.*

painted in heavy pigments, which have flaked off in some places.

The same technique of opaque pigments with some gold and silver was used in the miniature of Christ in Majesty (Fig. 43) on f.796v. The whole is enclosed in an orange-red border decorated with alternate squares and lozenges. Christ is enthroned, with two attendant angels in the central medallion, and the four evangelists with their symbols occupy the angles between it and the outer border. The lozenge-spangled red of the border is repeated in one of those around the medallion; the other, inner one has a zigzag ribbon motive of red and blue, rendered in light and shade to suggest a plastic effect. Both technique and decoration are reminiscent of late antique practice; the border motive is much like those seen in the Vatican Vergil miniatures (Fig. 4). The banded skies of the Vergil illustrations also are reflected in the backgrounds of the standing evangelists—horizontal stripings of blue, shading from light to dark and contrasted with bands of pink. Such a setting for these figures has no precedent in either the elaborate architecture or neutral gold of Byzantine style (Figs. 23, 24), but a reasonable comparison can be found in the landscape environment of their counterparts in the mosaics of San Vitale at Ravenna.[52] All these characteristics of the Christ in Majesty miniature confirm the hypothesis, advanced in discussing the Ezra portrait, that the model followed by the Amiatinus artist or artists was in the Latin style of late antiquity. In a way, the aesthetic limitations of the Amiatinus miniatures allow a clearer understanding of the nature of the models available to them.

Miniatures in a number of manuscripts from the middle to the end of the eighth century that are believed to have been made in Canterbury itself are equally dependent on models in late antique style. A Psalter in the British Museum (Cotton Vespasian A. i.),[53] which dates from about 750, contains, on f.30v, a miniature of David as Musician, seated under an arch with his four collaborators.[54] It is executed in opaque colors with gold, and the flesh surfaces of the faces and hands are carefully modeled. Another Canterbury manuscript from the same general period is in the Royal Library at Stockholm (Ms. A. 135).[55] A Gospel-book, it is known as the *Codex Aureus* from the lavish use of gold in script and miniatures, often on folios of purple parchment. It contains two Evangelist portraits—of Matthew on f.9v,[56] and of John (Fig. 44) on f.150v.

The figure is seated on a cushioned throne under an arch, between curtains drawn back and looped around the columns. The Evangelist's eagle symbol is in the lunette above. Gold is used for the nimbi and the decorative discs on the curtains, and the heavily painted colors are dominated by the blue and pink of the backgrounds, with accents of blue and red in the decorative details, and violet for the column shafts.

Many features of the St. John miniature in the Stockholm *Codex Aureus* resemble details of the Gundohinus Gospel St. Matthew (Fig. 41), such as the architectural setting with columns supporting an architrave and the lunette above with the Evangelist's symbol. But it is clear that the Canterbury artist understood these features of his model better than his Merovingian contemporary. The columns have capitals and bases instead of the simple slabs representing them in the Autun miniature, and the slanting zigzags on the shafts suggest the spirals of the prototype rather more effectively than the angled strips in the continental miniature. The blue background of the curtained space in which the Evangelist sits is shaded to suggest depth, and the face is modeled, however summarily, with light and shade. Even the ornament, in part, is in the tradition of late antiquity, for the motive on the archivolt is the so-called double-axe or pinwheel in a form that came into use about the beginning of the Christian era.[57] But appearing along with these echoes of late classical style are other elements, which derive from another stylistic tradition, primarily decorative rather than representational. The draperies of the figure and the curtains looped around the columns have been formalized into flat, linear patterns, and the unarchitectonic medallions above the column capitals are decorated with a motive not previously encountered—the spiral. This, especially when it appears as it does here with trumpet-shaped appendages that seem to have spun off the perimeter of the whirling shape, is one of the distinctive characteristics of the other and non-Mediterranean component of pre-Carolingian insular art—the Celtic.

From the outset, books played an important part in the establishment and diffusion of Christianity in Ireland. It is stated in the Book of Armagh that St. Patrick distributed books of the Law and the Gospels to his foundations, and one of his successors, St. Columba (521–599), is reported by his biographer Adomnan[58] to have copied more than three hundred "noble books" with his own hand. One of these, indeed, was involved in the circumstances leading to the establishment *c.* 563 at Iona, off the west coast of Scotland, of one of the most important later centers of manuscript illumination. Columba secretly copied a psalter belonging to his mentor, St. Finian, working at night by light coming miraculously from his own fingers. Finian claimed the copy and the ensuing argument had to be resolved by King Diarmuid of Ireland, who decreed that Columba should go into exile as a missionary to northern Britain. A foundation of Iona at Lindisfarne in Northumbria is identified with one of the most distinguished Celtic manuscripts, the Gospel-book of Lindisfarne in the British Museum in London (Cotton Ms. Nero D IV). Properly speaking, the style of this and the other manuscripts illuminated in the Irish monasteries and their dependencies should be termed Anglo-Celtic, to distinguish it from contemporary work originating in the Canterbury orbit like the *Codex Amiatinus* and the Stockholm *Codex Aureus,* which can be called Anglo-Italian.

Anglo-Celtic and Anglo-Italian illumination is found almost exclusively in texts of the Scriptures[59]—Gospel-books for the most part, although there are some psalters—unlike the situation on the Continent, where pre-Carolingian book decoration is predominantly in liturgical texts. This can be accounted for, in part at least, by the different spirit and purposes of the propagators of Christianity in the insular centers, missionaries as they were, from the more theological interests of their continental counterparts. The same sentiment explains the Celtic practice of providing these books with costly and elaborate containers of precious metals and jewels known as *cumdachs.*[60] Thus enshrined, the scriptural texts were easily accorded the awed reverence due the Word of God.

In view of the importance of books in early Celtic Christianity, it is surprising that the known history of their decoration begins at a relatively late date.[61] It is now generally held that the Gospel-book in Trinity College Library at Dublin (Ms. 57 (A. lv. 5),[62] called the Book of Durrow (Fig. 45, Plate V, and Fig. 46), cannot be dated before the middle or latter part of the seventh century, and no earlier example among the few Celtic manuscripts known, such as the so-called Cathach of St. Columba,[63] a psalter of about mid-sixth century (possibly that copied by the saint), can give more than rudimentary indication of any native antecedent to its decorative style and repertory.[64] But it is pertinent to

note that, among the metal objects found in 1939 in the excavation at Sutton Hoo in East Anglia of the tomb of a Saxon prince who died *c.* 640,[65] practically every motive of the Anglo-Celtic decorative repertory can be found. These are the interlace of ribbons or braids, the interlace of animal forms called lacertines, a pattern of steps or diagonal frets, and the spiral. All except the ribbon interlace, moreover, are found in one form or another in pre-Christian Celtic art,[66] and can be traced back to the Iron Age of the fifth century B.C.

The possibility cannot be overlooked that, through the accidents of history, only a little has survived of what may once have been a considerable body of Celtic illumination antedating the seventh century. Pertinent to this consideration, however, is the analogous phenomenon of the monumental Celtic and north British carved stone crosses,[67] none of which can be dated with certainty before the latter part of the seventh century. Nordenfalk has suggested[68] that the proceedings of the Synod at Whitby in 664 created the atmosphere in which both book illustrations and stone carvings could be created. In that year, the meeting began in which the dogmatic differences between the Celtic monasteries of Ireland and north Britain, and the Benedictine and Augustinian foundations of Canterbury were ultimately resolved. Books and crosses alike shared the ornamental repertory developed in earlier and contemporary metal-work, whether Irish or English; as Nordenfalk also points out, by the end of the seventh century, Hibernian and Saxon elements were intermingled and mutually fructifying.

A unique feature of Anglo-Celtic Gospel-book illumination is the so-called carpet page of almost purely decorative design found at the beginning of each Gospel (Fig. 45, Plate V). They are placed on the versos of folios facing the opening passages of their respective Gospels, which are decorated with ornate initials.[69] Though the several carpet pages in the Durrow Book differ in detail, the central motif is usually a cross in a medallion surrounded by other decorative forms (circular plaits in the one on f.192v), all enclosed in a circular border. The entire folio is framed by rectangular panels in which various patterns appear, such as interlaces or spirals.[70] The latter are of the type described in discussing the medallions surmounting the capitals and supporting the arch of the Stockholm *Codex Aureus* portrait of St. John (Fig. 44). In its seeming rotary movement, it appears to have thrown

Fig. 46.
Dublin, Trinity College Library, Ms. 57 (A. IV. 5), f.191v.
The Book of Durrow, Evangelist Symbol preceding St.
John's Gospel.

off an end that expands into a trumpet-shaped terminal, which is immediately merged with another, however, so the impression is of continuous and uninterrupted motion.

On f.192v of the Durrow Book (Fig. 45), the border is of rectangular panels filled with interlaced biting animals called lacertines. These fantastic beasts seem to derive ultimately from the same sources as their pre-Carolingian continental counterparts, like the birds dangling from the Alpha and Omega of the cross on f.3v of the Gelasian Sacramentary (Fig. 37). But in their interlacing, they become dynamic like the trumpet spirals, and contribute to an effect quite different from that of their Merovingian morphological counterparts. In like fashion, the interlaced plaited ribbons framing the symbol on f.191v in the Durrow Book (Fig. 46) are akin to the stylized borders of Roman mosaic pavements, of which there are still many in Britain. But they too have become dynamic in the impression they create of an unceasing continuity changing only from one color to another in endless patterns. The step or fret pattern, which also is found in the Durrow Book illumination (on. f.248), is clearly derived from the meander or Greek key pattern, but the four-square stability of classic prototype is characteristically transformed into a dynamic diagonal in Celtic usage.

Other Celtic characteristics of the miniature preceding the Gospel of St. John (Fig. 46) in the Book of Durrow include the small red dots in the interlaced bands of the side frame panels, used also in an overall pattern on the animal's head. They frequently outline the contours of the large initial letters on the opening text pages, create a background for the beginning text lines, and connect the large initials with the main body of the script passages. The color scheme is relatively simple—black or dark green for the backgrounds, a lighter green, yellow, and vermilion red for the ribbons and the animal's body.[71] The precise contours, stylized drawing, and the surface patterns found in all the Durrow symbols are clear indication that their makers were following the example of workers in metal. Rustic in their simplicity and somewhat coarse in draftsmanship, they stand in contrast in these respects to the equally simple yet assured patterns of the purely decorative motives, so beautifully disposed in coordinated rhythmic designs of extraordinary distinction.

The Latin text of the Gospels in the Book of Durrow is a version of St. Jerome's Vulgate revision, but the illustration follows the order of the pre-hieronymian recension, so that the lion (Fig. 46) is placed before the Gospel of St. John instead of that of St. Mark, where it is found in most illustrated Gospel-books. Also unusual, and indicative of an early iconographic tradition, is the portrayal of the Evangelists by their symbols alone, and the fact that they have neither wings nor nimbi. It has been suggested that these iconographic characteristics of the Darrow miniatures, as well as the concept of the carpet page, of which there are five in the book, were taken from Coptic practice.[72] It has also been observed, however, that these same features can be associated with one of the oldest traditions of Gospel-book decoration and textual organization, that embodied in the second-century *Diatesseron* of Tatian.[73] Though no example of that time has survived, a sixteenth-century copy of an illustrated Persian version in the Laurentian Library in Florence (Cod. Orient. 81) appears to be a trustworthy indication of its basic structure and illustrative program.[74] It is reasonable to assume that a *Diatesseron* would have been in the monastery founded by St. Columba at Iona, where it is equally reasonable to assume that the Book of Durrow was written and illuminated at some time after the middle of the seventh century.

In the Book of Durrow, the canon of Celtic illumination is defined. In the decoration of the Lindisfarne Gospels (London, B.M., Cotton Ms. Nero D IV),[75] Anglo-Celtic style is seen in its most distinguished form. Also known as the Book of Durham, since it was kept in the Shrine of St. Cuthbert there from the end of the tenth until the twelfth century, its date and place of origin are given in a long colophon on f.259:

> Eadfrith, bishop of Lindisfarne, wrote this book to the glory of God, of St. Cuthbert, and of all the brotherhood of saints upon this island; and Ethelwald, bishop of Lindisfarne, made outside the binding and decorated it with his utmost skill; and Billfrith the hermit forged the outer metalwork and set the gold and gems within it; and Aldred, the unworthy humble priest, wrote with the help of God and St. Cuthbert the glosses in English.

This is written in the same Northumbrian dialect as the glosses, and the Aldred who wrote them and the colophon was probably the one who was bishop of Durham from 946 to 968. Eadfrith, whether actually the writer or during whose incumbency the book was made, held that post from 698 to 721, to be succeeded by Ethelwald from 724 until 740. The authenticity of this colo-

Fig. 47.
London, British Museum, Ms. Cotton Nero D. IV, f.95.
The Lindisfarne Gospels. Incipit of St. Mark's Gospel.

phon has never been seriously questioned, and the Lindisfarne Gospels can thus be dated with certainty in the early years of the eighth century.

Lindisfarne was established by St. Aidan in 635 as a foundation of Iona, on an island in the North Sea off the east coast of Northumbria. The decoration of its great Gospel-book follows the same general scheme as that of Durrow—Evangelist miniatures, carpet pages, and developed initials at the beginning of each book, and arcaded canon tables. But the scale is more monumental and the execution more sophisticated. The initial letters (Fig. 47) are developed by organizing the entire page in intricate designs that include all the opening text lines, rather than only the beginning words as in the Book of Durrow. Illustrated is Mark 1:1—*Initium evangelii Iesu Christi filii Dei. Sicut scriptum est in Esaia propheta*—"The beginning of the gospel of Jesus Christ, the Son of God. As it is written in Isaiah the prophet. . . ." The full repertory of Celtic ornament seen in the Durrow Book is also found here—spiral, lacertine, fret, and interlace—but infinitely more involved, and executed with the utmost finesse. The interlace is of narrow edged bands instead of the broad ribbons of Durrow, the spirals are more complex, and the lacertines turn back on each other until the whole of their panelled sections is filled. Also different from Durrow is the more limited use of the red dot pattern, which is used only as a linear motive in Lindisfarne and not as an all-over background element. Red, yellow, and green are used, as in the Durrow Book, but blue and purple are added, occasionally heightened with gold.

Even more significant is the different imagery of the Evangelists in the Lindisfarne Gospels (Fig. 48, Plate VI). Each author portrait is accompanied by his symbol, shown in a rectangular frame of thin bands with knots of interlace at the angles. Evangelists and symbols are identified by inscriptions. In the carpet pages, the cross is the central element, as it is in many of the Durrow examples (Fig. 45, Plate V), but whereas it is on such a diminutive scale there as to be almost overlooked, it is enlarged in the Lindisfarne designs to dominate the entire scheme.[76]

The Vulgate text of the Gospels appears in both the Durrow and Lindisfarne books, the majuscule script in both is very similar, and, as has been seen, the decorative repertory is much the same in both. Such parallels as these support the suggestion[77] that the two manuscripts were the work of artists trained in the same scriptorium, or at least grounded in the same general tradition. Cer-

tain of the differences between them—the enhanced scale, the greater finesse, and the more complex designs of Lindisfarne—could thus be accounted for as the result of development within the atelier over a period of time. But that period could not be very long—not so much as a century if Durrow be placed as early as mid-seventh century and Lindisfarne c. 740 toward the end of Ethelwald's bishopric, and considerably less than that if, as seems more likely, Durrow be dated in the last quarter of the seventh century and Lindisfarne identified with the Eadfrith (698–721) named in the colophon as the writer of the book.

But the most striking difference between the two manuscripts, not to be accounted for by a period of time between the dates when they were made, is seen in the portraits of the Four Evangelists with their symbols, which take the place in Lindisfarne of Durrow's unaccompanied emblems. That of Matthew (Fig. 48, Plate VI) on f.25v shows him seated and writing within a rectangular frame decorated at the angles with knots of interlace. Above and behind him is his symbol, the winged man inscribed *imago hominis,* Latin for "image of man"; the Evangelist is identified, however, as *O agios Mattheus,* the Latin *Sanctus* usually found being replaced by a transcription of its Greek equivalent. The names of the other Evangelists are also prefixed by the Greek title and their symbols are also identified in Latin.[78]

There are differences in style and composition as well as iconography between the Lindisfarne Matthew and its counterpart in Durrow, or in another manuscript of about the same period as Lindisfarne, the Echternach Gospels (Paris, B. N. Ms. lat. 9389).[79] The latter is traditionally believed to have been taken by the Northumbrian missionary Willibrord to the Celtic monastery at Echternach in western Germany when he established it in 698; it is usually dated c. 690. In both Durrow and Echternach, the human figure is rendered as a two-dimensional, stylized arabesque, as was the Durrow Lion (Fig. 46), with no suggestion of modeling in the figure or of depth in space. The Lindisfarne Matthew is no more three-dimensional as a form than his counterparts in the other two books, with his blue hair outlined against a red-bordered yellow nimbus, his purple robe, and his green mantle slashed with red. But his bench extends backward at an angle to the plane of the bordering frame, and his feet rest on a carpet, which, without apparently lying on the floor, projects itself back to touch the corner of a hanging red curtain partially concealing a nimbed figure, uninscribed, who has not as yet been satisfactorily identified; he may be a male counterpart of the unidentified feminine figure in the author portrait of Mark in the Rossano Gospels (Fig. 9, Plate II).

The nature of the source of these representational elements in the Celtic style of Lindisfarne, and the reason for their appearance, are matters of some interest. That it was Mediterranean rather than northern can hardly be doubted. The use of both Greek and Latin in the Evangelist title suggests this, as does the parallel between the unidentified companions in the Rossano Mark and the Lindisfarne Matthew.[80] But a more immediate source than these can be found in the Ezra miniature of the *Codex Amiatinus* (Fig. 42, Plate IV). From it, the Lindisfarne artist took almost line for line the contours of the figure and the cushioned bench, omitting the footstool and the author's sandals (though copying the thongs by which they were attached), and replacing the writing desk and bookcase of the Amiatinus composition with the curtain and the unidentified figure. He failed, however, to understand the light and shade patterns in his model, whether it was the Amiatius miniature itself or the one from which it was copied in the *Codex Grandior* of Cassiodorus, since they could not be reduced to two-dimensional linear patterns. Comparable representational elements appear in the other Evangelist portraits in the Lindisfarne Gospels, Mark on f.93v, Luke on f.134v, and John on f.209v. There are no such immediate prototypes or parallels for them as for Matthew in the Amiatinus miniature, but they appear in the order of St. Jerome's Vulgate sequence, i.e., Mark's symbol is the lion and John's is the eagle, instead of the reverse as in the Book of Durrow.

Historical circumstances would seem to account for the appearance in the prevailingly Celtic style of the Lindisfarne illumination of the representational elements that have been identified in insular manuscript production, with the Anglo-Italian group represented by the Amiatinus Codex and the Stockholm *Codex Aureus*. The Council of 664 at Whitby was presided over by a Greek, Theodore of Tarsus, and the resolution at that synod of the dispute between the Celtic monasteries of Ireland and north Britain on the one hand, and the Benedictine and Augustinian foundations allied to Canterbury on the other, was a prologue to the establishment of the Benedictine community of Jarrow-Wearmouth. This is not far distant from Lindisfarne,

and it is reasonable to assume friendly relations between the two establishments. As these developed, the model from which the Amiatinus version of the Ezra portrait had been made by a painstaking if uninspired illustrator presumably trained in the idioms of representational style, was transformed a short time later, if at all, by the brilliant decorative imagination of the Anglo-Celtic Lindisfarne illuminator. The subsequent history of the Anglo-Italian manner has been noted in the Stockholm *Codex Aureus* author portrait (Fig. 44) of the mid-eighth century from Canterbury. The nearest equivalent aftermath of Lindisfarne style is seen in the Cutbercht Gospels (Vienna, NB, Ms. lat. 1224)[81] of the last quarter of the eighth century, possibly the work of a south English artist. But an even more striking development is seen in the Book of Kells.

The Book of Kells (Dublin, Trinity College Library, Ms. 58 A. I. 6)[82] contains the text of the four Gospels (there are some lacunae in Mark, Luke, and John), the prefaces and summaries of Jerome, and the Eusebian Canon Tables. Its decoration is very rich, including all the features found in the Book of Lindisfarne and the majority of illuminated Celtic Gospel-books. There are eight pages of arcaded canon tables, two Evangelist portraits[83] (two have been lost), and a full initial page at the beginning of each Gospel. Also preceding each Gospel is a page with the Evangelist symbols placed between the arms of a cross,[84] an earlier example of which is found in the Book of Durrow. There is but one carpet page (f.32),[85] but a number of subjects not otherwise found in Irish illumination are represented. These are the Virgin and Child on f.7v,[86] Christ Enthroned on f.32v facing the single carpet page, Christ Taken Captive on f.114,[87] and Christ Tempted in the Wilderness on f.202v.[88] There is some reason to believe that there may have been four more full-page narrative miniatures that have disappeared. In addition, there are developed initial letters for nearly every verse of text,[89] and elaborate line endings.[90] The sumptuousness of even the Lindisfarne Book is overshadowed by the luxuriant ornament of the Book of Kells.

The augmentation in the Book of Kells of the canonical Celtic pattern of Gospel-book decoration can be accounted for, in part, at least, by the date of the manuscript. This has been established with reasonable certainty as between *c.* 795 and 806,[91] and its place of origin as in the monastery at Iona, whence it was presumably taken, unfinished, to escape the invading Northmen who overwhelmed the island in that year. Some

Fig. 49.
Dublin, Trinity College Library, Ms. 58 (A. I. 6), f.34.
The Book of Kells, The Chi-Rho *Monogram.*

Fig. 50.
Dublin, Trinity College Library, Ms. 58 (A. I. 6), f.124.
The Book of Kells, Account of the Crucifixion, Matt. 27;
38.

Fig. 51.
Dublin, Trinity College Library, Ms. 58 (A. I. 6), f.2. The
Book of Kells, Canon Table, Canon I of 4.

work was done later (though the manuscript was never completely finished) at Kells in County Meath, where the monks who had fled from Iona reestablished an older foundation, whence the name of the book.

The full-page initials (Fig. 49) at the beginning of each Gospel and also of certain significant passages in them go even beyond those in the Lindisfarne Book (Fig. 47) in complexity and largeness of scale. Illustrated are the first words of Matthew 1: 18, on f.34,[92] following the listing of Christ's ancestors. The Latin words are *Christi autem generatio*—"Now the birth of Christ was on this wise," in the King James version. The first three letters—XRI—form a monogram that was a traditional sacred symbol known as the Chi-Rho from its letters in Greek. This the artist has developed to such a degree that the last three letters of the first word in the phrase and nearly all the second word are swallowed up in a fabulously intricate pattern, the completion of the sentence, the m of *autem* and *generatio,* being written in Irish majuscule letters at the bottom of the page. Here, as in all the initial pages as well as some with more text, is seen in ultimate degree the realization of the Celtic artist's purpose, to transform the written word by illumination and so define and convey its transcendental content.

A further case in point is provided by the illuminated text of Matthew 27:38 on f.124 (Fig. 50). The facing verso of f.123 is blank, possibly to have been filled with a representation of the Crucifixion. The text describing it—*Tunc crucifixerant XRI cum eo duas latrones*—"Then were there two thieves crucified with Him"—rendered in a pattern of forms that interlace and cross to the point of being almost unreadable, but the content of which is made all the more clear, if anything, by the shapes and colors of the design. It is in such dynamic patterns as these rather than by representation that the Celtic temperament found the most expressive means of conveying its profoundest concepts and emotions.

The full repertory of traditional Celtic ornament is found in the decorated initials and canon tables (Fig. 51) of the Book of Kells, but augmented by others not previously noted in Irish illumination. These include foliate forms like the rinceaux and rosettes in the archivolt of the canon table of parallel readings in all four Gospels on f.2. Animal forms other than lacertines and the human figure, apart from author portraits, also appear. Many of the verse initials incorporate animal heads, fish, and the like, and in the space above the trumpet spiral medallion at the base of the Chi-Rho monogram (Fig. 49) there is a remarkably convincing representation of cats watching mice at play.[93] On the same page, there are winged angels to the left of the long arm of the letter X, fitted into the spaces between the arm and a series of spiral medallions, and a human head is the end of the rounded terminal of the P in the monogram. In the next-to-outer columns of the canon table, full-length figures stand on the shoulders of others.

Human these forms may be, but not naturalistic. Striking a note of realism in the all-pervasive abstraction of line and color that is the Celtic artist's ideal would have defeated his expressive purpose and method. For in the Kells initial, even more than in that of the Lindisfarne Book (Fig. 47), it is the endless dynamic rhythm of lines drawn with unbelievable subtlety and precision, weaving through motives that change from one form to another with kaleidoscopic unpredictability, that is at once the expressive component and the unifying element in the design. Nowhere is the two-dimensional rhythmic imperative of Celtic style more apparent than in its treatment of the human figure, as in the author portrait of St. Matthew (Fig. 52) on f. 28v of the Book of Kells. This is the Anglo-Celtic interpretation of the motive that was seen through Anglo-Italian eyes in the portrait of John in the Stockholm *Codex Aureus* (Fig. 44) from Canterbury. The evangelist is placed under an arch between two inverted L-shaped bands of spirals. Between these bands and the border are the ox and eagle heads of Luke and John, with Mark's lion shown twice on either side of Matthew's nimbus to complete the quartet of the authors. These Evangelists' symbols would appear to be the terminals of the arms and back of a monumental throne. Their relationship to the inverted L-bands is such that the lion heads on the throne's back seem farther away in space. But so little was the artist interested in or concerned with a naturalistic effect that it is impossible to tell whether the Evangelist is sitting on his throne or standing in front of it. The inverted L-bands are conceivably the translation into Celtic idiom of the columns flanking the figure in the hypothetical prototype; just such columns with half-circular bases and square capitals can be seen in the canon tables.

In transforming the forms of organic life—floral, animal, human—into abstract pattern, the Celtic artist reveals his indifference to the naturalism whose beauty

Fig. 52.
Dublin, Trinity College Library, Ms. 58 (A. I. 6), f.28v.
The Book of Kells, St. Matthew.

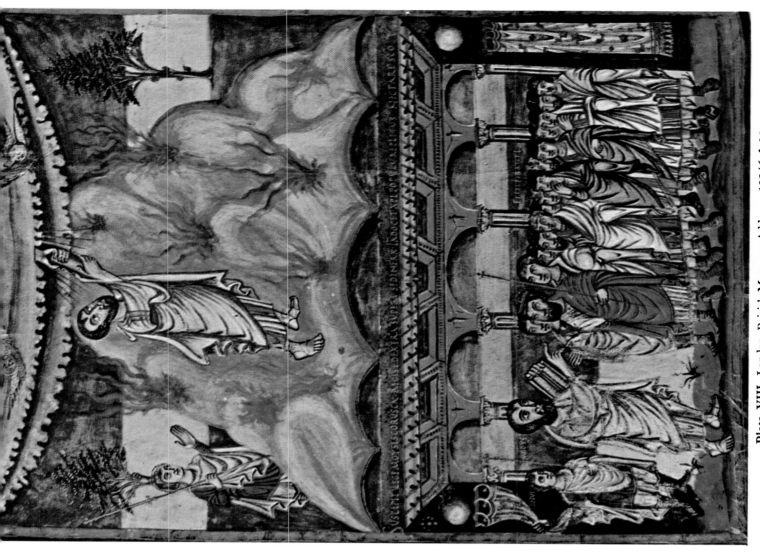

Plate VIII. London, British Museum, Add. ms. 10546, f. 25v.
The Moûtier-Grandval Bible, Moses Receiving and
Giving the Tablets of the Law.

SALUUMMEFAC   LINGUAMAGNILOQUA   LOQUIADNIILOQUA
DNEQMDEHCITSCS   UIDINERUNTLINGUA   CASTA ARGENTUM
QMDEMINUTAESUNT   NOSTRAMMAGNIHI   IGNEEXAMINATUM
UIRITATISAFIIIISHO CABIMUS·LABIANOS   PROBATUMTERRAEPUR
MINUM·   ILAANOBISSUNT·   GATUSEPTUPLUM·
IANALOCUTISUNT   QUISNOSTERDNSEST   IUDNESERUABISNOS

Plate VII. Utrecht, University Library, Script. eccl. 484, f. 6v.
The Utrecht Psalter, Illustration of Psalm XI (12).
(Photo author)

Plate IX. Rome, San Paolo f.l.m., Unnumbered ms., f. 26v. The San Paolo or San Callisto Bible, Moses Receiving and Giving the Tablets of the Law. (Photo author)

Plate X. Rome, San Paolo f.l.m., Unnumbered ms., f. 11v. Genesis *incipit* Initial. (Photo author)

inspired the antique tradition reflected, however dimly, in the Amiatinus Ezra (Fig. 42, Plate IV) and the St. John of the Stockholm *Codex Aureus* (Fig. 44). Yet, in its own way, the form created by his process of abstraction has an incomparably monumental quality. This is owing in part to the remarkable unity of the linear idiom that defines the forms in an ever-changing rhythm and achieves a vitality and grace that is all the more distinctive because it exists in its own right, a realism that is none the less real because it resembles nothing but itself. Color also plays a part in this, richer and more subtle than even the augmented Lindisfarne palette, to which the Kells artists added nuances of yellows coupled with blue, in pigments that are sometimes thick and opaque and sometimes translucent as enamel. Gold, which appears occasionally in the Lindisfarne miniatures, is lacking in Kells, but this is in accordance with earlier Celtic usage.

The non-Celtic character of some motives in the decoration of the Book of Kells has already been noted —the animal heads, for example, in many of the verse initials. Although they are always much more lively and dynamic than their Merovingian counterparts (cf. Fig. 38), there seems little doubt that they were inspired by continental pre-Carolingian examples.[94] The subjects from the life of Christ that augment the iconography of Gospel illustration in the Book of Kells are infrequent in eighth- and early ninth-century Occidental illumination, but do occur in Eastern manuscripts, a source to which the lavish use of purple and yellow in the Kells miniatures has also been referred.[95] The prototype of the Evangelist under an arch framing his head is almost certainly to be found in the author portraits of Carolingian manuscripts in the Rhineland or "Ada" group (Fig. 55), and one of the non-Celtic elements in the Kells canon tables has been identified beyond any question with such manuscripts in the discussion by Friend cited above.[96] This is the appearance in the top lunette of the Four Evangelist symbols, a detail of Kells that is unique in Celtic illumination. It is found, however, in a number of Carolingian manuscripts in the category mentioned (Fig. 56), which include one in the British Museum (Ms. Harley 2788) of *c.* 800.[97] This, as Friend points out, cannot be the specific model of the Kells "beast canon tables," for there are some differences in detail, but his demonstration that both Kells and Harley 2788 copy the "beast canon tables" of the same model is conclusive.

Viewed overall, the initial impression of pre-Caro-

lingian manuscript illumination in the Occident is of such variety and diffuseness that any valid generalization seems almost impossible. There is apparently nothing in common between the miniatures of the Ashburnham Pentateuch (Fig. 35), the Gelasian Sacramentary (Fig. 37), the Amiatinus Codex (Fig. 42, Plate IV), and the Book of Kells (Fig. 52), save that all in their way are expressive of the Christian belief of their creators. Yet a common reference can possibly be found in the relationship of all, whether positive or negative, to the stylistic tradition of late antiquity, which was, after all, the early Church's idiom of artistic expression.[98] To the extent that this idiom was continued, ignored, assimilated, or transformed, it provides a norm by which the stylistic character of the three categories of pre-Carolingian illumination discussed can be defined.

It goes without saying, of course, that even such a patent attempt to continue the method and vocabulary of late antiquity as the Amiatinus Ezra (Fig. 42, Plate IV) is conditioned by the outlook and individuality of its creator; there can be no doubt of its late Seventh-century date and quality, both stylistic and expressive, for all the quasi-archaeological intention of the artist. But so far as he was able, he remained faithful to the pictorial purpose and method of the tradition transmitted to him, as did also the painter of the St. John of the Stockholm *Codex Aureus* (Fig. 44). It is quite otherwise in the decoration of the Gelasian Sacramentary (Fig. 37), whose artist drew upon his barbarian inheritance of northern, non-Mediterranean, zoomorphic forms, borrowed originally from Persia in all likelihood by the Scytho-Sarmatian peoples of the southern Slavic countries, to be taken from them in turn by the nomadic tribes making their way westward in the time of the great migrations. Such was the propensity of these people for nonrepresentational abstraction in design that, when confronted by the demands of realistic portrayal imposed by Christian imagery (Fig. 41), only grotesque ugliness could result.

By contrast, the Celtic genius, of similar barbarian origin and equally committed to abstraction as a fundamental expressive mode, found a way to turn such forms to a positive end (Fig. 52), even though completely transforming them. As C. R. Morey has put it, "Whereas on the Continent, the collision between the two cultures, barbarian and Latin, neutralized the beauty of both, in Ireland the barbarian style was carried on to high sophistication, and to a perfection of technique and taste that makes the best of Irish works stand out as historic masterpieces of ornamental design."[99] But Celtic illumination at its best is more than striking and original pattern. An age that finds expressive power in the looping whorls and massive accents of pigmented color in twentieth-century abstract expressionism cannot but sense the same quality in the spirals and interlaces of the Books of Durrow and Lindisfarne and Kells. These, in the final analysis, engage the observer's interest and ultimately provide him satisfaction in the intense vitality and sense of impulsive movement in patterns that have all the unpredictability and un-expectedness of nature itself. To call this realistic, as Morey does, may seem paradoxical, yet realistic it is in giving form to the artist's desire to find expression for the content of his theme in patterns of unquestioned and specific individuality. In the art of Charlemagne's "renaissance," it was the capacity of the northern temperament to create dynamic patterns of inherently expressive vitality that infused new life into forms borrowed once again from late antiquity by its immediate Early Christian and Byzantine descendants.

NOTES

1. Cf. *EDA,* cited in n. 15, chap. 2.

2. *Mediaeval Art,* p. 195.

3. Cf. Roberts, "The Codex", cited in Introd., n. 6; pp. 203–4.

4. E. R. Curtius, *European Literature and the Latin Middle Ages* (New York: Harper Torchbooks, 1963).

5. *Codicis Vergiliani qui Augusteus apellatur reliquiae quam simillime expressae . . . praefatus est,* ed. R. Sabbadini, Codices e Vaticanis selecti, vol. 15 (Turin, 1926).

6. C. Nordenfalk, "En senantik initialhandskrift," *Konsthistorik Tidskrift* 6 (1957):117–27.

7. B. Lehane, *The Quest of Three Abbots* (New York: Viking, 1968). G. W. C. Thomas, *The Circle and the Cross* (New York: Abingdon, 1964).

8. F. Wormald, *The Miniatures in the Gospels of St. Augustine, Corpus Christi College,* Ms. 286 (Cambridge: Cambridge University Press, 1954).

9. Reproduced in color in *EMP,* p. 100.

10. Reproduced in color in *EDA,* fig. 147.

11. Cf. *EMP,* p. 46.

12. Cf. Wormald, pl. xi.

13. There is little agreement about the date of these miniatures. In the catalogue of an exhibition at Berne in 1949 (*Kunst des frühen Mittelalters,* No. 67, p. 38), they are said to be Ottonian copies of late antique models, but of such good quality that they have been taken for sixth-century originals. This last is the assumption of E. Baldwin Smith, *Early Christian Iconography and the School of Provence* (Princeton: Princeton University Press, 1918), p. 64. Porcher (*EDA,* p. 138, with reproductions in color) assigns them to the ninth century.

14. Volbach, *Early Christian Art,* pls. 100–101.

15. Cf. *Speculum* 8 (1933): 150 ff. The motive also appears in adaptation, as Porcher has observed (*EDA,* p. 139), in an early seventh-century fresco of the Martyrdom of Sts. Cyrus and Giulitta in Santa Maria Antiqua of Rome in an analogous style (cf. Grabar-Nordenfalk, *EMP,* p. 49).

16. *EDA,* figs. 216–17; cf. also A. M. Friend, Jr., "Notes on two pre-Carolingian ivories," *American Journal of Archaeology,* 2d ser. 27 (1923):59.

17. *ECA,* p. 177.

18. O. Von Gebhardt, *The Miniatures of the Ashburnham Pentateuch* (London: Asher & Co., 1883). W. Neuss, *Die katalanische Bibelillustration um die Wende des ersten Jahrtausends und die altspanische Buchmalerei* (Bonn-Leipzig: Shroeder, 1922). Cf. Grabar-Nordenfalk, *EMP,* pp. 102, 103–5 for some reproductions in color.

19. Neuss, p. 61.

20. *AB* 43 (1961):251.

21. Cf. below, chap. 4.

22. E. A. Lowe, "The 'Script of Luxeuil,'—A Title Vindicated," *Revue Benedictine* (1953), pp. 132–42.

23. Cf. A. Boeckler, *Abendländische Miniaturen bis zum Ausgang der romanischen Zeit* (Berlin-Leipzig: Lietzmann, 1930), pp. 7–9. Porcher, *EDA,* pp. 136–37, 165–74.

24. Cf. *EDA,* pp. 214–43.

25. Reproduced in color in *EDA,* figs. 175, 189.

26. Cf. also *EDA,* figs. 180, 181, 185, 191.

27. *EMP,* p. 128.

28. Cf. Boeckler, *AM,* p.. 12.

29. *EMP,* p. 126.

30. B. Teyssèdre, *Le sacramentaire de Gellone et la figure humaine dans les manuscrits francs du VIIIᵉ siècle* (Toulouse: Privat, 1959).

31. Reproduced in color in *EDA,* figs. 198–203.

32. E. A. Lowe, *Codices latini antiquiores* 5, no. 618 (1950).

33. Teyssèdre, p. 11, dates it 773 on palaeographic grounds; Porcher (*EDA,* p. 358) puts it a little later, *c.* 790–95.

34. Reproduced in color in *EMP,* p. 130.

35. Cf. *EDA,* fig. 131.

36. Cf. also Porcher, *EDA,* p. 188.

37. M. C. Ross, *Arts of the Migration Period* (Baltimore: Walters Art Gallery, 1961).

38. *EDA,* fig. 199.

39. Zimmerman, *Vorkarolingische Miniaturen,* pp. 59–61, 182–84, pls. 78–84.

40. *CR,* fig. 61.

41. *Mediaeval Art,* p. 181.

42. Cf. above, n. 8.

43. Cf. above, chap. 1.

44. H. J. White, "The Codex Amiatinus and its Birthplace," *Studio Biblica*, 2 (1890):283. P. Battifol, *The Amiatinus Codex* (Paris, 1895).

45. G. Biagi, *Reproductions from Illuminated Manuscripts. Fifty Plates from the Laurentiana* (London: Quaritch, 1914).

46. Reproduced in color in *EMP*, p. 119.

47. Reproduced in color in *Evangelium Quattuor Codex Lindisfarnensis. The Book of Lindisfarne* p.p. T. D. Kendrick, T. J. Brown, R. L. S. Bruce-Mitford, H. Roosen-Runge, A. S. C. Ross, E. G. Stanley, A. E. A. Warner. 2 vols. (Olten-Lausanne: Urs Graf, 1956–1960).

48. "Eastern Style Elements in the Book of Lindisfarne," *Acta Archaeologica*, 13 (1942):157–69.

49. A. Boeckler and A. A. Schmid, "Die Buchmalerei," *Handbuch der Bibliothekswissenschaft* vol. 1 (Stuttgart: K. F. Koehler Verlag, 1950), p. 272.

50. M. Rickert, *Painting in Britain: The Middle Ages* (Baltimore: Penguin, 1954), p. 15.

51. *Mostra Storica Nazionale delle Miniature: Palazzo di Venezia, Rome,* no. 31, (Florence: Sansoni, 1954), p. 22.

52. Volbach, *Early Christian Art,* pl. 160.

53. *The Vespasian Psalter;* introd. by D. H. Wright and A. Campbell, (Copenhagen: Rosenkilde & Bagger, 1967).

54. *PiBMA,* pl. 160.

55. C. Nordenfalk, "A Note on the Stockholm *Codex Aureus,*" *Nordisk Tidskrift för Bok-och Biblioteksväsen,* 38 (1951):145–56.

56. Reproduced in color in *EMP,* p. 123.

57. R. B. O'Connor, "The Mediaeval History of the Double-Axe Motif," *American Journal of Archaeology,* 2d ser. 24 (1920):151–70.

58. A. O. and M. O. Anderson, *Adomnan's Life of Columba* (Camden: Nelson, 1961).

59. P. McGurk, "The Irish Pocket Gospel-Books," *Sacris Erudiri* 8 (1956):249 ff. Idem, *Latin Gospel-Books from A.D. 400 to A.D. 800* (Paris-Brussels-Antwerp-Amsterdam: Érasme, 1961). O.-K. Werckmeister, *Irisch-northumbrische Buchmalerei des 8. Jahrhunderts und monastische Spiritualität* (Berlin: De Gruyter, 1967).

60. F. Henry, *Irish Art during the Viking Invasions (800–1020 A.D.)* (Ithaca: Cornell University Press, 1967), pls. 57–58.

61. Cf. Porcher, *EDA,* pp. 136–37, 157.

62. *Evangeliorum quattuor Codex Durmachensis. The Book of Durrow,* p.p. A. A. Luce, O. Simes, P. Meyer, C. Bieler, 2 vols. (Olten-Lausanne: Urs Graf, 1960).

63. H. J. Lawlor and W. M. Lindsay, "The Cathach of St. Columba," *Proceedings of the Royal Irish Academy* (1916) (C), pp. 241 ff.

64. C. Nordenfalk, "Before the Book of Durrow," *Acta Archaeologica,* 18 (1947):141–74.

65. C. Green, *Sutton Hoo; the excavation of a royal ship burial* (London: Merlin Press, 1963).

66. C. Fox, *Pattern and Purpose—A Survey of Early Celtic Art in Britain* (Cardiff: National Museum of Wales, 1958).

67. F. Henry, *Irish Art in the Early Christian Period (to 800 A.D.)* (Ithaca: Cornell University Press, 1965), pp. 117–58. G. B. Brown, *The Arts in Early England,* 8 vols. (London: Murray, 1903–30).

68. *EMP,* p. 124.

69. *IAEC,* pl. 61; *AM,* pl. 8.

70. *IAEC,* pl. 31.

71. *IAEC,* pl. E, opp. p. 168, for a reproduction in color. The Durrow St. Matthew Symbol and the St. John Carpet Page are reproduced in color in *EMP,* pp. 110–11.

72. *IAEC,* pp. 64–65, 168 .

73. Cf. above, chap. 1.

74. Nordenfalk, "An Illustrated Diatesseron," cf. chap. 1, n. 56.

75. Cf. n. 47.

76. Reproduced in color in *EMP,* pp. 116–17.

77. Rickert, *PiBMA,* p. 14.

78. The portrait of St. Luke on f. 137v is reproduced in color in *EDA,* fig. 173.

79. The Durrow and Echternach Matthew portraits are reproduced in color in *EDA,* figs. 170, 174.

80. Interesting analogies in a group of Byzantine ivories in the Museo Archeologico of Milan have been pointed out by Nordenfalk, n. 48, p. 161.

81. H. J. Hermann, *Die illuminierten Handschriften und Inkunabeln der Nationalbibliothek in Wien,* vol. 1 (Leipzig: Hiersemann, 1923), pp. 50–56, pls. xi–xx.

82. *Evangeliorum quattuor Codex Cenannensis. The Book of Kells.* Contributions by E. H. Alton, P. Meyer, G. O. Simms, 3 vols. (Olten-Lausanne: Urs Graf, 1950).

83. The portrait of St. John is reproduced in color in *EDA,* fig. 169.

84. *IAVI,* pl. 28.

85. *Ibid.,* color pl. C.

86. *Ibid.,* pl. 17.

87. *Ibid.,* color pl. G.

88. *Ibid.,* color pl. B.

89. *Ibid.,* pls. 22, 26.

90. *Ibid.,* color pl. F.

91. A. M. Friend, Jr., "The Canon Tables of the Book of Kells," *Mediaeval Studies in Memory of Arthur Kingsley Porter,* vol. 2 (Cambridge, Mass.: Harvard University Press, 1939), pp. 611–66.

92. Reproduced in color in *EMP,* p. 115.

93. *IAVI,* pl. 24.

94. Porcher suggests (*EDA,* p. 157) that the Celtic foundation at Bobbio in northern Italy, established by St. Columbanus in 612, played an important role.

95. Rickert, *PiBMA,* p. 23.

96. Cf. n. 91 above.

97. *CR,* fig. 69.

98. There is an exact analogy in the development of regional styles of writing, all based on Roman example, as Thompson points out (*GLP,* pp. 371 ff), but arriving at different forms, of which the Irish are among the most individual.

99. *Mediaeval Art,* p. 181.

 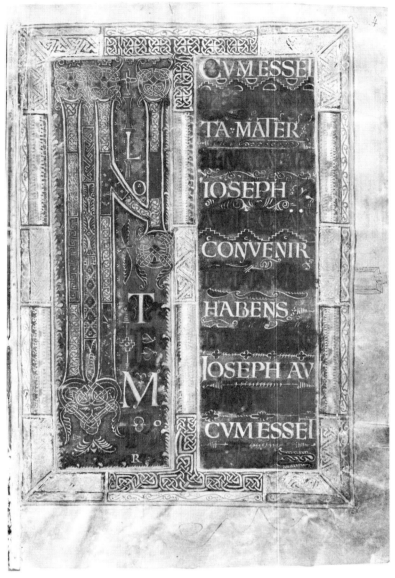

Fig. 53.
Paris, Bibliothèque Nationale, Ms. n.a. lat. 1203, ff.3v–4.
The Godescalc Gospels, The Fountain of Life: Incipit of
the Vigil of the Nativity.

4

Carolingian and Ottonian Illumination

A. Carolingian Illumination

Occidental illumination in the ninth century was dominated by developments of the innovations initiated by Charlemagne (768–814) in the so-called Carolingian Renaissance. So influential were these, and so far-reaching their effect, that Carolingian style continued with remarkable consistency even after Charlemagne's death, unlike the disintegration of the political structure he had created in the Holy Roman Empire and of which he had been crowned the leader by Pope Leo III on Christmas Day in 800. For, unhappy as may have been the political fortunes of the Empire under his successors, Louis the Pious (814–840), Lothaire (840–855), Louis II (855–875), and Charles the Bald (875–877), elaborately illuminated manuscripts commissioned by or identified with all of them are rightly considered among the most notable examples of book art. For in this sense, the Carolingian illuminated codex took on the public character of its Byzantine counterpart; the scriptoria in which they were produced were monastic, but their patronage was royal. In this, as in the total culture of his time, Charlemagne sought to renew or recreate the glory of ancient Rome.

Charlemagne's reforms were motivated initially by his awareness of the low level of literacy in his time. He himself could write only with difficulty, according to his biographer, Einhard,[1] although he could understand Greek and spoke Latin as well as his native Teutonic tongue. But he was profoundly impressed by the fact that even many churchmen of his day were poorly educated, and those who could read were forced to depend on texts that often were almost illegible (cf. Fig. 36). Largely because of these circumstances, the liturgy itself had become corrupted to such an extent that its most fundamental meaning was obscured. It was to renew and correct the degenerated texts and provide training in writing better ones that Charlemagne summoned outstanding scholars of the day into his service, men like Paul the Deacon, a historian from the Benedictine monastery at Monte Cassino in southern Italy, and Alcuin of York, a Saxon from English Northumbria, who founded the palace school at Aachen, Charlemagne's capital, in 782.

Among the first reforms of major importance brought about by Charlemagne was that of writing. The history of mediaeval paleography, as the study of textual script is known, is complex and involved,[2] but there is some agreement on a few major points. Generally speaking, Latin script in its basic forms is either majuscule or minuscule. A line of majuscule letters lies between two upper and lower limits—MDLP—and would be called upper case or capitals. Minuscule letters, on the other hand, lie between four lines—mdlp—two inner lines and one above and another below, and would be called

"lower case" by a printer today. In the basic forms described, the majuscule book-hand is derived from inscriptions carved in stone;[3] a late Latin example can be seen in the Vatican Vergil (Fig. 4). The minuscule hand, by contrast, is associated from the outset with writing rather than carving, whether on wax tablets, papyrus, or vellum, in none of which does the marking instrument encounter much resistance to its movement over the surface. The more rounded form of the resulting script is often called cursive. Majuscules or capitals subjected to the same rounding procedure, particularly in certain letters like A, E, and M, are called uncials; an example can be seen in the rubrics of the Gellone Sacramentary (Fig. 40). In a modified form called half-uncial, it is seen in many Celtic books, e.g., the word *generatio* at the bottom of f.34 in the Book of Kells (Fig. 49).

The Carolingian or Caroline minuscule was developed in the scriptoria founded by Charlemagne to produce a unified script with the clarity and legibility of uncials, yet which would flow nearly as easily from the scribe's pen as cursive. The success of the Carolingian script is attested by its rapid spread through the scriptoria in all parts of Europe, and by the fact that when humanistic sentiment stimulated a reaction against Gothic black-letter script in the manuscripts and later in the printed books of the fifteenth century, it was to the ninth-century Carolingian minuscule that designers turned for models, though from the mistaken notion that its model was in the writing of the Romans. But with the exception of some attempted innovations in twentieth-century typography, it is not exaggerating to say that the various type designs in printed books from the sixteenth century to the present owe their character largely to humanistic models following Carolingian example. Just when or where the Carolingian minuscule was first used is much debated, but it does appear early in the chronological tables on ff.121v–126 of a Gospel-book in the Bibliothèque Nationale in Paris (Ms. n. a. lat. 1203), known as the Godescalc Gospels from the name of the scribe who wrote it for Charlemagne between 781 and 783.[4]

The content of Carolingian books is a further indication of Charlemagne's intention to renew the culture of the past rather than to create one anew. In the scant remains of literary production of the time, histories like that of the Longobards by Paul the Deacon, and Einhard's biography of Charlemagne are noteworthy. The critically corrected texts of the Scriptures—Bibles,

Psalters, and Gospel-books—were written and illuminated to provide better understanding of ideas that had become vague or distorted, and the commentaries and theological treatises essential for comprehension by the still limited Latinity of the day continued to be produced. But the full measure of Charlemagne's intent to raise the intellectual level of his empire is best indicated, perhaps, by the great number of secular and even pagan texts that were copied and illuminated.[5] All that is known today of the Chronograph of 354, for instance, is from copies of copies made in Charlemagne's time. The same can be said of scientific treatises on medicine and astronomy,[6] and such pagan works as the *Comedies* of Terence (Fig. 57).[7] Nothing could give a clearer idea of Charlemagne's image of the glory that had been Rome.

Viewed overall, Carolingian illumination, like its book-hand, was an eclectic phenomenon. From what has been said of the places from which Charlemagne obtained the scholars who supervised the textual and liturgical reforms he set in motion, it follows that the models used must have been drawn from various sources. The presence of the Saxon Alcuin of York, first at Aachen in 782 and subsequently as abbot of St. Martin at Tours from 796 to 804, accounts for the appearance of much Anglo-Celtic ornament in Carolingian illumination. Charlemagne's interest in Italy is equally well documented, particularly Ravenna, where the church of San Vitale was the model for his own chapel-mausoleum at Aachen, and from whence also came many of the Western elements of style and iconography in the illuminated books made for him and his times. From the Christian Orient came yet other influences, explained, in part at least, by political and ecclesiastic relationships between the Rhineland and Constantinople; at one time, Charlemagne even contemplated marrying the iconodule Byzantine Empress Irene in the hope of consolidating the Eastern and Western empires. The results of assimilating these many influences on Carolingian illumination were given even greater variety by their production in the different monastic centers where the reforms were established, centers whose names are usually given to the "schools," as they are termed, with which groups of related manuscripts are identified. Though scholars are not in entire agreement as to either the number of these schools or the relationships between them, certain broad categories can be established.

The Godescalc Gospels referred to above is a key

work. As much is known of its date and authorship from the dedicatory verse or colophon on ff.126v–127 as of any major manuscript of the period. It is stated there that the book was written by the scribe Godescalc between Easter 781 and 783, for Charlemagne and his queen Hildegarde, whose death in the latter year gives the date before which the book must have been completed. The book was written to commemorate the baptism of Charlemagne's son, Pippin, by Pope Hadrian in the baptistery of San Giovanni in Laterano at Rome on Holy Saturday in 781. The miniatures on ff.3v–4 (Fig. 53) refer specifically to this event as further explained in the colophon.[8]

On f.3v, to the left, a circular building topped by a conical roof supporting a cross is flanked by a number of birds and a deer-like animal. Facing it, on f.4, are the opening lines of the pericope, or reading for the Mass, of the Vigil of the Nativity, beginning *In illo*

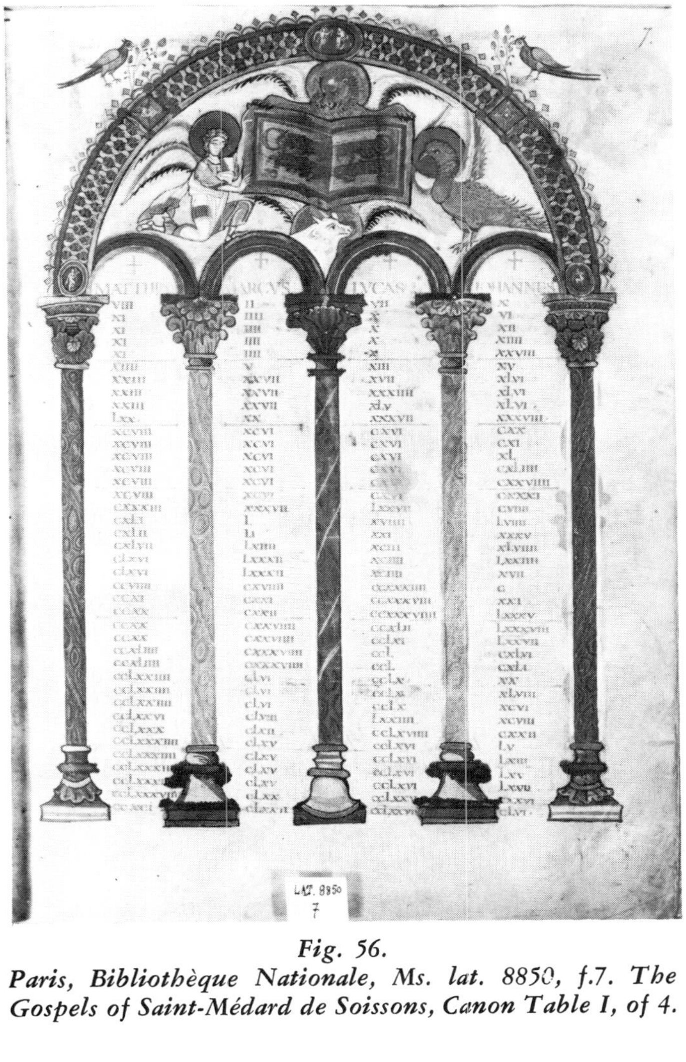

Fig. 56.
Paris, Bibliothèque Nationale, Ms. lat. 8850, f.7. The Gospels of Saint-Médard de Soissons, Canon Table I, of 4.

tempore (Matt. 1:18–21). Its letters are written in alternate lines of gold and silver, the latter so oxydized as to be nearly illegible, laid on a purple background. Both folios have elaborate borders of rinceaux, interlaces, and bands of small lozenges in differing colors of red, white, and blue conveniently termed a rainbow motive.[9]

The symbolism of the architectural form and the accompanying birds and beasts has been determined with certainty in the study by Paul Underwood referred to in note 8. The building is the Fountain of Life, its circular form with conical roof being a reference to that of the Holy Sepulchre as seen in the lower register of the Crucifixion miniature in the Rabula Gospels (Fig. 13). Here it signifies specifically the octagonal font in the Lateran Baptistery in which Pippin had been baptized. The deer-like animal is a hart, traditionally associated with the baptismal rite from the passage in Psalm 42:1 (King James version), "As the hart panteth after the water brooks, so panteth my soul after thee, O God." The peacocks at the base of the conical roof were a traditional symbol of immortality, and the smaller birds above them, at the base of the cross, are recognizably waterfowls. They are identified in Eastern theological commentaries as symbols of the apostles— "fishers of men"—who look back at the cocks symbolizing the Old Testament prophets in whose sayings the coming of Christ was foretold, the authority for the preaching of the apostles. A similar but somewhat more elaborate Fountain of Life is on f.6v of the Gospels of Saint-Médard de Soissons[10] (Paris, B.N. Ms. lat. 8850), which was probably also made for Charlemagne.

So far as sources can be determined for the symbolic ideas incorporated in the Godescalc Fountain of Life, they are in the Near East. This is also true of the architectural form, a particularly close parallel being seen in a little circular building on f.5v of a Gospelbook in the Patriarchal Library at Etschmiadzin in Armenia (Gospel 229).[11] The Armenian miniature is of the tenth century and so later than the Carolingian, but Underwood has given conclusive proof that the concept harks back to much earlier times, and that both Eastern and Western examples stand in the same symbolic tradition. There are also Oriental overtones in the Godescalc ornament. The rainbow bands in the borders of both miniatures can be compared directly with those used the same way in the Vienna Dioscurides manuscript (Fig. 7), and they also occur in the Rabula Gospels. In like fashion, the use of gold script on purple parchment throughout the Godescalc book harks back to the sixth-century Near Eastern purple manuscripts like the Vienna Genesis, the Rossano Gospels, and the fragment from Sinope.

Yet mingled with these derivatives from the Near Eastern ornamental repertory are others equally clearly of Western origin. The letters IN on f.4 occupy nearly the full height of the folio and are filled with panels of interlace and the fret pattern that are certainly directly or indirectly of insular origin. Interlaces also appear in the border of the author portrait of St. John (Fig. 54) on f.2v of the Godescalc Gospels. Yet other features of this latter miniature can be referred to Occidental prototypes in the late antique manner. In the upper right border angle, the double-axe motive appears, as it does in the archivolt of the Stockholm *Codex Aureus* portrait of St. John (Fig. 44); it recurs frequently in manu-

scripts of the general Carolingian group, which includes the Godescalc Gospel-book.[12] The setting of the Godescalc John, on the other hand, is a simplified version of the type seen in the Greco-Asiatic Byzantine miniature of St. Mark in Gospel-book No. 43 in the Stauronikita Library (Fig. 23) on Mount Athos, and is even closer to that of the sixth-century mosaic representing the seaport of Classis in Sant' Apollinare Nuovo in Ravenna.[13] Also from Ravenna must have come the wingless symbols in the other three Evangelist portraits in the Godescalc Gospels;[14] the closest parallel, as noted in the discussion of the wingless symbols in the Book of Durrow (Fig. 46), is in the Evangelist mosaics of San Vitale .

In both technique and style, the Godescalc miniatures reveal a different conception and understanding of late classical models from those seen in their Anglo-Italian counterparts like the Cambridge Gospels (Fig. 33, Plate III) and the Stockholm *Codex Aureus* (Fig. 44). They are painted in rather thick and opaque pigments, and color is used to model the forms, especially the faces in which red and brown patterns on one side with green shading into blue and gray on the other create an effect of light and shade that is quite convincing. The strong lines of contours and drapery folds also contribute to the plasticity of the forms, and there is some attempt to suggest perspective depth in the setting.

A number of other manuscripts whose miniatures contain somewhat similar stylistic and ornamental features can be grouped with the Godescalc Gospels and associated with Charlemagne. One of them, a Gospel-book in the Stadtbibliothek at Trier (Codex 22), contains a statement that it was made for a certain ADA ANCILLA DEI—"Ada, handmaiden of God"—who has been thought to be a sister of Charlemagne. From this, the entire group is sometimes referred to as the "Ada School" of Carolingian illumination.[15] There are some reasons to associate it with the scriptorium of the monastery at Trier, and, in any event, with the East Frankish region of the empire, suggested by the term "Rhineland School" preferred by some for the group as a whole.[16] The portrait of St. Mark (Fig. 55) on f.59v of the Ada Gospels is painted in thick and opaque colors like the Godescalc St. John,[17] the Evangelist's red mantle over a purple robe set against the dark green drapery over the back of the throne. Reds, pinks, and purples appear in the architectural setting, and in the lunette the lion symbol (winged this time) holds a blue scroll. Much gold is used, in the nimbi and for

Fig. 57.
Vatican, Biblioteca Apostolica, Ms. lat. 3868, f.2. The Comedies of Terence, Portrait of the Author.

highlights and decorative ornament, and the face and hands are modeled in much the way seen in the Godescalc evangelist.[18]

Although the date of the Ada Gospels is not specifically recorded, as it is for Godescalc's book, the part containing the portrait of Mark is thought to be a little later, perhaps shortly before 800. This conclusion is supported by the greater plasticity of the modeled forms, the more ornate and monumental character of the composition, and by still further assimilations from late classical art like the simulated antique gems inserted in the rainbow faceted archivolt. In all these characteristics and details, the illuminator is moving closer to the spirit of his model as well as a more correct use of its forms, achieving an effect not unworthy of comparison with contemporary Byzantine work (Fig. 23). Much the same quality is found in what is often considered the finest manuscript in the Ada or Rhineland group, the Gospels of Saint Médard of Soissons (Paris, B.N. Ms. lat. 8850).

The Soissons Gospels are named from their association with the monastery of Saint Médard to which the book was given by Charlemagne's son, Louis the Pious, at Easter time in 827, with some other objects known to have been made for Charlemagne; from this it has been assumed that the Gospel-book was once his and consequently to be dated before his death in 814. Its decoration is luxurious. The text is in gold uncials, an archaic hand by the ninth century for the most part, but "employed in adding a further air of splendour to the costly MSS. of the Carolingian monarchs."[19] The usual Gospel complement of canon tables and Evangelist portraits is augmented by a full-page miniature of the apocalyptic Vision of the Adoration of the Lamb, and a Fountain of Life developing the Godescalc version in a number of ways.[20]

Reference has already been made to one of the most individual features of the Soissons Gospels, the canon tables (Fig. 56). Illustrated is the first table on f.7 in which parallel passages in all four Gospels are cited. The architectural arcade provides ample scope for the classical decorative motives characteristic of the Rhineland group books—well-proportioned columns with complete bases and capitals, the double-axe pattern of the archivolt accented by simulated gems or cameos, and the birds and flowers in the spandrels outside the arch. There is an innovation, however, in the appearance of the Four Symbols in the lunette of the principal arch, Luke at the bottom, Mark at the top, Matthew and John to the sides, all holding or supporting an opened book inscribed in gold CANON PRIMVS IN QUO QVATTUOR, i.e., the first canon of readings from all four Gospels. The "beast canon table" also appears in another "Ada" manuscript in the British Museum (Ms. Harley 2788),[21] which can also be dated about 800, as well as in the Book of Kells (Fig. 51), where it is unique in early Celtic illumination. Another point of interest in the Harley 2788 canon tables is the two contrasting styles seen in them. The arcades of the first three (ff.6v–7v) are flat and two-dimensional, while the later ones have marbelized shafts and some of them are spiraled like those in the Soissons page.[22] It has been suggested with plausibility[23] that this change in style came when Alcuin left the supervision of the Ada-Rhineland scriptorium in 796 to Einhard, later Charlemagne's biographer. In any case, the trend toward more three-dimensional and organic forms noted in comparing the figures in the Ada Gospels with those in Godescalc's book is indication of the increasing concern with plastic values, more closely approximating those of late antique style, that developed within the atelier itself.

Much the same quality is found in the illustrations of a manuscript that can be identified with either the monastery at Corbie near Amiens, a royal foundation of c. 660, or its Saxon branch at Corvey established by monks from Corbie in the early ninth century. The manuscript in question, a copy of the *Comedies* of Terence, is in the Vatican Library (Ms. lat. 3868). An inscription on f.3 states that it was painted by the monk Adelricus of Corvey during the abbacy of Adelardus, one of the earliest datable names of illuminators rather than scribes, for Adelardus' regime lasted from 822 until 826. The author portrait (Fig. 57) on f.2 is of a type discussed at length by Weitzmann.[24] The bust-length likeness appears against a light blue background, with a darker blue border enclosed in a wider yellow band with gold ornament. This is framed, in turn, in a square field of dark blue decorated with a white foliate motive and bordered with red bands accented with gold lozenges. It is supported on a marbleized base by two figures wearing masks like those shown on a rack on f.3, by which the characters in the comedy *The Andria* are identified. The opaque colors, thickly applied within heavy contours, define surfaces modeled with bluish-white highlights. The flanking supporting figures are painted directly on the parchment, as are all the illustrations of scenes in the various plays in the manuscript.

The Vatican Terence is one of the oldest of thirteen

copies made between the early ninth and twelfth centuries of an edition of Terence's six comedies compiled in Rome by a certain Calliopius in the fifth century.[25] Of them all, the Vatican copy is closest to the assumed prototype, as the analysis of style and technique makes clear, even to the gold lozenges in the red border of the frame held by the supporters, precisely comparable to the borders of the Vatican Vergil illustrations (Fig. 4). There are but scant indications of linear perspective and none of atmospheric depth in the illustrations of scenes in the comedies, for they are painted directly on the parchment, but they too follow directly in the classical tradition in being inserted at the precise places called for in the text; the plasticity of the figures is actually enhanced by the neutral backgrounds. The folios are almost square in format, again following late antique precedent. In every sense, then, the Vatican Terence is a typical expression of Carolingian desire to renew the classical past, in style, technique, and general expressive character, to say nothing of the secular content of these thoroughly pagan comedies.

Another aspect of Carolingian style is seen in manuscripts written and illuminated in the monastery at Fulda, in what is now called the province of Hesse-Nassau in West Germany. Founded by the Anglo-Saxon Boniface in 744, its abbot from about 820 on was Hrabanus Maurus, a disciple of Alcuin at Tours. A learned man who was much concerned with the study of pagan authors[26] and an enthusiastic supporter of the pictorial arts, he directed the scriptorium at Fulda in one of its most creative periods, the middle part of the ninth century.[27] Among its most individual products was a series of illuminated codices of a poem composed by Hrabanus Maurus himself, called *Liber de Laudibus Sancti Crucis*—"The Book of Praise of the Holy Cross"; the original is believed to be in the Vienna National-bibliothek (Cod. 652),[28] with copies in the Vatican Library (Ms. Reg. lat. 124) and in the Biblioteca Nazionale of Turin (Ms. K. II. 20). Louis the Pious, Charlemagne's son, is portrayed on f.4v of the Vatican example (Fig. 58), wearing the armor and carrying the shield of a warrior but nimbed and holding a staff cross. His tunic is blue, the cuirass and buskins brown, the shield and cross staff a bright orange, and the nimbus is a yellow circle. The pigments are opaque and rather thickly applied. The composition of the folio is framed in simple narrow bands of green, which also enclose the most novel feature of the miniature, the text of one of Hrabanus Maurus's hymns in praise of

the Holy Cross, written in fine Caroline minuscules across the uncolored parchment and painted figure alike, but in such a way that the letters inside the outline of the form make up words and sentences by themselves as well as being part of the lines extending across the page.

Carl Nordenfalk has pointed out the source of these devices in the poetry of a fourth-century writer named Publillus Optatianus Porfyrius who was in the service of Constantine the Great.[29] The writing of words to form representational shapes is called *technopaignon*, literally "art games;" another Carolingian example is an Aratus manuscript about astronomy in the British Museum in London (Ms. Harley 647), again, significantly, a fourth-century secular treatise. The representation of Louis the Pious as a Christian warrior hero may have been inspired by the statue of Constantine in Rome that celebrated his victory over Maxentius. Nordenfalk also suggests the possibility that these ideas of design and composition may have reached the Carolingian continent from Canterbury in England. Touching on this is the fact that in the Hrabanus Maurus manuscripts, colored folios are occasionally interspersed among white ones, as was the case with Porfyrius' *carmina figurata* (literally "figured songs"), of which there is known to have been a copy at Canterbury around 750. Purple and white folios are also found together in the Stockholm *Codex Aureus*, a Canterbury book,[30] in which the *technopaignon* device also appears, as well as different colors of ink in the text. All these technical characteristics seem to have been suggested by Constantinian models, and the same can be said of the Fulda manuscripts under consideration, whether directly from Rome or indirectly by way of Canterbury.

As has been noted, the manuscripts of the Ada-Rhineland group have associations with the imperial household, even if the scriptoria that produced them cannot be precisely identified. In this respect, the case is different with another group also quite closely connected with Charlemagne, generally called the Palace school.[31] All are Gospel-books, and all are believed to date from the early ninth century. One is still in the Treasury of Aachen Cathedral, for which it conceivably was made.[32] A second is the Gospel-book from Xanten in the Bibliothèque Royale in Brussels (Ms. 18723).[33] A third volume in the group is the Gospel-book from Cleves in the Berlin Deutsche Staatsbibliothek (Ms. Theol. lat. fol. 260), and the fourth is the Coronation Book in the Schatzkammer or Treasure Room in the

Fig. 58.
Vatican, Biblioteca Apostolica, Ms. Reg. lat. 124, f.45.
Hrabanus Maurus, De Sancti Crucis, *Louis the Pious.*

Fig. 59.
Vienna, Kunsthistorisches Museum, Schatzkammer, Un-
numbered Ms., f.15. The Coronation Gospels, St. Mat-
thew.

Kunsthistorisches Museum in Vienna (unnumbered). The miniatures in all have much in common stylistically, and also iconographically to some extent, although they are not entirely consistent in this respect. The key work that establishes the association with Charlemagne is the Schatzkammer or Coronation Gospels, traditionally the book on which the kings of Germany took their oath of office, for it is said to have been found on the knees of the dead Charlemagne when his sepulchre was opened in 1000 by Otto III. If it were, as seems to be the case, a personal volume of the emperor, it could not have been executed after his death in 814.

The Schatzkammer Gospels are written in gold uncials on purple parchment. At the beginning of each book, there is a portrait of the author, seated in a landscape and writing or being inspired to write (Fig. 59),[34] framed in a heavy border of narrow bands separated by a wider band of foliage. The heavily painted colors are more or less consistent in all four miniatures. The draperies are bluish-white with gray shadows, the landscape is in dark brown tones with touches of gray, and there are also gray overtones in the blue skies. The faces are russet brown with bluish-white highlights. This rather sombre color scheme is vividly set off, however, by accents of brilliant red in the stool cushions, and the gold of the nimbi, stools, desks, and writing utensils, and in the narrow bands of the borders.

It is clear at once that the Schatzkammer Evangelists derive from a different tradition, iconographically and stylistically, from that of their Ada-Rhineland counterparts (Fig. 55). Unusually for the time, they are seated in landscapes, as are also those of the Cleves Gospelbook and the one still in Aachen, in which all four appear in the same composition. The only precedent for such setting of the Evangelists is in the often-cited choir mosaics of San Vitale in Ravenna, discussed in connection with the wingless Evangelist symbols in the Book of Durrow. There are no symbols at all, however, in the Schatzkammer Evangelist portraits, which allies them with Greek tradition, rather than the Latin, which followed St. Jerome's identification of the evangelists with the four apocalyptic beasts (Rev. 4:7).

This intimation of Greek rather than Latin elements in the Schatzkammer Evangelist iconography is paralleled and reinforced by their style, a style no less suggestive of classical antiquity than that of their Ada-Rhineland counterparts, but of Hellenistic rather than Greco-Attic and Latin strain. Matthew's folding chair and his costume are authentic reproductions of classical

forms, and his pose can be compared directly with those of figures in such lingering manifestations of Hellenism as the Vienna Dioscurides Discovery miniature (Fig. 7) and the portrait of St. Mark in the Rossano Gospels (Fig. 9, Plate II). The Coronation Book Matthew also shares with these a style that is pictorial rather than plastic, impressionistic rather than linear, a distinction that can also be observed between the late sixth-century miniatures of the Rabula Gospels (Figs. 12, 13) and the St. Luke in the Corpus Christi Gospels at Cambridge (Fig. 33, Plate III). In the Ada Gospels St. Mark (Fig. 55), the figure is a pattern of heavy contours and inner lines, rendered plastic by touches of modeling light and shade in color in the face and arm. In the Palace School St. Matthew (Fig. 59), line as such plays little, if any, part. Instead, the figure is built of loosely brushed color areas, with carefully graduated patterns of tone and value, which also create an atmospheric space in which the impressionistically rendered volumes of the form exist in full reality.

There is no specific explanation of this infusion of Hellenistic style in the Palace School miniatures, but that there were Greeks in Charlemagne's court is historically certain. Diplomatic missions were exchanged and relations between Aachen and Constantinople were such that in a treaty of 812, the Byzantine emperor referred to Charlemagne as his "brother." The Greek name Demetrius is written in gold rustic capitals on the opening page of Luke in the Coronation Book, allowing the inference that Greeks may have had something to do with its making; unfortunately nothing indicates what

Fig. 60.
Epernay, Bibliothèque municipale, Ms. 1, f.18v. The Ebbo Gospels, St. Matthew.

part Demetrius may have had in it.[35] In any event, once introduced, the impressionistic pictorialism of the Palace School style was not long in developing in its own way, which is seen in its most distinctive aspect in a group of manuscripts making up the so-called Reims School.

It is so designated from the inscription in a Gospel-book in the Bibliothèque Municipale at Epernay (Ms. 1) to the effect that it was made for Ebbo, archbishop of Reims from 816 to 835, by Peter, who was abbot of the monastery at nearby Hautvillers. It was probably made before 823, for Ebbo was in disfavor after that year and it is unlikely, in the circumstances, that he would have been given a book of such distinction. The text of the Ebbo Gospels is in gold minuscules, and the miniatures include a set of canon tables and portraits of the Four Evangelists;[36] that of Matthew (Fig. 60) is on f.18v. There are some points of similarity with the corresponding miniature in the Coronation Book (Fig. 59)—the landscape setting, the reading desk with its heavy molded shank, and the bright minium red cushion on the Evangelist's seat. Ebbo was a foster brother of Charlemagne's son, Louis the Pious, and a member of the royal household, so he presumably knew the Schatzkammer book. But the changes are many and significant. The robes worn by the evangelists in Ebbo's book are white, as they are in the Coronation Book author portraits, but shot through with gold, which is used much more lavishly throughout—in the desk and bench, in the linear patterns of the landscape, and in the windswept acanthus design in the border—than in the Coronation Book miniatures. The landscape is accented with trees and buildings, unlike the austere environment of the Schatzkammer Evangelists, and the writers' symbols also appear. Matthew bends to the task of transcribing the words on the scroll held by his angel; the others look with painful intensity at their symbols, as if seeking further light.

No less striking is the transformation of technique and style in the Ebbo miniatures. The sober and carefully applied brush strokes used by the Schatzkammer artists to create a broadly impressionistic pictorial effect have given way to a whirling melee of short lines, and the surfaces they define flicker with light as the quiet silhouettes of the Coronation miniature figures break up into jagged staccato outlines. The entire composition is pervaded by vibrant movement; even the inkwell becomes a horn held fast in the writer's hand instead of standing beside his book. The foliage of the border, a series of symmetrically disposed palmettes in the Coronation Book, is a twisting spiral in the Ebbo miniature.

The Ebbo Gospels canon tables also show how close their creator was to classical forms. The numbers referring to the passages are arranged between columns as usual, but these are topped by architraves and surmounted by pediments in the antique manner instead of the semicircular arches of the Ada-Rhineland compositions (Fig. 56). Animals, flowers, and humans are placed above them, but caught up in the same frenzied movement that pervades the full-page Evangelist miniatures. The distinction between the classicism of the Coronation Book and that of Ebbo's Gospels is that between a skillful reemployment of antique idiom and vocabulary in the one, and an interpretation or translation of the same elements in the other for new and different expressive purposes. Just as the Anglo-Celtic artists of Lindisfarne and Kells gave new meaning to the forms they borrowed from older prototypes, so the Ebbo painter invested his transformation of comparable models with a characteristically northern, not to say barbarian, content. As the human figure lost its representational significance in the interest of decorative expressionism in the miniatures of the insular scriptoria, so in the Reims manuscripts it becomes part of an essentially dynamic and emotionally expressionistic unity.

In the one hundred and sixty-six drawings illustrating the Psalms and Canticles in the Utrecht Psalter (Utrecht, Bibliotheek der Rijksuniversiteit, Script. eccl. 484),[37] the expressionistic transformation of classical pictorial style seen in the Ebbo Gospels is carried to a unique and unparalleled climax. There is no inscription or colophon, as in the Ebbo Gospels, to identify its date and place of origin, but there is fairly general agreement that it, too, was made c. 820, at or near the monastery of Hautvillers, and possibly for the same Archbishop Ebbo who owned the Gospel-book. There are several distinctive characteristics. The text is written in rustic capitals[38] resembling those of the Vatican Vergil (Fig. 4), an archaic script for the time and uncommon, if indeed it was used at all, in Christian texts before the eighth century. Unusual too is the arrangement of the text in three columns. It follows the Gallican version of St. Jerome, and includes the Psalms and Canticles, the Lord's Prayer, the Apostolic and Athanasian Creeds, and the Apocryphal Psalm.

The illustrations of the Utrecht Psalter are uncolored pen drawings in brown or bistre ink, placed at the

Plate XI. New York, Pierpont Morgan Library, Ms. 755,
f. 16v. The Wernigerode Gospels, Initial Page.

Plate XII. Munich, Bayerischesstaatsbibliothek, Ms. Clm. 4453, f. 139v. Gospels of Otto III, St. Luke.

beginning of each psalm or unit of the text. They are unframed, and the designs, drawn directly on the parchment, illustrate the text with an almost naïve literalness that is at the same time highly original and intensely dramatic. The text of the 11th Psalm (King James 12) and its pertinent illustration are on f.6v (Fig. 61, Plate VII). Verse 1 reads "Help, Lord; for the godly man ceaseth; for the faithful fail from among the children of men"; on a hill right of center, the psalmist addresses his plea to the Lord. Verse 2: "They speak vanity every one with his neighbor"; in the lower right angle are those who speak "with flattering lips and a double heart" among a group of soldiers. Verse 3: "The Lord shall cut off all flattering lips"; below the psalmist, an angel threatens the vain ones with the butt of his spear. Verse 5: "For the oppression of the poor, for the sighing of the needy, now will I arise, saith the Lord"; above, left of center, the Lord has arisen from His aureoled throne of the earth and follows a beckoning angel toward the psalmist. Verse 5: "I will set him in safety from him that puffeth at him"; the gesticulating figures around a hill on the left side. Verse 6: "The words of the Lord are pure words: as silver tried in a furnace of earth, purified seven times"; upper right, workers smelting metal in a furnace. Verse 9: "The wicked walk on every side, when the vilest men are exalted"; lower left, a group of men moving around a circular object, a direct reference to the idea phrased somewhat differently in verse 9 of the Latin Vulgate (in which this is Psalm 11) which reads *"In circuiti impii ambulant"*—"The impious go around in circles." Occasionally themes drawn from other sources than the text are pictured.[39] The four men in a turnstile, bottom center, apparently illustrate St. Augustine's commentary on this verse: "the ungodly walk in a circle, that is the desire of temporal things, as a cycle of seven days which revolves as a wheel."

The Utrecht manuscript is one of the earliest lavishly illustrated Occidental psalters. As such, particular interest attaches to the sources of its illustration, and a determination of the degree, if any, of their originality. There is fairly general agreement now that the composition of the text to include the Canticles and added hymns was a Carolingian compilation of the late eighth century.[40] It has also been pointed out that some details of the illustration were not inspired by the Gallican version of the text actually found in it, but by images suggested in the Hebraic variant also compiled by St. Jerome,[41] as well as in commentaries like the Augus-

tinian passage cited above. This suggests a rather eclectic procedure, and such appears to have been the case with the formal elements of the illustration as well.[42] The prototypes, as would be expected, must have been in the antique tradition, some Latin, no doubt, but predominantly eastern Mediterranean and, more specifically, Hellenistic. Such details as the rolling hills of the landscapes partially concealing buildings, the forms of trees, the poses and gestures of figures, and the formulae for representing animals can all be traced to the stylistic tradition of the Paris Psalter (Figs. 14, 15) and the Joshua Roll (Fig. 17), the tradition continued in the Christian Orient of Byzantium in the decorative formalism of the miniatures in the Menologium of Basil II (Fig. 25) and the still later Octateuchs (Fig. 16). Pertinent to this implication of Hellenistic rather than Latin sources is the major division of the text in two parts, following Greek usage, rather than the eight found in Latin psalters.

But only the formulae are Greek. The use made of them is Occidental and northern, a true renovation of antique concepts to give expression to the content of Christian faith. As in the Ebbo Evangelist (Fig. 60), the shapes and patterns that painstaking analysis can trace back to classical norms take on a different meaning when translated into expressive line, here freed even of the decorative restraints of color. The carefully related patches of light and dark that gave substance to three-dimensionally modeled forms in the prototype (Fig. 17) are whipped and torn into streaming lines that thrust hands out and heads forward from hunched shoulders. The reticence that bestows gravity and significance upon the classic figure (Fig. 14) is shattered by the emotional content that disregards symbolism and allegory and arrives at a direct statement of specific and concrete meaning. The Lord who arises—*Nunc exsurgam*—moves immediately to answer the psalmist's plea with forceful action, leaving behind the aureoled symbol of His divine power.

Such is the Carolingian expression of the content to which Celtic genius had given form in the dynamic patterns of carpet pages (Fig. 45, Plate V) and initials (Fig. 49), investing ornament with such vitality that it has existence and hence reality in its own right. To achieve comparable concrete reality in figured compositions, the Carolingian artist had first to find and then adapt them to his implicit purpose—to affirm the reality of the written word that became the Word of God in the magic of the line that whips the forms of hills and

trees, of buildings and animals and men, all given
meaning by the divine afflatus driving them in the
windswept arabesques that so clearly convey the content
of the psalmist's anguished plea.

Ebbo's Gospel-book and the Utrecht Psalter are the
key manuscripts of the Reims group with which others
can be associated. Two leaves from what must have been
an elaborately illustrated evangelistary or selections
from the Gospels, bound with a later volume in the
Düsseldorf Landesbibliothek (Ms. B. 113), have drawings of scenes from the life of Christ in a style so close
to that of the Utrecht Psalter that they must have come
from the same atelier.[43] Painted miniatures in styles
related to that of the Ebbo Gospels can be found in a
number of books,[44] including one in the Morgan Library
in New York[45] (Ms. 728) that originated in the dio-
cese of Reims in the time of Archbishop Hincmar
(845–882), one of Ebbo's successors. St. Matthew is
portrayed in f.14v (Fig. 62). The composition is based
on a different model from the one in Ebbo's book
(Fig. 60), and the linear patterns are less agitated, but
the essential characteristics of Reims pictorial style are
clear. The pigments are heavy and opaque in a color
scheme dominated by the dark blue of the background,
which sets off the dull purple of the mantle and the
typical bluish-white of the robe. Gold is used for the

highlights of the accessories, with sharp white accents to model the flesh surfaces. The effect is less dynamic than that of the Ebbo Matthew, a little closer in this respect to the Schatzkammer example, but there are typical Reims touches in the rolling hills of the landscape and the intense communication between the evangelist and his symbol.

Elsewhere in northwestern France, an important center of manuscript illumination whose style derived in some measure from that of the Reims group began to develop around mid-ninth century at Metz. There are not many books from its scriptorium, but the central example, the Sacramentary of Drogo (Paris, B.N., Ms. lat. 9428) is of major importance. An inscription on f.128 indicates that it was probably made for Drogo, an illegitimate son of Charlemagne, who was archbishop of Metz from 826 to 855; it is to be dated *c.* 850. On f.71v is the reading for the Feast of the Ascension of Our Lord (Fig. 63), written in gold uncials around a great letter C, with which the office begins.[46] Elaborated initials are a distinctive feature of Anglo-Celtic illumination, as has been seen, but in the Ada, Palace, and Reims manuscripts, although chapter and verse initials may be accented, they are not the central feature of the book decoration as they are in Drogo's Sacramentary, which contains twenty. All follow the same general scheme. The letter and its twining acanthus are gold, with a background of purple or pale green. Each initial contains a group of figures, moreover, illustrating the episode in the life of Christ or the saint commemorated in the reading, making them among the earliest examples of the "historiated" initial destined to become so popular in later Romanesque and Gothic illumination.

Although there is reason to believe that narrative cycles of Christ's life were known in Anglo-Italian illumination of the eighth century, they did not play a very important part in the early phases of Carolingian art. Tiny vignettes of New Testament themes do appear in some of the full-page miniatures of the evangelists and some of the *incipit* folios of the Soissons Gospels,[47] but on such a small scale that they pass almost unnoticed. Their purpose, moreover, is to illustrate certain points in the Priscillian Prologues in the prefatory passages to the four Gospels[48] rather than the Gospel text itself. On the other hand, it can be assumed from the Reims style fragment in Düsseldorf, referred to above, that such cycles were at least known in early ninth-century Carolingian illumination. To Reims can

Fig. 63.
Paris, Bibliothèque Nationale, Ms. lat. 9428, f.71v. The Sacramentary of Drogo, The Ascension of Christ.

also be traced the lively animation of the Drogo initials, the rather small figures with their brisk, forceful gestures and fluttering draperies, and the writhing acanthus stems treated with a subtlety that makes them quite close to the antique prototypes that were their ultimate inspiration.

Elaborately developed initials are also the distinctive feature of the so-called Franco-Saxon group of manuscripts,[49] which date in general in the last half of the ninth century. A typical example is the *In principio* at the beginning of the Gospel of St. John (Fig. 64) on f.8 of a Gospel-book in the Bibliothèque Municipale of Arras (Ms. 233). The idea of a monumentally decorative initial like this was clearly inspired by Anglo-Celtic examples. All evidence points to the scriptorium of Saint-Amand as its place of origin, a monastery not far from Echternach, where, as has been

Fig. 62.
New York, Pierpont Morgan Library, Ms. 782, f.14v.
Gospel-book from Reims, St. Matthew.

Fig. 64.
Arras, Bibliothèque municipale, Ms. 233, f.8. Gospel-book
from Saint-Vaast of Arras, John incipit.

noted earlier, a Celtic foundation had been established by St. Willibrord in 698. The panels of interlace in the borders and the terminal knots of the principal initials, as well as the animal heads of the N in *IN,* leave no doubt of their Irish derivation, also suggested by the distinctive acid green in the scroll ends of the cross bars of the I. It is possible that this manuscript is one of those said to have been given to the monastery of Saint-Vaast in Arras by Ermentrude, first wife of Charles the Bald, who died in 869. In any case, the manuscript is to be dated early in the second half of the ninth century.

Franco-Saxon style in initial ornament continued for some time. Examples that differ in principle but little from the earlier ones are found as late as the tenth century in manuscripts identified with the monastery at Bobbio in northern Italy. That, as has been mentioned, was a Celtic foundation of St. Columbanus in 614; from its library came a number of manuscripts of which some, including fragments of an eighth-century Irish Gospel-book are in the Biblioteca Nazionale at Turin (Ms. O. IV. 20).[50] Even more specific evidence of the continuing use of Celtic models in continental scriptoria is seen in a Gospel-book in the Cathedral Treasury at Trier (Ms. 61 [134]),[51] written about 775 by a scribe who signed his name, Thomas, on f.5v, either at Echternach in Luxembourg or nearby Trier. In any case, his model was the Celtic Echternach Gospels (Paris, B.N. Ms. lat. 9389),[52] itself derived from the Book of Durrow. According to tradition, the Echternach Gospel-book was taken to the monastery there by its founder Willibrord in 698, where it was copied in the later book at least in the Evangelist symbol miniature on f.lv and some of the initials. The canon tables and the Matthew *incipit* miniature, on the other hand, are almost equally certainly not based on Celtic models; the practical architecture of the former and plasticity of the latter anticipate later Ada style, and were doubtless based on Greco-Asiatic or Latin prototypes. Another Gospel-book (Trier, Statdbibliothek, Ms. 23) of the ninth century repeats the wingless Evangelist symbols of Durrow and Echternach on the *incipit* folio of St. John's Gospel, but draws the faces of the evangelist and Matthew's angel according to the Byzantine formula of proportions, yet following it on the next folio with a typical Franco-Saxon initial at the beginning of the text proper.[53]

Of all the Carolingian schools of illumination, the products of the school of Tours can be most precisely localized as to provenance. It was to become abbot of the monastery of St. Martin at Tours that Alcuin of York left Aachen in 796, holding the post until his death in 804. The Carolingian minuscule as a style of writing had undoubtedly been in use before Alcuin went to Tours, e.g., the *capitularia* of the Godescalc Gospels, but there is no doubt that its further development took place there.[54] Alcuin's vital concern with textual reforms made the scriptoria of St. Martin's and its affiliate at nearby Marmoutier the centers of scholarship in scriptural texts, and the revision produced there of the Latin text of St. Jerome's Vulgate version of the Bible set the standard for the period and some time thereafter.[55]

Alcuin's primary concern was with the textual content of books rather than with their decoration. Such ornament as is found in Tours manuscripts from the period of his incumbency understandably reflects the insular modes his English origin would lead one to expect, mingled with the birds and fishes of pre-Carolingian continental usage.[56] His successors Fridugis (807–834) and Adalhard (834–843) had more interest in such matters; during their regimes, a series of books begins—Bibles, Gospel-books, and lectionaries—from whose decoration the style of the later masterpieces was to emerge.[57] The ornament of a volume in the Staatsbibliothek at Bamberg (Misc. class. Bibl. 1) called Alcuin's Bible is characteristic, though it was probably produced at Marmoutier in Adalhard's time, *c.* 840. A full-page miniature on f.7v (Fig. 65), preceding the Old Testament, is of the Genesis story from the Creation of Adam through the Murder of Abel.[58] The narrative is recounted in small figures arranged in a series of friezes across the page. They are painted in gold and silver silhouettes, outlined occasionally in red, and with touches of green, yellow-brown, and violet. The only precedent for this technique is in the gold-glass work of late antiquity, involving a thin film of gold applied to glass with the details incised or tooled;[59] in some ways, these tiny figures also suggest textile designs. Such characteristics as these, and the simple yet well-integrated design of the page as a whole, have led to the speculation that there must have been an illustrated Latin Bible in the library at Tours, decorated in a style like that of the Vatican Vergil (Fig. 4). In his definitive study of the Tours school, Koehler advances the idea that it or its prototype was produced in Rome in the time of Leo the Great (440–461). In any case, the most individual products of the Tours

Fig. 65.
Bamberg, Staatsbibliothek, Misc. class. Bibl. 1, f.7v. The
"Alcuin Bible," The Story of Genesis.

school were one-volume Bibles with Alcuin's version of the Vulgate text, illustrated with full-page miniatures of the Old and New Testament stories.

One of these, the Moûtier-Grandval Bible in the British Museum (Add. Ms. 10546), was produced at St. Martin of Tours at about the same time as the Alcuin Bible, c. 840. There are four full-page miniatures, one each preceding Genesis, Exodus, and the Gospels, and one at the end of the Apocalyptic Vision described in Revelation 4 and 5.[60] The Exodus miniature on f.25v is of Moses receiving the Ten Commandments and giving them to the Children of Israel (Fig. 66, Plate VIII).[61] It is composed in registers, like the Bamberg Genesis miniature, an upper and lower one separated by a purple band inscribed in gold letters identifying the scenes above and below. But unlike the Bamberg example, the Moûtier-Grandval Exodus picture is painted in full color, in opaque pigments heightened with gold in the drapery folds, the trees in the upper register, the wings and nimbi of the angels, and the like. And also unlike the two-dimensional silhouettes of the Bamberg Bible miniature are the figures, strongly modeled by firm contours, and the curving lines of the draperies, and the creation of volumes of space to accommodate them. Moses presents the Law to Aaron and the Israelites in a basilica with Corinthian columns, decorative figures in the arcade spandrels, and roofed with a foreshortened coffered ceiling. To all these reflections of a model in the late antique style of the Vatican Vergil should be added the horizontal bands—purple, blue, pink, and white—of the backgrounds, reminiscent of the shaded colors of classic illusionism to suggest atmospheric depth.

Pride of place among the Tours manuscripts must be given to those produced when Count Vivian was secular abbot of St. Martin's (845–851). One of these, now in the Bibliothèque Nationale in Paris (Ms. lat. 1), was presented by him to the emperor, Charles the Bald, about 846 on the occasion of a ceremonial visit to St. Martin's. This information is found in a dedicatory inscription on f.422r and v at the end of the volume, preceding a full-page miniature on f.423 of its presentation to the monarch (Fig. 67). This dedication page, the earliest surviving portrayal of a contemporary event in mediaeval illumination, established a type that was to become very popular; it is only one of several themes added to those of the Moûtier-Grandval Bible in this volume, which is known both as the Vivian Bible and the First Bible of Charles the Bald. Its other illustrations

are the story of St. Jerome (f.3v), the Creation and Fall of Man (f.10v), Moses and the Law (f.27v), David and his Musicians (f.215v), Christ in Majesty (f.329v), the story of St. Paul (f.386v), and the Apocalyptic Vision (f.415v).[62] Canon tables on ff. 326–327v, introductory titles in gold on purple bands, gold and painted initials at the beginning of each book, and a similarly designed concordance of the Pauline Epistles on ff.383v–384 complete the decoration of the volume.

The narrative miniatures in the Vivian Bible are composed, like those of the Moûtier-Grandval volume, in frieze-like bands, separated by purple-backed inscriptions written in gold, and the figures are generally similar in proportion and movement; three different artists appear to have shared in the enterprise.[63] There is less concern with perspective space, however, and the forms are related in a series of stepped planes, one above the other, to suggest depth. This device also appears in the full-page presentation miniature on f.423 (Fig. 67). Charles the Bald is enthroned between curtains drawn back under a golden arch. He is flanked by guards and warriors, and reaches out to accept the book offered him with veiled hands by three monks. In the foreground are Count Vivian and other participants in the ceremony. From the crown of the golden arch, the hand of God blesses the emperor, and in the spandrels two feminine figures symbolizing Virtues extend crowns toward him. Two columns with well-proportioned Corinthianesque capitals support the arch, their shafts twined with leafy stems of foliage instead of being decorated with flutes or spirals. This is a device often found in the Tours school canon-tables, too, as is also the squaring up of the composition by enclosing the arch in a rectangular frame.

Canon Table 1, with readings from the four Gospels (Fig. 68), is on f.326 of the Vivian Bible. It is the opinion of many that such canon tables were the most inspired creations of the Tours scriptorium, allowing free choice in the decorative repertory of late antiquity without posing the problem of adapting an organic representational figure style to the requirements of the two-dimensional page design. Purple and gold dominate the color scheme of the forms painted directly on the parchment. Occasionally, as under the three inner arches, a line of red dots suggests the insular contribution to the Turonian reforms, but the ornament is drawn for the most part from classical models. Acanthus leaves fill the outer border and the archivolts, and appear in

Fig. 67.
Paris, Bibliothèque Nationale, Ms. lat. 1, f.423. The
Vivian Bible, Abbot Vivian Presenting the Bible to
Charles the Bald.

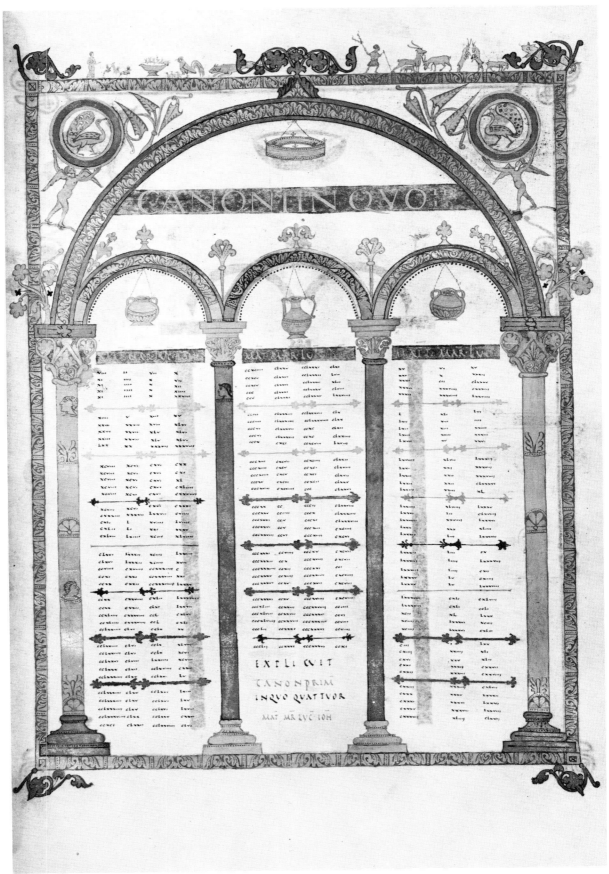

Fig. 68.
Paris, Bibliothèque Nationale, Ms. lat. 1, f.326. The
Vivian Bible, Canon Table I, of 4.

the capitals. The crown suspended from the keystone of the main arch and the vases hanging from the inner ones, a unique motive of the Tours scriptorium, also reproduce classical shapes. Profile heads on the shafts to the left imitate the medallion portraits on antique coins, the Turonian counterparts of the simulated classical gems in the Ada-Rhineland archivolts (cf. Fig. 55) from which the idea may have been derived.[64]

There are occasional symbolic forms like the peacocks in medallions supported by angels in the spandrels, but the tiny figures on the top of the rectangular border, like the two dogs similarly placed in the presentation miniature, can have no such significance. A woman feeds a flock of fowls, a fox swoops on a cock, a goatherd tends a flock of lively goats—a Turonian counterpart of the cats and mice in the Chi-Rho initial in the Book of Kells in anticipating the drolleries of later times. The Vivian Bible is equaled in impressiveness among Tours manuscripts only by the Gospel-book of King Lothaire, Charles the Bald's half brother (Paris, B.N. Ms. lat. 266), executed between 849 and 851. It contains the usual Gospel-book decoration of canon tables and author portraits, and also a representation, on f.lv, of Lothaire enthroned with two soldiers,[65] a reduction of the monumental presentation and dedicatory composition in the First Bible of Charles the Bald.

It is no more than coincidence, perhaps, that the *floruit* of Tours illumination came at a time when Charles the Bald had followed the example of his grandfather Charlemagne in calling Alcuin of York to the palace school at Aachen, and invited Johannus Scotus Erigena—"John the Scot born in Ireland"—to become part of the palace school at Tours. In any event, it was an act in keeping with Charles's great concern that the earlier reforms should be continued, manifest also in the emperor's interest in books, which led to the writing and illumination of a number of impressive volumes during the third quarter of the ninth century, and this despite the turmoil and confusion of a time when the raids of Norse pirates on his West Frankish kingdom were increasing constantly in frequency and severity.

Among the manuscripts made for Charles the Bald are a Psalter (Paris, B.N., Ms. lat. 1152), a Sacramentary (Paris, B.N., Ms. lat. 1141), a prayer-book in the Munich Residenz, a Gospel-book known as the *Codex Aureus* of St. Emmeram of Regensburg (Munich, Bayerische Staatsbibliothek, Clm. 14000), and a Bible, sometimes called that of San Callisto, now in the library of S. Paolo fuori le Mura at Rome. The psalter in Paris[66] and the Munich *Codex Aureus* are signed by the scribe Liuthard, collaborating with his brother Berenger in the latter, and Liuthard is also recorded as the painter of a Gospel-book in Darmstadt (Landesbibliothek, Cod. 746). Several of the books are dated, by inscription in the Munich *Codex Aureus* (870), or presumptive internal evidence in the instances of the psalter in Paris (between 842 and 869), and the San Paolo Bible (871). There is no inscription to identify the Paris Sacramentary[67] with Charles the Bald, but its miniatures are stylistically similar to those in the other books, and the one of a coronation on f.2v has been thought to refer to his being crowned king of the West Franks in 843, or to the occasion when he became king of Lorraine at Metz in 869, more probably the latter.

More than general contemporaneity and similarities in workmanship relate the manuscripts in this group to each other. In all, there is a fondness for strong, heavily painted colors and much use of gold and purple, dense acanthus-leaf borders often dotted with white creating an effect of flickering light, marbelized columns and other architectural forms, and a general striving for opulence of color and pattern. Because of this consistency, the style of the group is sometimes called that of Charles the Bald for there is no certain identification of it with any specific productive center. Corbie, the foundation near Amiens, has been suggested, for Charles the Bald is known to have had some interest in it. But this is even more pertinent to Saint-Denis near Paris as the base of operations of artists in Charles's employ. He maintained his residence and his personal library there, and became its lay abbot in 867. Cogent reasons have been advanced,[68] both stylistic and iconographic, to consider Saint-Denis as the most probable place where the variety of sources implied by the notable eclecticism of the group as a whole could be found. Although some details of the reasoning leading to this conclusion have been argued, it remains the most persuasive thesis so far advanced.

The *Codex Aureus* of St. Emmeram (Munich, Bayerische Staatsbibliothek, Clm. 14000) is so called because it was given to the monastery of that name at Regensburg about 893 by the emperor Arnulf, who had succeeded Charles the Bald on the imperial throne. Remarkably well preserved and still retaining its magnificent cover of gold repoussé panels and jewels,[69] the *Codex Aureus* is a preeminent example of late Carolingian manuscript illumination. In addition to the usual canon tables and Evangelist portraits, there is a full-page dedicatory miniature on f.5v, followed by a Christ in Majesty with prophets and evangelists, and the Adoration of the Lamb by the Twenty-four Elders from the Apocalypse.[70]

The stylistic eclecticism of the miniature in the *Codex Aureus* of Regensburg and its related manuscripts is well shown in the dedicatory miniature on f.5v of Charles the Bald Enthroned (Fig. 69). The color scheme is like that of the Tours volumes, but with even more lavish use of purple, as in the field of the minuscule inscriptions in gold, the latter also being used for architectural details of the emperor's canopy and throne, and in his mantle. In the background are horizontal bands of color like those in the Vivian Bible presentation miniature (Fig. 67). The acanthus border is more like that seen in the Reims Ebbo Gospels (Fig. 60), but here characteristically accented by white dots and stripes. The theme is clearly derived from the Vivian Bible picture, but monumentalized by transforming the two-dimensional arch of its frame into a three-dimensional canopy or baldacchino with the golden crowns hanging in the lateral arches. The content is also different. It is not a book that the emperor receives, but the homage of his armies in the persons of the two warriors beside him; his kingdoms are personified in the two crowned female figures with flowering cornucopias standing beside the canopy. There is a comparable allegory in the miniature of Christ Enthroned on f.6 of the Coronation Sacramentary,[71] where two figures representing Sea and Earth in truly classical fashion as reclining nudes symbolize Christ's authority over the universe. In the *Codex Aureus* miniature, the glorification of the emperor approaches apotheosis.

In the canon tables of the Munich *Codex Aureus,* there are also references to an earlier work, but this time to an Ada-Rhineland book. The Soissons Gospels (Fig. 56) had been given by Charlemagne's son, Louis the Pious, to the monastery of Saint-Médard at Soissons in 827. At some time, the illuminators of the Munich *Codex Aureus* must have had access to it, for the canon tables of the latter repeat the designs of those in the earlier book almost exactly, differing only in greater opulence of effect and the characteristic mingling of features from other schools in some details. Thus the table of Canons VI–VIII on f.11 (Fig. 70) is enclosed in a rich acanthus border that squares up the page in the manner of Tours, although this feature does not appear in the Soissons example. But in the lunette, the

four Evangelist symbols appear with a circular colonnaded structure topped by a conical roof symbolizing the Fountain of Life, just as it does in the same canontable on f.11 of the Soissons Gospels[72] where, as Underwood has pointed out, it is pertinent to the content of the passages listed below. Even the birds in the spandrels of the *Codex Aureus* canon-table page follow the Soissons example. But the typical concern of Charles the Bald's artist for enhanced decorative effect is also apparent—in the white-tipped and crocketed acanthus leaves, the marbleized column shafts, and, characteristically, the lozenge-shaped panels with the Evangelist symbols in the columns of the arcade, as if they were framed and hung from the shafts.

No less monumental than the Munich *Codex Aureus* and the First Bible of Charles the Bald is the Bible now in the library of San Paolo fuori le Mura (unnumbered) also called the Bible of San Callisto. Its three hundred and fifty-four folios contain the full Vulgate Bible text, and its decoration is more extensive than in any other Carolingian book. There are twenty-three full-page miniatures; one of the story of Job is now missing but left an offset impression on f.74, which it originally faced. They include a dedication page on f.1,[73] the story of St. Jerome,[74] and fourteen Old Testament subjects,[75] and, in the New Testament, a Christ in Majesty page, the Evangelist portraits and miniatures of Pentecost, the story of St. Paul, and the Apocalyptic Vision. In addition to these narrative or figural compositions, there are decorative miniatures of four full-page canontables, and thirty-seven full or part-page initials for the principal books of the Old and New Testaments, with less elaborate designs for the New Testament epistles. There are also gold *tituli* on purple bands enclosed in elaborate borders on the rectos of the narrative miniature folios, which are usually painted on the versos.

Many characteristics of the San Paolo Bible miniatures invite comparison with Tours illumination. All eight full-page miniature subjects in the Vivian Bible are found in the San Paolo book, where many of them are divided into registers by purple bands with gold inscriptions. Even in them, however, the incidents portrayed are not always the same, and there are differences in style. Moses receives the Law and transmits it to Aaron and the Children of Israel on f.26v of the San Paolo Bible (Fig. 71, Plate IX), just as he does on f.25v of the Moûtier-Grandval volume (Fig. 66, Plate VIII). For all the general similarities, there are noticeable differences. In the presentation scene, the

Fig. 69.
Munich, Bayerischesstaatsbibliothek, Ms. Clm. 14000, f.5v.
The Codex Aureus of St. Emmeram of Regensburg,
Charles the Bald Enthroned.

Fig. 70.
*Munich, Bayerischesstaatsbibliothek, Ms. Clm. 14000,
f.11. The Codex Aureus of St. Emmeram of Regensburg,
Canon Tables VI–IX, of 2.*

basilica of the earlier version has been made two-dimensional, and the figure group is related to it as another plane instead of being enclosed in its space. Mount Sinai in the upper register is a convoluted silhouette with neither foreground nor background, although the sky is painted in arching bands of pink shading into blue above.

These differences might seem to be further steps in the line of change distinguishing the style of the Moûtier-Grandval Bible from the First Bible of Charles the Bald, but there are also distinctions in the figure style. In the San Paolo Bible, the forms are more slender and more brisk and articulate in movement than in either of the Tours volumes. A point of iconographic interest is Moses' reception of the Tables of the Law with ceremoniously veiled hands like those of the monks presenting Vivian's Bible to Charles the Bald in the dedication miniature of the Paris book (Fig. 67) whereas he accepts them with bare hands in the Moûtier-Grandval version. There may be an explanation of the non-Turonian elements in the San Paolo style in the acanthus ornament in the upper and lower borders. Most of the San Paolo miniatures are simply framed in striped borders of silver, gold, and red, but an outer band of foliage has been added to the Moses composition. The gold acanthus on green of the top and bottom bands suggests Reims more than anything else, paralleling the more galvanic drawing and movement of the figures. However, in all the narrative miniatures of the San Paolo Bible, the artists must have drawn, like their predecessors at Tours, on an elaborately illustrated model of the late antique-Early Christian period, selecting even more generously from it than had the illuminators of St. Martin's and Marmoutier.

In the full-page initial designs that introduce most of the major books of both Old and New Testaments in the San Paolo Bible, the gift of its artists for elegant eclectic decorative pattern is obvious. The beginning of Genesis is on f.llv (Fig. 72, Plate X). In the majority of the *incipits* in the book, the letters and foliage sprays are of gold. Some are filled or touched with color—red, green, light blue-gray, and lilac—and many have painted purple backgrounds, as here, though some leave it in the natural color of the parchment. The IN of *In principio* can be compared directly with the same letters on the Mark *incipit* folio in the Book of Lindisfarne (Fig. 47), to suggest the ultimate ancestry of the interlace panels, but the geometric shapes and animal-headed terminals and more disciplined organization

point to the Ada-Rhineland and Franco-Saxon channels through which they undoubtedly came to Charles the Bald's artists, from whence came also the sprays of foliage that fill every space within and around and between the principal letters.

A dedicatory inscription in handsome gold minuscules at the beginning of the San Paolo Bible states that it was made by the scribe Ingobertus for a certain king Charles—*Rex Carolus.* The scribe has not been further identified, but there are several possibilities for the King Charles who commissioned the volume, as stated in the prologue, and donated it to Christ. A dedicatory miniature on f.1[76] shows the king seated as he is in the St. Emmeram *Codex Aureus* page (Fig. 69) and receiving homage. Among those who honor the monarch are two veiled women who have no counterparts in the St. Emmeram miniature, and the king holds a gold disc inscribed with a monogram. By elimination, the emperor has been thought to be either Charles the Bald or his successor Charles the Fat, who ascended the throne in 881. In the most perceptive study of the problem,[77] he has been identified as Charles the Bald, and the compilation of the volume explained as a celebration of his marriage in 870 to his second wife, Richildis, whose name is given in the monogram on the golden disc. The same study tends to confirm the identification of the manuscript and its illumination with the scriptorium of the abbey at St.-Denis.[78]

Among the leading scriptoria outside France proper in the later ninth century was that of St. Gall in Switzerland. Founded in 612 by Gallus, a disciple of St. Columbanus, the Celtic missionary, its library still contains important Irish manuscripts and a number decorated in Merovingian, pre-Carolingian style.[79] It was not until the latter half of the ninth century that a distinctive style began to develop, however, in the time of Abbot Grimvald (841–872). There are overtones of Reims and Tours in the style of St. Gall figure compositions of this period,[80] but St. Gall initials develop an individual form quite early. A Psalter in the monastery library (Stiftsbibliothek, Cod. 23) is identified in an inscription on pp. 26–27 as the work of a certain Folchard, who is listed as a scribe in the monastery from about 855 on; the manuscript can be dated around 870. Figured themes are not extensive, occurring for the most part in the lunettes of canon-table-like frames of the text of the litanies.[81] But the initial letters of the principal divisions of the psalter text are elaborated in a way that constitutes one of the hall-

Fig. 73.
St. Gall, Stiftsbibliothek, Cod. 23, p. 31. The Folchard
Psalter, Initial B.

marks of the scriptorium. The Initial B (Fig. 73) is on page 31, the beginning of the opening words of the first psalm in Latin—*Beatus vir*. Within a frame of gold rinceaux on a purple ground, the letter is constructed of panels and curving motives which are also filled with rinceaux. In the openings in the letter, interlaced and plaited ribbons, also of gold with touches of green and light blue, end sometimes in animal heads, sometimes in leafy fronds. A distinctive feature of the St. Gall rinceaux is the accenting of the stems with buds that occasionally spiral back on themselves or are transformed into interlaces. The effect is no less rich than in the San Paolo Bible initial (Fig. 72, Plate X), but it is also more clear, for in its sensitively balanced organization, the plain surfaces and spaces count as much as the elaborate decorative motives they set off. In later St. Gall work like the Golden Psalter or *Psalterium Aureum* (Cod. 22), there is some loss of the rhythmic structure that makes the Folchard Psalter initials so elegant, but they are a major point of departure for the forms developed in the manuscripts of the Ottonian schools of illumination in the late tenth and early eleventh centuries.

B. Ottonian Illumination

Ottonian illumination takes its name from the dynasty in power during the greater part of the tenth century in the eastern portion of what had been Charlemagne's kingdom. There a succession of weak rulers in the late ninth and early tenth centuries had permitted the consolidation of feudal principalities or duchies only nominally loyal to the reigning monarch. A measure of centralized authority was established by Henry the Fowler (919–936) and confirmed by his successor Otto I (936–975), whose dynasty was continued by his son Otto II (973–983) and grandson Otto III (983–1002), and, after the latter's death, Henry II (1002–1024). It is with these rulers and the monasteries under their patronage that Ottonian illumination[82] is identified.

Ottonian illumination is closely related to the reforms and spread of monasticism initiated by a group of Benedictine monks at Cluny in east central France, where a monastery had been founded in 910. Directed against abuses of churchly authority that had been unchecked by a succession of ineffective popes, the Cluniac reforms were the beginning of a moral and spiritual regeneration that was to stimulate and lead

to the creation of some of the most distinctive examples of mediaeval art. Foundations forming part of the Cluniac community were to be the creative centers for the better part of a century and a half, encouraged by royal patronage that sought to realize an alliance of Church and Crown, making common cause against the feudal nobility.

Books were among the most impressive symbols of institutional power and authority, a point made clear by the elaborate dedication pages of many outstanding Ottonian manuscripts (Fig. 79). Under the patronage of royalty and the ecclesiastical hierarchy, the output of the Ottonian scriptoria was voluminous. The influence of Carolingian example upon the books produced in the Ottonian scriptoria was understandably great; the value placed upon such models is indicated in a recorded restoration of Charles the Bald's *Codex Aureus* (Figs. 69, 70) by Ramwold, abbot between 975 and 1001 of the monastery of St. Emmeram at Regensburg, to which the book had been given around 893 by Arnulf, one of the last Carolingians. But no less important was a renewed infusion of Byzantine influence, symbolized by the marriage of Otto II in 972 to Theophano, daughter of the Byzantine emperor Romulus II. Illuminations in which these influences can be discerned are in books of somewhat more limited range of subject matter than in Carolingian times. There are very few Bibles, for example, like those of Tours, and only a small number of psalters. Old Testament subjects occur less frequently, and illustrated copies of late antique secular works—the comedies of Terence and astronomical treatises like the Aratus—are not found at all in Ottonian manuscripts, nor are the moralizing treatises harking back to Latin times of Prudentius and the Physiologus. But as if to compensate, the New Testament scenes that are but scantly represented in Carolingian illumination assume great importance, in Gospel-books, in pericopes, as selected Gospel readings are called, and in sacramentaries, which, like other liturgical texts, enjoyed great popularity in Germany during the reign of the Ottonian emperors.

The distinctive character of Ottonian illumination is first suggested in examples from the third quarter of the tenth century, in the last years of Otto I's reign, among them the dowry scroll listing gifts to the Byzantine princess Theophano when she was married to Otto II in 972.[83] Executed in gold on purple parchment with an all-over pattern of lions and griffons and the margins

Fig. 75.
Göttingen, Universitätsbibliothek, Cod. theol. fol. 231,
f.60. Sacramentary from Fulda, Christ Before Pilate, and
the Crucifixion.

Fig. 76.
Cividale, Museo Archeologico Nazionale, Codex Gertrudianis, *ff.16v–17.* The Egbert Psalter, Egbert Receiving
the Psalter from Ruodprecht. *(Photo Ciol)*

decorated with medallion busts of Christ, the Virgin, and saints, it resembles nothing so much as a textile design, pervaded throughout by suggestions of Byzantium. It is believed to have been made in the monastery at Corvey, a Carolingian foundation in Lower Saxony. No less opulent are the initial letters on the introductory pages of the Wernigerode Gospels (Fig. 74, Plate XI) in the Pierpont Morgan Library in New York.[84] Also believed to come from Corvey, it may be dated to the third quarter of the tenth century. The letters are gold, the I ornamented with Franco-Saxon interlace and with leaf and animal-head motives; they are placed in a green border surrounded by a margin of leaf-and-interlace of purple on a dark blue background. Much of this is clearly derived from Carolingian example, but the all-over foliate background of the inner green frame is Byzantine, suggested, no doubt, by textile patterns.

St. Boniface at Fulda was another Carolingian foun-

dation and manuscripts written and illuminated there in the Ottonian period understandably continue the tradition established in the ninth century.[85] One of its most distinctive early Ottonian books is a Sacramentary in the Universitätsbibliothek at Göttingen (Cod. theol. fol. 231), illuminated around the year 975. The readings of the various offices are preceded by full-page miniatures of New Testament subjects, scenes from the lives of the saints, and so on. The Crucifixion, with Christ before Pilate below, is on f.60 (Fig. 75). The figures are rather short and heavily proportioned, descendants of those who people the narrative scenes in manuscripts like the Carolingian Terence from Corbie (Fig. 57), but with a typically Fuldaesque note of animation in the whipping hems of the garments accented with white edging, a detail—also appearing in foliate motives in Fulda miniatures—that seems to derive from earlier Saint-Denis practice. Another distinctive trait of the Fulda scriptorium is the framing of the lower scene

Fig. 77.
Cividale, Museo Archeologico Nazionale, Codex Gertrudianis, *f.67.* The Egbert Psalter, Initial Q.

between two classical columns, found in most narrative miniatures in Fulda books; they often support fully developed architraves. Unlike the Carolingian manuscripts of the Ada-Rhineland group, with which many Fulda books can be related,[86] the color scheme in these Ottonian miniatures tends toward the cool side—blues with gray overtones, greens, lilac-purples, and yellows— possibly derived from Byzantine practice, which is also suggested by the Oriental full-length colobium of the crucified Saviour (cf. Fig. 13).

Among the most productive and influential Ottonian scriptoria were those in the monasteries at Trier or Trèves in the Rhineland, and at Reichenau on an island in Lake Constance. The Cluniac reform had been established in both communities, St. Maximin at Trier in 934, and Reichenau in 972. Both scriptoria were particularly favored by Otto II and III for their sumptuous Gospelbooks, evangelistaries, sacramentaries, and pericopes. Trier, it will be recalled, was an important center in Charlemagne's time, and thought by some to have been the locale of the Ada-Rhineland school. Reichenau was founded in the ninth century and produced some books

before 900, but its *floruit* came after the Cluniac reform and is distinctively Ottonian.

Relationships between Trier and Reichenau appear to have always been close.[87] One of the most important early Reichenau manuscripts, the psalter now in the Museo Archeologico at Cividale in northern Italy, where it is called the *Codex Gertrudianis*,[88] was made for the archbishop of Trier, Egbert, and presented to him in 983; a double miniature on ff.16v–17 (Fig. 76) shows him receiving it from the scribe Ruodprecht. Still earlier Reichenau books, notably the volume of pericopes called the Gero Codex (Darmstadt, Landesbibl. Ms. 1948)[89] can be demonstrably proven to derive from Ada-Rhineland models,[90] in this case the Lorsch Gos-

pels.[91] In the Presentation miniature of the Egbert Psalter, as it is also known, Ada influence is apparent in the technique of heavy and opaque colors, the linear patterns of the highlights, and the plastic rendering of the drapery folds. In the initial pages marking the principal divisions of the Psalter text (Fig. 77), like the letter Q on f.67, the plait-work and crocketed tendrils can be compared with St. Gall (Fig. 73), but the fantastic animals of gold on the purple background in the spaces between the initial and the border are distinctly Byzantine. A notable characteristic of such Reichenau initials as this is the dynamic design; where a St. Gall initial lies quietly within its border, the Reichenau letter thrusts violently against and through it, as the

entire rhythm of the plaits and interlaces is stepped up.

At about the time when the Cividale Psalter was being created in the Reichenau scriptorium, another book was being made for Egbert, the volume of pericopes or lectionary, a selection of Gospel readings now in the Stadtbibliothek at Trier (Cod. 24) called the *Codex Egberti;* it was the work of two Reichenau monks, Kerald and Heribert, and is to be dated about 980.[92] Four hands have been distinguished in its quite considerable illustration, which includes a Presentation miniature, the portraits of the Evangelists, and fifty-two episodes in the life of Christ, from the Annunciation to Pentecost—one of the most extensive early cycles extant in Western illumination. One of these, the Massacre of the Innocents (Fig. 78) on f.15v, is the work of a highly gifted illuminator who apparently had access to a model in the style of the fourth-century Quedlinburg *Itala* (Fig. 3), and, moreover, to have understood it. The horizontal composition is framed in a red border

spotted with gold lozenges like those of the Vatican Vergil illustrations (Fig. 4). The uptilted green plane of the ground shades to a darker value as it recedes, to meet a sky modulated with great subtlety from blues through pinks, quite unlike the arbitrary stripings used by the Tours miniaturist of the Moûtier-Grandval Bible (Fig. 66, Plate VIII) working from a presumably comparable model. The pigments are thick and applied in varying tonal intensities, so that the plastic quality of the heavily contoured figures is stressed. In every sense, in his understanding of pictorial form and space and his method of defining them in line and color, this artist is closer to the spirit of the late antique art from which he takes his formal ideas than is almost any other artist of the period. Only in the emphatic emotional characterization of the figures by pose and gesture does he give form to the imperative of expressionism that also finds outlet in the writhing interlaces and tendrils of the Cividale Psalter initial (Fig. 77).

Fig. 78.
Trier, Stadtbibliothek, Codex 24, f.15v. The Codex Egberti, *The Massacre of the Innocents.*

Fig. 79.
Trier, Stadtbibliothek, Ms. 1711/626. Epistles of Gregory the Great, Gregory attended by Peter the Deacon. Chantilly, Musée Condé, Ms. 14. Epistles of Gregory the Great, Emperor Otto II or III Enthroned. (Photo Giraudon).

A detailed and perceptive study of the personality of this illuminator[93] identifies him as the author also of two miniatures that were the dedicatory illustration (Fig. 79) of a manuscript of the Epistles of Gregory the Great, commissioned by Egbert about 985.[94] This is deduced from a poem of dedication, in which reference is made to the death of Otto II in 983; the enthroned emperor may be either Otto II or III, hence the poem is commemoratory if it be the former, adulatory if the latter. The two miniatures are now separated; that on the left is in the Trier Stadtbibliothek (Ms. 1711/626), the other in the Musée Condé at Chantilly (Ms. 14). In the Trier miniature, Gregory is dictating to his secretary, Peter the Deacon, the words inspired by the dove of the Holy Spirit; they are from Proverbs 3:13, "Happy is the man that findeth wisdom, and the man that getteth understanding." They refer to the emperor in the Chantilly miniature receiving homage from four crowned female figures; they are inscribed GERMANIA FRANCIA ITALIA ALEMANIA, the provinces of his realm.[95]

Such glorification of the emperor[96] has been seen in Carolingian books like the Vivian Bible (Fig. 67) and the *Codex Aureus* of Charles the Bald (Fig. 69), the latter with similar allegorical figures of the provinces. The style of the Gregory Master miniature is like that of the Massacre of the Innocents in the *Codex Egberti* (Fig. 78), closer, really, to the late antique than the Carolingian. The red borders with gold lozenges, the subtle shading of color in the background to suggest atmospheric depth, and the well-proportioned, reasonably articulated figures outlined in long and rhythmic curves bespeak this. Only in the general color scheme does the Gregory Master seem to have made any significant change from a prototype that can be reasonably assumed to have been in the manner of the fifth-century Vatican Vergil (Fig. 4); strong blues and reds and greens are harmonized with light pinks and yellows, and gold is used lavishly. The overall effect is of brightness, almost gaiety.

Many of these stylistic characteristics in the miniatures of a Gospel-book given to the Sainte-Chapelle in Paris by Charles V of France in 1379[97] place it too in the oeuvre of the Gregory Master, but one of them, on f.1, representing Christ in Majesty,[98] shows that he had access to Byzantine models as well. The background of the central mandorla is gold, the first such in Western illumination, although in very general use earlier in

Byzantine miniatures. No less Byzantine is the iconography of the glorification of the emperor, comparable in spirit to the prevailing sentiment in the Eastern imperial court from which the princess Theophano had come to wed Otto II and to hold the regency during the early years of his son's reign.

The theme recurs in a Gospel-book made for Otto III at Reichenau around the year 1000 (Munich, Stadtsbibliothek, Clm. 4453).[99] The composition on ff.23v–24 (Fig. 80)[100] is clearly related to that by the Gregory Master (Fig. 79), but in a style that can best be characterized as a crystallization and stylization of the prototype. The inscribed provinces have displaced Gregory and his scribe in the verso miniature and advance toward the emperor in a single plane of profiles repeated against a striped background. The monarch is rigidly frontal, seated in front of a flattened architecture instead of the canopy-in-perspective of the Gregory miniature. The fixed regard, almost a stare, of his eyes, is given nearly hypnotic concentration by the side glances of his suite, which repeat the peering regard of the symbolized provinces. The draperies, softly modeled in the earlier miniature, have become rigid and metallic, succumbing to the decorative imperative of Byzantinism.

Paradoxically enough, the stiffening of the style creates a more intense expressive effect, which is produced not by gesture and pose, as in the *Codex Egberti* Massacre of the Innocents (Fig. 78), but by the sharply angular rhythms of the linear patterns and the arbitrary juxtapositions of tints and modeling tones in the colors. Among the most striking statements of Ottonian expressionism are the Evangelist portraits in the Gospels of Otto III; that of St. Luke (Fig. 81, Plate XII) is on f.139v. The Evangelist, seated in a mandorla, extends his arms upward, not so much in support of anything as to allow the emanation from them of the overlapping glories of light in the arch above. A River of Paradise flows from the hill on which his mandorla is poised, with two animals drinking from it. Above the Evangelist's head is his symbolic ox and the enveloping arcs of other glories filled with inscribed figures of Old Testament prophets surrounded by angels, all streaming rays of light. Against the gold background of the arch, the figures and their aureoles are set in greens and brownish-purples shading into pinks, contributing to a deep and sonorous harmony, very different in effect and expressive character from the delicate color schemes preferred by the Gregory Master.[101] Also playing a part in this is the gradual movement upward from the solidly modeled forms of the drinking animals through the flattened shapes of the Evangelist's figure and mandorla to the dematerialized angels and prophets floating in glories of light at the top, a complete expression of the transformation of substance into spirit through the seer's rhapsodic vision of transcendental truth.

Otto III's Gospel-book was produced in the Reichenau scriptorium and is one of a group of manuscripts called that of "Liuthar," from the name of its scribe or donor in another Gospel-book also made for Otto, now in the Aachen Cathedral treasury. In still another Reichenau manuscript of pericopes or Gospel readings made for Henry II between 1002 and 1014 (Munich, SB, Clm. 4452),[102] a somewhat later phase of the style is seen. There are a number of full-page New Testament scenes in which a further stage of expressionism has been reached. The Annunciation to the Shepherds (Fig. 82) on f.8v is framed in a border of red bands with gold lozenges; this and the rounded bullet-shaped heads of the shepherds are all that remains to echo dimly a far-removed prototype in the style lying behind that of some of the *Codex Egberti* miniatures. The graded colorism of an atmospheric sky has given way to a band of pink above an expanse of gold that is the background of the announcing angel directing his message to the shepherds from atop a mound of hillocks.[103] The pale yellow and blue-gray of his robes are repeated in the sheep. The garments of the seated shepherds are deep green and brownish-gray, and those of the standing one are light blue and a sharp minium red. The contours of the faces, hands, and fingers are lined with white, the sole reminder of the Gregory Master's modeling highlights; here, rather than suggesting plastic form, they underscore the two-dimensional linear rhythms of the fingers that writhe and twist with the dynamic impulse of the message given and received. The peering-sideways glances of the eyes, black dots circled with white, also contribute to the intense expressionism of the whole, created in no small degree by the luminosity of the gold that seems to pervade the colors, the hallmark of Reichenau style at the climax of its maturity.

Ottonian style, shaped at Trier-Echternach and Reichenau in the late tenth century and reaching full development in the early eleventh-century manuscripts of the latter scriptorium, is largely dominated by its products for the better part of a half-century. Reichenau influence is especially evident in the ateliers of the southern monasteries of German territory like St. Gall and Einsiedeln. Elsewhere it was not so strong, and more individual manners were developed. At Cologne, a number of Gospel-books were illuminated in a style of some originality during the archbishopric of Heribert (999–1021), including one in the Biblioteca Ambrosiana at Milan (Ms. C. 53. sup).[104] The portrait of St. Matthew (Fig. 83) on f.19 is characteristic. There is no symbol, an omission to be noted in nearly all Cologne school Ottonian Evangelist portraits. This iconographic peculiarity indicates a Greek rather than Latin prototype and suggests quite evidently a comparison with the similarly symbol-less Evangelists of the Carolingian Palace School manuscripts like the Schatzkammer Gospels (Fig. 59). With the essentially pictorial as against linear forms of the Schatzkammer authors, the Cologne St. Matthew also shares a method of defining shapes by areas rather than contours, brushed instead of drawn as they are in the "Liuthar" Reichenau books, the tones graduated and accented with white lines. The color scheme is dark to the point of being sombre, dominated by the purple violet mantle to which the heavily painted blue-gray shading of the robe presents a restrained contrast. This too points to the derivation of Cologne Ottonian style from the Schatzkammer manner, as well as the stylized landscape elements of the background.

Along with the increasing expressionism of Ottonian style goes an increasingly greater symbolic content. One instance of this is seen in the inscribed prophets who figure so prominently in the Evangelist portraits of Otto III's Gospel-book (Fig. 81, Plate XII). They exemplify the foundation of the Gospels in Old Testament Scriptures from which the authority of their New Testament writings is confirmed. This heightened symbolic content in Ottonian illumination is particularly characteristic of the miniatures in manuscripts produced in the monastery at Regensburg in Bavaria during the time and under the patronage of Henry II.[105] It will be recalled that the *Codex Aureus* of Charles the Bald had been presented about 893 to the monastery of St. Emmeram there, and that it had been restored about a century later, testimony to the esteem in which it was held. A sacramentary made for Henry II in the first quarter of the eleventh century (Munich, SB, Clm. 4456) has a dedication miniature on f.11v[106] showing the enthroned emperor receiving the homage of his provinces, which follows the Carolingian model (Fig. 69) down to the cornucopias held by the personifications and the dome-like ciborium over the throne. The Regensburg miniature is as richly ornate in overall

Fig. 83.
Milan, Biblioteca Ambrosiana, Ms. C. 53, sup., f.19.
Gospel-book from Cologne, St. Matthew.

effect as the Carolingian prototype, but the somewhat ponderous color of the latter gives way to a much brighter scheme in the Ottonian adaptation. Byzantine methods are employed in it, the flesh surfaces being painted over a green ground, and the forms themselves are modeled in darker values of the reddish-yellow tint used for faces and hands. Gold is also lavishly employed.

Elsewhere in the same manuscript (f.11), Henry is shown receiving his crown from Christ, Who is seated in a mandorla above him.[107] His outstretched arms are supported by two figures identified by inscriptions as Saints Ulrich and Emmeram of Regensburg; the grouping suggests the Old Testament incident of Moses with arms upheld by Aaron and Hur in prayer for victory by the children of Israel over the Amalekites (Exod. 17: 10–12). A further note of imperial glorification is struck in the curious relationship between the emperor and the aureoled Christ placing the crown on his head; the divine ruler appears to be paying homage to the mortal. Inscriptions in the margins of the framing panels and the mandorla provide clues to the meaning of the forms.

Outstanding among products of the Regensburg scriptorium in which its artists sought to give expression to visionary content by exotic symbolism is the Evangelistary containing the lessons for the church services made for the abbess Uota of Niedermünster, a convent affiliated with St. Emmeram, between 1002 and 1025 (Munich, SB, Clm. lat. 13601). On f.3v, the Crucifixion appears in the upper medallion (Fig. 84, Plate XIII) and two figures inscribed VITA (Life) and MORS (Death) occupy the lower one.[108] The medallions are enclosed in a frame of gold bands with architectural and foliate forms in the spaces between. Square panels at the angles and lunettes at the midpoint of the long sides contain other figures, also identified by inscriptions. At the top are the sun and moon, the Church and Synagogue are in the lunettes, and in the square panels at the bottom are the Resurrection of the Dead and the Veil of the Temple rent asunder when Christ was crucified. Small blue letters on the foot of the gold cross are moralistic interpretations of the mathematical values of its proportions, and on the gold field below the arms of the cross are diagrams and legends defining the relationship between Music, Grammar, Mathematics, and Divine Law, summed up in the theory of the harmony of the celestial spheres.

Gold dominates the color scheme, as it does in most Regensburg miniatures, in the framing bands, the foliage between the medallions, and the cross and its background. Spots of dark blue, bright red, and green appear in the foliate patterns, and the costumes of the allegorical figures are light blue, pink, and brown. Christ's long robe is carmine red. This, the colobium of Near Eastern Crucifixion iconography (cf. Fig. 13), and the Saviour's crowned head, also Oriental, might suggest that Byzantine influences stimulated the proliferation of symbolism and metaphor in the Regensburg school. However, the immediate program for the Uota Evangelistary appears to have been the work of a theologian named Hartwic of Regensburg;[109] its literary intricacies and involved metaphors are a significant anticipation of the concepts and methods of later scholasticism.

Around the middle of the eleventh century, the scriptorium at Echternach emerges as one of the major Ottonian centers of illumination. It had been closely identified with Trier in the late tenth century, so it is understandable that some influence of its style is descernible in the Echternach oeuvre, although it ultimately developed along its own individual lines. The Gospel-book in the Germanisches Museum at Nuremburg known as the *Codex Aureus Epternacensis*[110] is one of its most distinguished exemplars. It was probably made between 1035 and 1040 during the abbacy of Humbert (1028–1051), a monk from Trier who established the Cluniac reform in the Echternach community. Unlike many of the most distinguished Ottonian manuscripts, the Echternach Golden Gospels appears to have been made for the monastery itself rather than an imperial patron. It easily stands comparison with the royal books, however, with its canon tables, Evangelist portraits and grand initial pages, its extensive cycle of New Testament narrative scenes, and, as its name implies, the golden minuscule text. Distinctive too are several decorative pages of animals, birds, and flowers arranged in trellis-like patterns somewhat like the miniature of birds in the Vienna Dioscurides manuscript of the sixth century; executed in gold on purple-dyed parchment,[111] they must have been inspired by Byzantine textile designs. The narrative scenes (Fig. 85) like those on f.18v beginning with the Annunciation and ending with Herod receiving the Magi (Luke 1:26–56; 2:7–20; Matt. 2:1–8) are composed in page-width friezes, divided by purple bands inscribed in gold, somewhat like those in the Carolingian Bibles from Tours. But the animated figures with their peering eyes, the importance of spatial values in the settings, and the striped backgrounds of shaded colors are directly descended from the *Codex Egberti* (Fig. 78). The head types are a little different from those in the earlier book in tapering rather sharply from the rounded skulls to the long chins, but the later date of the Echternach miniatures accounts for this stylistic difference.

Salzburg in the eastern reaches of the German Empire was also a center of book production in the eleventh century.[112] Some of the earlier works, like a book of pericopes in the Pierpont Morgan Library in New York (Ms. 781),[113] show a noticeable relationship to Reichenau production, but a pronounced Byzantine quality is evident in others of the later eleventh century. A lectionary signed by an otherwise unknown *"Custos Berthold"*—Berthold the Custodian—also in the Morgan Library (Ms. 780) illustrates this aspect of Salzburg style. The Warning to Joseph on f.1v (Fig. 86) is presented in a gabled frame surmounted by architectural forms and with marbleized columns with foliate capitals, which are among the touchstones of the Salzburg school. On the plain gold background, the colors are predominantly blue-green and pink in pigments rather

Fig. 85.
Nuremberg, Germanisches Nationalmuseum, Ms. 156 142,
f.81v. Codex Aureus Epternacensis, *Scenes from Christ's*
Early Life.

chalky in texture, like pastel. The faces are painted in the Byzantine manner, in which successively lighter coats are laid over a dark underpaint. Equally Byzantine are the strongly stylized drapery patterns, in which the rhythmic designs of the V-shaped folds of the bed cover and the curving lines of Joseph's robe define the volumes they conceal. Salzburg's location on the principal trade route from western Europe to Byzantium undoubtedly accounts for the considerable element of Byzantinism in much of the illumination produced there. In the form it takes in the Berthold Lectionary

miniatures, in details like the aedicules surmounting the gable of the frame but even more in the broadly simplified linear rhythms and the general hardening of the style, the Romanesque manner of the twelfth century is foreshadowed.

Ottonian style in illumination is primarily one of painting, but the Utrecht Psalter tradition of line without color is also continued. An example is seen in the Gospel-book in the Herzog-August-Bibliothek at Wolfenbütel (Cod.Guelf.16.1.Aug.2°), dating from the third quarter of the tenth century or perhaps a little

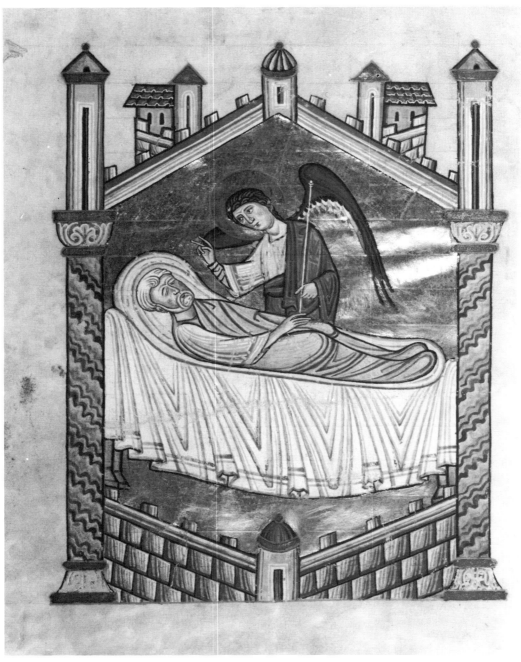

Fig. 86.
New York, Pierpont Morgan Library, Ms. 780, f.1v. Lectionary, Joseph Warned by an Angel.

Fig. 87.
Wolfenbüttel, Herzog August Bibliothek, Cod. Guelf 16.
1 Aug. 2°. Gospel-book, The Adoration of the Magi.

later. The Adoration of the Magi (Fig. 87) is represented in a pen drawing in brown ink on f.18v. Light tinted washes have been added in some of the five other Gospel scenes in the book, and the four Evangelist portraits are painted in opaque colors, but there is no reason to think that the drawings were preliminary sketches with colors to be added, for the manuscript is a finished work, with painted purple initial pages preceding all the four Gospels. Such details as the proportions and architectural elements of the canopy bespeak the same Byzantine influences seen in contemporary painted miniatures (Fig. 80), but the line that defines and animates the forms has descended directly from Carolingian Reims. In this respect, the Wolfenbüttel drawings are more akin to manuscript illustrations produced in those parts of Europe that were neither dominated politically by the Ottonian rulers and their Salic successors, nor allied to the monasteries that played such an important part in stabilizing the German empire. Such were the Anglo-Saxon and related centers in northwestern France and Flanders, the more southerly regions of France and Spain, and, to a lesser degree, Italy. During the ninth and tenth centuries, styles of illumination developed in these regions, which, while somewhat influenced by Carolingian and Ottonian ideas, tended to evolve independently and, ultimately, in different directions.

NOTES

1. *Vita Caroli Magni* (*Life of Charlemagne*), foreword by S. Painter (Ann Arbor Paperbacks, University of Michigan Press, 1960), chap. 25, pp. 53–54.

2. Cf. Introd., n. 1, 3.

3. Cf. Introd.

4. W. Koehler, *Die Karolingischen Miniaturen, II. Die Hofschule Karls des Grossen*, 2 vols. (Berlin: Deutscher Verein für Kunstwissenschaft, 1958).

5. M. Manitius, *Handschriften antiken Autoren in mittelalterlichen Bibliothekskatalogen*, ed. K. Manitius (Leipzig: Harrassowitz, 1935).

6. G. Thiele, *Antike Himmelsbilder* (Berlin, 1898). F. Saxl and H. Meier, *Verzeichnis astrologischer und mythologischer illustrieter Handschriften des lateinischen Mittelalters*, vol. 3, *Handschriften in englischen Bibliotheken*, ed. H. Bober (Heidelberg: C. Winter, 1953).

7. L. W. Jones and C. R. Morey, *The Illustrated Manuscripts of Terence*, 2 vols. (Princeton: Princeton University Press, 1931).

8. P. Underwood, "The Fountain of Life in Manuscripts of the Gospels," *Dumbarton Oaks Papers*, 5 (1950):43–138.

9. Reproduced in color in *EMP*, p. 139.

10. *CR*, fig. 75.

11. Cf. Underwood, figs. 34–38.

12. Cf. *CR*, figs. 76, 77.

13. G. Bovini, *Ravenna Mosaics* (Greenwich: New York Graphic Society, 1956), pl. 25.

14. Cf. *CR*, figs. 64, 65.

15. A. Goldschmidt, *German Illumination*, 2 vols. (Paris-Florence: Pantheon, 1928).

16. Cf. *CR*, p. 369, n. *Ada*.

17. Reproduced in color in H. Swarzenski, *Early Medieval Illumination* (New York-Toronto: Oxford, Iris Books, 1951), pl. ii.

18. Cf. *CR*, pls. 66–68 for the Matthew and John in the Trier "Ada Gospels."

19. Thompson, *GLP*, p. 297.

20. Cf. *CR*, pls. 73–76; also R. M. Walker, "Illustrations to the Priscillian Prologues in the Gospel Manuscripts of the Carolingian Ada School," *AB*, 30 (1948):1–10.

21. Cf. *CR*, pl. 69.

22. Cf. Koehler, n. 4, pls. 42–44, 48–49, 52.

23. Nordenfalk, *EMP*, p. 140.

24. *ABI*, pp. 116–27.

25. Cf. Jones and Morey, n. 7; *ABI*, p. 150, n. 1.

26. One of the most faithful copies of the classical treatise on land surveying, known as the *Codex Agrimensores* and now in the Vatican Biblioteca Apostolica (Ms. Pal. lat. 1564), was made at Fulda.

27. E. H. Zimmerman, *Die Fuldaer Buchmalerei in karolingischer und ottonischer Zeit*, Kunstgeschichtliches Jahrbuch der K. K. Zentralkommission 4 (Vienna, 1910), pp. 1–104.

28. Cf. *CR*, fig. 178.

29. *EMP*, p. 92.

30. Cf. Nordenfalk, chap. 3, n. 55.

31. W. Koehler, *Die karolingischen Miniaturen, III. Die Gruppe des Wiener Krönungsevangeliars, Metzer Handschriften*, 2 vols. (Berlin: Deutscher Verein für Kunstwissenschaft, 1960).

32. Cf. Swarzenski, n. 17, pl. iii; *CR*, fig. 82.

33. C. Gaspar, and F. Lyna, *Les principaux manuscrits à peintures de la Bibliothèque Royale de Belgique*, 2 vols. (Paris: Soc. fr. de la reprod. de mss. à peintures, (1937–45). Cf. Swarzenski, chap. 1, n. 34.

34. *CR*, figs. 79–81.

35. A study by D. Tselos, "A Greco-Italian School of Illuminators and Fresco Painters," *AB* 38 (1956): 1–30, seeks to establish a considerable artistic production by Greek artists in southern Europe in the late eighth and early ninth centuries. Cf. also Porcher, *CR*, pp. 92–123.

36. For illustrations, some in color, cf. *CR*, figs. 92–97, 242, 285–89.

37. E. T. DeWald, *The Illustrations of the Utreche Psalter*

(Princeton: Princeton University Press, 1933).

38. Cf. Thompson, *GLP*, pp. 283–84.

39. F. Wormald, *The Utrecht Psalter* (Utrecht: Institute of Art History, 1953), p. 9.

40. Wormald, p. 13.

41. Dora Panofsky, "The Textual Basis of the Utrecht Psalter Illustrations," *AB* 25 (1943):50–58.

42. D. Tselos, *The Sources of the Utrecht Psalter Miniatures* (Minneapolis, 1955). J. Engelbregt, *Het Utrechts Psalterium, een Eeuw wettenschappelijke Bestudering (1860–1960)* (Utrecht: Haentjens Dekker & Gumbert, 1964).

43. Cf. *CR*, fig. 107.

44. Cf. *CR*, figs. 89–91, 100–105, 109; also W. D. Wixom, *Treasures from Medieval France* (Cleveland: Cleveland Museum of Art, 1967), 1–4, p. 19.

45. B. da C. Greene and M. P. Harrsen, *Exhibition of Illuminated Manuscripts held at the New York Public Library*, Introd. by C. R. Morey (New York: Pierpont Morgan Library, 1934), no. 6. Miner, *IBMAR*, No. 4.

46. Reproduced in color in *CR*, fig. 146; cf. also *EMP*, p. 149.

47. Cf. *CR*, figs. 73, 76.

48. Cf. Walker, n. 20.

49. A. Boutemy, "Le style franco-saxon de Saint-Amand," *Scriptorium* 3 (1949):260–64.

50. Cf. Henry, *IAVI*, pls. 37–40; other books written and illuminated at Bobbio now in the Turin Biblioteca Nazionale include a Gregory *Moralia in Job* (Ms. F. I. 6), a Life of St. Columbanus (Ms. F. 14. 12), and a Lectionary (Ms. F. II. 20), all of the tenth century and with initials of the simplified interlace type seen in the Arras Gospel-book.

51. Cf. Goldschmidt, n. 15, vol. 1, pls. 5–8.

52. *Ibid.*, pls. 3, 4.

53. *Ibid.*, pls. 9, 10.

54. Thompson, *GLP*, p. 367.

55. E. K. Rand, *A Survey of the Manuscripts of Tours*, 2 vols. (Cambridge: Mediaeval Academy of America, 1929). *Ibid.* and L. W. Jones, *The Earliest Book of Tours* (Cambridge: Mediaeval Academy of America, 1934).

56. Cf. Micheli, Introd., n. 10; also *CR*, figs. 111–12.

57. W. Koehler, *Die karolingischen Miniaturen, I. Die Schule von Tours* (Berlin: Deutscher Verein für Kunstwissenschaft, 1930–33). Cf. also *CR*, figs. 114–16.

58. Reproduced in color in *CR*, fig. 122.

59. Cf. Volbach, *Early Christian Art*, pls. 11, 60.

60. Three are reproduced in color in *CR*, figs. 123–25.

61. Reproduced in color in *EMP*, p. 152.

62. Cf. *CR*, figs. 126–29.

63. Cf. Porcher, *CR*, p. 137.

64. Cf. Porcher, *CR*, pp. 127–30.

65. Cf. *CR*, figs. 132–33 for reproductions in color.

66. Reproduced in color in *CR*, figs. 134–36.

67. Reproduced in color in *CR*, figs. 140–43, and EMP, p. 155.

68. A. M. Friend, Jr., "Carolingian Art in the Abbey of Saint-Denis," *Art Studies* 1 (1923):67 ff.

69. Cf. *CR*, fig. 235.

70. G. Leidinger, *Der Codex Aureus der Bayerischen Staatsbibliothek in München*, 6 vols. (Munich: Hugo Schmidt, 1921–25). Cf. *CR*, figs. 106, 137–39 for reproductions in color.

71. Cf. *CR*, fig. 142.

72. Cf. Underwood, n. 8, fig. 29.

73. Cf. *CR*, fig. 130.

74. *Ibid.*, fig. 131.

75. Cf. *EMP*, p. 153; Boeckler, *AM*, pl. 26.

76. Reproduced in color in *CR*, fig. 130.

77. E. H. Kantorowicz, "The Carolingian King in the Bible of San Paolo fuori le Mura," *Late Classical and Mediaeval Studies in honor of A. M. Friend* (Princeton: Princeton University Press, 1955), pp. 287–300.

78. Cf. also, A. M. Friend, Jr., "Two Manuscripts of the School of St. Denis," *Speculum* 1 (1926):59–70.

79. A. Merton, *Die Buchmalerei in St. Gallen*, 2d ed. (Leipzig: Hiersemann, 1923).

80. Cf. *CR*, figs. 157–62.

81. Cf. *CR*, fig. 165.

82. A. Goldschmidt, *German Illumination*, 2 vols., *Ottonian Illumination*, Vol. 2 (Paris-Florence: Pantheon, 1928). H. Jantzen, *Ottonische Kunst* (Munich: Münchener Verlag, 1946).

83. Wolfenbüttel, Braunschweigisches Landes-Hauptarchiv. Cf. H.v. Sydel and Th. v. Stickel, *Kaiserverkunden in Abbildungen* (Berlin, 1891), p. ix, pl. 2.

84. Reproduced in color in *EMP*, p. 196.

85. Cf. n. 27 above.

86. E.g., the *Codex Wittechindeus* (Berlin, D.S.B. Cod. theol. lat. fol. 1). Cf. A. Boeckler, *Der Codex Wittekindeus* (Leipzig: Harrassowitz, 1938)

87. A. Boeckler, "Die Reichenauer Buchmalerei—Die Kultur der Abtei Reichenau," *Erinnerungschrift zur 1200 Wiederkehr des Gründungsjahres des Inselklosters* (Munich, 1925), pp. 956–98. E. Braun, "Beiträge zur Geschichte der Trier Buchmalerei im früheren Mittelalter," *Westdeutsche Zeitschrift f. Gesch. u. Kunst*, Erg.-Heft 9 (1895). C. R. Dodwell and D. H. Turner, *Reichenau Reconsidered* (London: Warburg Institute Surveys 2, 1965).

88. Unnumbered. A. Haseloff and H. V. Sauerland, *Der Psalter Erzbischof Egberts von Trier*, Festschrift der Gesellschaft f. nützliche Forschungen (Trier, 1901).

89. A. Schmidt, *Die Miniaturen des Gero-Kodex* (Leipzig: Hiersemann, 1924).

90. W. Koehler, "Die Tradition der Ada-Gruppe und die Anfänge des ottonischen Stils in der Buchmalerei," *Festschrift zum 60. Geburtstage von Paul Clemen* (Bonn, 1926), pp. 255–72.

91. Cf. Goldschmidt, *German Illumination*, 1, pls. 38–41; 2, pls. 17–18.

92. Reproduced in facsimile in *Codex Egberti*, ed. H. Schiel (Basel: Alkuin-Verlag, 1960).

93. C. Nordenfalk, "Der Meister des Registrum Gregorii," *Münchener Jahrbuch der Bildenden Kunst*, 3 Folge, Bd. 1 (1950), pp. 61–77.

94. Reproduced in color in *EMP*, p. 192, and H. Swarzenski, n. 17, pl. v.

95. J. Prochno, *Das Schreiber-und Dedikationsbild in der deutschen Buchmalerei bis zum Ende des 11. Jahrhunderts* (Berlin, 1929).

96. P. E. Schramm, *Die deutschen Kaiser und Könige in Bildern ihrer Zeit bis zur Mitte des 12. Jahrhunderts* (Leipzig: W. Götz, 1928–29).

97. Cf. *La Librairie de Charles V*, no. 99 (Paris: Bibliothèque Nationale, 1968), p. 41.

98. Cf. Goldschmidt, *German Illumination* 2, pl. 9.

99. G. Leidinger, *Das sog. Evangeliarium Kaiser Ottos III, Miniaturen aus Handschriften der Kgl. Hof-und Staatsbibliothek* 1 (Munich: Riehn & Tietze, 1912).

100. Reproduced in color in G. Leidinger, *Meisterwerke der Buchmalerei* (Munich: Schmidt, 1920), pl. 5.

101. Reproduced in color in *EMP*, p. 198; cf. also H. Swarzenski, n. 17, pls. ix–xi.

102. G. Leidinger, *Das Perikopenbuch Kaiser Heinrichs II, Miniaturen aus Handschriften der Kgl. Hof-und Staatsbibliothek* 5 (Munich: Riehn & Tietze, n.d.). *Idem., Evangeliarium aus d. Domschatz in Bamberg, Miniaturen aus Handschriften der Bayer. Staatsbibl.* 6 (Munich: Riehn & Tietze, 1921).

103. Reproduced in color in Swarzenski, n. 17, pl. xii.

104. H. Ehl, *Die ottonische Kölner Buchmalerei,* Forschungen zur Kunstgeschichte Westeuropas 4 (Bonn-Leipzig: Schröder, 1922). A. Boeckler, *Kölner ottonische Buchmalerei,* Beiträge zur Kunst des Mittelalters (Berlin, 1950), pp. 144–49.

105. G. Swarzenski, *Die Regensburger Buchmalerei des 10. und 11. Jahrhunderts* (Leipzig: Hiersemann, 1901).

106. A. Boeckler, *AM,* pl. 39.

107. Goldschmidt, *German Illumination* 2, pl. 72.

108. Reproduced in color in Swarzenski, n. 17, pl. xv.

109. B. Bischoff, *Literarisches und künstlerisches Leben in St. Emmeram während des frühen und hohen Mittelalters,* Studien und Mitt. zur Geschichte des Benediktiner-Ordens 51 (1933): pp. 102–42.

110. P. Metz, *The Golden Gospels of Echternach* (London: Thames & Hudson, 1957).

111. Cf. Metz, pl. i.

112. G. Swarzenski, *Die Salzburger Malerei von den ersten Anfängen bis zur Blütezeit des romanischen Stils.* Denkmäler der süddeutschen Malerei des frühen Mittelalters 2 (Leipzig: Hiersemann, 1913).

113. Cf. *IBMAR,* no. 10, pl. vi.

5

Illumination of the Tenth and Eleventh Centuries in Non-Germanic Countries

A. Anglo-Saxon Illumination

Even before the onset of the Vikings on the British Isles during the ninth century, the imaginative vigor of Anglo-Celtic illumination had begun to wane. Books like the MacRegol Gospels in the Bodleian Library at Oxford (Ms. Auct. D. 2. 19) and a Gospel-book in the Vatican Library (Ms. Barb. lat. 570) that has been thought to have come from a scriptorium in southern England, both of the late eighth or early ninth century,[1] show either a degeneration of the remarkable precision and vitality of the style at its prime, or a hardening of its patterns into formula. The Book of MacDurnan (London, Lambeth Palace, Library) of the end of the ninth century and the "Southampton Psalter" (Cambridge, St. John's College Library, Ms. C. 9) of the late tenth century show the continuation of these trends.[2] The destruction wrought by the invaders was immeasurable. Alfred the Great (871–899), who finally made peace with the Danes in 878, suggests this when he wrote "I remembered also how the churches throughout all England stood filled with treasures and books." Yet it is doubtful that, even had the ninth century been a time of peace and quiet in Britain, it would have been a period of creative artistic activity, for the old tradition was exhausted.

Alfred himself seems to have taken the first steps in creating a new one by encouraging the arts of literature and education, and his son Edward the Elder (899–925) busied himself with the rebuilding of such institutions as New Minster Abbey at Winchester, aided by monks from the Carolingian continent. It was not until King Edgar's reign in the third quarter of the tenth century (957–975), however, that a significant regeneration began. This is not to say that there was no activity earlier in the century. A copy of Bede's *Life of St. Cuthbert,* made about 930 for Edgar's predecessor, Aethelstan (Cambridge, Corpus Christi College Library, Ms. 183), has a miniature on f.1 of the monarch presenting the book to the saint, and there are inserted miniatures in a small psalter also made for Aethelstan (London, BM, Cotton Ms. Galba A. xviii) including a Christ in Majesty on f.21 of about the same time.[3] In both composition and technique, these miniatures associated with Aethelstan reflect continental models, however, and there is little about them that can be considered Anglo-Saxon.

Much more significant are the developments attendant upon the monastic reforms during Edgar's reign in the later tenth century. Three distinguished clerics were identified with them—Dunstan, Aethelwold, and Oswald—all of whom had been associated at some time

Fig. 88.
Oxford, Bodleian Library, Ms. Auct. F. iv. 32, f.1. St.
Dunstan's Classbook, Christ adored by St. Dunstan.

with continental monastic centers in which the Cluniac reform had been established. Dunstan, abbot of Glastonbury from about 943 to 957, had been exiled to St. Peter's in Ghent in 957–8, but returned to England to be the Archbishop of Canterbury from 959 until 988. Aethelwold, a monk under Dunstan at Glastonbury, was once associated with the Benedictine monastery at Fleury, as Saint-Bénoît-sur-Loire was once known, and later became Bishop of Winchester from 963 to 983. Oswald had also been at Fleury for a time, and subsequently was Archbishop of York from 972 until 992. Supported in their activities by Edgar and encouraged by him to bring about similar reforms in the English monasteries, all of these men, particularly Dunstan and Aethelwold, gave particular attention to founding the scriptoria that were the principal centers of Anglo-Saxon illumination.[4]

An inscription on a drawing of Christ being adored by a prostrate figure in monk's clothing (Fig. 88) identifies the worshiper as St. Dunstan. It is the frontispiece of a collection of miscellaneous texts in the Bodleian Library at Oxford (Ms. Auct. F. iv. 32) known as St. Dunstan's classbook, and may indeed be by the hand of St. Dunstan himself, as the inscription suggests. There is no color but the red disc of the cruciform nimbus and a few touches in the saint's robe; the monumental plastic effect is attained solely in terms of line. It is more than probable that the exemplar of Christ's figure was a continental miniature of the Ada-Rhineland school,[5] but the Anglo-Saxon draftsman has transformed the heavily pigmented surfaces and contours of the assumed prototype into pulsating arabesques of line that define and model the form and articulate its mass. Such dependence on line as a structural and expressive device is not new in insular illumination; the involved patterns of Anglo-Celtic miniatures (Figs. 46–49) are basically purely linear constructions. But knowledge of continental models, made possible by the Cluniac reform to which the English monasteries subscribed, brought the abstract and depersonalized linear idiom of Anglo-Celtic style to bear on the representational problem posed by the human figure. The resulting effect is comparable, in an Anglo-Saxon way, to that created by the Carolingian draftsmen of the Utrecht Psalter (Fig. 61, Plate VII).

There is reason to believe that the drawing of Dunstan bowing before Christ was made before 959 when he became Archbishop of Canterbury, for the saint wears a monk's robe instead of the prelate's garb appropriate to his later station. Some years thereafter, in 966, the charter in book form of King Edgar recording the founding of the reformed order in the New Minster at Winchester (London, BM, Cotton Ms. Vesp. A. viii) was provided on f.2v with a frontispiece (Fig. 89) in a different style. Line plays an important part in the design, but the forms outlined against the purple parchment are washed with color, and the same is true of the border, a trellis of parallel bars enclosing a stem of acanthus leaves spreading over and twining around the bands.[6] Touches of color are also seen in the lines that model the forms within the contours. The figures below are King Edgar with the Virgin Mary and St. Peter, who were the patron saints of the Winchester New Minister; the king offers the charter to Christ enthroned in a mandorla supported by angels in the sky. Composition and figure style[7] invite comparison with continental work. The subject is in the vein of the Turonian dedicatory miniatures (Fig. 67), the leaf-work has more than a little in common with that in Drogo's Sacramentary from Metz (Fig. 63), and the text of the charter is written in golden Carolingian minuscules throughout.

However much the iconography and some decorative elements of the New Minister charter miniature may suggest Carolingian influence, the border is an Anglo-Saxon invention. The espalier frame, to use Nordenfalk's felicitous term,[8] occurs here for the first time, but was destined for continuing popularity in English illumination until well into the twelfth century, and to be copied on occasion in continental manuscripts (cf. Fig. 113). Distinctively English and Wincastrian is the specific form of the acanthus leaf found in these espalier frames; unlike those in Carolingian manuscripts like the Drogo Sacramentary, where they lie flat on the page, the tips of the leaves in the Anglo-Saxon variety may curl out or around the frame band, adding a play of line in the third dimension to the surface patterns and thus augmenting the expressive dynamism inherent in the style.

In the New Minster Charter miniature frame, the bands carry through to the angles and turn the corners. In the next and most distinguished example of Winchester style[9] to be considered, the frames become even more elaborate, with great knots or sprays of foliage at the angles or developing into capital-like forms supporting archivolts also filled with acanthus leaves.[10] This is the Benedictional of Aethelwold,[11] formerly in the collection of the Duke of Devonshire at Chatsworth but now in the British Museum (Add. Ms. 49598). The

Fig. 89.
London, British Museum, Ms. Cotton Vesp. A. viii, f.2v.
Charter of New Minster, Winchester. King Edgar offering
the Charter to Christ.

text is of blessings to be pronounced by a bishop during the Mass; like the New Minster Charter, the golden script is in Carolingian minuscules. A long introductory poem at the beginning states that it was the work of an artificer named Godeman, to whom Bishop Aethelwold gave instructions that the figures were to be painted *multigenis miniis pulchris*—"in many different and beautiful colors," using the word *minium* to mean all hues and not red alone as in other usage—and that they were to be in *circi*, meaning the frames of the narrative scenes or groups of figures and the initial letters of the prayers contained in the Benedictional text. The manuscript was probably made between 975 and 980 while Aethelwold was Bishop of Winchester.

Like all the completed miniatures in the book, the Baptism of Christ (Fig. 90, Plate XIV) on f.25 is painted in thick and opaque colors with much gold.[12] Pink, blue, and purple are used for the curling acanthus of the angle knots and the panels between them. The background of the Baptism scene is reddish-purple, the sky is light blue, and the River Jordan is in a darker value of the same color. It flows from a jar held by a semi-nude male figure on the left side in front of the frame. From the sky comes the golden dove of the Holy Spirit, carrying in its beak a double phial of holy oil that symbolizes Christ's dual role of King and Priest.

Both composition and iconography of the Aethelwold Benedictional Baptism can be traced to Carolingian models, specifically an ivory casket in the museum at Brunswick in Germany,[13] where the dove carries a double oil flask and the same personification of the river *all' antica* is seen. There are similar parallels between the Nativity on f.15v in the Benedictional and the version on the casket, which is dated toward the end of the Carolingian period and assigned to the school of Metz by Adolph Goldschmidt in his monumental study of mediaeval ivories.[14] The plastic rendering of the curling acanthus leaf tips in the Winchester foliage might easily be the consequence of using such sculptured models also, and the occasional suggestion of later Metz and Saint-Denis figure style, as well as the curious wavy cloud patterns somewhat like those in Reims manuscripts (Fig. 60), supports the conclusion that models in many styles were available to Godeman in Aethelwold's scriptorium at Winchester.[15]

Continental models also contributed to the further development of manuscript illumination at Canterbury, where St. Dunstan was Archbishop from 958 to 988. The Psalter in the British Museum (Ms. Harley 603) appears to have been executed there about the year 1000. Its illustration of Psalm 11(12) on f.6v (Fig. 91) is so much like the corresponding one in the

Fig. 91.
London, British Museum, Ms. Harley 603, f.6v. Psalter
from Canterbury, Illustration of Psalm XI (12).

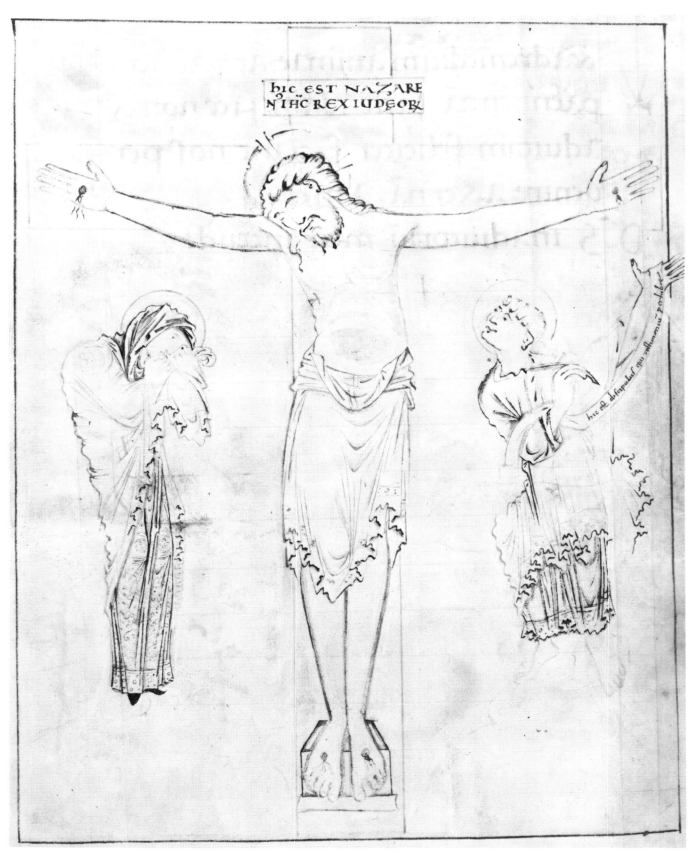

Fig. 92.
London, British Museum, Ms. Harley 2904, f.3v. Psalter
from Ramsey Abbey, The Crucifixion.

Utrecht Psalter (Fig. 61, Plate VII) that there seems to be no doubt that the Anglo-Saxon artist had the Carolingian manuscript immediately before him. Several different hands can be identified in the total illustration and their reactions to the model are not identical, but the one who drew the illustration of Psalm 11 was remarkably faithful to it. All compositional details are the same. The Logos rises from His throne to answer the psalmist's plea, the silversmiths and the impious going about in circles appear in both the Utrecht and Harley versions in identical arrangements. But the Anglo-Saxon artist, even when meticulously accurate in reproducing the lines of the model, reveals his predilection for decorative rhythms. The shapes become more elaborate and the curving lines multiply. As in the Utrecht Psalter, the drawings in Harley 603 that can be assigned to the beginning of the eleventh century (several in the middle of the book appear to have been done later) are unframed insertions in the text, which also follows the prototype in the unusual three-column arrangement.

Yet even while remaining faithful to the model in most respects, a further and very significant change, again of a decorative nature, has been made in the Harley drawings. Those of the Utrecht Psalter are monochrome, in brown ink. In Harley 603, they are in a variety of colors—purple, brown, green, and red—used without any consistent scheme or pattern, as the artist's decorative instinct dictated. Although not an innovation in Harley 603, this is an early and excellent example of the combination of line and color that is a characteristic of one aspect of early eleventh-century Anglo-Saxon illumination. In the Harley drawings, the contour lines may be in different colors, but in other instances a monochrome outline will be shaded in color. This can be seen in the Crucifixion (Fig. 92) on f.3v of another psalter in the British Museum (Ms. Harley 2904), believed to have been made in the late tenth century at Ramsey Abbey, founded about 968 by Oswald, the third member of the great Anglo-Saxon monastic triumvirate. The outlines are brown, shaded with red and blue and accented with black. The design has the monumentality of the continental model that must be assumed, but translated into a distinctive and characteristic Anglo-Saxon idiom.[16]

Although the painted style of the Aethelwold Benedictional seems to be identified with Winchester in its early phases and the linear idiom with Canterbury, no consistent distinction can be based on the different techniques as to place of origin, for both may appear in the same book. In the Ramsey Psalter, for instance, the initials are painted in opaque colors like gouache. What distinguishes early eleventh-century Anglo-Saxon illumination above all is the characteristic figure style, inspired by the expressionism of works like the Utrecht Psalter drawings and taking over many of their forms, as has been seen. But even at its most dynamic, as in the rising Christ of the illustration for Psalm 11 (Fig. 61, Plate VII), the Utrecht Psalter forms retain a measure of classical balance and stability; the movement of the figure is always to be referred to a central vertical axis. This the Anglo-Saxon artist changes by preference to a diagonal, as in the St. John of the Ramsey Crucifixion, accentuating the effect in the draperies that twist and coil in fluttering hemlines around the ankles and knees and fly out behind, and by thrusting the head forward from the hunched shoulders against the gesticulating left arm.

Many of these characteristics also appear in the por-

Fig. 93.
London, British Museum, Ms. Add. 34890, f.114v. The Grimbald Gospels. St. John.

trait of St. John (Fig. 93) on f.114v of the Grimbald Gospels in the British Museum (Add. Ms. 34890). Made at Winchester in the early eleventh century, the miniature shows some enlargement of the Winchester repertory seen in the Aethelwold Benedictional (Fig. 90, Plate XIV). The trellis frame (of which some bands are silver, unusually, which has oxydized) is filled with figures instead of foliage. The Trinity appear in the three medallions at the top, with prophets, apostles, angels, and saints below making up the Court of Heaven. And instead of curling, tipped acanthus leaves, the wings and fluttering robes of the angels create the whirling rhythm which combines with that generated in the draperies and gestures of the Evangelist. Comparison with the painted Evangelist in the Reims school Gospelbook in the Morgan Library (Fig. 62) will show the same distinction between Anglo-Saxon and Carolingian style already noted in discussing the drawings in the Utrecht Psalter and Harley 603. Also characteristic of developed Winchester style is the transparent effect of the unpainted parchment background. It is as if even when vigorous color (here predominantly blue with touches of green, red, russet brown, and purple, with gold and silver)[17] was available to the artist, the simple clarity of pure line on light surface was desired. It is this that makes possible the extraordinary feeling of tension wherein lies the expressive power of the design. The Evangelist's symbol and its scroll barely touch the inner edge of the border. The twisted curtain above the author depends only from the wing and fluttering drapery of an angel and Christ's mandorla. Yet it is almost as if a powerful current streams through them, galvanizing the forms and at the same time holding them fast in their appointed places.

Winchester and Canterbury were the principal centers of Anglo-Saxon illumination in the early eleventh century, but there were also important scriptoria elsewhere. A psalter in the Vatican Library (Ms. Reg. lat. 12) has been identified by a note in the Easter calendar as a product of Bury St. Edmunds.[18] Its illustration (Fig. 94) might be regarded as combining the marginal principle seen in some Byzantine manuscripts (Figs. 21, 22) with the animated linear style of Reims. Christ's Ascension on f.73v is the illustration of Psalm 67(68):18, "Thou hast ascended on high," the precise words being designated by the lower end of the scroll held by the angel in the upper left angle of the page. At the very top, in the center, the Saviour disappears in an ascending mandorla, only His feet being visible; in the lower

side margins are the eleven apostles and the Virgin Mary, their astonishment expressed in upturned heads and vigorous gestures. This iconography of the Ascension with the vanishing Christ is peculiarly Anglo-Saxon, continuing until well into the twelfth century. Whether it be an example of early mediaeval realism in purporting to show the miracle from the spectators' point of view,[19] or was imposed upon the draftsman by the limited space at the top of a text-filled page, it was an iconographic scheme that lent itself well to the expressive intention of the Anglo-Saxon draftsman.

Two miniatures in the Bury St. Edmunds Psalter in the Vatican Library are painted in full color,[20] the initial B of *Beatus* beginning the first verse of Psalm 1 on f.21, and the Q of *Quid gloriaris* opening Psalm 51(52) on f.65. Both have the espalier frames with curling acanthus leaves gripping the bars of Winchester style, but somewhat simplified. A tiny figure in monk's attire is seated at a desk in the central medallion of the *Beatus* B, possibly the scribe or illuminator, and the "mighty man who boasteth himself in mischief" (Ps. 51:1) is in the Q on f.65. These comparatively early examples of historiated initials have continental analogues, e.g., the Drago Sacramentary (Fig. 63), where a more orthodox Ascension iconography is seen. A nearer source, geographically, is suggested by the figured initials of a ninth-century psalter from Corbie in northwestern France,[21] executed in a linear style allied to Reims. But the majority of the Bury St. Edmunds psalter illustrations are in red and brown outline, largely unshaded, and with only occasional touches of color like the green and gold of Christ's nimbus in the illustration of Psalm 13(14) on f.28.[22] The line is still remarkably expressive, though a little harder than in the Ramsey Crucifixion (Fig. 92) and the illustrations of Harley 603, an indication of the general tendency toward crystallization and formula by the time it was executed, probably *c.* 1035.

Winchester style reached an expressive climax shortly before the middle of the eleventh century in such works as the Gospels of Judith of Flanders (New York, Pierpont Morgan Library, Ms. 709), named from her acquisition of it when she married Count Tostig of Northumbria in 1051.[23] The Evangelist portraits in this manuscript have fully developed Winchester borders, but the Crucifixion (Fig. 95) on f.1v is framed in simple gold bands. Mary and John stand on either side of the cross and an unnimbed feminine figure embraces its foot. She may represent Judith of Flanders and the

Fig. 94.
Vatican, Biblioteca Apostolica, Ms. Reg. lat. 12, f.73v.
Psalter from Bury St. Edmunds, Illustration of Psalm
LXVII (68).

miniature may have been inserted in the volume when she acquired it; the Evangelist portraits appear to have been done between 1040 and 1050. The colors are light and clear, unlike the opaque pigments of the Aethelwold Bendictional miniatures, transparent washes heightened with touches of gold. At the same time, they are quite bright—blue for the cloud-filled sky, the Virgin's mantle, and the loin-cloth of the Crucifix; yellow for the Virgin's robe; green and light red for St. John's garments; and gray for those of the kneeling woman. Christ's hair and beard are Titian red. The background is unpainted, contributing to an effect of open transparency, like that of the Grimbald Gospels Evangelist portrait (Fig. 93).

Lyric as the color scheme may be, the expressive content is profoundly poignant. This stems not alone from the pathos of such motives as the suppliant clasping the cross or the Virgin's gesture to stem the flow of blood from Christ's side, moving as these are. It is created by the angular patterns of the figures, their swaying stances accentuated by the fluttering draperies, and the jagged outlines of the sombre gray, rough-hewn cross, brought

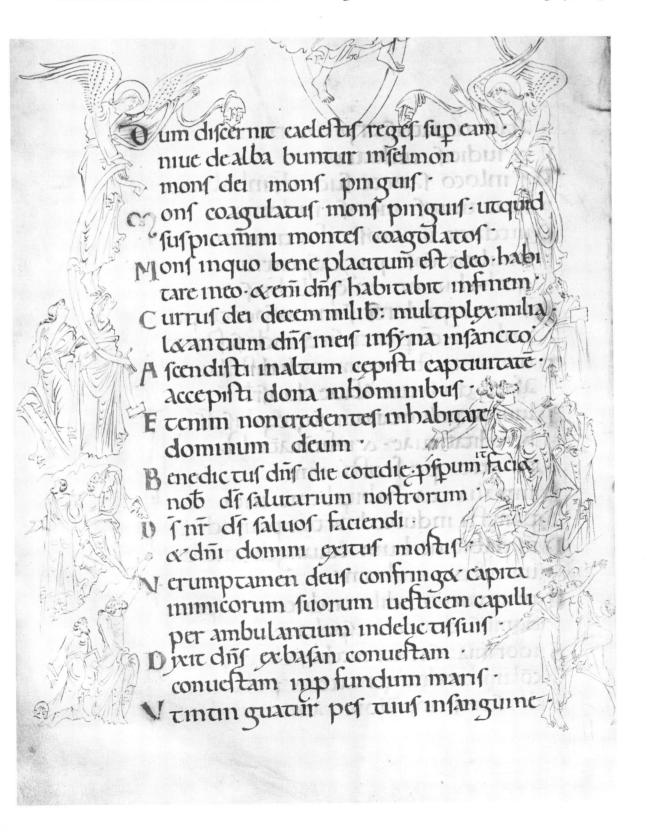

to focus in the broken body of the Saviour. Nothing could illustrate better the genius of the northern, Anglo-Saxon artist for the embodiment of deeply felt emotion in patterns of expressive line.

Judith of Flanders' Gospel-book is believed to have been made between 1040 and 1050 at New Minster of Winchester. A little over ten years later, *c.* 1060, the same scriptorium produced a psalter (London, BM, Ms. Arundel 60) in which a Crucifixion (Fig. 96) on f.52v is of more than usual interest. There are some points of difference from the version of the same subject in Mor-

gan 709. Two trees flank the cross, instead of the Virgin and St. John. The border is a foliated trellis with the Evangelist symbols in the angle medallions, and the cross on a hillock of rolling forms is not the rough-hewn shape of the earlier miniature but is painted in colored stripes within a jointed, bamboo-like border. Christ's body is in a Z-shape, as it is in the Morgan 709 Crucifixion, but the anatomy of limbs and torso is indicated by blue and pink lines, and the roundness of the head with its stylized features is accentuated by the black hair and beard. There are touches of yellow and

Fig. 96.
London, British Museum, Ms. Arundel 60, f.52v. Psalter
from New Minster, Winchester, The Crucifixion.

Fig. 95.
New York, Pierpont Morgan Library, Ms. 709, f.1v. Gospels of Judith of Flanders, The Crucifixion.

green in the espalier border, but the central theme is in dull pink, blue, and vermilion, applied thickly in opaque pigments.

Some acanthus leaves in the trellis border curl around the bars in established Winchester fashion, but others, tipped with white, lie flat as they emerge from the stem. All are soft and plastic, quite different from the wiry and sharp foliage of earlier Winchester miniatures. The sense of the third dimension thus revealed is also indicated by the modeling, however stylized, of the Crucifix, accented by the hard edges and metallic shapes of the flattened loincloth which are quite different from the fluttering edges and looping folds in the Judith of Flanders miniature. The effect is solemn rather than poignant, hieratic rather than emotional, standing in much the same relationship to earlier examples in this respect as later Ottonian works (cf. Fig. 83) to their predecessors. It is more than probable, in fact, that the factor differentiating the style of the Crucifixion on f.52v of Arundel 60 from the one in Morgan 709 was a renewed continental influence, conceivably Ottonian, bringing with it an element of Byzantine decorative expressionism. Compare, for example, the rolling hillock of Golgotha in the Anglo-Saxon miniature with that on which the announcing angel stands in the Reichenau miniature from the Gospels of Otto III (Fig. 82).

In its more hieratic and monumental quality, the Crucifixion on f.52v of Arundel 60 anticipates the Romanesque manner of the twelfth century. Contrary to what might be imagined, the Norman invasion of 1066 was not the catastrophe artistically that it was politically, from the Anglo-Saxon point of view. A perceptive study of this point[24] shows that while there may have been a lapse in manuscript production for a time after the Conquest, and though new influences came to bear when it was resumed, there is a strong continuing tradition of style in English illumination from the ninth century until well into the twelfth, and even later in some respects. Moreover, the impact of Anglo-Saxon style in some areas of eleventh- and twelfth-century continental illumination was as certain, if not as extensive, as that of the earlier Anglo-Celtic manner had been, as will be seen.

B. *Spanish Illumination*

Spanish illumination of the early Middle Ages, capable of producing the Ashburnham Pentateuch, was effectively isolated from other continental developments after the Moorish invasions. These, begun in 711 and crossing the Pyrenees by 720, reached an ultimate geographic point in 732, when the battle of Poitiers between Abd el Rahman and Charles Martel resulted in Moorish defeat and subsequent retreat into the Iberian peninsula. There the Moslems were firmly established, save only for the small principality of the Asturias, a narrow strip of territory lying north of the Cantabrian mountains separating Galicia from the rest of Spain. Christianity maintained a foothold in this region, and such manuscript illumination as there was in the eighth and ninth centuries is found where the Visigothic tradition had been established earlier. It was not until the tenth century, however, that a distinctive style appeared, in books made in the monasteries of León, San Millan de la Cogolla, San Pedro de Cardeña and Santo Domingo de Silos, to name only the most important. The provenance and dating of these Spanish manuscripts can be spoken of with much more assurance than in discussing Carolingian, Ottonian, and Anglo-Saxon examples, for their scribes and illuminators very frequently signed and dated them in colophons that often give the locale of the scriptorium as well. One of these has been cited in the Introduction.

Mozarabic is the term designating the style of Spanish illumination in the tenth and eleventh centuries, the work of artists who were Christian but influenced by Moslem formal tradition. It can be best characterized as an amalgam of elements still retaining some vestiges of late antique style and others from the Visigothic tradition, along with yet further influences from Near Eastern and north African or Coptic sources. One of the earliest dated examples is a Bible in León Cathedral (Codex 6), written and illuminated in 920 by two monks named Vimara and Juan at the monastery of San Martin de Albeares. The text is written in a minuscule script with excessively tall verticals or *hastae* in letters like b, d, and l—called the Visigothic hand; it bears some faint resemblance to the Luxeuil script of seventh-century Merovingian books like the Lectionary in the Bibliothèque Nationale in Paris (Ms. lat. 9427: Fig. 36). Another point of comparison with Merovingian example is the representation of the Evangelist symbols in the canon table lunettes by zoomorphs with human bodies and animal heads.[25]

Each of the four Gospels in the Bible of 920 is introduced by a full-page miniature like that for Mark (Fig. 97) on f.204v. A winged figure carrying the appropriate Evangelist symbol on his shoulders is enclosed in a

Fig. 97.
León, Cathedral, Cod. 6, f.204v. The Bible of 920, Symbol
preceding the Gospel of St. Mark.

circle with sections of circles projecting diagonally into the corners of the page. The circles are variously decorated, a spatulate motive for those in the angles interrupted by fish-like forms overhanging the perimeter, while the large one may have a geometric design or an inscription.[26] The colors—yellow, orange-red, green, blue-green, and violet—are laid directly on the parchment and there is no background, nor are the figures modeled, hence the design is a flat one of line and color on the neutral two-dimensional plane of the parchment. The introduction of the four Gospels by symbols rather than Evangelist portraits has been seen before in the Celtic Book of Durrow (Fig. 46), where it was recognized as stemming from an early iconographic tradition. Nor are the Mozarabic symbols winged or nimbed, another point suggesting the derivation of both Spanish and Celtic forms from a common tradition. Stylistically they are quite different; early Spanish drawing like this is bold but not sophisticated and attains its effects more in terms of line than color. The kinship of the color scheme in the 920 Bible miniatures to those in Merovingian books is patent, attesting the Oriental element in both.

In its early phases, then, Spanish Mozarabic illumination seems to have some characteristics in common with Merovingian work. But where the latter style, as has been seen, was unable to maintain its initial individuality once it came under the influences of insular and Carolingian procedures, its Iberian counterpart, partly because the peninsula had its own tradition and partly owing to influences brought by the Muslim invaders, was able to develop a specific and characteristic manner of its own. Another Bible made at León and now in the Collegiate Church of San Isidoro there (Cod. 2) is signed as the work of the scribe Florencio and his assistant Sancho in 960; they are shown on f.515v (Fig. 98, Plate XV), standing beneath the lobes of a great Omega, holding chalices and congratulating each other for their joint accomplishment described in the colophon. Islamic decorative elements are prominent—the stylized trees, the leaves with curvilinear notched edges and curled ends hanging from the initial, and the network of fine curving lines filling the interspaces of the Omega. But the plaitwork in the letter, though not without Islamic parallels, is comparable to Franco-Saxon work (Fig. 64), and although the figures are two-dimensional and schematized, they are drawn with distinct outlines and articulate drapery patterns. As in the Bible of 920, the pigments are laid directly on the parchment,

but they are thick and the color scheme has changed.[27] Instead of the relatively thin washes of the earlier miniature, these are strong—chrome yellow, red ochre, blue, and green, the latter sometimes mixed with white and accented with gold, reminding one of Carolingian technique if not effect.

A number of narrative scenes in the Old Testament portion of the Bible of 960[28] are interspersed in the text columns in a way that suggests the possibility at least of an Early Christian prototype so illustrated. There is some indirect evidence that a model of the same sort was in the stylistic ancestry of the most distinctively Spanish of all illustrated mediaeval books—the Commentaries on the Apocalypse or the Revelation of St. John the Divine, and the prophecies of Daniel, compiled about 786 at the latest by the Spanish monk Beatus of Liébana (c. 730–798). The Beatus text is not original, for it consists largely of excerpts from the patristic fathers, but the illustrative tradition of the twenty-three known copies owes nothing to the Carolingian one represented by the illuminated Apocalypse in Valenciennes (Bibl. Mun. Ms. 99), which is apparently based on an Anglo-Italian prototype of c. 700, or those in Trier (SB, Cod. 31), Cambrai (Bibl. Mun. Ms. 386), and Bamberg (SB, Ms. 116)[29] which can be traced more or less directly to an Italian exemplar. Moreover, none of the northern illustrative cycles approaches that of the Beatus commentaries in lavishness. More than a hundred subjects are found, including Evangelist portraits, genealogical tables, a map of the world to illustrate the prologue *De ecclesia et synagoga,* in addition to those required by the Apocalyptic and Daniel texts. No two are exactly alike, even in copies made in the same scriptorium like that created for Ferdinand I and Sancha of León in 1047 after an earlier one of 970 now in the University Library at Valladolid; both were written and illuminated in the monastery of San Isidoro at León. With all individual differences taken into account, the known examples fall into two main groups,[30] which share the distinction of embodying the most singularly dramatic and forceful interpretation that the theme of the world's ending was to have until Albrecht Dürer's in the closing years of the fifteenth century.

No Beatus manuscript of the time when the textual compilation was made in the late eighth century is known to exist, but Neuss surmises that the text was illustrated from the outset, presumably in a style with late antique overtones, as would be expected in illustrations of the patristic writings from which the Beatus

Fig. 100.
Madrid, Biblioteca Nacionale, Ms. B. 31, ff.183c–104.
Beatus Commentary on the Apocalypse, The Woman Clothed with the Sun.

text was excerpted. The earliest reasonably complete example presently known is in the Pierpont Morgan Library in New York (Ms. 644). The colophon gives the name of Magius as the miniaturist and a date of 922, but some erasures preceding the latter may have removed other numbers and it is at least possible that the year given is for the beginning rather than the completion of the volume. It can be taken in any case as a work of the second quarter of the tenth century, perhaps as late as *c.* 950.

Verses 1–2 of Revelation 7 are illustrated (Fig. 99, Plate XVI) on f.115v of Morgan 644, "And after these things I saw four angels standing on the four corners of the earth, holding the four winds of the earth, that the wind should not blow on the earth, nor on the sea, nor on any tree. 2. And I saw another angel ascending from the east, having the seal of the living God: and he cried with a loud voice to the four angels, to whom it was given to hurt the earth and the sea." Like the figures in the Bible of 960, those in Magius's Beatus are painted in strong, heavy colors with emphatic contours and drapery lines, but here they are provided with fully colored backgrounds—salmon red, purple, and chrome yellow in this instance.[31] The irregular ser-

rated band of the sea enclosing the earth is dark blue, with a lighter value of the same hue for the fish. The cocoon-like clouds in the angles from which the angels come are green and purple, overlaid with darker stripes of the same colors, against which the red, yellow, and green robes stand out in patterns of sinuous lines. The background of violently contrasted colors suggests comparison with the compositions in registers of the Ashburnham Pentateuch (Fig. 35), and the angels' wings ending in spirals at the top are also analogous to similar details in the older manuscript, supporting Neuss's suggestion that such was the style of the Beatus illustration prototype. But the border of the Spanish miniature is a series of sharply jagged motives, the Mozarabic transformation of the curvilinear guilloche of classical antiquity, a transformation that also makes harsh stylization and strident color the powerful vehicle for communicating the transcendental content of the vision of doom in all its baleful intensity.

Of the same general Beatus group as the Morgan manuscript is the one made in 1047 by Facundus the scribe for King Ferdinand I and Queen Sancha of León. Now in the Biblioteca Nacionale of Madrid (Ms. B. 31), it is one of the best preserved and most fully

illustrated of the known examples. On ff.186v–187 is the illustration of Revelation 12 (Fig. 100), the vision of the Woman Clothed with the Sun. It fills both pages, a unique feature of many Beatus compositions at the time. The Woman is seen in the upper left angle, approached by the seven-headed red dragon, whose tail, drawing the third part of the stars of heaven, stretches across the facing recto of f.187. Below left, the Woman flies into the wilderness with the wings of an eagle (v. 14), pursued by the flood from the dragon's mouth. Satan is cast into the earth (v. 9) to the right, below, and in the upper right, a group of winged and nimbed figures refers to verse 10: "And I heard a loud voice saying in heaven, Now is come salvation and strength."

The color scheme is dictated in part by the text, as in the red dragon, and is even more powerful, if possible, than it is in the Morgan Beatus. The hues are saturated, heavily painted and arbitrarily juxtaposed in relationships that are intensely dramatic. The linear conventions are equally emphatic. The colored horizontal background bands cut sharply across both pages, the spiral wing ends of the angels twist into volutes and spin off into spurs, and the fallen angels cast out with Satan fly uncontrolled over the field around him as they are pursued by the heavenly host. Paradoxical as it may seem, the heightened expressive intensity of the miniatures in the 1047 Beatus is a consequence of the more rigid and thorough conventionalization of the forms and patterns, in which even less remains to suggest the late antique style of the distant model than is seen in the Morgan volume. Facundus's book is, in fact, in the last and ultimate stage of Mozarabic style in its pure form. Another manuscript made for Ferdinand and Sancha a few years later, the Diurnal in the University Library at Santiago de Compostela, is signed as the work of Fructuosus and dated 1055. A miniature of f.3 of the artist giving the book to his patron[32] is composed like the Ottonian dedication pages, and the figures are drawn with a comparable feeling for form and functional drapery.

Mozarabic illumination was a product of northern and western Spain, the region protected by the Cantabrian mountains from the Moors occupying the southern plains of the Iberian peninsula. From the time of Alfonso III (866–914), it was the locale of the continuing opposition to Islamic political control of which the consistency of Mozarabic manuscript style was the artistic counterpart. But it was equally isolated from trans-Pyrenean influences during the ninth and tenth centuries;

not until the mid-eleventh century did developments in the continental scriptoria appear to have been known in Christian Spain, and their influence even then was far from general. A Beatus manuscript from Santo Domingo de Silos (London, BM, Add. Ms. 11695) was written between 1073 and 1091 by the calligraphers Domingo and Nuño, and illustrated by Prior Petrus, whose task was completed in 1109. Although this date falls well within the Romanesque early twelfth century, its miniatures, based on a model like that of the Morgan Beatus, are predominantly Mozarabic in style and show only a few Romanesque characteristics.[33]

By contrast, the splendid Beatus manuscript made for abbot Gregory Muntaner of the Gascon monastery at Saint-Sever in the western Pyrenees (Paris, BN, Ms. lat. 8878) is illuminated in a style that has many continental overtones.[34] The name Stephanus Garsia on a column of the genealogical tables on f.6 may be that of the scribe or illuminator, and since the book must have been done during the abbacy of Gregory Muntaner from 1028 to 1072, it can be dated about the middle of the eleventh century. The miniature of the Angels with the Four Winds and the Seal of God (Fig. 101) on f.119 is of the same subject as that on f.115v of the Morgan Beatus (Fig. 99, Plate XVI), and the compositional scheme is the same in both. The circular band of the sea filled with fishes encloses the angels and groups of people on the windless earth, with trees above and below here as in Magius's miniature. But there are significant differences in style. The Saint-Sever figures are well proportioned, with rounded heads and carefully delineated features and modeling contours. Equally functional are the drapery patterns in which overlapping folds are carefully delineated and others occasionally fly out from arms and ankles. The color scheme of the Saint-Sever Beatus is as vivid as in the earlier volume, dominated by the strong hues of the striated or compartmented backgrounds, but the colors are reds and oranges combined with yellows, blues, and greens, creating an effect that is brilliant rather than striking the sombre note that gives such baleful meaning to the Mozarabic miniature.

In all these respects, the Saint-Sever Beatus is closer to eleventh-century illumination north of the Pyrenees than to its Mozarabic congeners, notwithstanding the assurance that its illustration derives from the same cycle. This is also true of incidental decorative motives like palmettes, rinceaux, and interlaced knots, which can be more easily referred to Carolingian and Ottonian

Plate XIII. Munich, Bayerischesstaatsbibliothek, Ms. Clm. lat. 13601, f. 3v. The Uota Evangelistary, The Crucifixion with Symbolic Figures.

Plate XIV. London, British Museum, Mss. Add. 49598, f. 25.
The Benedictional of Aethelwold, The Baptism of
Christ.

types than those used in the Spanish scriptoria. In like fashion, the minuscule script in the text and inscriptions in the Saint-Sever book has no relationship to the Mozarabic hand found in the other Beatus manuscripts of the tenth and eleventh centuries. It seems obvious, therefore, that the model of the Saint-Sever Beatus illustrations must have been in a style very close to that of the Ashburnham Pentateuch (Fig. 35), and that its artist was trained in and accepted that tradition instead of translating it into the Mozarabic idioms of the Asturian ateliers. In the opinion of some, the Saint-Sever Beatus is a retranslation of a Mozarabic model into a more naturalistic manner. It seems more likely, however, that it lies in a direct line of descent from an original that was probably illustrated in a style related to that of the Ashburnham Pentateuch though possibly separated from it by intermediate examples that no longer exist.

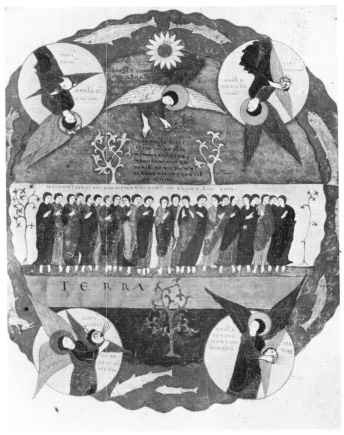

Fig. 101.
Paris, Bibliothèque Nationale, Ms. lat. 8878, f.119. The Saint-Sever Beatus. Angels with the Four Winds and the Seal of God.

This reasoning is further supported by the fact that some themes in the Saint-Sever book are unique and do not occur in the other copies of Beatus's Commentary.

In Catalonia in northeastern Spain, the scriptorium of Santa María di Ripoll was a notable center of manuscript production under the abbacy of Oliva (1002–1018).[35] Two copiously illustrated Bibles are particularly interesting, one called the Bible of Roda in the Bibliothèque Nationale in Paris (Ms. lat. 6), and the Farfa Bible in the Vatican Biblioteca Apostolica (Ms. lat. 5729); both are from the first quarter of the eleventh century. Catalonia is close to Spain, and ties between the two regions were constant, but the style of the miniatures in the two Catalan Bibles shares with those of the Saint-Sever Beatus an unmistakably continental, rather than Mozarabic, quality, implying an influence which is also suggested by the Carolingian minuscule text and the Franco-Saxon interlaces of the initials at the beginning of each book.[36] These are frequently quite elaborate, unlike those of the Mozarabic Bibles and Beatus manuscripts, in which they are usually relatively simple. The single volume of the Vatican Bible has miniatures illustrating the prologue of nearly every book, as well as narrative compositions, many of them full-page, immediately preceding their scriptural texts, save only the Apocalypse.

The illustration of the Book of Daniel (Fig. 102) is on f.227v. Beginning in the upper left with Nebuchadnezzar's dream of the shattered idol (2:31–35), it continues in a series of registers or friezes through the king's madness (chap. 4), Belshazzar's Feast (chap. 5), Daniel in the Lions' Den, and the death of his accusers (chap. 6). The forms are drawn in outline, the contours filled with thin washes like watercolor of red, yellow, blue, and green. Some have not been thus tinted,[37] allowing the firm and assured drawing to be seen. The backgrounds are plain, and there are no borders, the main compositional pattern being the arrangement of the episodes in frieze-like bands across the page. There are some Mozarabic touches, horseshoe arches in the architecture[38] and towers like those in the scene of Belshazzar's Feast in the next-to-bottom register portrayed in a checkerboard pattern of different colors.[39] But the most distinctive feature of the Farfa Bible miniatures is the organic figure style, in which curving contours model the forms and articulate their movements. In this and the frieze-like narrative strips, there seems to be yet another reference to the late antique prototype that can be assumed for the Catalonian Bibles as it

Fig. 102.
Vatican, Biblioteca Apostolica, Ms. lat. 5729, f.227v. The
Farfa Bible, The Story of Daniel.

has been for those of Carolingian Tours.[40] However, in the Catalonian Bibles as in the Saint-Sever Beatus, the animating spirit is not so much a quasi-archaeological approach to the forms of late antiquity, as it was in the Turonian volumes, but is rather an anticipation or foreshadowing of the more consistently organized and monumental conceptions of Romanesque style.

C. Italian Illumination

There is but little evidence of the nature of Italian manuscript illumination in the seventh and eighth centuries in surviving books, and the few that do exist seldom have more than occasional decorated initials and simple ornamentation. The tradition of figure style represented by the portrait of St. Luke in the Cambridge Corpus Christi Gospels (Fig. 33, Plate III) had little effective continuation in the land of its birth during the chaotic years in which temporal power dissolved into anarchic confusion, created by the multitude of warring factions that emerged in the declining years of the Western Empire. When the illustrated book as a distinctive form reappears in Italy in the ninth century, there is a clear division stylistically between manuscripts created in northern and southern centers, but in both regions, those centers were in monasteries. In the north, as has been seen, Bobbio owed its continuing vitality to the Celtic ties that understandably contributed to its production the insular and Franco-Saxon stylistic qualities found in most north Italian work of the time. In southern Italy, the Benedictine monastery at Monte Cassino and its many dependencies were the principal centers.

As in the north and central European scriptoria, there was a reform in writing in those of south Italy, producing a characteristic script usually called Beneventan, although "South Italian" might be more accurate since it was in general use in the whole region.[41] It is on palaeographic grounds that a manuscript in the Laurentian Library in Florence (Ms. Plut. 73, 41) has been attributed to the Cassinese or south Italian circle and dated in the early ninth century.[42] The text is a compilation of varied authorship and includes treatises on herbs and animals, and the illustration contains among other subjects sixteen drawings showing various types of medical operations (Fig. 103). That on f.122 shows the surgeon about to puncture the patient's torso in places indicated by red spots with an instrument that has been heated in a brazier by his assistant. Apart from the label beside the surgeon's head, there is no text; apparently the visual indication of where the heated instrument should be inserted was thought sufficient in this ninth-century copy of a text believed to be of Alexandrian origin in the early Christian period.[43] In copying what must have been a model in late antique style, the draftsman eliminated practically all pictorial elements of modeling and chiaroscuro, and reduced the forms to simple outlines, emphasizing the elongated head and angular drapery patterns of the surgeon's figure and tilting the patient's couch into a two-dimensional plane. Yet, for all the rude simplicity of the drawing, it exemplifies one of the basic elemental concepts of book illustration, the amplifying and clarifying of the written word by representational forms.

Linear simplification is a characteristic also of the miniatures in a collection of hymns called a Gradual, in the Biblioteca Angelica in Rome (Ms. 123), which was written and illuminated in 1039 in the monastery at Nonantola near Modena in northern Italy. On f.31 (Fig. 104), the hymn for the Feast of the Nativity begins with the words *Puer natus est nobis*. The Madonna is seated with the Christ Child, who is giving the Benediction, inside the circle of the P. Its perimeter is decorated with jewel-like lozenges and rectangles, and the vertical *hasta* filled with an acanthus pattern, ends above and below in knots of plait-work. The classical elements in this decoration are unlike anything in the Laurenziana treatise, but in a form more suggestive of a transalpine model than anything Italian or Byzantine. There are initials on other pages of the same manuscript, formed of birds, animals, and human figures somewhat like those in Merovingian books (Figs. 36–39), and as a whole, the illumination of the Nonantola Gradual seems to refer to northern example, transformed into linear patterns in much the same way that the Laurenziana medical artist adapted the forms of his late antique model. Colors are few in the predominantly linear design—red, yellow, and blue with some touches of black—applied in thin washes, and counting for little more than decorative accents in it. The drawing is rather rough and the forms are crudely rendered, yet the whole is remarkably expressive, an admirable complement to the abstract decorative patterns of the musical neumes and the minuscule script of the text.

A psalter with the Ambrosian redaction of the text, and thus almost certainly produced in Milan, is now in

Fig. 103.
Florence, Biblioteca Laurenziana, Ms. Plut. 73, 41, f.122.
Scientific Miscellany, A Surgical Operation. (Photo Pineider)

hic puer est natus qui soluit uincula reatus

Fig. 104.
*Rome, Biblioteca Angelica, Ms. 123, f.31. Gradual from
Nonantola, Initial P with the Madonna and Child.*

Fig. 105.
*Vatican, Biblioteca Apostolica, Ms. lat. 83, f.12v. Am-
brosian Psalter, David and his Musicians.*

the Vatican Library (Ms. lat. 83); datable in the last quarter of the tenth century, its miniatures show a rather more ambitious assimilation of transalpine influences than those of the Nonantola Gradual.[44] David and his Musicians (Fig. 105) are portrayed on f.12v, the king enthroned with his assistants beside and below him. The background is a vivid green, which is also used in the modeling touches of the faces, and the contours are red. Much gold is employed too, in the columns and archivolt of the framing arch, and in the throne and the costumes. The drawing of the figures is coarse, and their articulation indifferent, but the composition as a whole suggests that its model must have been in a fairly competent representational style. That it was transalpine can hardly be doubted. The patterns of forms and colors in the column shafts strongly resemble those of Carolingian goldsmith work, and the panels of braid-work in the arch and the upper angle terminals is Franco-Saxon, especially the protuberant animal heads (cf. Fig. 64). The form of the column capitals and the particular shade of the green background also seem to be Franco-Saxon. Elsewhere in the same book (f.206), a Crucifix in the initial letter of *Te Deum* beginning the 150th Psalm is in a more sophisticated figure style, but with ornamental details like those noted in the David miniature. This and very similar figures in another Milanese Ambrosian Psalter[45] of the late tenth century are also clear indications that Byzantine exemplars were available, a very probable contingency in view of close relations between Constantinople and western Europe at the time. Closely related to this more Byzantine manner in pre-Romanesque north Italian illumination are a group of manuscripts produced in the monastery at Ivrea in the Val d'Aosta, a little west of Milan,[46] in the time of Bishop Warmund (996–1001).

From the latter part of the eleventh century comes a series of illuminated Bibles[47] that are almost as distinctively Italian as the Beatus manuscripts are Spanish. This is not because of the originality and inventiveness of their illustration but their considerable size—so large, in fact, that they are called "Bibbie atlantiche" or "giant Bibles." Few of the fairly considerable number of these giant Bibles measure less than two feet in the longer dimension. They continued to be produced into the twelfth century, in central and north Italian centers for the most part, although the question of their provenance is somewhat in dispute. One in the Vatican (Bibl. Apost. Ms. lat. 10405) is called the Bible of Todi, a city not far from Orvieto in central Italy. Its principal illustra-

tion is a series of initials with figures of the authors or individuals mentioned in the various books. They are painted directly on the parchment, without frame or background, sometimes at the beginning of the text proper but as often prefixed to the prologue separating the initial from the body of the text. They are placed within the width of the text column,[48] following the principle of intercalation of text and illustration dating back to classical antiquity. The initial frames are usually divided into compartments filled with leaf and braid-work in which there are frequent suggestions of Carolingian practice, particularly Turonian and Franco-Saxon.

In the full-page miniature on f.4v of the Todi Bible (Fig. 106) representing the Creation scenes described in Genesis, as well as in the author and hero figures of the initials, late antique style is dimly reflected in the horizontally striped backgrounds, but the figures modeled with broad highlights and fluttering drapery folds bespeak a Byzantine model. This, however, provided only the formulae of the drawing. The abruptly angular movements of the compactly constructed forms, e.g., the crossed legs of the Logos confronting Adam and Eve with knowledge of their sin in the third register from the top, gives them an expressive power that is amplified by the linear translation of Byzantine decorative pictorialism, a premonition of the monumental expressionism of developed Romanesque forms.

Even more distinctively Italian than the "giant" Bibles are the liturgical scrolls produced in the southern scriptoria of the monasteries associated with Monte Cassino during the late tenth and eleventh centuries and continuing into the thirteenth.[49] Although the scroll form continued to be employed for legal documents until late in the Middle Ages, it was seldom used for liturgical purposes except in this group of south Italian examples. With but few exceptions, like a Pontifical in the Biblioteca Casanatense in Rome (Ms. 724), the texts of these scrolls are for the Easter feasts, the *Benedictio fontis* when the baptismal font was blessed, and the hymn sung on Easter Eve, *Exultet iam angelica turba caelorum,* "Now let the angelic trumpet of the heavens sound," when the blessing of the paschal candle culminated in its lighting as a symbol of the Pillar of Fire that led the children of Israel through the wilderness. Although there are some Byzantine liturgical scrolls, the Exultets are uniquely Italian, for the ceremony of blessing the candle was not in the Byzantine liturgy. The subjects illustrated vary somewhat among the twenty

Fig. 106.
Vatican, Biblioteca Apostolica, Ms. lat. 10405, f.4v. Giant
Bible from Todi, Creation Scenes.

or more known examples, but the sequence usually begins with a Christ in Glory,[50] followed by the enlarged initial E of *Exultet* and the sounding of the angelic trumpets. Thereafter the scenes are narrative, liturgical, or symbolic, as determined by the text. The miniatures are inverted in the text, allowing the assembled faithful to see them in the proper sense as the rotulus unrolls over the edge of the pulpit while it is being read.[51]

Christ's Descent into Limbo (Fig. 107) following His death on the cross to bring salvation to the deserving of the Old Dispensation is a subject found in nearly all the Exultet scrolls. The example illustrated is from one written for Pandulfus II of the monastery of St. Peter in Benevento between 981 and 987 (Vatican, Bibl. Apost. Ms. lat. 9820, m. 9). The style has some Byzantine overtones, but it is so closely related to that of late 9th-century south Italian frescoes, like those in the chapel of San Lorenzo in the church of San Vicenzo at the source of the Volturno River,[52] that it must be considered indigenous. The simple color scheme of light blue-gray and red accentuates the firm linear patterns suggesting the movement of the Lord as He lifts Adam and Eve from Hell. The drapery folds, quiet over the figure, become animated in the flying robe to convey the sense of the articulated form they cover. Like the earlier south Italian illustration in the Laurenziana medical treatise (Fig. 103), the miniatures of the Vatican Exultet Roll represent a revaluation of a stylistic tradition that still retains vitality, capable of suggesting movement and gesture with considerable assurance. Closely related are the illustrations in the *Benedictio fontis* made for Landolfo I, archbishop of Benevento from 957 to 984.[53] Compactly built forms, lightly tinted and touched with gold, in well-composed groups, illustrate the Biblical and liturgical scenes appropriate to the text of the ceremony in which the baptismal font is blessed.

In the early eleventh century, south Italian illumination comes increasingly and more strongly under Byzantine influence. This can be observed in an early stage in an Exultet scroll in the archive of the cathedral at Bari, and in the earliest of three belonging to the cathedral at Gaeta,[54] both dating after 1000. The trend comes to a climax in manuscripts produced at Monte Cassino during the abbacy of Desiderius in the last half of the eleventh century (1052–1087). An example is the Lectionary in the Vatican (Bibl. Apost. Ms. lat. 1202),[55] which also contains the lives of the principal Benedic-

tine saints. From the history of Monte Cassino, the *Chronicon Cassinense* of Leo of Ostia and Peter the Deacon, it is known that Desiderius did much to strengthen artistic ties between the monastery and Constantinople, calling on Byzantine artists for bronze doors, silver statues, and mosaics to decorate the basilica begun in 1066. That his interest extended to books also is clear from a list of his desiderata in the same chronicle, and the dedicatory miniature on f.2 of the Lectionary in the Vatican[56] shows him presenting a book to St. Benedict, with an accompanying prayer that he accept others along with the newly completed monastic buildings.

Most of the illustrations of the lives of the Benedictine saints in the Desiderian Lectionary are intercalations in the text columns, painted in opaque colors directly on the parchment and without frames or backgrounds (Fig. 108). Technically they follow mid-Byzantine usage, such as would be found in contemporary or slightly earlier work, like the Menologion of Basil II (Fig. 25), as they do in some stylistic qualities as well. The colors, for instance, are much more effective than in the Exultet Roll of Pandulfus II, in patterns of strong reds, greens, and blues, and in such details as the reddish flesh tones with modeling shadows of green in the faces. Also Byzantine are the slender figures and their reticent movements, the carefully controlled contours and inner modeling lines, and the resulting monumentality of effect. At the same time, the forms are not so rigidly schematized as in mid-Byzantine work, and there is some integration of the forms with the enveloping space.

Quite as distinctively Desiderian as the figure style in the Lectionary miniatures are the decorative initials. In late ninth-century initials like those of the Casanatense Exultet Scroll,[57] the outline of the letter is carefully retained in the alternate plain and plait-work panels, with foliate tendrils at the ends that merge with or are tied to dog-like forms that always lie outside the body of the letter. Such intermingled ribbon braids and animals suggests a possible transalpine or even insular influence; could this be demonstrated, it would have had to be direct, rather than through Carolingian or even north Italian intermediaries. Many of these same elements appear in initials of Monte Cassino manuscripts from Desiderius' time, like the C on f.44 (Fig. 108), but treated in a different way. Rinceaux and braid-work alternate in the panels of the body of the letter, and intertwine to fill the central opening. The canine forms

Fig. 107.
Vatican, Biblioteca Apostolica, Ms. lat. 9820, m. 9. Exultet
Scroll, Christ's Descent into Limbo.

Fig. 108.
Vatican, Biblioteca Apostolica, Ms. lat. 1202, f.44. Lectionary from Monte Cassino, Scenes from the Life of St. Benedict.

Fig. 109.
New York, Pierpont Morgan Library, Ms. 333, ff.84v–85.
Gospel-book of Odbert, St. John and Incipit *Page.*

crawl in and out of the trellis-like armature of the initial, instead of lying outside, and much gold is used along with the colors. There is no doubt that the elaborate patterns of foliated trellises and the lavish use of gold in Desiderius' manuscripts were inspired by Ottonian illuminations, specifically those of a Regensburg book now in the Vatican Library (Ms. Ottob. lat. 74) known as the Gospels of Henry II.[58] It had been given to Monte Cassino by Henry II after he had been cured of an illness there in 1022; a note in Beneventan script on f.176v indicates that it was there during the eleventh century. Only the color scheme of the initials in the Desiderius Lectionary differentiates them from the Regensburg type of those in the Gospel-book of Henry II.

Under Desiderius' successor, Oderisius, the quality and distinction of Monte Cassino manuscripts declined considerably. The established traditions of style were powerful, however, and south Italian illumination of the early twelfth century continued using the Monte Cassino formulae even if with waning inspiration. The Chronicle of Santa Sofia of Benevento (Fig. 124) of *c.* 1120 contains miniatures and initials of the type seen in the Desiderius Lectionary, in patterns that approach the textile-like effect also found in late Byzantine

work. Much of the illumination in Roman scriptoria of the twelfth century was influenced in the same way by the late eleventh-century Monte Cassino style.

D. French Illumination

Manuscript illumination in the region ultimately to be known as France presents an overall picture with little more homogeneity than that of pre-Romanesque Germany or Italy. During the tenth century, in fact, it can hardly be said to have existed, a symptom of the catastrophic confusion resulting from the collapse of centralized authority in the post-Carolingian period, and the successive incursions of Norse invaders from the north and Saracens in the south. Only in the reforms of the Benedictine order originating in and guided by the great abbey at Cluny was there any promise of spiritual strength and creative activity in the dark period that was the tenth century in France. The culmination of these reforms, symbolized in another way by the pilgrimage to the tomb of St. James the Greater at Santiago de Compostela in northwestern Spain, which was sponsored by Cluny, came during St. Odilo's directorship of the order (994–1049). It was not coincidence

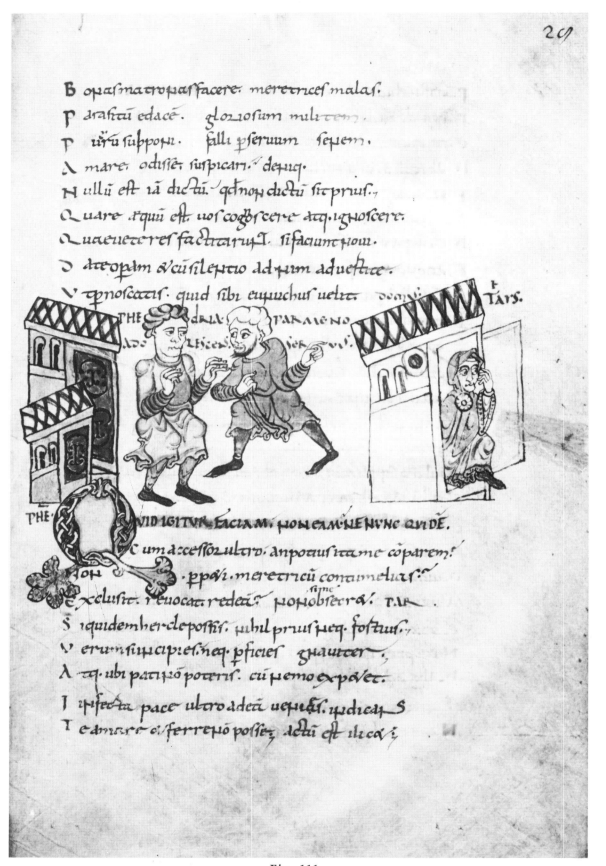

Fig. 111.
Leyden, University Library, Ms. Voss. lat. Q, 38, f.28. The
Comedies of Terence, The Eunuchus, act. i, sc. 1, Parmeno,
Phaedria and Thais.

Fig. 112.
Paris, Bibliothèque Nationale, Ms. lat. 5058, ff.2v–3.
Josephus, De Bello Judaico, Josephus presenting the book
to Titus and Vespasian.

that this same period in the closing years of the tenth century witnessed the beginning of centralized temporal authority in France when Hugh Capet ascended its throne in 987. Although far from an effective ruler himself, the regime he initiated was the one that made France into what was to become the power known in history.

Unlike the styles of illumination that developed in England during the eleventh century, which, for all their individuality, have some characteristics in common, those that evolved in France show, understandably, very marked regional traits. Thus it is not surprising that in the northwestern area fronting on the English Channel, including some Flemish regions, there should have been direct contacts with the art of Anglo-Saxon England and an intermingling of ideas. So much was this the case, indeed, that the term "Channel School" has been used to designate manuscripts identified with the region as a whole, in which the principal scriptorium was in the abbey of Saint Bertin at St. Omer. There, during the abbacy of Odbert (986–1007),[59] who was responsible himself for the decoration of a number of manuscripts, a distinctive group of books was produced, including a psalter in the Bibliothèque Municipale at Boulogne-sur-Seine (Ms. 20)[60] and a Gospel-book in

the Pierpont Morgan Library in New York (Ms. 333), among others. In both, he had the collaboration of the scribe Dodolinus, with whom he is shown presenting the book to Saint Bertin in a drawing on f.84 of the Morgan book.[61] The date is in the early eleventh century, before 1008.

Overleaf from the drawing just referred to is the portrait of St. John (f.84v), facing the beginning of his Gospel (f.85) (Fig. 109). It is apparent at once that Odbert was familiar with late tenth-century Anglo-Saxon illumination. The borders show characteristic Winchester foliate types, although not in trellis frames, and if certain characteristics of drawing in the palmettes seem to derive from Carolingian usage, it is clear that Odbert drew chiefly on Anglo-Saxon sources for his ideas. The Ascension of Christ at the top of the Incipit page shows the Saviour vanishing from view, as He does in the Bury St. Edmunds Psalter (Fig. 94); other interesting iconographic details in this miniature are the Four Rivers of Paradise, the Church and Synagogue, personifications of Earth and Sea, as well as Christ's Descent into Limbo and the Three Holy Women at His Empty Tomb. It is possible, indeed, that English illuminators were working in Odbert's scriptorium; a Nativity and Annunciation to the Shepherds in another

Fig. 113.
Poitiers, Bibliothèque municipale, Ms. 250, f.21. Life of
St. Radegonde, Bishop Fortunatus writing the saint's life.

Saint Bertin Gospel-book in Boulogne-sur-Mer[62] could very well be by an English hand. The rippling drapery edges and the dark lines of the folds accented by white streaks derive from the same general source. Only the somewhat less attenuated figures and their poses, not quite so angular as in Anglo-Saxon miniatures, distinguish these exemplars of the "Channel School" of illumination from their English cousins. Like the Saint Bertin scriptorium, others in northwestern France or nearby Flanders like Saint-Vaast at Arras, Saint-Amand, and Marchiennes developed styles in which the calligraphic Anglo-Saxon linear idiom is combined with decorative motives more closely related to continental usage.

The north French and Flemish scriptoria just mentioned had been centers of manuscript production in earlier times, although they were not among the major ones like Tours, Reims, and Saint-Denis. These latter also contributed to the revival of French illumination in the early eleventh century in works which understandably inherited something of their traditional styles. Thus a late eleventh-century psalter from Saint-Germain-des-Prés (Paris, BN, Ms. lat. 11550) contains a miniature on f.6 of the Crucifixion[63] in a linear style, but one that drew on Carolingian Reims precedent rather than Anglo-Saxon, not surprising, however, since Saint-Germain-des-Prés was a dependency of Saint-Denis. From Saint-Denis itself came a missal of *c.* 1050 (Paris, BN. Ms. lat. 9436) in which a Christ in Majesty[64] is painted in opaque pigments on a purple background, the figures modeled with bluish-white highlights, and the whole framed in a border of white-tipped acanthus leaves, giving the composition a remarkably Ottonian look. This is understandable in view of the generally eclectic character of Saint-Denis style. A mid-eleventh-century date is indicated by the more slender figures and their rather angular movements, as well as those representational elements so laboriously adapted from the antique in Carolingian style, which have now crystallized into decorative abstractions.

Ottonian art with its Byzantine elements also played a significant role in forming the style of illumination developed at the abbey of Cluny, the *fons et origo* of the Benedictine reform in the tenth century. This is not surprising in view of the fact that its abbot in the later eleventh century, St. Hugh (1049–1109), was godfather of Henry IV, the emperor of Germany (1056–1106). Unhappily, but little remains today of its library, much of which was destroyed during anti-clerical riots

between 1809 and 1813, but Carl Nordenfalk has identified one manuscript executed there in the late eleventh century.[65] It is a treatise in praise of the Madonna, *De virginitate Sanctae Mariae* by St. Ildefonsus, which is in the Biblioteca Palatina at Parma (Ms. 1650). The decorated initials and much of the illustration have obvious Ottonian overtones in the somewhat inarticulate figures and lavish use of gold, silver, and purple, a little reminiscent of the rather sombre scheme of early eleventh-century work at Cologne. However, two miniatures in the latter part of the book are in a different style. They have to do with the transmission of the original text to France where it was presented to Godescalc (Fig. 110, Plate XVII), the archbishop of Le Puy,[66] by abbot Gomesanus. It is much more Byzantine than the other miniatures in the book, in details like the diaper pattern of the seated archbishop's robe, the stylized architecture with its flattened acanthus capitals, and the greater variety of the color scheme in which red, green, lavender, and light and dark blue are added to the restrained and sober gamut of the more Ottonian miniatures. The technique is also different, for the Cluniac miniatures are executed in rather delicate gouache pigments, unlike the heavier impasto of the others. But most significant of all is the heightened monumentality of the forms, plastically conceived and organically articulated, achieving an effect of solid volumes that directly anticipates the impending Romanesque manner.

Manuscript illumination of the eleventh century in southwestern France has been referred to earlier in comparing the style of the Saint-Sever Beatus with Mozarabic examples. Its powerful and individual manner is almost isolated in time and place, for no other southwest French volume approaches it in the lavishness of its illustrative cycle, the absolute assurance of its style, and the superb quality of its execution. Even in an ambitious project like the so-called "First Bible of S.-Martial of Limoges" (Paris, BN, Ms. lat. 5), a massive two-volume work from the late tenth century, the decoration consists only of elaborated initials and the canon tables of the Gospels;[67] the omission of narrative miniatures is the more unusual since the Limoges Bible derives, in part at least, from Turonian models. Nor have the extensive researches of the late Jean Porcher and the staff of the Bibliothèque Nationale in Paris[68] as yet found more than incidental reflection of the Saint-Sever manner in other books of comparable date and provenance. Among the few instances are the jugglers and dancers in a Troper-Proser,[69] a collection of musical paraphrases of liturgical offices (Paris, BN, Ms. lat. 1118) of the mid-eleventh century from the region of Auch not far from Moissac.

Tours in the Loire Valley has already been noted as one of the most important centers of Carolingian illumination, but successive raids by the Saracens beginning in the late ninth century reduced the output of its scriptoria to much more modest volumes than the Moutier-Grandval and Vivian Bibles (Figs. 66 [Plate VIII]–68), and but little from the succeeding century has been identified with them. However, some books were produced in the general region of western France, like an illustrated copy of Terence's *Comedies* in the University Library at Leyden (Codex Vossianus 38).[70] It can be dated in the late tenth century for palaeographic reasons, and assigned to a center in the Loire region on the same grounds, supported by a fifteenth-century note on f.135v that it was made for the monastery of Saint-Maurice at Angers. In Act I, scene 1 of *The Eunuchus,* illustrated on f.28 of the Leyden book (Fig. 111), Parmeno the slave attempts to dissuade his master Phaedria from returning to the courtesan Thais who had dismissed him from her favors. The illustrations of the Leyden Terence stand alone in the thirteen cycles studied by Jones and Morey, no one of the others being like it except in a very general way. In the same scene in the other versions,[71] for instance, master and slave appear alone, neither the building they stand in front of here nor that in which the listening Thais is seated being shown. It is possible that an otherwise unknown model was used by the Leyden Terence illustrators or, as Jones and Morey suggest, that the text was copied from an unillustrated version for which the scenes were invented in a style not immediately related to or directly influenced by another. The braids and foliate tips of the initial are in the general decorative repertory of the period, however, and the style of the figures is very expressive. The large heads, hands, and feet of the short and massive bodies combine with the varied poses and vigorous movements in giving visual form to the comic spirit of the text.

The Leyden Terence style can be best characterized as derived from the late antique canon but unaffected by the modifications to which it had been subjected in Carolingian and Ottonian circles. It appears to have been characteristic of the west central French region, for other manuscripts like a Prudentius, also at Leyden (Codex Vossianus oct. 15), of the early eleventh century and probably from Saint-Martial at Limoges,[72] and a Psychomachia or Conflict of the Virtues and Vices of the late tenth or early eleventh century from Moissac (Paris, BN, Ms. lat. 2077) are illustrated in a comparable style.[73] By the end of the eleventh century, however, this style indigenous to west central and southern France had been transformed by outside influences to the degree apparent in the dedicatory miniatures on ff.2v–3 (Fig. 112) of a copy of Josephus's "History of the Jewish People" (*De Bello Judaico*) in the Bibliothèque Nationale in Paris (Ms. lat. 5058); the manuscript came to the Bibliothèque Nationale with others from Moissac and probably was made in or near Saint-Sernin at Toulouse. The miniatures show Josephus presenting his book to the emperors Titus and Vespasian in a style having some features in common with the Terence miniature. The author's rounded head with its casque of curls,[74] the slanting glances of his eyes and those of the ruler on the right, the broad gestures and animated poses of the crowd following the author are all details to the point.

Yet, related as these details of the two miniatures may be, there are noteworthy stylistic differences between them. The figures in the Josephus manuscript are attenuated and slender rather than stocky and compact. The author's diagonal stance projects him toward his seated patrons, whose robes ripple around the edges of folds that sometimes fly out on the sides or fall in v-shaped patterns between the spread knees. In these characteristics, the figures of the Josephus miniatures are closer to those found in early eleventh-century Anglo-Saxon manuscripts than any others save those that derive directly from such insular models as the products of the so-called Channel School (Fig. 109). With these latter the Josephus miniatures also share the predominantly linear technique in which the figures are drawn directly on the parchment with only a few washes of red, yellow, and green, and some touches of blue.

There is nothing to suggest that Anglo-Saxon artists may have worked in the Aquitanian scriptoria as they did in Odbert's at Saint-Omer, nor is there any reason to think there was a particularly close relationship between the monastic communities of England and southern France. There is documentary evidence, however, that illuminated books from England were in the Aquitanian region in the eleventh century and that they were held in some regard. The account of a council at Limoges in 1031 contains the following passage:

Plate XV. León, Colegiata de San Isidoro, Cod. 2, f. 515v.
The Bible of 960, The Scribes Florencio and Sancho.

Plate XVII. Parma, Biblioteca Palatina, Ms. 1650, f. 102v. Ildefonsus, *De Virginitate Sanctae Mariae,* Presentation of the book to Archbishop Godescalc.

Plate XVI. New York, Pierpont Morgan Library, Ms. 644, f. 115v. Beatus Commentary on the Apocalypse, Angels with the Four Winds and the Seal of God.

Illud quoque mihi memorandum est, quod ante nos septem annos rex Anglorum duci Aquitaniae regalis muner misit, simulque *codicem* literis aureis scriptum, in quo nomina sanctorum distincta cum *imaginibus* continebantur. Quod volumen jam olim in concilio Pictavensi, dum hac eadem de re quaestio esset, idem dux Wilielmus literis edoctis in testimonium antiquitatis pontificibus ostendit.[75]

Nothing in this states specifically that the book was Anglo-Saxon, to be sure, but this could be reasonably assumed in the circumstances.

It is demonstrable, moreover, that southwestern French illuminators drew some of their ideas from such models. On f.21 of a Life of Saint Radegonde in the Bibliothèque Municipale of Poitiers (Ms. 250) is a full-page miniature (Fig. 113) of Bishop Fortunatus of Poitiers writing the saint's biography; the manuscript is of the late eleventh century and is believed to have been written and illuminated in the saint's convent of Sainte-Croix which is known to have had some relations with England. The border of the miniature is the espalier-trellis type identified with Anglo-Saxon Winchester, with its accenting angle and lateral medallions of leaves with curling tips (cf. Fig. 90, Plate XIV). The figure of the author is not so dynamically conceived as might be expected, nor are those in the other twenty-one miniatures in the book,[77] but the decorated initials throughout are comparable to Anglo-Saxon work in much the same way and to the same degree as the border of the author portrait.

Jean Porcher points out the kinship in form and spirit between the figure of Josephus (Fig. 112) and the contemporary sculptured reliefs of angels and apostles flanking the enthroned Christ in the ambulatory of Saint-Sernin at Toulouse.[78] His comments are equally applicable to other examples. Enough remains of the mutilated historiated capitals in the cloister of Saint-Pierre at Moissac dating from the last years of the eleventh century to reveal robustly expressive figures very much like those in the Leyden Terence miniatures (Fig. 111), created by quite similar formal means. And the large reliefs of Durandus, abbot of Moissac, and several apostles carved on pier slabs in the same cloister, are realizations in stone of the same formal and expressive concepts embodied in the standing Evangelists introducing their writings in a Gospel-book of the very end of the eleventh century (Paris, BN, Ms. lat. 254) that was written and illuminated in or near Moissac itself. The strongly frontal figure of St. Matthew (Fig. 114, Plate XVIII) on f.10 is framed by slender colonnettes surmounted by tourelles and stands on an imbricated slab, just as his sculptured counterparts do.[79] Either could well have been the model for the other, just as the enlaced human and grotesque animal forms decorating the capital L beside it, with which Matthew's text begins, is different from the sculptured trumeau of the adjoining church at Moissac[80] only in being two- rather than three-dimensional. Painted and carved forms are alike in the monumentally expressive content that is the essence of fully developed Romanesque style.

NOTES

1. Cf. Henry, *IAVI*, pp. 60–61; pls. 34, iv, v: also Rickert, *PiBMA*, pls. 11b, 12.

2. *IAVI*, pls. I, K, L, M, N, O, 36, 42–45.

3. *PiBMA*, pl. 20a, b.

4. E. Millar, *English Illuminated Manuscripts from the Xth to the XIIIth Century* (Paris-Brussels: Van Oest, 1926).

5. F. Saxl and R. Wittkower, *British Art and the Mediterranean* (London: Oxford University Press, 1948), pl. 20, no. 8.

6. F. Wormald, *English Drawings of the 10th and 11th Centuries* (London: Faber & Faber, 1952).

7. Cf. *CR*, fig. 157.

8. *EMP*, p. 182.

9. O. Homburger, *Die Anfänge der Malerschule von Winchester im 10. Jahrhundert*, Studien über christliche Denkmäler 13 (Leipzig, 1912). J. B. L. Tolhurst, "An examination of two Anglo-Saxon Manuscripts of the Winchester School: the Missal of Robert de Jumièges and the Benedictional of St. Aethelwold," *Archaeologia* 83 (1933):27–74.

10. Cf. F. Wormald, *The Benedictional of St. Ethelwold* (New York: Yoseloff, 1959), pls. 3, 4.

11. F. G. Warner and H. A. Wilson, *The Benedictional of Aethelwold* (Oxford: Roxburghe Club, 1910).

12. Reproduced in color in *EMP*, p. 180.

13. Cf. Homburger, n. 9.

14. A. Goldschmidt, *Die Elfenbeinskulpturen aus der Zeit der karolingischen und sächsischen Kaiser*, 4 vols. no. 96 a–e (Berlin: Deutscher Verein für Kunstwissenschaft, 1914–26), pls. xliv–xlv.

15. Cf. Wormald, n. 10, pp. 13–15.

16. C. Niver, "The Psalter in the British Museum, Harley 2904," *Medieval Studies in Memory of A. Kingsley Porter*, vol. 2 (Cambridge, Mass.: Harvard University Press, 1939), pp. 681–87.

17. Reproduced in color in *EMP*, p. 181.

18. Cf. Wormald, no. 56, n. 6.

19. As suggested by M. Schapiro, "The Image of the Disappearing Christ, The Ascension in English Art around the year 1000," *Gazette des Beaux-Arts*, 23 (1943):135–52.

20. F. Wormald, "Decorated Initials in English Manuscripts from A.D. 900 to 1100," *Archaeologia* 91 (1945):107–35.

21. Amiens, Bibliothèque Municipale, Ms. 133; cf. *EDA*, figs. 204–10.

22. *PiBMA*, pl. 39a.

23. M. Harrsen, "The Countess Judith and the Library of Weingarten," *Papers of the Bibliographical Society of America*, 24 (1930):1–13.

24. F. Wormald, "The Survival of Anglo-Saxon Illumination after the Norman Conquest," *Proceedings of the British Academy*, 30 (1944):127–45.

25. J. Dominguez Bordona, *Spanish Illumination*, 2 vols. (Florence: Pantheon, 1930). Idem, *Exposiçion de códices miniados españoles* (Madrid: Sociedad española de amigos del arte, 1929).

26. Cf. Luke, reproduced in color in *EMP*, p. 164.

27. Reproduced in color in *EMP*, p. 167.

28. Dominguez Bordona, *Spanish Illumination*, vol. 1, pl. 11.

29. Cf. *CR*, figs. 167–69.

30. W. Neuss, *Die Apokalypse des hl. Johannes in der altspanischen und altchristlichen Bibel-Illustration*, Spanische Forschungen der Görresgesellschaft 2–3 (Münster-im-Westphalia, 1931).

31. Reproduced in color in *EMP*, p. 169.

32. Dominguez Bordona, *Spanish Illumination*, vol. 1, pl. 34.

33. Cf. *AB*, 21 (1930):313–74.

34. E. A. Van Moé, *L'Apocalypse de Saint-Sever* (Paris: Editions de Cluny, 1942).

35. W. Neuss, *Die katalanische Bibel-Illustration um die Wende des 1. Jahrtausends und die altspanische Buchmalerei*, Veroffentl. d. roman. Auslands-Instituts d. Rhein. Bonn 3 (Bonn-Leipzig: Schröder, 1922).

36. Cf. Boeckler, *AM*, pl. 61.

37. Dominguez Bordona, *Spanish Illumination*, vol. 2, pl. 41.

38. *Ibid.*

39. Cf. *EMP*, p. 173.

40. Cf. Bordona, *Spanish Illumination*, vol. 2, p. 30.

41. B. L. Ullman, *Ancient Writing* (New York: Longmans, Green, 1932), pp. 94–100.

42. E. A. Lowe, *The Beneventan Script* (Oxford: Clarendon, 1914), pp. 18–19.

43. K. Sudhoff, *Beiträge zur Geschichte der Chirurgie im Mittelalter*, 2 vols. (Leipzig: J. A. Barth, 1914–18), p. 90.

44. P. D'Ancona, *La miniature italienne du Xe au XVIe siècle* (Paris: Van Oest, 1925). P. Toesca, *La pittura e la miniatura nella Lombardia* (Milan: Hoepli, 1912), p. 72. Boeckler, *AM*, p. 66.

45. Munich, SB, Ms. lat. 343; cf. *AM*, pl. 65.

46. L. Magnani, *Le Miniature del Sacramentario d'Ivrea* (Vatican City, 1934).

47. P. Toesca, "Miniature romane dei secoli XI e XII. Bibbie miniate," *Rivista del R. Istituto d'Archeologia e Storia dell' Arte*, 1 (1929):69–96. E. B. Garrison, *Studies in the History of Medieval Italian Painting*, 1, no. 1 (Florence, 1953).

48. Cf. the contemporary initials in a Bible in the Biblioteca Palatina of Parma (Ms. Palat. 386); *AM*, pl. 68.

49. A. M. Latil, *Le Miniature nei Rotoli dell' Exultet: documenti per la storia della miniatura in Italia* 3 (Monte Cassino, 1899–1901). M. Avery, *The Exultet Rolls of South Italy* (plates only) (Princeton: Princeton University Press, 1936).

50. M. Salmi, *La Miniatura Italiana* (Milan: Electa Editrice, 1956), pl. 1.

51. Grabar-Nordenfalk, *RP*, p. 147.

52. Cf. *EMP*, p. 221.

53. Rome, Biblioteca Casanatense, Ms. 724–II; *AM*, pl. 70; Avery, no. 49, pls. 110–17.

54. Avery, pls. 4–11, 30–32.

55. M. Inguanez and M. Avery, *Miniature Cassinesi del secolo XI illustranti la vita di San Benedetto*, dal Cod. Vat. lat. 1202 (Monte Cassino, 1934).

56. É. Bertaux, *L'art dans l'Italie méridionale* (Paris: Fontemoing, 1904), fig. 66.

57. *AM*, pls. 70a, 72.

58. H. Bloch, "Monte Cassino, Byzantium and the West in the Earlier Middle Ages," *Dumbarton Oaks Papers*, no. 3, (1946), pp. 178–87.

59. A. Wilmart, "Les livres de l'abbé Odbert," *Bull. de la Soc. des Antiquaires de la Morinie*, 14 (1924):169–80. A. Boutemy, "Un grand enlumineur du Xme siècle; l'abbé Odbert de Saint-Bertin," *Annales de la Federation archeologique et historique de la Belgique*, 32 (1947):247 ff.

60. A. Boutemy, "La Miniature (VIIIe—XIIe)," *L'Histoire de l'Eglise en Belgique*, 2 (Brussels, 1946):323. J. Porcher, *Medieval French Miniatures* (New York: Abrams, 1959), p. 17, fig. 13.

61. W. D. Wixom, *Treasures from Medieval France* (Cleveland: Museum of Art, 1967), p. 23.

62. *MFM*, p. 17 and pl. v.

63. *MFM*, pl. iii.

64. f. 15v; *MFM*, pl. ii.

65. *RP*, pp. 188–89; cf. also M. Schapiro, *The Parma Ildefonsus* (New York: New York University Press, 1964).

66. Reproduced in color in *RP*, p. 189.

67. *MFM*, p. 27 and fig. 25.

68. *Les manuscrits à peintures du viie au xiie siècle* (Paris: Bibliothèque Nationale, 1954).

69. *MFM*, pl. xvi.

70. Jones and Morey, chap. 4, n. 7; Ms. N.

71. Jones and Morey, 1:130–51; 2, figs. 167–70.

72. Woodruff, chap. 1, n. 27.

73. Cf. also Porcher, *MFM*, p. 12.

74. Reproduced in color in *MFM*, pl. xix.

75. "I must also recall the fact that seven years before my time the king of the Angles sent royal gifts to the Duke of Aquitaine, and on the same occasion a codex written in letters of gold, in which were contained the names of the saints illustrated with images. Earlier, at the Council of Poitiers, when the same question was under discussion, this same Duke William had, in a learned letter, pointed out this very volume to the pontiffs as evidence of this antiquity." G. D. Mansi, *Sacrorum conciliorum nova*, 19, col. 521, D—E. *Concilium Lemovicensis*, 2, 1031.

76. M. E. Ginot, *Le manuscrit de Ste.-Radegonde de Poiters et ses peintures du xie siècle*, Bulletin de la Soc. fr. de Reproductions de Mss. à peintures, 4 (1914–20). F. Wormald, "Some illustrated manuscripts of the Lives of the Saints," *Bulletin of the John Rylands Library* (Manchester, 1952), pp. 248 ff.

77. Cf. *MFM*, fig. 31.

78. *MFM*, pp. 28–29.

79. G. Marchiori, *Il Chiostro di Moissac* (Florence: Sansoni, 1965), pls. 10, 14.

80. *Ibid.*, pls. 18, 22.

Fig. 115.
Cambridge, Trinity College Library, Ms. R. 17. 1, f.20.
The Eadwine Psalter, Illustration of Psalm XI (12).

6

Romanesque Manuscript Illumination

Romanesque is the term employed in the history of art for the twelfth and early thirteenth centuries. Its implication—related to, yet different from, the art of Roman antiquity—is as fully realized in western European manuscript illumination as in the architecture and sculpture of the time, for Romanesque illumination characteristically maintains the individuality of both text and illustration, often separating them from each other by frames (cf. Fig. 4), so that the two elements of page design are coexistent rather than integrated. Also, particularly in those regions where the influence of late antiquity had been strong, either directly or through Byzantine intermediaries, regions such as the German provinces where the styles of Carolingian Ada and Ottonian Reichenau were strongly entrenched, or southern France and Italy where the late antique was the indigenous tradition, the Romanesque styles of the twelfth and early thirteenth centuries retain a feeling for plastic values reminiscent of those in classical art. Elsewhere, notably in England, Flanders, and northern France, the dynamic and linear idioms of earlier periods is continued in the Romanesque, sometimes developing even more intense and angular rhythms in the initial phases, though assuming more reticent form as the proto-Gothic manner begins to evolve in the early thirteenth century.

Some idea of the changes in style and expressive content during the twelfth century can be gained from the miniatures in two copies of the Utrecht Psalter made during the latter part of the period. It will be recalled that the Carolingian book was almost certainly in Canterbury around the year 1000, when it was copied in the Psalter now in the British Museum (Ms. Harley 603) (Fig. 91). About 1150 it was copied again at Christ Church, Canterbury, by the monk Eadwine, whose portrait appears on f.283v (Fig. 116) of the volume now in Trinity College Library in Cambridge (Ms. R. 17. 1).[1] The text is tripartite, with the Hebrew, Roman, and Gallican versions of the Psalms in three parallel columns. As in both the Utrecht Psalter and Harley 603, each psalm and canticle is preceded by an illustration filling the full width of the folio, and each of the three text columns begins with an elaborate initial, the Gallican more ornate than the others.

The illustration of Psalm 11 (12) on f.20 (Fig. 115) contains the same elements as in Utrecht and Harley (Fig. 61 [Plate VII] and Fig. 91)—the Lord arising from his throne at the top, the smelters of silver, and the evil men ambulating about—and the composition is also the same. Also, as in the earlier versions, the illustrations are line drawings and are, like Harley, in color—blue, green, vermilion, and brown. But the

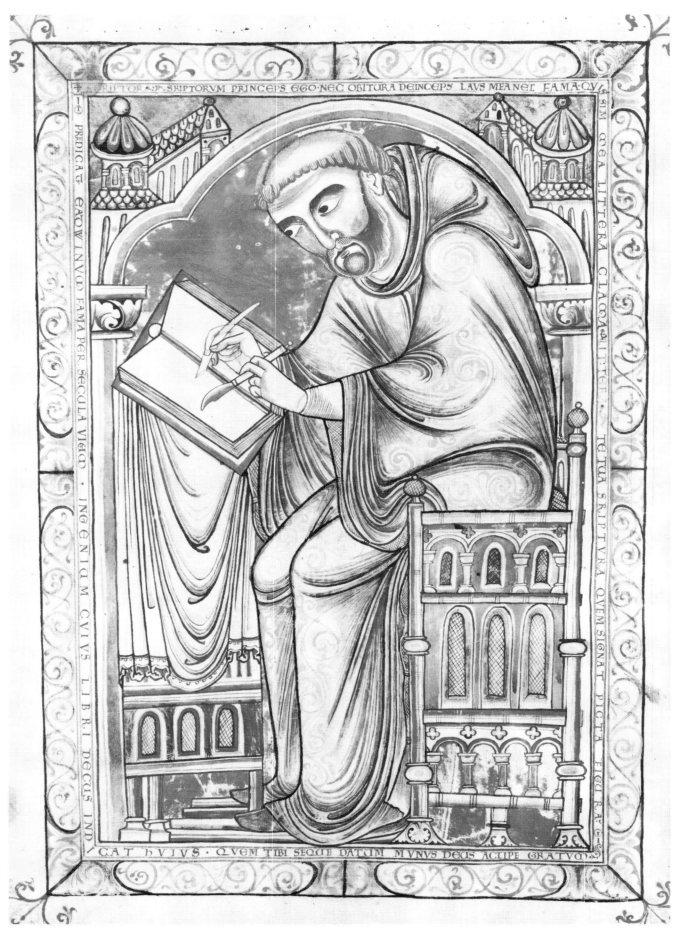

Fig. 116.
Cambridge, Trinity College Library, Ms. R. 17. 1, f.283v.
The Eadwine Psalter, Eadwine the Scribe.

Eadwine Psalter illustrations differ from those in the
earlier Anglo-Saxon version in several noteworthy respects.[2] The colored lines do not replace the monochrome of the Carolingian prototype, but run parallel
to the contours and the inner modeling strokes. Even
more significant is the fact that the Eadwine drawings
are framed, instead of being scattered over the parchment surface and appearing to be on the same plane
as the accompanying text, as they are in the Harley
designs. A similar tightening and decorative consolidation is noted in the style of the forms and figures. The
latter have the same attenuated bodies and small heads
seen in Harley 603, and there is the same sinuous ground
line for the hills, punctuated by small buildings based
on antique types, but the line defining these forms is
precise and specific instead of being free and sketchy;
the flying drapery fold of the angel attacking the soldiers
in the lower right is as rigid as a metal scroll instead of
floating on the wind of his swift movement. The initials
of twining ribbons ending in leaves or animal heads are
fully colored, painted rather than drawn, in red, blue,
and green, heightened with white and accented with
gold, a distinctive feature of twelfth-century Canterbury
illumination.

The portrait of Eadwine the Scribe (Fig. 116) on
f.283v of the Psalter named for him is unusual in a

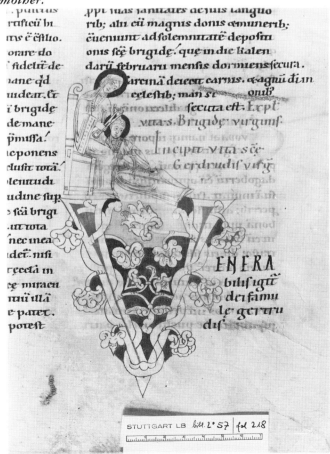

Fig. 119.
Fulda, Hessisches Landesbibliothek, Ms. Aa 35. Lectionary
by Odalricus custos, The Holy Women at the Tomb.

Fig. 120.
New York, Pierpont Morgan Library, Ms. 710, f.16v. The
Berthold Missal, The Nativity and Annunciation to the
Shepherds.

number of respects. The color scheme is the same as in the illustrative miniatures, predominantly blue and green with touches of vermilion and brown. As in the narrative miniatures, the contours and drapery patterns are accentuated by colored lines, but color is also used to model the face and head, in which accents of green, red, and brown are set against the blue beard and hair. Though the tradition of color usage established in eleventh-century English illumination is thus continued, a decorative function is added; flat areas create planes organized on the two-dimensional surface, and there is little effort to suggest three-dimensional form or space. Equally notable is the new expressive content, implicit in the concept of the portrait, in its full-page dimensions, and stated at length in the inscription in the border:

SCRIPTOR S.D. S(C)RIPTORVM. PRINCEPS. EGO. NEC.
    OBITVRA. DEINCEPS
LAVS MEA NEC FAMA. QVIS SIM MEA LITTERA CLAMA.
LITTERA S.D. TE TVA S(C)RIPTVRA. QVEM.
SIGNAT PICTA FIGVRA I.O.
PREDICAT EADWINVM FAMA PER SECULA VIVUM.
INGENIUM CVIVS LIBRI DECUS INDICAT HVIVS
QVEM TIBI SEQVE DATVM MVNVS DEUS ACCIPE GRATVM.

Fig. 121.
Munich, Bayerischesstaatsbibliothek, Ms. Clm. 15903, f.5v.
Pericopes of St. Erentrude, Joseph warned by an angel.

Eadwine's fulsome self-praise could hardly breathe a more different spirit than the humble words of Georgius, who wrote the mid-eighth-century copy of Gregory's *Dialogues* at Bobbio, or those of Prior Petrus in the colophon of the Silos Beatus Apocalypse in the British Museum.

Around 1200, the Utrecht Psalter compositions were once more adapted in a Psalter, presumably written and partly illuminated at Canterbury, which is now in the Bibliothèque Nationale in Paris (Ms. lat. 8846).[3] Psalm 11 (12) is illustrated on f.20 (Fig. 117). As in the Eadwine copy, the general composition and the individual elements are as they are in the Utrecht proto-type (Fig. 61, Plate VII), but it seems probable that Eadwine's book was the immediate model.[4] The style, however, has been greatly transformed. The miniature is painted in full, heavy color, predominantly red and blue with a background of highly burnished gold, and framed in colored bands. The gestures of the figures are much the same, but the forms are larger in scale and fill more of the picture area. The rolling landscape of the Eadwine drawing has been further systematized in a series of flat, sinuous bands, dividing the composition into two-dimensional areas with convoluted edges, peopled with figures outlined in slowly moving con-tours, clothed in ponderous draperies, and with strongly modeled faces. No trace remains of the suggestion of atmospheric space still retained in the Utrecht Psalter from its late antique source, conveyed by the sketchy lines and wind-whipped contours of its forms. And the lingering reminiscence in the Eadwine miniature of classical architecture in the shop of the silver smelters has vanished in the systematic conventionalizing of all the shapes that eliminates any vestige of spatial per-spective, sacrificed to what Erwin Panofsky has aptly termed "surface consolidation."[5] Gone too is the ani-mated narrative that gives such vitality to the Utrecht and Harley miniatures. Instead, there is a new gravity and monumentality that is the very essence of Roman-esque content, implicit in the stately rhythms and strong colors of the two-dimensional patterns.

In these respects, Romanesque manuscript illumina-tion is analogous in style and content to the other representational arts of the time—mural painting, sculpture, and ivory carving, enamel, and goldsmith work.[6] However, manuscript illumination in the twelfth century and thereafter loses something of the pride of place it enjoyed, numerically speaking at least, in earlier

Fig. 122.
Darmstadt, Landesmuseum, Ms. 680, f.24. Gospel-book
from Cologne, Christ in Glory.

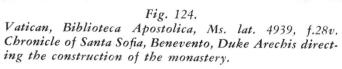

Fig. 124.
*Vatican, Biblioteca Apostolica, Ms. lat. 4939, f.28v.
Chronicle of Santa Sofia, Benevento, Duke Arechis direct-
ing the construction of the monastery.*

Fig. 123.
*ttgart, Württembergische Landesbibliothek, Cod. H.B.
Bibl. 24, f.91v. The Landgraf Psalter, Christ's Descent
o Limbo.*

times. The law of survival undoubtedly had something to do with this, but it is also owing in part to the changing role of book illustration in relationship to the other arts. Pre-Romanesque illumination frequently provides the norm or frame of reference for the other media; in the Romanesque period, it is more likely to move along lines first charted in other arts, notably monumental sculpture. Herein lies one reason for the continuation of Romanesque style in illumination in some regions long after it had given way to the Gothic in other art forms.

There are many more illuminated manuscripts from the Romanesque period than from earlier comparable time spans, and while survival assuredly was a factor, this must also be a consequence of changes in the general culture and economic system that made possible the increase in church building that began in the eleventh century, bringing a greater demand for scriptural and liturgical texts, which was met by the establishment of many new scriptoria. Instead of the relatively few major centers of production in the eleventh century, there were many in the twelfth. The majority of these were still largely monastic, but more various and individual styles quickly developed. At the same time, there was more interaction between styles, indicating a considerable movement of books from place to place, as had been the case with the Utrecht Psalter, but on a much wider scale. Thus a Gospel-book in the Laurentian Library in Florence (Ms. Acq. e Doni 91) with Evangelist portraits and a miniature of the Ascension, apparently written and partly illuminated in the late tenth or early eleventh century in an Ottonian scriptorium, probably Reichenau, had the initial Gospel pages decorated a century or so later in what appears to be a Tuscan style.[7]

German Romanesque illumination of the twelfth and early thirteenth centuries was, understandably, long under the influence of Ottonian eleventh-century style. This is true in particular of the earlier phases, in which reminiscences of classical form transmitted by eleventh-century intermediaries are quite apparent. Later on, continuing and strengthening ties with more western centers, and renewed contact with Byzantine art, led to the formation of a highly dynamic manner, characterized by sharp linear patterns and angular movements, the so-called jagged style, which is almost baroque in quality and spirit. Many new centers came into existence, with recognizable regional characteristics, replacing the Ottonian scriptoria. This was partly the result of changing circumstances of patronage. There is little in German Romanesque illumination to compare with the royal and state commissions of the late tenth and early eleventh centuries. Instead, the most productive centers were in the monasteries where the Cluniac reform had been introduced.

Suebia and the area around Lake Constance formed one such region. At Hirsau, one of the German monasteries in the Cluniac community, a Passional of the second decade of the twelfth century (Stuttgart, Landesbibliothek, Cod. bibl. fol. 56–58) was illuminated with miniatures executed in a predominantly linear manner (Fig. 118). The one on f.218 (Cod. fol. 57) is of St. Gertrude the Virgin and her mother, the latter cutting her daughter's hair as she prepares to leave the temptations of the world for life in the cloister. The text is a characteristic product of a time in which an unusually large number of women appeared to be seeking spiritual guidance. The rather slender figures are in a linear style which continues one aspect of Ottonian art (Fig. 87), but their rather static quality and the geometric pattern of the whole are of the twelfth century.

An outstanding center of Romanesque illumination in Suebia was the monastery of Weingarten near Lake Constance, not far from Reichenau. This geographic factor was one influence on the style of Weingarten miniatures, but even more important was the patronage of the monastery by the aristocratic Guelph family. For it was to a member of this family that Countess Judith of Flanders was married after the death of her Anglo-Saxon husband, Tostig of Northumbria, at the battle of Hastings. As patroness of the Benedictine monastery at Weingarten, she left it her library in 1094, including the Gospel-book named for her (N. Y., Pierpont Morgan Library, Ms. 709: cf. Fig. 95) along with some other Anglo-Saxon and Flemish manuscripts.[8] Within the first quarter of the twelfth century, the influence of the several styles is evident in Weingarten books produced during the regime of Abbot Cuno (1109–1132), such as a lectionary (Fulda, Landesbibliothek, Ms. Aa. 35), which is probably among those listed in the abbey archives as the work of "Odalricus custos." The miniature of the Three Holy Women at the Tomb and Christ appearing to them (Fig. 119) is clearly related to Ottonian work of the "Liuthard group" in the rather short figures with rounded heads and the details of the foliage. But the figures move with something of Anglo-Saxon and Franco-Flemish animation (Figs. 94, 109), and the border foliage, for all its echoes of Reichenau (Fig. 77), is disposed in a trellis that could have been inspired only by a Winchester prototype (Fig. 96).

Weingarten illumination reached a climax about a century later in a group of books identified with Abbot Berthold, among them the Missal bearing his name (N. Y., Pierpont Morgan Library, Ms. 710) in which there is a list of books he commissioned during his abbacy from 1200 until 1232. The Nativity and Annunciation to the Shepherds (Fig. 120) is on f.16v. The strong, saturated colors and vigorous drawing construct forms of such plasticity that they seem almost to have been sculptured. The pictorial technique, especially the modeling color of the shadows and the white highlights, follows Byzantine usage, while the dramatic gestures and intense expressions that make the figures so expressive reveal the impact of Anglo-Saxon style on the Weingarten miniaturist. But the composition as a whole is the achievement of a highly original artist. The miniatures of the Berthold Missal are approached by but few others of its time and surpassed by none in the sense of abstract power created by the patterns of interwoven curving lines in the figures, the forceful juxtapositions of vigorous colors, and the lavish use of gold and silver in the backgrounds and decorative motives.

At Salzburg, manuscript illumination in the early twelfth century continued the tradition established in Ottonian work of the eleventh century with little change. A group of large Bibles like the one from Admont (Vienna, NB, Ser. Nov. 2701)[9] are illuminated in a style continuing the refined Byzantinisms of "Custos Berthold's" manner (cf. Fig. 86). Later in the twelfth century, there is evidence of a strong and more direct influence from Byzantium in the miniatures of the Pericopes of St. Erentrude (Munich, SB, Ms. lat. 15903) which can be dated around 1150. The Angel Awakening Joseph (Fig. 121) on f.5v repeats the theme and many features of Custos Berthold's version, like the gabled building of the setting, but in a style that is much more animated. The composition is more vertical, the drawing more dynamic; the difference between the two is a paradigm of the change from pre-Romanesque to Romanesque quality. The opaque colors are strong and the drawing is forceful, creating forms that are much more plastic than in the Ottonian miniature. The overall effect is an expressionism that is more reticent than the intense Weingarten quality, but none the less monumental for that. If the Weingarten miniatures invite comparison with contemporary sculpture, the spirit of

the Salzburg Pericope illustrations is no less evident in mural paintings like those in Kloster Nonnberg at Salzburg itself.[10]

Cologne was an important Romanesque center in all the arts. Notable styles in ivory carving and enamel work were developed there in the twelfth century, and many illuminated manuscripts were produced in the numerous monasteries of the region.[11] A Gospel-book of about 1130 (Darmstadt, Landesmuseum, Ms. 680) contains, along with the usual Evangelist portraits, a Christ in Glory (Fig. 122) on f.24. The relatively sober color scheme suggests comparison with earlier Ottonian work, with its pronounced Byzantinisms (Fig. 83), and the formula of structural proportions is also in the Byzantine tradition, particularly in the face and head. But the prevailingly pictorial Ottonian manner has given way to a pronounced linearism. The drapery folds are reduced to a few curving lines and the contours are simplified, creating an effect of monumental quietude. This, along with the gold background and the slow rhythm of the emphatic contours, invites comparison with contemporary work in enamel, which is not surprising since Cologne was an important center of this art, as has been mentioned. It proximity to the Flemish metal-work centers should also be taken into account. Indeed, just as the stylistic orientation of the more easterly centers like Salzburg was toward Byzantium, that of Cologne was westward, to Stavelot and later to the work of Nicholas of Verdun.[12] The relationship between him and Cologne Romanesque illumination is very apparent in the miniatures of a Gospel-book of the early thirteenth century in the Bibliothèque Royale of Brussels (Ms. 9222).[13]

Saxony in northern Germany had been the locale of important manuscript production in the Ottonian period, in centers like Corvey and Hildesheim. Around the middle of the twelfth century, the latter assumed new importance from the canonization of Bernward, its great abbot in the early eleventh century. From then and thereafter came a number of distinctive Hildesheim books, such as the Ratman Missal in the city cathedral treasury.[14] It may also have been in Hildesheim that a number of important works were commissioned in the early thirteenth century by Landgrave Hermann of Thuringia.[15] Two of these are outstanding, the Landgraf Psalter made for Hermann himself (Stuttgart, LB, HB II Bibl. 24),[16] and the so-called Psalter of St. Elizabeth in the Biblioteca Communale at Cividale in northern Italy (Codici sacri 7). The former can be dated 1212

Fig. 126.
*Perugia, Biblioteca Augusta, Ms. L. 59, f.2. Bible, The
Creation of the stars, fish and birds.*

with some certainty, and both were executed before the Landgrave's death in 1217.

Christ's Descent into Limbo (Fig. 123) on f.51v of the Landgrave Psalter illustrates the style well. Red and blue dominate the color scheme of the figures, which appear against a burnished gold ground and are contained within a plain banded border. They are strongly modeled by a system of highlights in which renewed Byzantine influence is seen, but it is used in conjunction with drapery patterns of hard and jagged folds that give great animation to the whole. A particularly effective touch is the harsh intersection of the border by the flying hem of Christ's robe. Although approximately contemporary with the Berthold Missal miniatures (Fig. 120) and comparable to them in expressionistic intention, the angular patterns of the Landgrave composi-

tions create a strikingly different content, which eminently justifies their characterization as "baroque."

The prominence of Byzantine elements in this thirteenth-century Saxon style has been explained by renewed contacts with the Near East during the Crusades, and a parallel has been seen in the somewhat similar phenomenon in work contemporary with it in the Hohenstaufen provinces of lower Italy. A pattern book in the Landesbibliothek at Wolfenbüttel (Ms. Aug. 8°. 61/2),[17] a precious example of the models used by mediaeval illuminators, shows that mid-Byzantine prototypes were widely used and understood at the time, but the static and rigid forms of the model were given new and characteristic energy by the harshly angular rhythms and movements of Saxon style. The structure of the developed initials in these Thuringian manu-

scripts[18] expresses the same energetic spirit. The plaited interlaces and curling tips of the foliage twining around humans and animals are a clear indication of the artist's familiarity with English work, a conclusion supported by both the type of book involved, the Psalter, and certain iconographic details. Luxury manuscripts of the psalm texts like these, intended for private use, were first developed in the early twelfth century in England; later, the Psalter became the preferred book for personal as distinguished from public devotions when selected prayers were combined with it in the Book of Hours. The theme of Christ's Descent into Limbo, or the Harrowing of Hell as it is also known, is a subject first used in England in illustrating psalter texts.

Romanesque style in Italian illumination is like that of Germany in taking form rather early in the twelfth century and continuing for some time into the thirteenth. Also as in Germany, regional characteristics established earlier tend to continue, but all ultimately are subjected to recurrent influences from Byzantium. Thus, although Monte Cassino declined as a productive center after its floruit under Desiderius (1052–1087) its influence remained strong in scriptoria like the one at Santa Sofia in Benevento, as can be seen in the miniatures of the monastery chronicle (Vatican, Bibl. Apost. Ms. lat. 4939), which was written about 1120. On f.28v, its founder, Duke Arechis, supervises the construction of the monastery (Fig. 124). The strongly Byzantinizing character of the style developed in Desiderius' books (cf. Fig. 108) is unmistakable. The forms are painted in thick, opaque pigments, directly on the parchment and with modeling white highlights on the darker flesh surfaces. Byzantine too is the all-over pattern of medallions painted in white dots on the duke's vermilion robe, as well as the architecture of the building. Only in its more plastically realized forms and the freer gestures of the figures are there indications of the chronological separation of the Santa Sofia miniature from its proto-Romanesque predecessor. The IN of plait-work, foliage, and animals at the top of the page is equally in the Monte Cassino tradition, with juxtaposed bands of gold and color lined with white dots.

In a modified form, the Monte Cassino initial type appears in a Gospel-book in the Biblioteca Vallicelliana in Rome (Ms. E. 16), which is dated 1104. The manuscript belonged to the monastery at Farfa, near Rome, in the thirteenth century; it may have been written at Subiaco or in Rome itself. Although there was an important school of mural painting in Rome earlier in the Middle Ages, scholars do not agree on the possibility of a distinctive Roman tradition in manuscript illumination.[19] It is thought by some that the mid-eleventh-century "giant Bibles" (cf. Fig. 106) may have originated in the Roman region, but this has been argued. The Evangelists in the Vallicelliana Gospel-book, like St. Luke (Fig. 125, Plate XIX) on f.96, wear particolored robes, green and red in this instance, and this is possibly a Roman stylistic convention. For the rest, the frontally seated figure and the aedicule of his throne follow Byzantine precedent, but the attenuated body, with its spread knees and tilted head, are Romanesque in the sense of movement and animation. Even the large initial Q, for all its obvious derivation from the Monte Cassino type of mingled plait-work and foliage, differs from it in the open design with color only in the background, the more florid leaf patterns, and the restricted use of animal forms.

Whether or not the eleventh-century "giant Bibles" were a Roman creation, there is no doubt that most of their twelfth-century counterparts were produced in central Italy;[20] an example is in the Biblioteca Augusta of Perugia (Ms. L. 59). As the generic name implies, it is quite large, measuring 54 by 35.5 cm (21.25 x 14"). At the beginning are several miniatures illustrating the Creation scenes from Genesis, among them the Creation of the Stars, Fish, and Birds (Fig. 126) on f.2 as related in Genesis 1:14–22. The opaque colors are heavily painted, red and blue predominant with touches of green and lavender. The bands of the border are gold, as are the nimbi of the Creator and the rim of His aureoled throne.[21] In technique, the dark flesh tones with broad whitened highlights follow Byzantine practice, but the drawing seems more Ottonian, particularly the rhythmically curving patterns of robes and fingers (cf. Fig. 82), as does also the stately and formal composition. The color harmonies are distinctly Italian, however, and the monumental quality of the plastic forms and their design is characteristically Romanesque. The Perugia Bible is also a typical expression of twelfth-century sentiment in being a monumentally embellished text of the entire Scriptures. Although such all-inclusive Biblical texts were produced in pre-Romanesque times (e.g., Figs. 65, 66 [Plate VIII]–68, 97–98 [Plate XV]), most of the books then illuminated were for liturgical use—Gospel-books, lectionaries, and the like. The twelfth-century Bibles, on the other hand, were intended for more general use, for study and contemplation, and for reading aloud at meal times in the mo-

Fig. 127.
Vatican, Biblioteca Apostolica, Ms. lat. 4922, f.7v. Life of Matilda of Tuscany, Donizonus presenting the book to the Countess.

nastic refectories.[22] More than any other period, the twelfth century was that of the illuminated Bible in all parts of the Occidental Christian world.

In north Italian Romanesque illumination, there are strong trans-Alpine overtones as in pre-Romanesque work. From the early years of the twelfth century comes the Life of Matilda of Tuscany (Vatican, Bibl. Apost., Ms. lat. 4922), the biography of the redoubtable countess written by a monk Donizonus in the monastery at Canossa not far from Reggio Emilia. There is some reason to believe that the Vatican copy was corrected by the author for his patroness, hence it may be dated before her death in 1115.[23] She is shown in the miniature (Fig. 127) on f.7v receiving the volume from the author, enthroned between him and an armed dignitary. The concept is similar to that in the Carolin-

gian dedication pages (Fig. 67) and their Ottonian descendants, even to the heavily painted purple background. The flattened Byzantinesque forms and the decorative patterning of the wide gold bands of the Countess's robe and its sleeves were doubtless of similar derivation. But the emphatically contoured silhouettes of figures in other miniatures in the book,[24] which are only partially colored, and the movement of their bent knees and elbows, are fully Romanesque in their animation.

Ottonian overtones are even more pronounced in the miniatures of an Evangelary (a compilation of Gospel readings or pericopes for the principal church festivals) in the treasury of the cathedral at Padua.[25] It is signed as the work, both written and painted, of a certain Isidoro, *doctor bonus,* whose portrait also appears in the colophon on f.85v, where the date of 1185 is recorded as well. The Nativity and Annunciation to the Shepherds (Fig. 128) are portrayed on f.1v, one of the eight full-page miniatures of New Testament subjects illustrated in the book, which also contains numerous initials with human and animal figures and grotesques. The stylistic characteristics that have led to comparison with the Reichenau "Liuthar" group of Ottonian miniatures[26] are obvious. The gables and turrets of the architectural setting of the Nativity are like those in much Ottonian illumination (cf. Fig. 86). But the rather small figures in the Annunciation to the Shepherds, with their flowing contours and rhythmic drapery folds, gesturing animatedly with long-fingered hands, their small bullet heads having sharply peering eyes, are the immediate descendants of those enacting the same theme in the Pericopes of Henry II (Fig. 82). From the same general stylistic source came the color scheme—shaded greens and pinks and lavenders, with spots of blue, vermilion, and purple, set against a plain gold ground. The somewhat coarse drawing is the most distinctively Romanesque quality of the style as a whole.

English illumination after the Conquest of 1066 shows no marked differences immediately from the Anglo-Saxon style of the earlier part of the century, as has been seen. At the same time, in miniatures like the Crucifixion in the Psalter (B.M. Arundel 60) from Winchester New Minster (Fig. 96), the more monumental and decorative quality of Romanesque style is foreshadowed. What that manner was to be by mid-twelfth century has been touched upon in the discussion of the Eadwine Psalter, a manner that had been anticipated in the first half of the century in manu-

Fig. 128.
Padua, Biblioteca Capitolare del Duomo, unnumbered ms., f.1v. Evangelary of 1170, The Nativity and Annunciation to the Shepherds.

Fig. 129.
Florence, Biblioteca Laurenziana, Ms. Plut. 12, 17, ff.3v–4.
St. Augustine, De Civitate Dei, St. Augustine and his
followers. (Photo Pineider)

scripts from a number of English scriptoria that became important then, along with the older centers at Canterbury and Winchester. The individual styles of these centers are usually quite distinctive, yet they all have formal and expressive characteristics in common that make them representative of developed Romanesque concepts.

A manuscript of St. Augustine's *City of God (De Civitate Dei)* in the Laurentian Library in Florence (Ms. Plut. 12. 17), which once belonged to Piero de' Medici, is believed to have come from St. Augustine's at Canterbury. Written and illuminated in all probability about 1130, it contains two miniatures, among others, that represent St. Augustine, as an author accompanied by his disciples, and a group of clerics in animated discussion (Fig. 129), on ff.3v/4.[27] The linear patterns of the arguing figures are executed in red, green, and brown, with a minimum of shading. It is a style in the expressive impressionistic tradition of the early eleventh century, as in the Harley 603 copy

of the Utrecht Psalter (Fig. 91) but carried a step farther than is seen in the late eleventh-century Crucifixion of Arundel 60 (Fig. 96). St. Augustine and his companions on f.3v are also drawn, rather than painted, but the patterns of colored lines portraying them are placed against red and green backgrounds, colors that also fill the spaces between the leaves and tendrils of the foliage in the borders. The leaves still turn back at the tips to clutch the trellis bars, but both they and the stems have a curiously metallic quality, revealing the Romanesque predilection for pattern over representation that is one of the significant points of difference between eleventh- and twelfth-century styles, underlying the more monumental quality of the latter.

That continental influences contributed at least in part to these changes in style and content in English Romanesque illumination cannot be doubted. The turrets and spires of the architectural frames are directly comparable to similar forms in Ottonian miniatures (Fig. 86), as are also the medallion heads in the borders of the miniature of the arguing clerics.[28] But the grave dignity of the seated Augustine is Romanesque, resulting from the same restraint that controls the gestures and poses of his followers despite the linear animation of flying drapery folds, crossed legs, and jutting chins. For the line defining these forms has changed still more from the wispy arabesques that give such vitality to the drawings in Harley 603 than it had in Arundel 60. Ultimately it will become the idiom of crisp outlines by which the shapes in the drawings of Eadwine's Psalter (Fig. 115) achieve their essential character of pattern rather than representation. In the same way, the portrait of Eadwine (Fig. 116) is the complete statement of those characteristics of style and content that differentiate the Romanesque manner of the Augustine portrait from the proto-Romanesque of the late eleventh century.

Among the new centers of English manuscript illumination in the twelfth century was the Benedictine Abbey at St. Albans, a few miles north of London. Although an old foundation, its period of greatest affluence and authority came during rebuilding after the Conquest, marked in its first stage by the consecration of the abbey church in 1115. Shortly thereafter, between 1119 and 1146, the manuscript called the Albani Psalter[29] was written and illuminated there for an English anchoress of distinguished ancestry named Christina; it is now in the treasury of St. Godehard's Church at Hildesheim in Germany. Note has been taken of the special role of the psalter as a liturgical book in the twelfth century in addition to its traditional identification as the principal text for private devotions, as it was for the Carolingian and Ottonian emperors, for example. The change in the twelfth century, and earlier in England than elsewhere, came about, in part at least, in response to the desires of a new and different patronage—ladies of the aristocracy such as she for whom the Albani Psalter was made. In meeting it, changes were also made to include themes not previously much encountered in psalter illustration, in particular subjects from the life of Christ. There are forty-six such New Testament episodes in the Albani Psalter, one of the first examples of this type of illuminated psalter in which the calendar, traditionally the initial part of the book, is followed by the Biblical scenes. There are also miniatures of special saints, David and his musicians, and numerous decorated initials.

Three individual styles have been identified in the Albani Psalter miniatures, the most noteworthy in the forty-six dealing with the life of Christ. One of these

is the Annunciation (Fig. 130, Plate XX) on p. 19. As in the approximately contemporary miniature of St. Augustine in the Laurenziana City of God (Fig. 129), the forms are rendered as patterns of line rather than portrayed as shapes. The thin and attenuated figures, traditionally Anglo-Saxon in this respect, are somewhat angular in stance and gesture. But unlike most earlier English work and much of the same period, the miniatures are executed in full color—blues and greens, reds and purples—with strong contours and highlights of white lines that fan over the surfaces and are set off by shadows in darker tones of the base color.[30] This color scheme, for all its vivid hues, is a factor in creating a severe, not to say austere, effect, to which the solemn expressions and rhythmically measured gestures also contribute. The backgrounds are varicolored, and the whole composition is bordered with panels in which bird forms alternate with a modified meander motive rendered in perspective and shaded color.

Many of these characteristics of the Albani Psalter miniatures of the life of Christ, and others like the architectural details, suggest a more direct Byzantine influence on English style than any as yet seen, and one that is more fully understood. This has suggested to some scholars that the miniatures may be the work of an artist from a continental scriptorium, or that they were imported from such a center under strong and direct Byzantine influence.[31] However this may have been, the style proved to be immediately congenial, once it was introduced. A manuscript of the Life and Miracles of St. Edmund in the Pierpont Morgan Library (Ms. 736) from Bury St. Edmunds, another active center of illumination in the early twelfth century, shows it adapted to English taste in a work of about 1135.[32]

Illuminated texts of the complete Bible are among the most distinctive Romanesque books, as has already been mentioned. Understandably, such texts had always been important; note has been taken in discussing the Carolingian Bibles of Tours, of the probability that Early Christian prototypes of the fifth century were available as their models; the significance of the great Bible in the Laurentian Library in Florence, the *Codex Amiatinus,* for both illustrative and technical reasons has also been touched upon. But as a class, the Romanesque twelfth-century Bibles differ from earlier ones in a number of respects. Written for the most part in the larger minuscule[33] that distinguishes most twelfth-century script from earlier hands since the volumes were often intended to be read from aloud in public, their dimensions are considerable, and the text usually requires more than one book. The greater size of these multi-volume twelfth-century Bibles also provided more area to be decorated than their single-volume Carolingian predecessors, and the repertory of illustrative themes is much more rich and varied.

Giant Bibles were produced in all the principal Romanesque regions but nowhere on a more impressive scale and with greater variety of illustration than in England. An early example from Bury St. Edmunds (Cambridge, Corpus Christi College, Ms. 2)[34] is to be dated between 1121 and 1148, when payments were made to "Master Hugo" for work on it. Hugo was a secular artist, unusual at that time, and was renowned for his work in metal and sculpture as well as his illuminating. The Lambeth Bible (London, Lambeth Palace, Ms. 3, & Maidstone, Museum, Ms. P 5),[35] a product of Canterbury between 1130 and 1140, is a monumental work in two volumes, measuring 52.2 x 34.4 cm (20.5" x 13.5"). But perhaps the most notable English Romanesque Bible is the one made in the latter part of the twelfth century for Winchester Cathedral and now in its library.[36]

Although the illumination of the Winchester Bible was never completed, it is still one of the most lavishly ornamented English books of its kind. The original scheme called for an elaborated initial at the beginning of each book,[37] and more for some, like the Book of Psalms. In addition, two full-page miniatures were designed and drawn but not painted, whether as an afterthought or not is unclear,[38] and two more on the recto and verso of a detached folio were completed but seem never to have been part of the book; it is now in the Pierpont Morgan Library in New York (Ms. 619). It must certainly have been intended for the Bible, however, as its dimensions are the same (51.7 x 41.2 cm: 23 x 15.75"), the script of the chapter headings on the recto is identical with that of the book text, and the style of the illuminated scenes from the life of David (Fig. 131) on the verso is found also in some of its initials. The three registers of the miniature have heavily painted backgrounds of red, tan, and blue, against which the figures appear in almost sculptural relief. They are executed in a modeling technique strongly reminiscent of Byzantine practice with green shadows on rather yellow flesh tones.[39] The figures are somewhat elongated and their movements are rather angular, but they are not so extreme in these respects as those of the earlier Albani Psalter; their relatively greater naturalism is enhanced by the rhythmically modulated drapery patterns, which effectively express the plastic volumes of the forms they cover.

In these characteristics, the miniature in the Morgan Library and many of the initials in the Winchester Bible reveal the consequences of a new and rather direct wave of Byzantine influence on the English style of manuscript illumination. Though the degree of this influence varies among the five artists whose hands have been identified in the initials, the fact that there was such influence cannot be doubted, particularly in view of the appearance of a Byzantine technique in the use of gold in some of the later miniatures. In them, the metal was applied as gold leaf upon a viscous white base and burnished, whereas in what appear to be the earlier initials, it has the granular texture of liquid gold applied directly on the parchment usually found in Anglo-Saxon and English illumination of a preceding era.[40] Moreover, a direct relationship in style has been pointed out between that of the Morgan leaf artist and the manner of the mosaics in the cathedral at Cefalù in Sicily,[41] a country with which the English were frequently in contact during the twelfth century.[42] And the style of the Lambeth Bible differs from earlier English work in much the same way, anticipating the developments in the Winchester Bible.[43]

The miniatures of the latest copy of the Utrecht Psalter (Fig. 117) made at Canterbury between 1170 and 1200[44] also reveal Byzantine influence in the technique of massive impasto and burnished gold, and in the more convincing if still conventionalized realism of the figures. In this way, they exemplify, like the figures of the Winchester Bible miniatures and initials, the new monumentality of developed Romanesque style, concurrent with and expressive of the same ideals set forth in the massive stone architecture and the plastically conceived sculptured figures of the period. All are expressions in their individual media of the increasing humanism of twelfth-century thought, summed up in the eclectic philosophy of John of Salisbury (c. 1120–1180), which is often called a renaissance.[45] In art, it anticipates the Gothic spirit of the thirteenth century; one of the most characteristically English mediaeval books reveals much the same point of view—the Bestiary.[46]

The text of the mediaeval bestiary was drawn from a variety of classical scientific writings about the characteristics of animals, birds, and fish. By the time it was being compiled, from the eighth to the tenth centuries,

Fig. 131.
New York, Pierpont Morgan Library, Ms. 619, f.1v. Leaf
in the style of the Winchester Bible. Scenes in the Life of
David.

the interpretation of such natural forms as symbols of theological concepts had begun to take shape. Illustration of the text may have begun in Carolingian times, but the iconography does not appear to have been established before the twelfth century; one of the earliest illustrated examples known, in the Bodleian Library at Oxford (Ms. Laud. Misc. 247), is of about 1125, with drawings in brown ink.[47] But the theme soon became popular and a number of copies dating before the end of the twelfth century are known, including one in the Pierpont Morgan Library (Ms. 81) that was

probably written and illustrated near Lincoln about 1170. Several miniatures illustrate the nature and character of the Lion, the one on f.8 (Fig. 132) being of the passage describing how the lion cubs are born dead but come to life when the father breathes on them after three days. The text goes on to point out that this is symbolic of Christ's death and resurrection after the third day. The Saviour appears above, in the enlarged initial B with which the text begins.

In style, the miniatures of the Morgan Bestiary have the same frank red and blue coloring with burnished

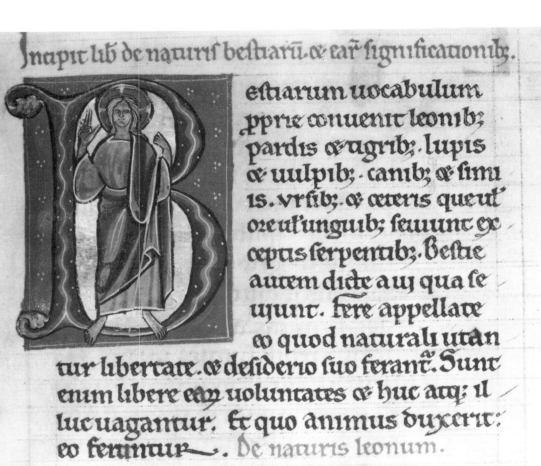

gold backgrounds observed in the other late twelfth-century English manuscripts that have been discussed. The Saviour's draperies fall in elegantly curvilinear folds, and the lions in the lower miniature are well modeled and plastically conceived, for all their physiological ambiguity. In these respects, they anticipate the larger scale and more monumental character of the Gothic, qualities in which the script of the text also shares. For although it still has the amplitude of Carolingian minuscule, the vertical strokes occasionally end in spikes and the curved ones in points. As a result, the letters appear longer and narrower, and the visual effect is no longer horizontal but vertical, the palaeographic parallel of the pointed arches that began about this time to replace the semicircular ones of Romanesque building.

Manuscript illumination of the early twelfth century in northwestern France and Flanders, the region of the so-called Channel School of the early eleventh century, continued under English influence. A portrait of John the Evangelist (Fig. 133, Plate XXI) is one of two, all that remains of an impressive Gospel-book made at Liessies during the abbacy of Wédric (1124–1147): it is in the Société Archéologique at Avesnes. Wédric is shown in the central medallion of the right border holding the Evangelist's inkwell, and episodes from the saint's life appear in those at the angles. The miniature is of considerable size (35.5 x 24 cm: c. 14.5 x 9.5″), befitting the monumental design. The border trellis and curling acanthus leaves gripping the bands harks back to Winchester (Fig. 90, Plate XIV). But the broad drapery patterns of continuous contours and interior lines fanning out in textured areas are so close to similar effects in mid-twelfth-century English work, particularly in Canterbury books like the Eadwine Psalter (Fig. 116) and the Lambeth Bible, that it has been thought to be by an English artist.[48] In other respects, like the doubling of the contours into an almost metallic rim and the white linear highlights, the style of the Liessies Evangelist is close to mid-ninth-century Byzantine practice, which was probably known through ivory carvings rather than paintings or miniatures.[49] As a whole, the Liessies miniature shows the decorative hardening or crystallization that foreshadows the developed Romanesque style of the later twelfth century.

The Romanesque decorative quality of the Liessies St. John is also a characteristic of the portrait of St. Gregory (Fig. 134, Plate XXII) that is the frontispiece (f.1v) of a copy of his *Letters* written and illuminated in the Flemish monastery of Saint-Amand (Paris, BN, Ms. lat. 2287) in the second half of the twelfth century. The matte gold background is covered with incised simplified rinceaux, the saint's red mantle falls from his shoulders in lines that fan out to cover the broad surfaces with a network pattern, and the blue-gray lower robe is disposed in broad ellipses of swirling lines over the thighs of the seated figure.[50] The shaded patterns of these folds creates an impression of form and three-dimensional plastic shapes, to which the modeling shadows of the hands, face, and neck also contribute. All this constitutes a definition of form in abstract terms, a form that is not naturalistic but nonetheless has the qualities of bulk and material substance, which are the elements of a more human conception than that embodied in the comparatively two-dimensional and graphic patterns of the Liessies Evangelist.

A large two-volume Bible (London, BM, Ms. add. lat. 17737–8) from Floreffe, near Namur in eastern Flanders, contains some miniatures characterized by much the same plastic quality noted in the Saint-Amand Gregory. The Ascension of Our Lord (Fig. 135) on f.199 appears above a symbolic representation of the New Dispensation. The manuscript may be dated about 1160. Floreffe is in the Maas or Mosan region of Flanders, where there was a long-established tradition of work in metal and enamel,[51] going back to Carolingian times, the style of which seems to have permeated the Floreffe Bible miniatures. The precise contours of the figures might enclose the colored enamels of a Mosan reliquary casket; the leaves of the foliate border are equally metallic in effect, and its inscribed outer band looks like nothing so much as the rim of an enameled plaque. The strong, saturated colors of draperies and background heighten the resemblance to goldsmith work. At the same time, the flowing contours and the treatment of the highlights create the same sense of three-dimensional form observed in the Saint-Amand St. Gregory. These are the characteristics of Mosan style that are echoed in some German work of the late twelfth and early thirteenth centuries, as noted in the discussion of the Cologne school. They are equally apparent in later twelfth-century illumination in western Flemish centers like Saint-Bertin, Saint-Amand, and Anchin; particularly striking examples can be seen in the miniatures of the Gospel-book of Hénin-Liétard from Saint-Bertin and a Life of St. Amandus from Saint-Bertin.[52]

Like many of the twelfth-century Romanesque Bibles,

Fig. 135.
London, British Museum, Add. ms. 17737–8, f.199. Bible
from Floreffe, The Ascension of Our Lord.

the one from Floreffe is very large, and while the illustration is not lavish, the changing thought of the time is revealed in its content. For example, the Ascension miniature on f.199 also contains a reference to the New Dispensation in the figure holding a scroll at the left end of the lower register. Its inscription equates Ezekiel's vision of the Four Beasts and the Wheel within a Wheel and the four-part account of Christ's life in the Four Gospels. The same concept is stated in the marginal inscription that the prophecies of the Old Testament are realized in the New. The idea that Old Testament subjects prefigured or foreshadowed New Testament truths is found earlier in Christian art; at least as early as the fifth century, it figures in the carved wooden doors of Santa Sabina in Rome[53] and is based on the *Dittochaeum* of the Early Christian writer Prudentius. But it appears in the Floreffe Bible miniature in a more systematic presentation anticipating the scholastic syntheses of the thirteenth century; it is as proto-Gothic in content as in its pictorial style.

One of the outstanding early twelfth-century scriptoria within the limits of modern France was in the Cistercian monastery at Cîteaux, near Dijon in Burgundy.[54] Its abbot from 1109 until 1133 was the English monk Stephen Harding, from Sherburne Abbey near Salisbury. He directed the completion of a great four-volume Bible begun by his predecessor, and was responsible for the writing and illumination of many other books, including a copy, also in four volumes, of a treatise by St. Gregory called *Moralia in Job.* (Dijon, Bibliothèque municipale, Mss. 168–170, 173); a colophon in the third volume gives the date of completion as 24 Dec., 1111.

A distinctive feature of the *Moralia in Job* illumination is the series of figured initials representing scenes and episodes in the daily life of the monks who, as Cistercians, were particularly concerned with such activities. The letter Q (Fig. 136) on f.92v of the fourth volume (Ms. 173) shows three monks making or dyeing cloth. Two standing ones bend over to form the circle, and the legs of the seated one are the queue. They are painted in opaque colors, red, pale yellow, and blue, handling the green cloth.[55] The theme is realistic in portraying an everyday incident of monastic life, and it is set forth in realistic terms. The figures are vividly characterized and differentiated, so much so that it has been surmised that the artist's fellow monks were his models and that he caricatured them amiably in representing them. The types, especially the standing figure on the

right with beak nose and heavy chin, might well be by an English artist, for such figures are at least foreshadowed in the vivid line drawings of late eleventh-century Anglo-Saxon manuscripts and paralleled in twelfth-century miniatures like those of the Eadwine Psalter (Fig. 115). But it is equally clear that using human figures to form initials rather than as adjuncts to them follows directly in the tradition of the eighth-century zoomorphic initials in Merovingian books (Figs. 38, 39). In any case, the humor of these lively vignettes of monastic life points the way to the marginal drolleries of later Gothic illumination.

A different spirit pervades the miniatures in another Cîteaux manuscript, a copy of St. Jerome's *Commentary on Isaiah* (Dijon, Bibl. Mun., Ms. 129), which was probably executed between 1125 and 1130. On f.4v, the standing Virgin with the Christ Child is actually part of a Tree of Jesse, so identified by the inscription *Egredietur virga* at the bottom of the page from Isaiah (11:1): "And there shall come forth a rod out of the stem of Jesse," and by the reclining figure from whose loins the tree grows. The symbolism is not stressed. Jesse and the tree are drawn in simple brown outline while the Virgin and Child and angels are touched and modeled with red, yellow, green, and blue,[56] a difference in emphasis that is an expression of the particular devotion of the Cistercian order to the Virgin Mary. And the appearance of the Jesse Tree theme even in this simple

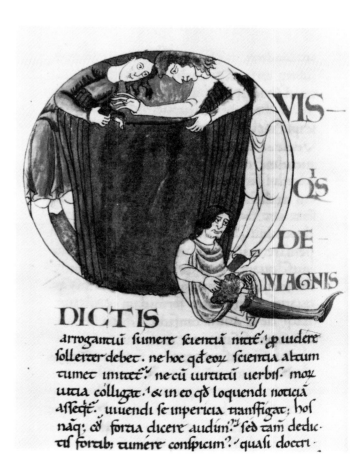

Fig. 136.
Dijon, Bibliothèque municipale, Ms. 173, f.92v. Moralia in Job, Initial Q—monks making or dyeing cloth. (Photo Remy)

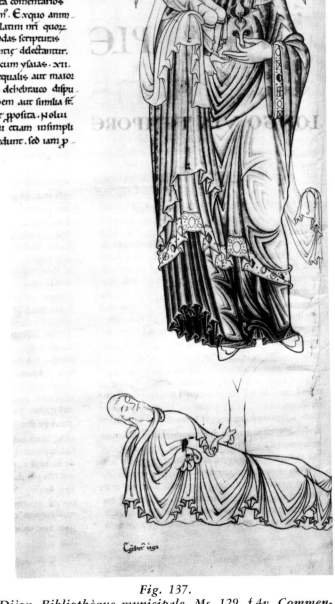

eidem unsionis tes platio devn. Duo ad gratiam li
bri. qui pseudographi putantur. & xxv. homelie
& chui co cie. quas nos excerpta possim appella
re. Eusebius quoq; pamphili. Juxta hystoricam ex
planatione quindecim edidit uolumina. Et didin
cui amicieris nup usi sum. ab eo loco ubi scriptum e
consolamini consolamini popim meu sacerdotes: loq
mini ad cor Inertm. usq; adfine uolumini decem
& octo edidit tomos. Appollinaris aut more suo sic
exposuit omia ut uniuersa transcurrat. & punctis
quibdam atq; interuallis. Jmmo compendiis. gran
dis uip spana preruolet. ut non ta comentarios
qua indices captom nos legere credam. Exquo anim
aduertis quante difficultatis sit ut latini mi quoq;
aures fastidiose sunt. & ad intellegendas scripturas
scas nauseant. plausuq; tanta doquentie delectantur.
m ignoscant si plixius locut fuero. cum ysaias. xii.
phis iuxta numeru uersuu aut equalis aut maior
sit. Sicubi aut pretermissit. Lxx. de hebraico dispu
tauit. illud incausa e quod aut eadem aut similia sit
pleraq; cu ceteris & duplici editione pposita. nolui
libros explanationis extendere qui etiam insimpli
ci expositione modu breuitatis excedunt. sed iam p
positum persequar.

form is prophetic of its later popularity, as in one of the famous stained-glass windows in the ambulatory chapels of Suger's church at Saint-Denis built a short time afterward[57] (Fig. 137).

More than symbolism, however, distinguishes the content of the Virgin and Child-Jesse Tree miniature from earlier Cîteaux work. As in the *Moralia in Job* initial, the forms are lightly indicated, but where they are rather sketchily rendered there, these figures are carefully drawn in lines that are, for all their lightness, firm and precise; the drapery fold hanging in mid-air by the Virgin's left knee is almost metallic in the exact certitude of its outlines. The same remarkable draftsmanship in the principal forms creates a sense of actuality in the figures, giving a monumental dignity to the whole on a scale far exceeding its modest physical dimensions. Again, as with comparable phenomena noted in other aspects of twelfth-century illumination, this new spirit seems to be the result of renewed Byzantine influences, influences which can be demonstrated in other Cîteaux manuscripts. In another Jesse Tree on f.40v of a Lectionary (Dijon, Bibl. mun., Mss. 641–642), the Virgin is identified by the Greek term *Theotokos,* and the border of a full-page miniature of Christ Enthroned with the Minor Prophets on f.2 of a *Commentary on Daniel* by St. Jerome (Dijon, Bibl. mun., Ms. 132) contains Cufic Arabic letters and Sassanian animals that could only have been copied from a Near Eastern model.[58]

Fig. 137.
Dijon, Bibliothèque municipale, Ms. 129, f.4v. Commentary of St. Jerome on Isaiah, The Virgin and Child and Tree of Jesse. (Photo Remy)

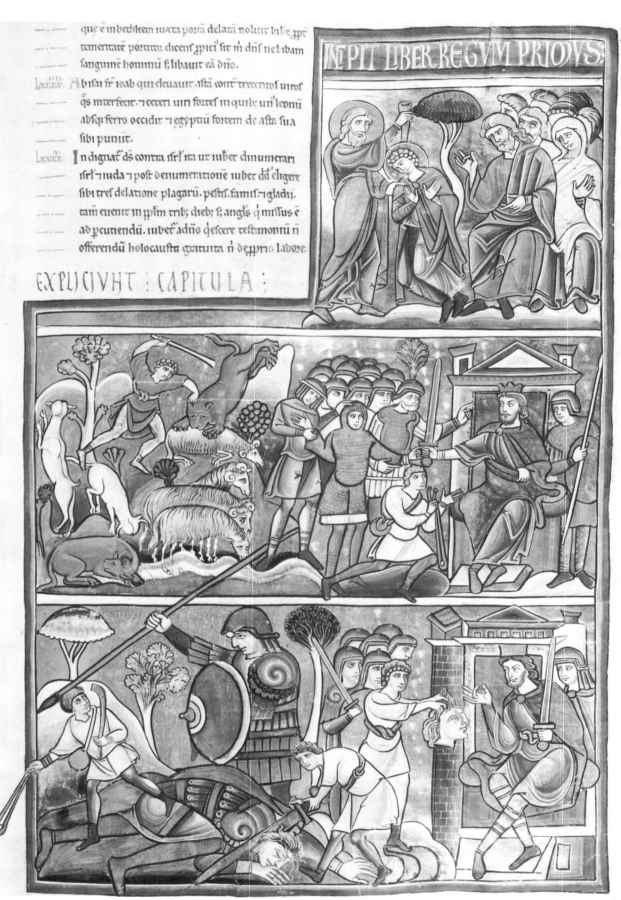

que e in bethleem iuxta porta delata noluit bibe ppt
temeritate portitor dicens ppiti sit m dns ne biba
sanguine hominu si libauit ea dno.

lxxiii. Abisai fr ioab qui eleuauit asta cont trecentos uiros
qs interfecit et ceteri uiri fortes in quib; un leonu
absq; ferro occidit et egyptiu fortem de asta sua
sibi puniit.

lxxxii. In dignat ds contra isrl ita ut iuber dinumerari
isrl et iuda et post denumeratione iuber dd eligere
sibi tres delatione plagaru. pestis. famis et gladii.
tam euenit in ppim trib; dieb; si angts q missus e
ad pcutiendu. iuber a dno qescere testimoniu n
offerendu holocaustu gratuita n de pprio labore.

EXPLICIVHT : CAPITULA :

INCIPIT LIBER REGVM PRIOVS

Fig. 138.
Moulins, Bibliothèque municipale, Ms. 1, f.93. The
Souvigny Bible, Scenes from the Life of David. (Photo
Giraudon)

The monastic life of manual labor at Cîteaux, so engagingly portrayed in the *Moralia in Job* initials, was an integral part of the Cistercian reform of the Benedictine order begun by its founder, Robert of Solesmes, and continued by Stephen Harding. The austere principles of its rule were set forth by an early member of the community near Dijon, Bernard, founder of the Cistercian house at Clairvaux in 1115. His *Apologia* of c.. 1130 includes the well-known fulmination against one aspect of the degeneracy, as he considered it, of the reformed Cluniac rule. He speaks in particular of the decorative carvings in Cluniac churches, but the reference is no less pertinent to the illumination of manuscripts:

> this formless decoration and decorative deformity. These dragons, monkeys, centaurs, tigers, and lions affronted or in combat, these soldiers fighting, these hunting scenes, and many-headed monsters, or two of them with one head, are of no use except to distract the eye, trouble attention, and disturb contemplation. *Proh Deo!* If we are not ashamed of such foolishness, do we not even regret its expense?[59]

In the light of this sentiment, it is not surprising to read in the rules of the order as revised in 1134: *"Litterae unius coloris fiant et non depictae"* (Letters are to be in a single color and without pictures). The admonition was obeyed for a brief moment and Cistercian illumination of the mid-twelfth century is characteristically restrained in color and ornament. Yet even during St. Bernard's life (+1153), his own house at Clairvaux could produce a magnificent Bible in five volumes (Troyes, Bibliothèque municipale, Ms. 27), in which fine parchment and the beauty of the script create an effect of restrained elegance, to which the cameo-like initials also contribute much.[60]

The five volumes of the Bible from Clairvaux are fairly large, making it a French Romanesque example of the giant type that was popular in all parts of Europe, as has been noted before. France produced a considerable number of them, in fact,[61] and although there is considerable variety in the group as a whole, many appear to have been made in or around Burgundy.[62] One now in the Bibliothèque municipale at Moulins (Ms. 1) belonged to the monastery at Souvigny in the fifteenth century and takes its name from it. It is a large book (56 x 39 cm: 22 x 15.25"), lavishly decorated with many historiated initials and a number of full-page miniatures. One of these on f.93 is of scenes from the life of David (Fig. 138), from his anointing by Samuel

through the slaying of Goliath. The episodes are arranged in registers, enacted by solidly modeled figures against a background of burnished gold. The Byzantine overtones of this technical characteristic are paralleled in the iconography of the crowded compositions, although in somewhat simplified form. In this and in some stylistic points, this late twelfth-century French Bible is comparable to its English contemporaries from Winchester (Fig. 131) and Canterbury, not least in its decorative sumptuousness. The color scheme of frank reds and blues, along with the gold grounds, anticipates later Gothic style.

Manuscript illumination in the southwestern region of France—Languedoc, Aquitaine, and the Limousin—had flourished in the eleventh century in styles significantly related to the contemporary monumental sculpture of Moissac and Toulouse. But whereas the art of stone carving continued to progress in the region, manuscript illumination of the twelfth century there loses much of the imagination and vitality of its eleventh-century exemplars. An exception is a Sacramentary from the cathedral of Saint-Étienne at Limoges (Paris, Bibliothèque Nationale, Ms. lat. 9438)[63] of the early twelfth century. Among its several full-page miniatures is the scene of Pentecost (Fig. 139) on f.87. The descending Holy Spirit is portrayed in the sinuous lines emerging from the Saviour's head, which divide and come to rest on the apostles seated below Him, a unique iconography of the subject. The elongated figures

Fig. 139.
Paris, Bibliothèque Nationale, Ms. lat. 9438, f.87. Sacramentary from Limoges, Pentecost.

Fig. 140.
New York, Pierpont Morgan Library, Ms. 44, f.1v. Scenes
from the Life of Christ, The Annunciation.

with over-large but remarkably expressive hands are in angular poses to which the turned heads and peering eyes give great emotional intensity. This quality of the miniature might seem to be accounted for by the inspirational content of the theme, but it is also found in others like the Baptism and the Ascension,[64] and is paralleled in the slightly later stone sculptures carved by Gilabertus for the cathedral of Saint-Étienne at Toulouse.[65]

A relationship has been suggested between the Limoges Sacramentary miniatures and Ottonian art in these characteristics of style and expression, and Byzantine iconographic parallels have also been cited. Both associations are quite possible in view of the far-flung connections of the Limousin monastery of Saint-Martial with other centers. But it is equally clear that the aesthetic of the Sacramentary miniatures is comparable to that of the enamel work for which Limoges is justly renowned. The strong colors are dominated by the blue of the backgrounds setting off the figures with their red, pink, and white robes, defined by emphatic curving lines like the cloisons separating the colors of an enameled plaque. The border resembles a band of metal set with jewels, and the four gold disks starring the blue sky around Christ's aureole are like nothing so much as the ornamental heads of pins fastening an enameled panel to a reliquary casket. The similarity in method and effect to the parallel between Mosan metal-work and illumination (Fig. 135) is obvious.

One of the paradoxes in the history of mediaeval art is the fact that there is nothing in the manuscript illumination of the region of the Ile-de-France, where monumental Gothic style was formed in the second and third quarters of the twelfth century, that is comparable in importance to the cathedrals and the sculpture that is a part of them. In the decade when Gothic art began at Saint-Denis, Chartres, Paris, and Laon, there is little if anything outstanding to be found in the manuscript illumination of the region. In the lengthy and detailed account of the building and decoration of the abbey church at Saint-Denis by its abbot Suger (1082–1152),[66] there is not a single reference to manuscripts among the descriptions of paintings, enamels, sculpture, and stained glass made at his command. Particular interest attaches, therefore, to a series of illustrations of the life of Christ (N. Y., Pierpont Morgan Library, Ms. 44) that have been associated with the stained-glass panels of the same subjects in the central western window of Chartres Cathedral, which date from about 1150.[67] The origin of these thirty miniatures is an enigma. Although they have also been associated with Limoges, there is nothing to support this attribution, and the style is unrelated to any manuscript originating there. An iconographic detail suggesting a possible north French provenance is the portrayal of the Saviour disappearing at the top of the Ascension on f.14, as in earlier Anglo-Saxon and "Channel School" versions.

In the Annunciation (Fig. 140) on f.1v, the protagonists stand before a plain gold background enclosed within a wide foliate border. The figures are painted solidly in opaque pigments, outlined by emphatic contours and with little or no modeling of the pinkish flesh surfaces. Apart from the gold background instead of the red of the same scene in the Chartres window, style and composition are very similar in the two. The figures in the miniature are a little taller and more slender than their counterparts, whose stockier proportions are in harmony with the almost square format of the stained-glass panel. But even in their greater slenderness, the Morgan figures can be compared with those enacting the same scene in the Virgin portal sculpture of the Chartres west front. Also related to the stained-glass aesthetic are the decorative motives in the borders throughout the series, and a preference for the red-blue color harmony that presages later Gothic usage.

The precise relationship of the Morgan 44 miniatures to the stained-glass panels at Chartres with which they have been compared is not easy to determine. But in any event, such a determination would not add to their importance as indicators of the parallels that had developed by mid-twelfth-century between illumination and the monumental arts of the Cathedral. It has already been pointed out that by that time, illumination was no longer the pioneering art it had been before; illuminators adapt innovations in style and content from the other arts, rather than the reverse. This was partly the consequence of changing patronage, which was itself a factor in bringing about the resurgence in the twelfth century of architecture and the monumental sculptural and pictorial decoration it required. Up to the latter part of the twelfth century, the creative artistic centers had been largely monastic.[68] But coincident with the developments that mark the transition from Romanesque to Gothic style in architecture and sculpture, the centers of intellectual and artistic creation were moving from the abbeys and monasteries to the cities and universities.[69] Several factors contributed to the different cultural climate in the urban centers. On the one hand, there were the ever-widening influences of expanding knowledge that was one of the consequences of the Crusades, bringing an increased awareness of the philosophical and scientific achievements of classical and Arabic cultures. There were also the changing social values created by the rise of the communes and the growth of bourgeois and mercantile classes. In the circumstances, it was inevitable that there should be demands for different types of books from those needed in earlier times. The illuminated book as an expression of religious exaltation, whether used in the service or treasured by prince or monastery, gives way to the codex decorated for the enjoyment of its owner or owners.

There is no text accompanying the miniatures of the Life of Christ in Morgan 44, and their exact purpose is uncertain.[70] But such scenes are often found in the illustrated psalters that began to be popular earlier in the twelfth century, such as the one made at St. Albans in England between 1119 and 1146 for an aristocratic anchoress. It is possible that the Morgan scenes were painted with some such end in view. In any event, psalters with scenes from the life of Christ preceding the psalm text, usually made for or identifiable with a person of high degree, begin to appear in considerable numbers early in the thirteenth century in the milieu of Paris.

An example in point is the Psalter of Ingeborg of Denmark, second wife of Philippe Auguste of France (Chantilly, Musée Condé, Ms. 1695).[71] It is not precisely dated but can hardly be far from the beginning of the thirteenth century, c. 1200–1205, and is not later than 1214 from internal evidence. A series of full-page miniatures includes the one of Christ's Entombment and the Three Maries at the Tomb (Fig. 141, Plate XXIII) on f.28v.[72] The two scenes are separated by an orange-red band with small white circles, and the top and bottom borders are the same color with gold stars, while the sides are blue with a wave-and-dot pattern. The costumes are painted in varying shades of blue and russet, with touches of bright green in Christ's bier and the tomb, set off by sharp reds in the sarcophagus lid, an ointment jar, and the cap worn by Joseph of Arimathea anointing the Saviour's body. The background is plain unburnished gold.

Opinions differ widely about the stylistic origins of the Ingeborg Psalter miniatures,[73] ranging from Porcher's conclusion that it stems from Ottonian sources[74] to that of André-Charles Coppier,[75] relating it to the enamel work of Nicholas of Verdun's Tournai Casket of 1205. Louis Grodecki concurs in this at least to the extent of associating the manuscript with a Franco-Flemish locale.[76] But Anglo-Saxon elements have also been pointed out,[77] particularly in the script, and the English origin of this particular type of illustrated psalter is not open to question.[78] At the same time, the textual organization follows Parisian usage, and, in view of its identification with a queen of France, it seems reasonable to conclude that the varied stylistic overtones rightly observed in its miniatures make them examples of the eclecticism of much Parisian illumination at the beginning of the thirteenth century.

Standing where it does chronologically, the Ingeborg Psalter has a place in the history of mediaeval illumination comparable to that of the late twelfth-century buildings and stone carvings in France, which are often termed transitional from Romanesque to Gothic. Certain details are characteristically twelfth-century, e.g., the neck and head of the figure at Christ's feet in the Entombment. But the humanization of the forms, for which Romanesque painters had striven in a variety of ways, has been much more fully realized in the plastic implication of bodies to which the ridged draperies, disposed in realistic folds instead of arbitrarily decorative patterns, make a significant contribution. The figures move more gravely and graciously, quietly rhythmic instead of violently dynamic, investing even the tragedy of the Entombment with noble serenity. The hands, which are characteristically exaggerated in size and gesture in earlier Romanesque forms, are reduced in proportion and restrained in action. Even the border which typically may share in the excitement of a Romanesque composition (Fig. 133) becomes a simple band limiting the proto-Gothic design.

Along with the innovations in pictorial style in the Ingeborg Psalter, modifications of the textual script are also found. The changes that took place in writing, especially during the twelfth century, were from the rounded minuscules of Carolingian letters toward shapes that occasionally ended in sharp points or spikes.[79] It is now generally accepted that fully Gothic script in which the rounded letters are made by separate strokes of the pen and the taller ones terminate in spiky ends or flourishes, creating an angular impression, is found first in the Ingeborg Psalter. Such, in any case, is the kind of writing found in Gothic books of the middle and later thirteenth century, illuminated with miniatures whose stylistic premises are those established in France in the scenes from the life of Christ in the Ingeborg Psalter.

NOTES

1. M .R. James, *The Canterbury Psalter* (London: Percy Lund, Humphries & Co., 1934). S. Dufrenne, "Les copies anglaises du Psautier d'Utrecht," *Scriptorium*, 18 (1964):185–97.

2. H. Roosen-Runge, Introd., n. 18; vol. 1, pp. 104–5.

3. S. Millar, chap. 5, n. 4, p. 46; H. Omont, ed., *Psautier illustré (xiiiͤ siècle), reproduction des miniatures du manuscrit latin 8846* (Paris: Bibliothèque Nationale, 1906).

4. Cf. James, n. 1, pp. 4–5.

5. E. Panofsky, *Early Netherlandish Painting*, 2 vols. (Cambridge: Harvard University Press, 1953), 1:14.

6. Cf. H. Swarzenski, *Monuments of Romanesque Art* (Chicago: University of Chicago Press, 1954).

7. G. Biagi, *Cinquanta tavole . . . da codici della R. Biblioteca Medicea Laurenziana* (Florence: Sansoni, 1914), p. 8, pls. 8–9.

8. Cf. Harrsen, chap. 5, n. 23; H. Swarzenski, *The Berthold Missal—The Pierpont Morgan Library Ms. 710—and the Scriptorium of Weingarten Abbey* (New York: Pierpont Morgan Library, 1943).

9. Cf. *RP*, p. 199.

10. P. Buberl, "Die romanischen Malereien im Kloster Nonnberg," *Kunstgeschicht. Jahrb. der K. K. Zentralkommission*, 3 (1909), pp .25–40; *RP*, pp. 122–23.

11. A. Boeckler, "Beiträge zur romanischen Kölner Buchmalerei. Mittelalterliche Hss.," *Festgabe für H. Degering* (Leipzig: Hiersemann, 1926), pp. 15–28.

12. Cf. H. Swarzenski, *MRA*, pp. 27–32.

13. L. M. J. Delaissé, *Miniatures médiévales* (Geneva: Deux Mondes, 1959), pp. 42–45, pl. 7.

14. Ms. 37; cf. *AM*, pls. 83–84.

15. A. Haseloff, *Eine thüringische-sächsische Malerschule des 13. Jahrhunderts.* Studien zur deutschen Kunstgeschichte 9 (Strasbourg: Heitz, 1897).

16. K. Löffler, *Der Landgrafenpsalter* (Leipzig: Hiersemann, 1925).

17. H. Hahnloser and F. Rücker, *Das Müsterbuch von Wolfenbüttel*, Wiener Gesellschaft für vervielfältigende Kunst (1929).

18. *AM*, pl. 86.

19. Cf. Boeckler, *AM*, pp. 67–69; Nordenfalk, *RP*, pp. 135–36.

20. Garrison, chap. 5, n. 47.

21. Reproduced in color in Salmi, chap. 5, n. 50; pl. iii.

22. Cf. Nordenfalk, *RP*, pp. 146, 163–70.

23. G. F. Warner, *The Gospels of Mathilda, Countess of Tuscany* (New York: Roxburghe, 1917).

24. A. Boeckler, *AM*, p. 102, pl. 103.

25. B. Katterbach, *Le Miniature dell' Evangeliario di Padova* (Rome: Danesi, 1931).

26. Boeckler, *AM*, p. 102.

27. Indifferent color reproductions in S. Mitchell, *Medieval Manuscript Painting* (New York: Viking, 1965), pls. 26–27.

28. Cf. Metz, chap. 4, n. 110; pls. i, 73, 74.

29. A. Goldschmidt, *Der Albani Psalter in Hildesheim* (Berlin: G. Siemens, 1895). O. Pächt, C. R. Dodwell and F. Wormald, *The St. Albans Psalter* (London: Warburg Inst., 1960).

30. Reproduced in color in *RP*, p. 171; cf. also Roosen-Runge, Introd., n. 18; i, pp. 81–94.

31. Cf. *PiBMA*, pp. 79–80.

32. *Ibid.*, pls. 65, 66.

33. Thompson, *GLP*, pp. 436–44.

34. C. M. Kauffman, "The Bury Bible," *Journal of the Warburg and Courtauld Institutes*, 29 (1966):60–81.

35. C. R. Dodwell, *The Great Lambeth Bible* (London: Faber & Faber, 1959).

36. W. Oakeshott, *The Artists of the Winchester Bible* (London: Faber & Faber, 1945).

37. *RP*, p. 176.

38. Oakeshott, p. 6.

39. The painting technique of the Winchester Bible miniatures is exhaustively analyzed by Roosen-Runge, cf. Introd., n. 18.

40. Oakeshott, p. 6.

41. *Ibid.*, p. 11.

42. C. H. Haskins, "England and Sicily in the Twelfth Century," *English Historical Review*, 26 (1911):43–73.

43. Dodwell, n. 35, pp. 8–11.

44. C. R. Dodwell, *The Canterbury School of Illumination* (Cambridge: Cambridge University Press, 1954), pp. 98–104.

45. C. H. Haskins, *The Renaissance of the Twelfth Century* (Cambridge, Mass.: Harvard University Press, 1933).

46. M. R. James, *The Bestiary* (Oxford: Roxburghe Club, 1928). T. H White, *The Bestiary—A Book of Beasts* (New York: Capricorn Books–Putnam, 1960).

47. *English Romanesque Illumination*, no. 7 (Oxford: Bodleian Library, 1951).

48. Cf. Dodwell, *Lambeth Bible*, pp. 16–18.

49. Cf. Porcher, *MFM*, p. 38.

50. Reproduction in color in *MFM*, pl. xxxiii.

51. Cf. Swarzenski, H. *MRA*, pp. 27–32.

52. Porcher, *MFM*, p. 34, pls. xxix, xxxiii.

53. Cf. Morey, *ECA*, pp. 137–40.

54. C. Oursel, *La miniature du xiiͤ siècle à l'Abbaye de Cîteaux* (Dijon: L. Venot, 1926).

55. Cf. Nordenfalk, *RP*, pp. 202–3.

56. Reproduced in color in *MFM*, pl. xxv.

57. Cf. E. Panofsky, *Abbot Suger: On the Abbey Church of Saint-Denis* (Princeton: Princeton University Press, 1946). A. Watson, *The Early Iconography of the Tree of Jesse* (Oxford-London: Humphrey Milford, 1934). Nordenfalk, *RP*, pp. 161–62.

58. Oursel, pls. xxxiii, xlv.

59. Morey, *Mediaeval Art*, p. 236.

60. L. Morel-Payan, *Les plus beaux manuscrits et les plus belles reliures de la bibliothèque de Troyes* (Troyes, 1935).

61. Cf. *Manuscrits à peintures du viiͤ au xiiͤ siècle* (Paris: Bibliothèque Nationale, 1954), nos. 329–40.

62. Cf. Nordenfalk, *RP*, p. 170.

63. J. Porcher, *Le sacramentaire de Saint-Étienne de Limoges* (Paris, 1953).

64. Wixom, chap. 5, n. 61, pp. 50–53. *MFM*, fig. 21, pl. xiv.

65. P. Deschamps, *French Sculpture of the Romanesque Period, Eleventh and Twelfth Centuries* (Florence: Pantheon, 1930), pl. 25.

66. Panofsky, n. 57.

67. B. da C. Greene and M. Harrsen, *The Pierpont Morgan Library: An Exhibition of Illuminated Manuscripts held at the New York Public Library,* no. 35 (New York, 1933), p. xiv.

68. Cf. F. Wormald, "The Monastic Library," *The Year 1200,* vol. 2, *A Background Survey* (New York: Metropolitan Museum, 1970), pp. 169–74.

69. Cf. Haskins, n. 45.

70. Porcher suggests (*MFM,* p. 45) that they may have been a pattern-book for stained-glass window designs.

71. F. Deuchler, *Der Ingeborgpsalter* (Berlin: Walter de Gruyter, 1967).

72. Reproduced in color in *MFM,* pl. xii.

73. J. Guignard, "La miniature gothique: le psautier d'Ingeburge," *Art de France,* 1 (1960):278–280.

74. *MFM,* p. 47.

75. "Le rôle artistique et social des orfèvres-graveurs français au Moyen-Age," *Gazette des Beaux-Arts,* 79, no. 1 (1937):270–71.

76. In *Le vitrail français* (Paris: Deux-Mondes, 1958), p. 118; cf. also "Le psautier de la reine Ingeburge et ses problèmes," *Revue de l'Art,* 5 (1969):73–78.

77. Millar, chap. 5, n. 4, p. 45; but cf. also D. H. Turner, "Manuscript Illumination," *The Year 1200,* vol. 2, p. 137.

78. C. Nordenfalk, "Insulare und kontinentale Psalter-Illustrationen aus dem XIII. Jahrhundert," *Acta Archaeologica,* 10 (1939):107–20.

79. Cf. L. E. Boyle, "The Emergence of Gothic Handwriting," *The Year 1200,* vol. 2, pp. 73–78.

7

Gothic Manuscript Illumination

In applying the term *Gothic* to manuscript illumination from about 1230 to the early decades of the fifteenth century, it is implied that miniatures so designated have characteristics comparable to and compatible with the architecture of pointed arches, ribbed vaults, and flying buttresses to which it was originally given. Such is the case, but it is to be noted that the Gothic phenomenon is not contemporary in the different media, a point referred to above in the discussion of later twelfth-century illumination. In the early stages of Gothic book decoration, the inventive leadership of the architectural arts is even more apparent than in late Romanesque examples like the New Testament illustrations of Morgan 44 (Fig. 140) and the Ingeborg Psalter (Fig. 141, Plate XXIII).

Changing patronage and methods of production were among the factors that shaped the nature of manuscript illumination during the Gothic period, as they had already begun to in the twelfth century, but to a more limited degree. In earlier times, de luxe manuscripts like the Gospels of Saint-Médard de Soissons (Fig. 56) or the *Codex Aureus* of St. Emmeram of Regensburg (Figs. 69, 70) may have been commissioned by individuals, but they were usually presented to a church or monastery. In the thirteenth century and thereafter, the most pretentious decorated books were not produced primarily for liturgical use but for princes and noblemen, for wealthy merchants and their respective spouses. Two of the many consequences of this were of particular significance. One was the proliferation of book collecting in the modern sense. Charles the Bald had been an enthusiastic patron of fine bookmaking in the ninth century, and owned a considerable number of extraordinary codices, as has been noted. But the late fifteenth-century bibliophile, Jean, duc de Berry, had nearly three hundred books in his personal library,[1] and the royal collection of his brother, King Charles V of France, contained nearly twelve hundred, amassed by inheritance, commission, and purchase.[2] The other consequence of the changing patronage of fine books in the Gothic period was the growing popularity of different types of books, many of them secular (romances like the *Roman de la Rose,* didactic treatises like the *Somme-le-Roi,* poetry such as the work of Guillaume de Machaut), but particularly the Book of Hours.

As has been noted, the psalter was the book most extensively used for private devotions in the earlier Middle Ages;[3] such was the purpose of manuscripts like the Albani Psalter (Fig. 130, Plate XX), the Landgraf Psalter (Fig. 123), and the Ingeborg Psalter (Fig. 141, Plate XXIII) of the early thirteenth century. It was only natural, then, that as the desire for a more personal touch led to the individualization of devotional books by the addition of prayers appealing to the owner's emotions or directed to patron saints, they should be incorporated with the psalter. These additional short prayers or offices were to be read or recited on special occasions, like the Office of the Dead, or at specified times of the day, the eight canonical hours, hence the name. Combined Psalters and Books of Hours are usual in the thirteenth century, but perhaps under the impetus of the piety of persons like St. Francis of Assisi or mystics like Hildegard of Bingen in the late thirteenth and fourteenth centuries, the Book of Hours then became an independent volume, far outnumbering in production all other types of service books.

Concurrent with changing patronage and the emergence of different types of books in the thirteenth century is a significant change in the circumstances and methods of manuscript production. By and large, until the thirteenth century, they were written and illuminated almost exclusively in monastic or ecclesiastical scriptoria; even the rather individual style of Charles the Bald's books must be seen in such a frame of reference. This was but natural in times when the monasteries were almost the only repositories of what learning there was and teaching was a function of monastic and cathedral schools like that established at Chartres by Fulbert about 1006, or William of Champeaux's cathedral school of Notre-Dame in Paris, which was to become the University of Paris by the middle of the thirteenth century. The transformation that began in the later twelfth century was a manifestation of the widening intellectual horizons of western Europe following on the Crusades, which opened the way for renewed and increased transmission of classical learning, especially Aristotle, through the Arabs and their scientific thought. Along with them came expansion of commerce, growth of population, and, as a negative factor, the declining authority, theological and intellectual, of the older monastic orders like the Benedictines and Augustinians. To meet the needs of this increasingly secular society, the monastic scriptoria were neither adequate nor competent in background. In the circumstances, it was only natural that secular workshops should have grown up to supply the needs of the new patronage. These were often located near the universities; in Paris, the bookmakers had their shops on the rue Erembourg de Brie, now called the rue de la Boutebrie.

Unlike Romanesque style, which was formed at more or less the same time in many regions and in comparatively independent schools, Gothic style began in a well-defined area and spread out from it. That area was northwestern France, including southern England at least in the earlier stages. As is the case of French Gothic style in architecture, French style in manuscript illumination

is the Gothic norm, dominated by Paris in the thirteenth century. Whatever the explanation of this may be[4]—the early intellectual primacy of its university, its importance as a center of commerce, its glory as the capital city of the Capetian realm—Paris was the creator of Gothic style in manuscript illumination, and books written and illustrated there created the standard of judgment for all Europe. It was not by chance that when Dante spoke to Oderisi, a manuscript illuminator of the thirteenth century from Gubbio, he called him an honor to *"quell' arte che alluminare chiamata è in Parisi"* (that art called illumination in Paris) (*Purgatorio* 11. 79–81).

To meet the growing demand for manuscripts in the thirteenth century and thereafter, new production methods were developed. In the earlier monastic scriptoria, artists would be provided with models, which they followed as faithfully as possible. Large books might be parceled out by gatherings among several assistants, but in a given section, the style would be more or less consistent. From the end of the thirteenth century on, the practice in the larger shops, particularly those catering to a wider public, was for the master illuminator to complete a few miniatures as a standard to be emulated by his assistants as best they could, sometimes aided by sketches in allotted places or the margins.[5] The actual execution of the miniatures was frequently divided into stages in which each color would be applied by a given assistant, the gold by yet another, and so on. It is increasingly more rare, as time proceeds, that a given book can be considered the work of one individual, save only in the case of very important commissions. Paradoxically, it was precisely this circumstance that created the environment in which the individual artist came into his own. More and more names of individual masters are recorded, whether the administrative supervisors of ateliers or painters, and personal styles can be much more clearly distinguished in the products of the many anonymous illuminators.

A Psalter traditionally associated with Blanche of Castille (1187–1252), the mother of Louis IX (Saint-Louis) (Paris, Bibl. de l'Arsenal, Ms. 1186), is a distinguished example of Parisian illumination in the first half of the thirteenth century. There is nothing to support such specific identification of the person for whom the book was made, but the text of a prayer on f.190 indicates that it was for a lady, and its rich decoration suggests that she was of high degree. The probable date is around 1230. Apart from the calendar illustra-

Fig. 142.
Paris, Bibliothèque de l'Arsenal, Ms. 1186, f.23v. The Psalter of Blanche of Castille, Christ's Betrayal and Flagellation.

tions and ten historiated initials in the text, its illumination consists of twenty-five full-page miniatures relating the Fall and Redemption of Man, most of them on ff.9v to 29v, preceding the text of the Psalms. The majority of these are composed like the Betrayal and Flagellation of Christ (Fig. 142) on f.23v, with each scene in one of the two interlocked medallions enclosed in a rectangular border. The burnished-gold ground sets off the figures outlined in simple sweeping curves. There is no indication of space and little attempt to model the figures save for spots of red on white planes laid over the brownish flesh tints of the faces. The designs are primarily linear and two-dimensional, echoing the rigidness of late Romanesque style (Figs. 117 and 141,

Plate XXIII), but the rhythms are slower, the gestures more grave, the content more monumental.

These premonitions of the High Gothic are the more significant in that the overall effect is much like that of a stained-glass window, heightened by the brilliant and saturated colors—dominated by reds and blues with touches of green, russet brown, and lavender—and accentuated by the gold.[6] The derivation of this aesthetic is even more apparent in the Tree of Jesse on f.15v of the Arsenal Psalter,[7] in which the compositional scheme of the central stem with flanking half-medallions framed in an arch could easily have been directly translated from a window like the one in the ambulatory of Suger's Abbey Church at Saint-Denis.

Much the same style but in a later phase is seen in the miniatures of the *Bibles moralisées* or Moralized Bibles,[8] one of the most remarkable products of French Gothic illumination. Three thirteenth-century copies are known: one in the National Library of Vienna (Cod. 1179; one divided among the Bodleian Library at Oxford (Ms. 270 B), the Bibliothèque Nationale in Paris (Ms. lat. 11560), and the British Museum (Harley Ms. 1526–7); and one in the Cathedral of Toledo in Spain, of which eight leaves are in the Pierpont Morgan Library in New York (Ms. 240). All are massive works, the latter two consisting of three volumes each, measuring about 17 x 12.25″, and illustrated with over five thousand subjects. These are arranged in groups of eight on a page in circular medallions with vertical columns of text (Fig. 143). Louis IX of France, Saint Louis, is portrayed on f.246 of the Vienna *Bible moralisée,* and he is also shown, with his mother, Blanche of Castille, above a scene of an ecclesiastic dictating to a scribe in a miniature in the Morgan frag-

ment, probably to indicate that the books were intended for the monarch. It is certain in any case that the *Bible moralisée* was created in the French royal milieu around the year 1250.

The *Bible moralisée* differs significantly from earlier illuminated Bibles in being primarily a compilation of illustrations with related texts. Thus on f.71v of the Paris book (Fig. 143), the odd-numbered medallions beginning on the left and reading down are interpretations of verses from the Song of Solomon (1:16–17, 2:1–3), "Behold, thou art fair, my beloved, yea pleasant: also our bed is green. . . . I am the rose of Sharon and the lily of the valleys. As the lily among thorns, so is my love among the daughters." The other four medallions are also visualizations, but of moralizing interpretations of or comments upon the Scripture passages. Thus the fourth medallion is a comment on the subject of the third, "Also our bed is green," visualized as life in a monastery.

Sometimes New Testament incidents are included, like Christ bearing His cross in the second medallion, while others are based on the *Postillae in Bibliam* of Hugues de Saint-Cher, a Dominican monk and theologian who died in 1252. Such confrontation of Old and New Testament subjects is not new, but in earlier instances, the comparisons are typological, the Old Testament themes prefiguring those of the New. What distinguishes the *Bible moralisée* comparisons from the earlier ones is their didactic and moralizing purpose, a direct outcome of the revision of the Vulgate text undertaken in the thirteenth century in the University of Paris. In the scholastic commentaries written in this connection, the interpretations move away from the purely objective and realistic ones. In the aggregate, the Bible passages are interpreted or moralized in four ways. Historically, the incident itself is shown. Allegorically, its exemplification of Christian faith is set forth. Tropologically, its moral implications are defined, and anagogically, its promise of hope for a future life in heaven is revealed.

In the illuminated folios of the *Bibles moralisées,* the parallel with contemporary stained-glass usage is even more striking than in the Blanche of Castille Psalter. The eight medallions are arranged in columns of four like the roundels of a window, and the backgrounds of the spandrels with semi-quatrefoils between them have the same mosaic or diaper patterns seen in the windows. The color scheme is also similar, dominated by red and blue in the costumes, the various border

Fig. 143.
Paris, Bibliothèque Nationale, Ms. lat. 11560, f.71v. Bible moralisée, *The Song of Solomon, chaps. i–ii.*

motives, and the diapered backgrounds of the medallion columns.[9] Even the burnished-gold backgrounds of the medallions contribute to this; laid on thick priming coats of gesso, they protrude from the parchment in curving surfaces that reflect light in glints like the sparkle of a cathedral window.

Certain characteristics of the *Bible moralisée* figure style are also related to contemporary monumental Gothic art, specifically the emphatic contours and the drapery formula of long, hairpin-like loops creating the effect of furrows. The relationship of this to contemporary sculpture can be seen in a drawing representing The Church (Fig. 144) on f.4v of the well-known Album of Villard de Honnecourt, a sketch-book of an itinerant architect in the early thirteenth century.[10] The hairpin-and-furrow formula is employed in it to graph the plastic values of a figure like those in the Visitation group in the central portal of the west façade of the Cathedral at Reims, intensifying the outlines to indicate the third dimension and accentuating the effect by the inner patterns. The *Bible moralisée* version of the formula is more elegant and the plastic values somewhat less emphatic, but the relationship between the two is clear. In the painted miniatures of the illuminated manuscript, the figures stand in relief from the gold backgrounds in the same way as their sculptural counterparts do in the stone embrasures of the cathedral portals.

Many features of the *Bible moralisée* style—the strong contours, the hairpin-furrow drapery formula, the plain burnished-gold grounds and minimal spatial effects—can be found in later thirteenth-century French manuscripts. One such is a small Psalter (Philadelphia, Free Public Library, Lewis Ms. 185)[11] of about 1260. The psalm text is preceded by twenty-five full-page miniatures beginning with a historiated B of *Beatus* and continuing with forty-eight scenes from the life of Christ in paired medallions, and twenty-four smaller medallions of the Zodiac signs and Labors of the Months illustrating the calendar. The Annunciation, Visitation, Nativity, and the Annunciation to the Shepherds (Fig. 145) are on ff.2v-3. As in the *Bibles moralisées,* balancing compositions are paired in color, i.e., a blue pattern like the diaper around the medallions on f.2v becomes red on f.3, and the semi-quatrefoils and angle ornaments on red grounds on f.2v are on blue on f.3. Even the borders, where decorative motives repeat those of the *Bible moralisée,* alternate in design and color in a given opening, creating an abstractly structural unity. A number of saints listed in the calendar were held

in particular veneration in the region of Sens, but this slight indication of provenance can hardly suggest more than a place of origin outside the Ile-de-France. This would be consistent with *retardataire* quality by now (*c.* 1260) of the *Bible moralisée* style in the Parisian ateliers, where it was giving way to another manner. The Lewis Psalter is a distinguished example of the style, nonetheless, of highest quality throughout in script and decoration, the uniformity of the fine, semi-transparent vellum, and the exacting precision and consistency of workmanship down to the smallest details.

The new manner that made its appearance in Parisian illumination shortly after 1250 is seen in a collection of Old Testament illustrations, of which the greater part (forty-three folios with eighty-six scenes) is in the Pierpont Morgan Library in New York (Ms. 638); two others are in Paris (BN, Ms. n.a. lat. 2294), and yet another is privately owned.[12] The history of the manuscript is unusual. Some of the marginal inscriptions indicate that it was in Italy in the fourteenth century; others in Hebrew and Persian were added to explain the Christian subjects to Shah Abbas the Great of Persia, to whom it was presented by Pope Clement VIII in 1608. Acquired by the English collector Sir Thomas Phillipps in 1834, it subsequently found its way, except for the detached folios, to the Pierpont Morgan Library.

The total of two hundred and eighty-three scenes begins with the Creation and ends with 2 Samuel 20; they may possibly have been, or been intended for, the introductory illustrations of a large Psalter, but nothing indicates their specific role. The battle described in 1 Samuel 13 is shown above in the miniature on f.23v (Fig. 146) of the Morgan manuscript, with Saul and his counsellors and a sacrificial scene below. Some of the backgrounds are burnished gold, while others are deep blue and red, contrasting the areas on different levels. Even more significant than this departure from the *Bible moralisée* scheme is the architectural enclosure of the several scenes in a framework on which participants in the episodes move, like the archer in the upper right angle and the catapulter in the left margin. This new and basically realistic element is found in other miniatures of the manuscript where figures are overlapped by the architectural forms of the Gothic frame as if they were moving behind it in space. A comparably new realism is seen in the figures. The draperies are no longer furrowed by shadowed hairpin folds but are disposed in large units defined by simple

Fig. 144.
Paris, Bibliothèque Nationale, Ms. fr. 19093, f.4v. Sketch-
book of Villard d'Honnecourt, The Church.

Fig. 145.
Philadelphia, Free Library, Ms. Lewis 185, ff.2v–3.
Psalter, The Annunciation, Visitation, Nativity, and An-
nunciation to the Shepherds.

curves that suggest plastic form without the stressed contours of the earlier Blanche of Castille and *Bible moralisée* formulae. This is, in essence, "High Gothic" style, in which a new and different system of linear conventions allows an integration of figures with space that without yet being visually three-dimensional is still unified and seemingly capable of existing both within and beyond the limits of the picture.

English manuscript illumination of the early thirteenth century was apparently the source of the style that influenced mid-thirteenth-century Parisian style as seen in the miniatures of Morgan 638.[14] An example of English style around 1200 has been seen in some miniatures of the copy of the Utrecht Psalter (Fig. 117) made in all probability at Canterbury. This style with its dynamic and two-dimensional patterns of strong contours and tense linear rhythms, of gold backgrounds and vigorous colors, was continued in the early thirteenth century; an outstanding example is the Lothian Bible in the Pierpont Morgan Library (Ms. 791),[15] probably a Canterbury manuscript. About a third of a century later, c. 1230, the miniatures of an Apocalypse (Cambridge, Trinity College Library, Ms. R. 16. 2)[16] are in a style standing in relationship to that of the earlier works in much the same way as the Blanche of Castille manner (Fig. 142) does to that of the Ingeborg Psalter (Fig. 141, Plate XXIII).

The two miniatures on f.7 of the Trinity College Apocalypse (Fig. 147) illustrate the Opening of the Sixth Seal (Rev. 6:12–17) and the Four Angels restraining the Four Winds while the Servants of God are being numbered (Rev. 7:1–8); they occur in a part of the book illuminated in a style that still owes something to the Byzantinizing manner of c. 1200, especially in the modeling of the faces. But the style for the most part is one of vigorous outlines defining areas that are sometimes uncolored and elsewhere enriched with modeling tones that deepen in the drapery folds in an effect somewhat like the furrows of the Blanche of Castille miniatures. The colors are rich, with backgrounds of red and blue with various all-over patterns for episodes taking place on earth, and tooled burnished gold for celestial scenes, like the heavens surrounded by the sea in the Four Angels and Four Winds miniature. Apart from the drawing and the subtly tinted faces with modeling shading around the eyes and pink spots on the cheeks, the figure style is different from that of late Romanesque work of c. 1200 in the slenderer proportions, the more angular yet better articulated move-

ment, and by the broadening of the heads at the top that continues in the later stages of Gothic manner. The Trinity College Apocalypse was probably made at St. Albans; in addition to the distinction it enjoys in its own right, it provides insight into the stylistic antecedents of the outstanding artist of the St. Albans scriptorium a little later, Matthew Paris. It is also important as an early and impressive example of the illustrated Apocalypse texts that are as characteristically, even uniquely, English in the thirteenth century as the Bestiary was in the twelfth.[17]

Even at the time when the Trinity College Apocalypse was being illuminated (c. 1230), a different manner appears in English miniatures produced in other centers. The Psalter of Robert de Lindseye (London, Society of Antiquaries, Ms. 59) was made for the abbot of Peterborough between 1212 and 1222; the miniatures of the Crucifixion and Christ Enthroned (Fig. 148) face each other on ff.35v-36. The forms are heavily painted in richly harmonious colors on gold grounds that are burnished and also tooled with decorative patterns, an early instance of this technique that was destined to great popularity in the later thirteenth century in both England and France. Compared with the Trinity Apocalypse figure style, the patterns in the Lindseye Psalter are simpler and more elegant. The lines of contours and inner drapery folds flow smoothly in defining the large quiet surfaces of the forms, unlike the more animated and nervous areas of the Apocalypse style. In a word, there is much the same contrast between these two early thirteenth-century English idioms as there is between their French contemporary manners in the *Bibles moralisées* and the Old Testament miniatures of Morgan 638. In view of the close relationships between England and northern France including Paris at the time, the conclusion that the slightly later French work was influenced by the English is inescapable.

Robert de Lindseye's Psalter is certainly dated before his death in 1222, and is thus an example of fully developed thirteenth-century English illumination.[18] There are a number of interesting details in addition to those touched upon. The leafy foliage of the cross is found in quite a few English examples, but only rarely elsewhere. It will be recalled that the cross is rough-hewn in the Crucifixion of Judith of Flanders' Gospels (Fig. 95) of the mid-eleventh century, a reference to the belief that it was made of wood from the Tree of Life; the foliation of the Lindseye cross has the same iconographic significance. Also to be noted as a thirteenth-century detail of iconography is the fastening of Christ's feet with one nail instead of the two found without exception in earlier versions (Figs. 13, 40, 75, 84 [Plate XIII], etc.). Adolf Goldschmidt has pointed out[19] that the three-nail Crucifixion type appears first in sculpture. In painting or a miniature, it contributes to an increase of plastic energy and greater freedom of movement, qualities that underlie the restrained yet poignant emotional content of the Lindseye Psalter version.

In France, where the *Bible moralisée* was presumably compiled in the milieu of Saint Louis himself, the style of its illumination has been considered that of the royal atelier, for all its conservatism, not to say archaism. This atelier was to react in its turn to the progressive English influences that had already become apparent in the Morgan 638 Old Testament miniatures (Fig. 146); the miniatures in a Psalter made for Louis himself (Paris, BN, Ms. lat. 10525) between 1253 and 1270 (probably *c.* 1256) are to the point. Its original ownership is attested in a fourteenth-century note on f.Av at the beginning, and the date has been established by necrological notices in the calendar. The latest of these in 1252 recorded the death of Louis's mother, Blanche of Castille, while the date of Louis's death in 1270 is the *terminus ante quem*. Saint Louis's Psalter is a small

Grant li aignel auint ouert le sime sel graunt
Trerremuer su fer. E le solail fu fer neir aust cumun
sac de peil. e tote la lune su fer cum sanc. e les estoile del
cel cheurent sur la tere. auis cum le fier lest cheir sun saus feur
kaunt il est mu de graunt uent. E le cel sen departi cu un
liure enuolupe. ↄ cheskeune muntaine e les isles sunt
mues de lur liu. E les reise les princes. e les balliff. e les
riches e les fors. e les serfs. e les frauns semusscerent en
foses. e en pertz des muntaines. E dient as muntaines.
e as peres. Cheez sur nus. e museces nus de la face al se
auint sur le throne. e del curus del aignel. pur co ke le
graunt uir de lur curus uient. E ki purra ester.

Le ouerture del sime sel apartent al deterer des gius e a la
pel des paens. Il ouert le sime sel kaunt il pempli poeure
co ke il auer auaunt dist. Grant te moc. Par la tere en est hu les
gius fust signefiez. Treremor est ter. kaunt ceste gent sut destruz p les
romains. Li solail ē fer neir. kaunt les gius ki par conusaunce
de un sul deu. e p la garde de lai resplendoient entre gent cu le
solail. e pus sut hais de rote gēt pur lur feloniees. La lune sig
nefie le synagoge. ke est cu sanc del saint ihu crist. par les este
les les pines des prestres. e les notarie e les pharisens sut enten
duz P le cel. le ueu testament. ki paser des gius treske a paens.
P les muntanes. ceus ki manenent en la cutez. p les isles. ce ki mane
nent es chaumpestres. P les reis e les bailliff. ce ki gouernenent le po
ple

Fig. 147.
Cambridge, Trinity College Library, Ms. R. 16. 2, f.7. The
Apocalypse, The Opening of the Sixth Seal; Angels with
the Four Winds and the Seal of God.

book (21 x 14.5 cm; *c.* 8.25 x 5.75″), typical of the reduced format of volumes meant for personal rather than liturgical use in the thirteenth century. Seventy-eight full-page miniatures precede the text, of Old Testament subjects from the Sacrifice of Cain and Abel through the Coronation of Saul, and there are eight historiated initials in the text proper.[20]

Typical of the full-page miniatures is the one on f.11v (Fig. 149, Plate XXIV) illustrating the story of Abraham sending his servant into Mesopotamia to find a wife for his son, Isaac, and the encounter with Rebekah at the Well (Gen. 14:1–20). Unlike the discursive narrative of the Vienna Genesis version of the subject (Fig. 8), only the dispatching of the servant and the drawing of water are shown. They read from left to right, separated by the panel of blue diaper work in the otherwise plain burnished-gold background. Comparison of the figures with those in the *Bible moralisée* and Lewis Psalter miniatures on the one hand (Figs. 143, 145) and in the Morgan 638 Old Testament scene on the other (Fig. 146) shows the closer affinity of the Saint Louis Psalter style with the latter. There are the same broadly simplified areas, supple movements, and gracefully elegant proportions, as against the emphatic plasticity of the others. Notable too is the sophisticated and decorative color harmony,[21] dominated as would be expected by deep blues and reds, but with effective foils in touches of green, lavender, and light blue. The whole is distinguished by the meticulous detail of the workmanship, the refinement and consistency of the execution, and the linear formulae, which are at the same time graphically integrated and plastically effective, marking the miniatures of Saint Louis's Psalter as one of the most noteworthy examples in French illumination of full-fledged High Gothic style.

The majority of the full-page miniatures in the Saint Louis Psalter have rectangular borders of foliate motives enclosing an architectural setting of gables with pointed and cusped arches, pinnacles, pointed and circular traceried windows, and salient buttresses, suggesting that the episodes take place along the side of a Gothic church. The parallels already noted between earlier French thirteenth-century illumination and the arts of sculpture and stained-glass are preparation for such an architectonic synthesis. Architectural elements appear in many earlier miniatures (Figs. 86, 90 [Plate XIV], 129, *et al.*) and they are comparable to the features of buildings of their periods. But the architectural settings in the Saint Louis Psalter miniatures have a different function from their symbolic purpose in earlier styles. This is anticipated in the spatial implications of the architectural framework in the Old Testament miniatures of Morgan 638 (Fig. 146),[22] implications that are carried still further here. For the fully plastic figures, in which a kind of actuality is attained (without being realistic in the usual sense), are integrated with the architectural setting in just the same way that the fully plastic figures of contemporary cathedrals are integrated with the buildings by the arched canopies in which they stand. So too the figures of the Saint Louis Psalter miniatures are placed on ground lines that ripple and wave, overlapping each other and the columns between the arches, to the end that their plastically realized forms exist in viable space. Compare the arbitrary treatment of the ground lines in the medallions of the Lewis Psalter miniatures (Fig. 145), whether they be the segmental curves of the Annunciation and Visitation or the sheep in the Annunciation to the Shepherds; in either case, there is no implication of space in the two-dimensional effect.

In taking over the vocabulary and grammar of Gothic building and arriving at a pictorial synthesis comparable to the architectonic one of contemporary architectural style, French illumination of the mid-thirteenth century would appear to have been immediately and directly influenced by its sister art.[23] And indeed, the system of arches, gables, pinnacles, and rose windows of the Saint Louis Psalter miniatures faithfully follows that of the exterior of the Sainte-Chapelle built in Paris by order of Louis IX between 1243 and 1246 as a shrine for the relic of the Crown of Thorns.[24] So close is the relationship between the design of the building and the pattern of the miniatures that the possibility has been suggested[25] that the scheme of the latter was directed by Pierre de Montreuil, architect of King Louis.[26]

From the same atelier that produced the Psalter of Saint Louis came a two-volume Evangeliary or Lectionary of Gospel readings (Paris, BN, Mss. lat. 8892 & 17326) made for the Sainte-Chapelle, probably between 1260 and 1270. There are no full-page miniatures in either volume, but each has a wealth of figured or historiated initials. Some in the first part of Ms. 8892 are related to the *Bible moralisée* style, but the remainder and all in Ms. 17326 are very close to the Saint Louis Psalter manner. On f.130v of the latter are two initials I (Fig. 150) introducing readings that begin, as they do all through the volume, *In illo tempore,* "Now in that time." In the one on the left, the small scenes are of the Calling of Matthew (Matt. 9:9–13); on the right are Christ confronting the Pharisees and John the Baptist preaching (Luke 7:28–29). Architectural canopies above the scenes on the right, and the diaper panels alternating with burnished-gold grounds in both initials are in the manner established in the Saint Louis Psalter, as is also the drapery formula of large and simple folds falling in quiet curves. Only in the color scheme is there any noteworthy change from the Psalter style. It tends toward a pastel gamut of pinks, roses, soft blues, and grays in a rather restrained overall effect that suggests a slightly later date for the Evangeliary.[27]

The plasticity of the figures and the incipient spatialism of the settings in the Saint Louis Psalter and Sainte-Chapelle Evangeliary style contribute to a closer approximation to visual reality than has as yet been seen in mediaeval illumination. But precisely those same characteristics tend to compromise the decorative unity of script and illustration that had been a fundamental principle of the illuminated book since pre-Carolingian times. On folios given wholly to illustration (Figs. 145 and 149, Plate XXIV), this is not so apparent. On others with both text and illumination (Figs. 146, 150), the potential incompatibility between the two-dimensional pattern of the script and the three-dimensional implications of the illustration cannot be discounted. To mitigate this dualism and maintain ornamental equilibrium in the design of the folio, the Gothic illuminator developed a new concept of the historiated initial; an early example (Fig. 151) can be seen on f.39 of the Lewis Psalter (Philadelphia, Free Public Library, Lewis Ms. 185) of *c.* 1260.

Fig. 148.
London, Society of Antiquaries, Ms. 59, ff.35v–36. The Psalter of Robert of Lindseye, The Crucifixion; Christ Enthroned.

Fig. 150.
Paris, Bibliothèque Nationale, Ms. lat. 17326, f.130v. Lectionary of the Sainte-Chapelle, New Testament Scenes.

At the top of the folio, the letter I of *In domino confido,* "In the Lord put I my trust," is the beginning of Psalm 10 (11), one of the psalms of supplication. In the upper half, King David addresses his plea to the Lord; the two figures in the lower half are the righteous of verse 5. This letter is arbitrarily inserted in the text, partially indented in the column, partially extending into the margin, and without effective formal or decorative relationship to either one. At the bottom of the same folio, in the initial S of *Salvum me fac,* "Help, Lord; for the godly man ceaseth" of Psalm 11 (12), the psalmist prays before a small building. From the lower left corner of the initial frame, a bar with a decorative foliate terminal hangs down, while from its upper right angle a leaf projects into the space immediately above the a of *Salvum.* By so extending the design of the initial beyond its form as a letter, it is effectively integrated with both the written script and the neutral parchment plane on which both text and illustration have their proper places, and ornamental unity, disregarded in the upper part of the page, is thereby achieved.

Although the concept of the decorated and historiated initial was not new, the particular form it took in thirteenth-century Gothic manuscripts was a major and inventive innovation. In pre-Carolingian Occidental

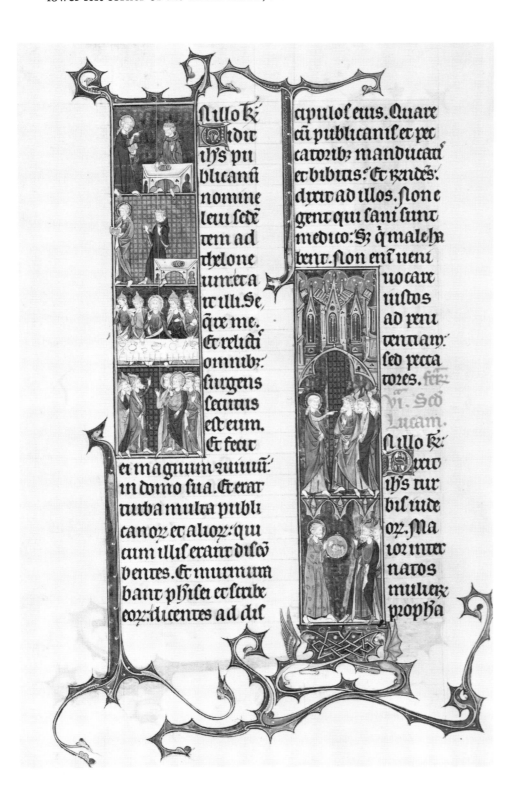

illumination, the general similarity of a natural form to a letter, or even of a theme like the Crucifixion, could suggest the figured patterns on the pages of books like the Luxeuil Lectionary (Fig. 36) and the Sacramentary of Gellone (Fig. 40). There is incomparable variety and imaginativeness in the figured initials of eleventh-century Anglo-Saxon books,[28] which carries over into the great twelfth-century English Bibles, in forms paralleled in kind if not in opulence in the products of many continental scriptoria. But even the most magnificent pre-thirteenth-century initials are embellishments of the letter itself, filling its form or elaborating its outline with flowers, leaves, animals, figures, and the like. Original as the Q of the Cîteaux *Moralia* in Job may be (Fig. 136), the design is determined by the form of the letter. The bar extension of the Gothic historiated initial, on the other hand, was developed to meet the need to reestablish the relationship between it and its associated text, a relationship endangered by the emerging realism of its figured patterns. Its basic purpose is structural: to recreate the formal unity of text and illustration.

Once conceived, the bar extension of the Gothic initial developed in a characteristic way. There is little

appreciable difference in date between the Lewis Psalter and the Sainte-Chapelle Evangeliary, but the latter is more advanced in the treatment of the initial, as it is in figure style, an understandable difference between the products of a sophisticated metropolitan atelier and a nonurban scriptorium. The bars of the initials on f.130v of the Sainte-Chapelle manuscript (Fig. 150) are extended on the left of the text columns, ending in leaf-like shapes that are repeated in the motives sprouting from the other angles. These foliate shapes have a rather indeterminate character but resemble the cusps or triangular projections from Gothic moldings as much as anything else. In due course, the foliate elements become specific and individual, just as the carved leaves do on the capitals of thirteenth-century cathedrals. They serve the Gothic illuminator in much the same way as the Gothic builder. The leafy tendrils that integrate script and miniature on the manuscript folio are the exact counterparts of the foliated stringcourse encircling the interior of Amiens Cathedral.

Precisely when and where the Gothic bar initial was first used cannot be certainly determined, but it is found in both northern France and England from the mid-

Fig. 151.
Philadelphia, Free Library, Ms. Lewis 185, ff.38v–39.
Psalter, Text—Psalm IX (10), v. 5 to Psalm XI (12), v. 1.

Plate XVIII. Paris, Bibliothèque Nationale, Ms. lat. 254, f. 10. Gospel-book from Moissac-Agen, St. Matthew.

Plate XIX. Rome, Biblioteca Vallicelliana, Ms. E. 16, f. 96. Gospel-book from Farfa, St. Luke. (Photo author)

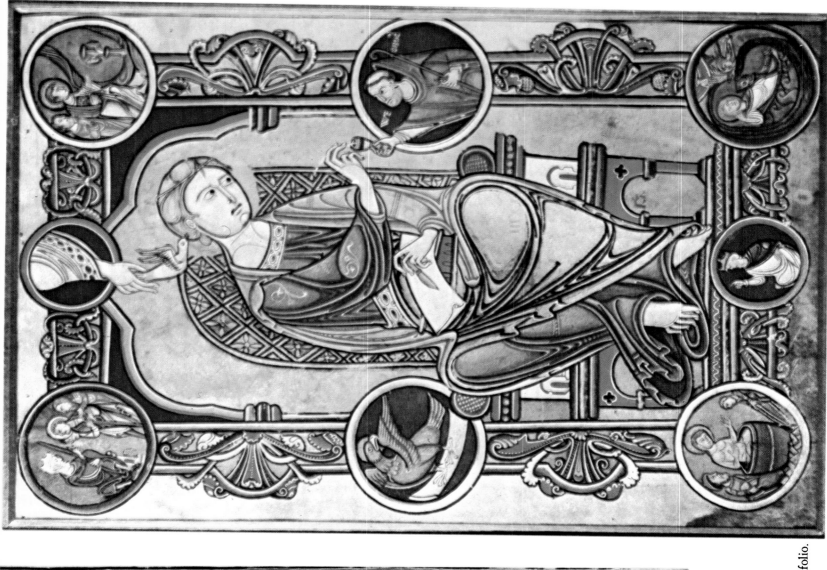

Plate XX. Hildesheim, St. Godehard's Treasury, unnumbered ms., p. 19. The Albani Psalter, The Annunciation.

Plate XXI. Avesnes, Société archéologique, detached folio. Gospel-book from Liesses, St. John.

thirteenth century on. It appears in an English Bible (London, BM, Royal Ms. 1 D. I) identified as the work of a scribe named William of Devon in a colophon on f.540v; on stylistic grounds, it can be dated *c.* 1250. The opening page of Genesis (Fig. 152) on f.5 begins with the I of *In principio* filling the full height of the left margin. It is decorated with a sequence of Creation scenes through Adam and Eve toiling, and, at the bottom, the Crucifixion. These scenes, with backgrounds of gold, red, and blue, are framed in Gothic arches rather like the canopies in the Sainte-Chapelle Evangeliary initials, but somewhat simpler. But the bar motive is considerably larger, extending across the top and bottom of the page, along the right margin, and dividing the two text columns. The bars are cusped and end in foliate forms or dragons. No place of origin is given, but Sts. Peter, Paul, and Martin are shown in the facing miniature on f.4v of the Crucifixion with the Enthroned Virgin and her Coronation;[29] all these saints were particularly venerated at Canterbury.

Even greater interest attaches to another element in the Genesis page decoration in William of Devon's Bible, the grotesque or drollery. Along the top bar are dogs chasing a rabbit and a stag. An archer poised on a leaf projecting in from the right-hand marginal bar draws an arrow at a rabbit above. The inverted-V bars at the bottom end in dragons and support herons and hybrid grotesques. These reappear on the horizontal bar above with two animals like wolves or foxes; one is dressed like a monk and the other wears a bishop's mitre, and carries a crozier. It goes without saying that these figures have nothing to do with the text, either as illustration or interpretation. There is no explanation for them, in fact, save that they play the same role in the Gothic manuscript as the gargoyles and grotesques that their stone counterparts do on the Gothic cathedral. All are expressions of the increasingly anthropocentric or "menschlich" orientation of Occidental thought in the thirteenth century.[30]

Like the Gothic initial, the Gothic drollery is not without ancestry. In the *Christi autem* monogram on f.34 of the Book of Kells (Fig. 49), cats are watching mice at play in the lower part of the miniature. It has been suggested that this may have been inspired by observation of what must have been a frequent occurrence in the monastic buttery, but nothing assures this interpretation.[31] Animals and grotesques often appear in the complex involutions of ribbons and foliage in the decorated initials of eleventh- and twelfth-century

manuscripts (Fig. 108), and the type persists into the early thirteenth, as in the *Beatus* initial of the Robert de Lindseye Psalter.[32] But like the decorative embellishments of pre-Gothic initials, the animals and grotesques of pre-Gothic illumination, diverting as they are, do not escape the confines of the letters. The Gothic drollery is independent of any restriction and appears where the whim of its creator pleases.

Early thirteenth-century English drolleries, intended like those in the William of Devon Psalter to entertain or amuse, can be found in two Psalters in the British Museum (Mss. Harley 5102 & Lansdowne 420),[33] and another (Belvoir Castle, Rutland Psalter)[34] of about mid-century contains literally scores. A monkey on f.38v of the Lewis Psalter (Fig. 151) is a reasonably early continental drollery of about 1260, and probably from northern France where it can easily be understood as a result of English connections. In like fashion, the Beatus page of a north French Psalter in the Walters Gallery of Baltimore (Ms. 45) has a complete bar border with foliation,[35] and although the illustration at the bottom or *bas-de-page* is of the Slaying of Goliath and thus pertinent to the text rather than being a drollery, it is comparable in general to the Genesis page in William of Devon's Bible (Fig. 152). On the basis of all evidence, it can hardly be doubted that the Gothic drollery was invented in England early in the thirteenth century and spread to the Continent, probably through northern France and Flanders, where it enjoyed a vogue comparable to its popularity in England. Granted the predilection for exaggerated characterization, which often became caricature in Anglo-Saxon and English illumination, as early as *c.* 1000 in the Harley 603 copy of the Utrecht Psalter (Fig. 91) and apparent even in the miniatures of the Albani Psalter (Fig. 130, Plate XX), it is not difficult to recognize the humor of the Gothic drollery as a thirteenth-century realization of this characteristically English trait.

Humor and vivid characterization are among the distinctive qualities of the Genesis scenes (Fig. 153) on one of six leaves (Cambridge, Fitzwilliam Museum, Ms. 330), which were possibly once part of a psalter. The date is about 1230–1250. Some of the subjects are unusual—God providing Adam and Eve with clothes in the upper left medallion, and Cain planning to murder Abel immediately beneath. The brisk, matter-of-fact way in which God attires the disobedient pair might be understood as the conception of an artist interpreting an untraditional theme, but Eve berating Adam in the

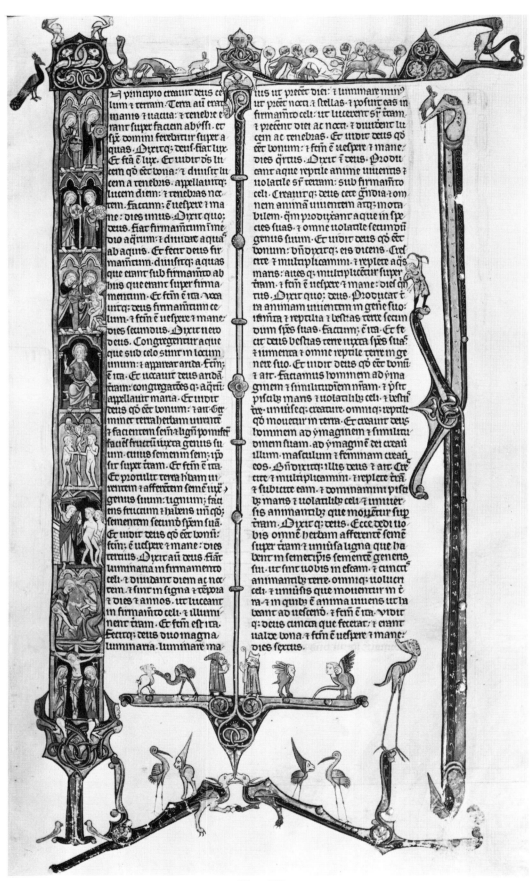

Fig. 152.
London, British Museum, Ms. Royal 1 D, I, f.5. Bible of
William of Devon, Creation Scenes and Drolleries.

Fig. 153.
Cambridge, Fitzwilliam Museum, Ms. 330. Bible Picture
Leaf by W. de Brailes, Scenes from Genesis.

upper right medallion, Cain gloating over Abel's death, and his expression and gesture of pretended innocence when accused of the crime are minute masterpieces of characterization, unprecedented in earlier illumination in England or elsewhere. The composition of the miniature is somewhat conventional, the arrangement of the pointed elliptical medallions somewhat resembling a stained-glass window. But the stocky figures with their vivid movements and expressive gestures are instinct with a new and realistic feeling for the very real human dramas they enact.

Were nothing else known of the Fitzwilliam Genesis miniature than what is seen in it, its interest would be considerable. Interest is augmented by the fact that its author is known. In a Last Judgment on another leaf in the Fitzwilliam collection, the bust of a tonsured cleric being snatched from the damned by an angel (Fig. 154) is inscribed *"W. de Brailes qui me fecit*—W. de Brailes who made me." Nor is this the only signature left by the earliest illuminator so to identify himself with his work. It appears also on ff.43 and 47 of a small Book of Hours of Sarum use, [37] which is of interest in its own right as one of the earliest-known Books of Hours as an independent volume, i.e., not combined with a psalter. Two villages in Warwickshire, Upper and Lower Brailes, may be the community from which the artist

Fig. 154.
Cambridge, Fitzwilliam Museum, Ms. 330, Bible Picture Leaf by W. de Brailes, Last Judgment, detail.

of her deceived servants are immediately communicated by the grotesque facial expressions, contrasted with Joseph's smug and mannered smile. The types are characteristic of de Brailes's work, the exaggerated features drawn in heavy lines on the brown flesh surfaces modeled with white highlights. The banded headdress is a favorite detail of contemporary costume. The miniature is framed in the Romanesque manner by simple blue bands, but the burnished-gold ground is tooled, and the figures are somewhat slenderer and more rhythmic in movement than in the Fitzwilliam miniature. This has led to the conclusion that the Walters leaves are a little later than the signed works, along with some of the elaborately decorated initials in a psalter in New College, Oxford (Ms. 322), which are distinctly Gothic in style.

Apart from the listing of William de Brailes (who may or may not have been the illuminator of the examples discussed) as living in Oxford in 1260, nothing more is known. By contrast, there is considerable information about his contemporary, Matthew Paris of St. Albans.[39] He was scribe, illuminator, painter, goldsmith, and historian of St. Albans from about 1236 until 1259, and also found time for a journey to Norway in 1248–49.[40] A signed work, the miniature of the Virgin and Child with Matthew Paris kneeling before them (Fig. 156) is on f.6 of a manuscript of the History of the English (*Historia Anglorum*) in the British Museum (Royal Ms. 14 C. vii). The last entry in the hand of the inscription on the miniature is for the year 1259. Also thought to be by Matthew Paris himself, and close to his style in any event, are some miniatures in another historical work, the *Chronica Maiora* (Cambridge, Corpus Christi College, Ms. 26), and the influence of his manner is seen in the illustrations of a number of other manuscripts.[41]

In the art of Matthew Paris, one of the most characteristic and specifically English techniques of illumination is seen again—outline drawing (cf. Figs. 88, 91, 94, *et al.*). It had never fallen entirely into disuse, but the plastic values and rigidly organized decorative schemes of late twelfth-century English miniatures (Fig. 117) were understandably better realized in patterns of gold and opaque color than in line. Some miniatures of the Trinity College Apocalypse (cf. Fig. 147) were executed in combined outline and painting techniques, however, and as it may well have been produced at St. Albans when Matthew Paris was there, it can be considered indicative of his background. The Enthroned

came, and a William de Brailes was listed among illuminators living in Oxford in 1260.

W. de Brailes's distinctive figure style has been recognized in a number of miniatures that are unsigned but certainly to be related to him or his atelier (Baltimore, Walters Gallery, Ms. 106).[38] The story of Joseph and Potiphar's Wife (Fig. 155) is on f.15, one of a series cut from a small book (5¼ x 3⅞″) and rebound; they may once have prefixed a psalter like the similar grouping at the beginning of Saint Louis's Psalter. The anger of the spurned woman (Gen. 39) and the wrath

Virgin and Child being adored by Matthew Paris has something still of Romanesque monumental design and solemn content in the forms defined by quietly flowing curves, which are heavy and forceful for the contours, lighter and delicately shaded with color in the inner lines of drapery folds. The same style is seen in the illustrated *Life of St. Alban* (Dublin, Trinity College Library, Ms. E. i. 40), certainly the one Paris is recorded as having executed, in which the implicit narrative content encouraged a more animated manner, filled with lively movement and characterized by expressive gestures that are typically Gothic.[42]

It has already been mentioned that the Apocalypse was a favored subject in English thirteenth-century illumination, and St. Albans seems to have been a major center of production. The grouping of the considerable number of Apocalypse manuscripts, whether textual[43] or stylistic,[44] reveals a consistency in the miniatures of the group assigned to St. Albans that must be the result, in part at least, of the continuing influence of Matthew Paris's style of illumination. Five manuscripts in particular are illuminated in the style he developed of tinted outline drawings on plain vellum,[45] and although their texts fall into both the principal groups identified by Delisle and Meyer, the themes chosen and the compositions are remarkably similar in all. The miniatures are executed in outline with delicate washes of red, blue, and green in plain tinted borders, and are peopled with figures in which English fondness for caricature and the grotesque is frequently apparent.

Other Apocalypses of the later thirteenth century have been ascribed to Canterbury, notably Ms. 209 in the Lambeth Library in London. Its miniatures[46] are painted in full color on backgrounds of gold or color, quite unlike the tinted drawings on plain parchment of the St. Albans books. Lying between the two in this respect is one of the finest Apocalypses of the period and one of the most distinguished manuscripts of any type, Ms. Douce 180 in the Bodleian Library at Oxford.[47] It was made for Edward I and his wife, Eleanor of Castille, before he ascended the throne in 1271, as they are shown in an initial on f.1 in the robes of prince and princess. Certain features of its ninety-seven miniatures have been thought to be French, but the manuscript has also been assigned to Canterbury, a center whose products often combined characteristics of illumination on both sides of the English Channel. But Millar,[48] and Hassall in the most recent study of the manuscript, are of the opinion that it might well have originated in the

Fig. 155.
Baltimore, Walters Art Gallery, Ms. 106, f.15. Scenes from the Bible by W. de Brailes, Joseph and Potiphar's Wife.

court circles of Westminster. In any case, the combination of figures painted on plain backgrounds and framed in bands that are sometimes decorated but as often simply colored, place the Douce Apocalypse somewhat apart from both the St. Albans and Canterbury manuscripts—"in a class by itself," as Millar remarks—for its technique and the refined power of its style.

St. John's vision of the Four Angels restraining the Four Winds (Fig. 157) on p. 19 of the Douce Apocalypse is an interpretation of the same subject (Rev. 7: 1–5) painted by Magius some three hundred and fifty years earlier in the Spanish Beatus manuscript (Fig. 99, Plate XVI) in the Morgan Library (Ms. 644). But where the Mozarabic artist presented the vision as it would appear to the observer, the anonymous artist of Douce 180 describes it as an experience of the apostolic visionary. In the Beatus miniature, the sea surrounding the earth fills the entire frame and nothing is represented but what is mentioned in the text. Nearly all the same elements appear in the Douce miniature but the angel with the "seal of the living God" (so identified by the cruciform nimbus also seen in the Trinity College Apocalypse version (Fig. 147) usually signifying God the Father or Christ) descends from the upper right angle of the banded frame above St. John seated with staff and book on a wooded hill and regarding the cosmic apparition. The Gothic artist's intention was to describe St. John having the vision; the Mozarabic painter's had been to describe the visionary's experience but addressed directly to the observer instead of indirectly through the eyes of the Evangelist.

A number of unfinished miniatures in the Douce Apocalypse allow the method of their execution to be determined.[49] All forms and details were carefully indicated by lines with no shading. The drapery folds are broad and simple, the forms they cover well proportioned and articulated. Gold was then applied for nimbi and other appropriate details, followed by successive layers of flat and rather thin washes of color, and finished off with darker and more opaque overpainting. The effect is sober, even sombre on occasion, appropriate to the content of the Apocalyptic theme, yet not lacking the graceful and lyric touches that are the essence of Gothic style. Notable also is the absence of the caricature and grotesquerie often found in St. Albans miniatures. In their monumental elegance, the Douce 180 miniatures share a quality of the most distinguished contemporary work in France, like the Psalter of Saint-Louis (Fig. 149, Plate XXIV) and the Evangeliary of the Sainte-Chapelle (Fig. 150). In so doing, they illustrate a well-made point[50] that a "Channel School" existed in the thirteenth century just as one did in the eleventh.

If French elegance made its way across the Channel to influence English style, continental illuminators were quick to take up the marginal drollery. It appears quite early in books identified with the north French and Franco-Flemish region, such as the elegant Psalter of Gui de Dampierre of *c.* 1270[51] (Brussels, Bibl. royale, Ms. 10607), which is also an example of the very small books (10.7 x 7.8 cm: *c.* 4¼ x 3″) intended for private and personal use that became very popular in the late thirteenth century and thereafter. A Breviary for use in the church of Saint-Sépulchre at Cambrai (Cambrai, Bibl. mun., Ms. 102)[52] of about 1290 shows the opulence with which marginal bar borders had developed by the end of the century, and their lavish popula-

tion of drolleries. The border is somewhat more restrained in a Psalter from Picardy in northern France of about 1290 (Paris, BN, Ms. lat. 10435), but it encloses the entire page and all kinds of animals and hybrid grotesques perch in the knots of interlace and the leafy sprays.[53] Eight large historiated initials are dispersed through the psalter text, the one illustrated (Fig. 158) being for Psalm 95 (96), which begins *Cantate domino canticum novum,* "O sing unto the Lord a new song." In the upper part of the large C is the Creation of Eve, with a group of choristers below. The figures, drawn with firm yet elastic contours, are lithe and graceful, well proportioned and effectively articulated in the gestures and movements, and with typically Gothic heads that are broad through the temples and taper to pointed chins. The nudes of the Creation scene and the heads and hands of the other figures are reserved in the natural color of the parchment, while the draperies are light purple-red, blue, and yellow, the figures placed on a ground of burnished and tooled gold. Between the outline of the C and the enclosing frame is a diaper pattern in red. Above the initial and below the horizontal bar border of the *bas-de-page* are red inscriptions identifying the subjects of the scenes in the initials; they seem to have been added by a one-time owner of the book.

Elsewhere in the Picardy Psalter, similar inscriptions give the specific names and places of the young people shown singing and playing musical instruments or dancing, as they are here. Written, no doubt, as a jest by the owner in identifying these engaging worldly intruders into the scriptural page with his friends, these inscriptions are in a local patois of the region of Picardie, as are also the place names. Nothing could illustrate more entertainingly the mundane and worldly sentiment that developed in the later thirteenth century, a concomitant of the growing feeling for realism that appears in the pictorial style as well.

It should not be assumed, however, that increasing realism of form and changing sentiment were indications of diminishing faith. Gothic feeling was communal, and its finest expression was in ensembles that bespeak collective belief defined by symbols. These, once established, could be treated with limitless freedom and individuality, whether playful, as in the Picardy Psalter, or poignant, as in certain miniatures in the Psalter and Hours of the Virgin made for Yolande de Soissons around 1275 (N. Y., Pierpont Morgan Library, Ms. 729).[54] She was the wife of Bernard V, sire de Moreuil

Fig. 156.
London, British Museum, Ms. Royal 14 C. VII, f.6. His-
toria Anglorum by Matthew Paris, The Virgin and Child
adored by Matthew Paris.

ost hec uidi quatuo2 ange
los stantes super quatuo2
angulos terre tenentes quatuo2
uentos terre ne flarent uenti su
per terram neq̃ super ullam arbo
rem. Et uidi alterum angelum
ascendentem ab o2tu solis habentē
signum dei uiui ꞇ clamauit uoce
magna quatuo2 angelis quibus
datum est nocere terre ꞇ mari dicēs
Nolite nocere terre ꞇ mari neq̃ ꞇ
arbonb; quoadusq̃; signemus ser
uos dei nostri in frontib; co2um. Et
audiui numerum signatorum cen
tum quadraginta.iiij. milia ex ꞇ

omni tribu filio2um isrł. Ex tri
bu iuda duodecim milia signati.
Ex tribu ruben: xij. milia signa
ti. Ex tribu gad. xij. milia signa
ti. Ex tribu aser. xij. m̃; signati. Ex
tribu neptalim. xij. milia signati.
Ex tribu manasse. xij. m̃; signati.
Ex tribu symeon. xij. milia signa
ti. Ex tribu leui duodecim milia
signati. Ex tribu ysachar duode
cim milia signati. Ex tribu zabu
lon duodecim milia signati. Ex tri
bu ioseph duo decim milia signa
ti. Ex tribu beniamin duodecim
milia signati.   Post hec uidi. ꞇ c̃

Fig. 157.
Oxford, Bodleian Library, Ms. Douce 180, p. 19. The
Apocalypse, Angels with the Four Winds and the Seal
of God.

near Amiens, and the book was probably written and illuminated in that region. It is small in format (18.2 x 13.1 cm: 7⅛ x 5⅛″) and contains four hundred and thirty-four folios with forty full-page miniatures, sixty-six historiated initials, and numerous drolleries and marginal borders with Yolande's armorial device throughout. In this and the numerous offices added to the traditional psalms and canticles, the Psalter and Hours of Yolande de Soissons is typical of the costly devotional books of the late thirteenth century.

The frame of the Crucifixion (Fig. 159) on f.345v is topped by gabled Gothic arcading to establish its architectonic character. The cross stands before a burnished-gold background, and is identified as the Tree of Life by its twelve leafy branches. Above the cross-bar, the pelican nurses its young with its own blood, a familiar symbol of the Saviour's sacrifice of His life for mankind. Below, the historical participants in the episode, St. John, the Virgin, and the Roman centurion, are accompanied by three other persons who were not present: Moses, Balaam, and Caiaphas, identified by their inscribed scrolls, and a sword is embedded in Mary's breast. Nearly all of these nonhistorical and therefor nonrealistic details are found here as symbols of one sort or another. Moses and Balaam bore witness in their prophecies to the divinity of Christ, as did also the Jewish high priest Caiaphas in his statement "that one man should die for the people, and that the whole nation perish not" (John 11:50). The meaning of the Pelican in Her Piety would be quite clear to a man of the thirteenth century, and the sword refers directly to Simeon's words to Mary when Christ was brought to the Temple—"Yea, a sword shall pierce through thy own soul also" (Luke 2:35).[55]

No less important than symbolism in conveying the expressive content of the figures in the Crucifixion of Yolande de Soissons's Psalter is their style. The background is burnished gold, as has been mentioned, although delicately patterned color is used for other miniatures in the book, like the one on f.232v of Yolande adoring the Enthroned Virgin and Child.[56] Against these backgrounds, the figures are two-dimensional projections of plastic forms, defined by vigorous contours and with what little modeling there is limited for the most part to the draperies. They stand on base lines rather than planes, and the architectural frames imply space even less than they do in the Saint Louis Psalter miniatures (Fig. 149, Plate XXIV). One detail, however, reveals an increasing awareness of plastic

values, even though couched in linear terms. Christ's body is fastened to the cross with three nails, as it is in the Lindseye Psalter version (Fig. 148), but here there is a double break in the figure since the left knee projects out over the right one. There is more emphasis on the plasticity of the forms as a result, and also on the tragic content of the theme, stressing as it does the broken lifelessness of the body. Yet, for all its expressiveness, the style of the miniatures in Yolande de Soissons's Psalter is marked by the elegance and dignity that distinguish French and specifically Parisian illumination of the late thirteenth-century from contemporary English and Franco-Flemish work like the Picardy Psalter (Fig. 158).

Several different artists worked on the Yolande de Soissons Psalter miniatures, and although the Crucifixion on f.345v is not by the most distinguished one, its style is clearly related to his. He was the artist of the miniature of St. Francis's Sermon to the Birds on f.2, a rather early instance of this theme in north European art, and of another Crucifixion on f.4v.[57] The inherent interest of the miniatures by this master, doubtless the head of the atelier, is made even greater by the close stylistic relationship between them and the work of one of the earliest named and identifiable illuminators in Paris, Maître Honoré.[58] Credited by document with the supervision and decoration of one book[59] with which others can be grouped for stylistic reasons, Honoré was a slightly younger contemporary of Matthew Paris and W. de Brailes in England.

Unlike his English counterparts, however, Honoré was not a monk or cleric but a secular professional illuminator who is listed in a tax roll of 1292 as having paid a levy of ten sous on his property on the rue Erembourc-de-Brie, where his atelier also included his son-in-law Richart de Verdun and his assistant Thomassin. This street is now called the rue Boutebrie, and opens off the present rue de la Parcheminerie, which used to be called the rue aux Ecrivains. These streets are in the region around the University of Paris, understandably the locale of considerable book production. It was from Honoré's shop on the rue Erembourc-de-Brie that the copy of Gratian's *Decretals* was bought for forty Paris livres in 1288, according to a note on f.351. Honoré is mentioned again in a tax list for 1293, and a notice in the accounts of the royal palace of the Louvre for 1296 records the payment to him of twenty Paris livres for a book for the king, Philippe le Bel. On the same page of the account book, a payment of 107 livres,

10 sous is noted for a breviary for the king, and while there is no specific documentary identification of this item in the accounts with the so-called Breviary of Philippe le Bel (Paris, B.N., Ms. lat. 1023), it is generally held to be the volume in question.

The Breviary of Philippe le Bel is a stout volume of five hundred and seventy-seven folios of relatively small size (20.5 x 13.5 cm: *c*. 8 x 5½″). Several items in the calendar indicate that it was made for a member of the royal family, the basis for identifying it with the Louvre accounts for 1296 mentioned above. The decoration consists of historiated initials, for the most part, but there is one full-page miniature of Scenes from the Life of David (Fig. 160, Plate XXV) on f.7v immediately following the calendar. It is composed in two registers with Samuel anointing David in the presence of Jesse and his brothers above, and the slaying and beheading of Goliath below. The upper scene has a gold background with a tooled rinceau design, the lower one a diaper lozenge pattern of blue and gold with white fleurs-de-lys on the blue surfaces.

Two components of Maître Honoré's style merit particular notice, the plasticity of the figures and their relationship to the space around them. The contours are as positive as in the slightly earlier miniatures in Yolande de Soissons's Psalter (Fig. 159), but the surfaces they define are vigorously modeled by variations in the tone of the local colors of the compact figures. These frequently overlap, like the forms in a sculptured relief, and the feet of figures in both registers and David's sword in the Beheading overpass the framing borders. As a result, although they still stand on a ground line rather than a ground plane, they do seem to exist in space—space delimited by the tooled or diapered backgrounds to which the figures are related by implication if not organically, but space none the less. In so affirming the "consubstantiality of form and space,"[60] Maître Honoré achieves an effect comparable in kind to that in the painting of his Florentine contemporary Giotto. Yet he does so within the continuing expressive tradition of the Gothic north, following the example of contemporary sculpture in attempting to liberate both form and space from the synthesis achieved in earlier thirteenth-century High Gothic art, e.g., the *Vierge Dorée* of Amiens Cathedral.[61]

English illumination in the closing years of the thirteenth century continued to reveal connections with French work, as would be expected, but there were also other developments of interest. The manuscripts called "East Anglian" from their known or presumptive origin in that region (Suffolk, Norfolk, and Essex counties) established a stylistic tradition that was maintained through the first half of the fourteenth century. Most of its exemplars are psalters, always popular in England and continuing to be so, such as the Windmill Psalter (N. Y., Pierpont Morgan Library, Ms. 102), so named from the building that figures prominently in the decoration of f.2, the beginning of the text (Fig. 161). The initial B of *Beatus* on f.1v is decorated with the Tree of Jesse, showing the genealogy of Christ (cf. Fig. 137) in the bows and Creation scenes in the vertical part of the letter. The four Evangelists and their symbols appear in the medallions of the border, which encloses a diaper background. An unusual note is struck, however, in the enlargement of the second letter of the opening word—E—to fill the entire upper part of f.2. Its decoration includes, in addition to the windmill, the Massacre of the Innocents above, and an angel below, who swoops down with outstretched arms holding a scroll with the remaining letters of the opening phrase of the psalm—*atus qui non abiit.*

There is no specific date or provenance for the Windmill Psalter,[62] but it is generally thought to be from the last years of the thirteenth century and stylistically related to slightly later East Anglian manuscripts. There are French overtones in the strongly modeled surfaces within emphatic contours of the figures, but the capricious, not to say wayward, treatment of the ornament is quite unlike anything in current Parisian practice at the end of the thirteenth century. The flair for the unexpected in the diving angel also appears in line endings, like the hybrid creature inserted after the opening verse on f.2 and the extravagant red and blue flourishes enveloping the E and filling its unpeopled interstices, and the typically English drollery of the cock pheasant perched on a stump in the lower margin. No less individual than the animated figure style and the lively ornament is the color scheme of eleven large initials in the book and the numerous drolleries and line endings. Particularly striking is a recurring shade of iridescent greenish-gold, set off by a glowing blue and soft rose-red.

English illumination is notable even in its early phases for vivid characterization often verging on caricature, and the irrepressible humor that is sometimes found in unlikely subjects. This has been observed in some of the qualities that distinguish the early eleventh-century Anglo-Saxon copy of the Utrecht Psalter from

antate
dño cã
ntatum
nouū:
quia
mira
bilia
fecit:Sal
uit ti
bi dex
tera ei͂
et bza
chium

Fig. 158.
Paris, Bibliothèque Nationale, Ms. lat. 10435, ƒ.117.
Psalter from Picardy, Initial Page of Psalm XCV (96).

Fig. 159.
New York, Pierpont Morgan Library, Ms. 729, f.345v.
Psalter Hours of Yolande de Soissons, The Crucifixion.

its model (Figs. 61 [Plate VII] and 91), in the facial types of the Albani Psalter miniatures (Fig. 130, Plate XX), and in the work of W. de Brailes (Figs. 153–155), to say nothing of the concept of the marginal drollery. Another example is seen on f.33v (Fig. 162) of a Psalter and Book of Hours in the Walters Art Gallery of Baltimore (Ms. 102) which was written and illuminated about 1300, possibly in the Augustinian monastery of St. Julian, not far from St. Albans. There are two illuminated initials sprouting the inevitable tendrils in the margins, grotesque line endings, and a slanting line of red and blue flourishes in the lower margin indicating the completion of the page. But more text has been added below, its initial attached by a rope

to the right hand of a monk, wearing red hose and capuchon and a blue cloak, who points with his left hand to the place where the line should have been written. The text is from Psalm 127 (128):3, *Uxor tua sicut vitas habundans in lateribus domus tue,* "Thy wife shall be as a fruitful vine by the sides of thine house." Its conclusion, *Filii tui sicut novelle olivarum in circuiti mense tue,* "thy children like olive plants round about thy table," is the added line at the bottom. Nothing could be more original than such a transformation of an obvious error on the scribe's part into a humorously decorative adjunct of the page design. Elsewhere in the same manuscript (ff.72–80), a sequence of drolleries portrays a fox's funeral with a cortege of birds and ani-

Fig. 161.
New York, Pierpont Morgan Library, Ms. 102, ff.1v–2.
The Windmill Psalter, Incipit *Psalm I.*

Sicut sagitte in manu potentis: ita filii
excussorum.

Beatus vir qui implebit desiderium
suum ex ipsis: non confundetur cum
loquetur inimicis suis in porta.

Beati omnes qui timent dominum:
qui ambulant in uiis eius.

Labores manuum tuarum quia man
ducabis: beatus es et bene tibi erit.

Uxor tua sicut uitis habundans: in
lateribus domus tue.

Ecce sic benedicetur homo: qui timet
dominum.

Benedicat tibi dominus ex syon: ut
uideas bona ierusalem omnibus diebus
uite tue.

Et uideas filios filiorum tuorum: pacem
super israel.

Sepe expugnauerunt me a iuuentute

Filii tui sicut nouelle oliuarum: in circuitu men
se tue.

Fig. 162.
Baltimore, Walters Art Gallery, Ms. 102, f.33v. Psalter
and Hours, Text of Psalm CXXVII (128).

mals following a dog carrying a crozier and wearing a red cardinal's hat.[63] It is cast in the same satirical mold as the popular mediaeval beast epic, *Reynard the Fox,* and sounds the same note as Chaucer's story of the Cock and the Fox in the "Nonne Preeste's Tale" a few decades later.

East Anglian style is fully developed in the Peterborough Psalter (Brussels, Bibliothèque Royale, Ms. 9961–2)[64] for which there is strong presumptive evidence of a date around 1299.[65] A relationship has been pointed out between a series of miniatures presenting parallels between Old and New Testament subjects in it[66] and some twelfth-century paintings of the same subjects once in the choir of Peterborough Cathedral, thus both date and provenance are established with some certainty. Apart from the full-page Old and New Testament miniatures, there is a decorated calendar and eight elaborate historiated initials, and fully developed borders preceding the psalms, which marked the usual principal divisions of the psalter text. The one for Psalm 109 (110) on f.74 (Fig. 163) begins with the words *Dixit dominus domino meo,* "the Lord said unto my Lord. . . ."

God the Father and Christ on His right form the Trinity with the dove of the Holy Spirit in the initial D. The heavy bars of the marginal foliage border are punctuated with long and deeply notched leaves, the "serrated cabbage leaves"[67] that are distinctively East Anglian in the early fourteenth century. The leaf of the upper border is transformed into a spear held by a figure in the roundel over the initial D; the lozenge-shaped device near its tip was joined later by the bearings on hanging shields, which were added by subsequent owners in the reigning houses of Limbourg and Flanders. In the *bas-de-page,* a dismounted knight rests in the company of a girl combing her hair, and a woman is about to throw a large stone at a stooping figure. Just what these figures mean, if anything, is hard to determine. In the right border are angels playing musical instruments, framed in mandorlas with gold backgrounds and at the top, a girl, crowned and lightly veiled, kneels in prayer. The text on this folio is written in gold Gothic script with blue rulings between the lines.[68] Elsewhere in the Peterborough Psalter, gold, blue, and red letters are used, often on the same page. Yet so delicate is the coloring, so sensitive the drawing, and so impeccable is the artist's decorative sense that there is no feeling of overcrowding or the disorganization found in some later East Anglian books.

Gothic style began in the thirteenth century, in the region comprising northwestern France and southern England, as has been noted. In continental Europe, when Gothic style appears, it usually reflects innovations originating in that region, and this is understandably more apparent in the products of those centers with closest relations to England and northwestern France. Thus late thirteenth-century Franco-Flemish manuscripts can often be distinguished from French and English work only by their liturgical offices, their provenance being established by references to local saints in the calendars. Once such provenance is determined, minute local stylistic differences can sometimes be discerned, but such distinctions usually have to be supported by other facts instead of being the basic criteria.

In the Netherlands proper, it is not until near the end of the thirteenth century that a regional version of Gothic style with much individuality develops in Flanders. A Flemish Psalter (London, BM, Royal Ms. 2 B. iii)[69] of about 1250 contains several miniatures of the life of Christ, but distributed among the Psalms rather than being gathered at the beginning of the book, as was more usual at the time. Save for the alternation of blue and red in the border frames and the somewhat elongated figures, there is little to distinguish them from Romanesque work. The raised backgrounds of burnished gold and the thick colors strongly accented with white highlights are also unlike anything in contemporary French and English illumination of high quality.

A small Flemish Book of Hours in the Walters Art Gallery in Baltimore (Ms. 37) is illustrated with fourteen full-page miniatures, a number of large and small historiated initials, calendar scenes, and numerous marginal drolleries.[70] In all these respects, its small size (9.2 x 7 cm: 3⅝ x 2¾"), and the illustrational scheme, it is comparable to contemporary French books like the Psalter of Guy de Dampierre and the Picardy Psalter (Fig. 158). Inscriptions in the book indicate that it was made for a member of the noble Figinnes family of Huy, near Liège, late in the thirteenth century. The full-page miniatures like the Deposition from the Cross (Fig. 164) on f.83v have frames of ornamented bars on the sides and bottom, topped by alternate pinnacles and trefoil Gothic arches. The three-nailed type of the Crucified Christ is consistent with the thirteenth-century date. The burnished-gold ground sets off the heavy black contours of the figures and the curvilinear drapery patterns conform to the prevailing Anglo-Frankish

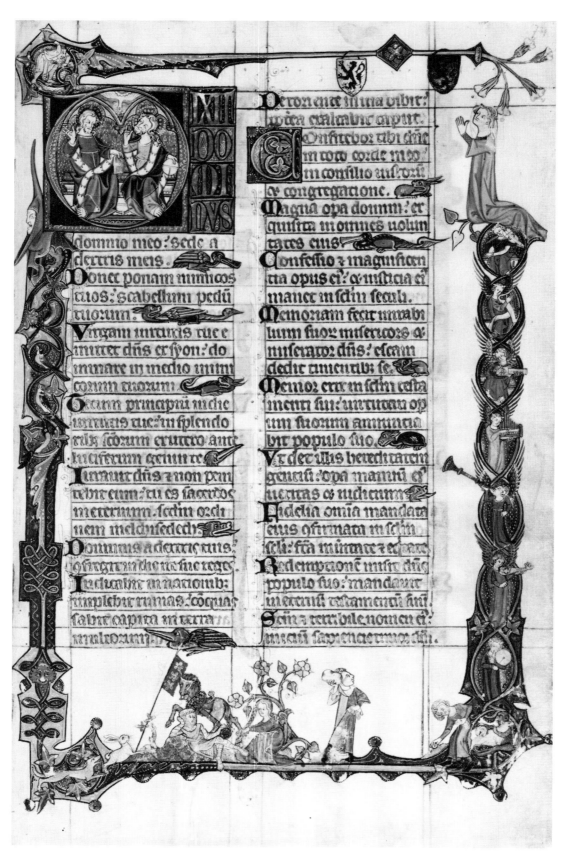

Fig. 163.
Brussels, Bibliothèque Royale, Ms. 9961–9962, f.74. The
Peterborough Psalter, Psalms CIX–CX (110–111).

Plate XXII. Paris, Bibliothèque Nationale, Ms. lat. 2287, f.
1v. Letters of St. Gregory, St. Gregory.

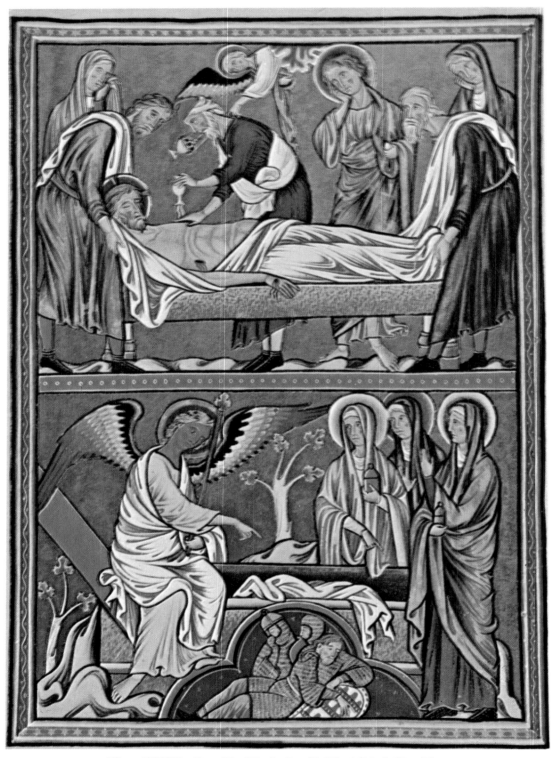

Plate XXIII. Chantilly, Musée Condé, Ms. 1695, f. 28v. The Ingeborg Psalter, Christ's Entombment and the Three Maries at the Tomb.

mode. Indeed, only in the simplified and slightly coarse drawing is there anything to distinguish the Figinnes Book of Hours as Flemish rather than north French in origin.

Both text and illustration are quite different in the book called *Le Vieil Rentier d'Audenarde* in the Bibliothèque Royale of Brussels (Ms. 1175).[71] Dated by internal evidence between 1291 and 1302, its text, implied by the title, is a record of revenues from about 1275 until 1291 of the revenues accruing to the unfortunately anonymous seigneur of Audenarde, a community north and east of Lille. The illustrations, like those of Farming Scenes (Fig. 165) on f.156v, are pen drawings with occasional accents of red, blue, and green, and the subjects are sometimes but not always suggested by the adjacent text. Many are identified in marginal notations written by the scribe of the text as instructions to the illustrator. There is no clue to the precise purpose of this unique volume, but the lively and spirited drawings strike the same fresh note of realism sounded in the marginal drolleries of contemporary Books of Hours. The conventions of draperies and movements are thoroughly Gothic, but the figures are closely observed and vividly characterized, and with more than a few passing touches of humor.[72] It is also more than incidentally interesting that drawing rather than painting should have been chosen for these lively vignettes with their direct and immediate interpretations of visual experience, continuing the centuries-old tradition of the Utrecht Psalter and related manuscripts.

In Germany, early thirteenth-century illumination maintained the tradition of style created by recurring Byzantine influences upon the modes inherited from Ottonian and Romanesque precedents. Only the heightened monumentality of the Berthold Missal miniatures (Fig. 120) and those of the Landgraf Psalter (Fig. 123) suggests the new spirit that was to be given such impressive expression in the thirteenth-century sculptures of Bamberg and Naumburg. By the third quarter of the century, its potential was realized in miniatures like the Resurrection of Christ (Fig. 166, Plate XXVI) on f.1 of a partially preserved Cistercian missal, which was made in all probability about 1260 in Mainz (Hamburg, Stadtbibliothek, Ms. in scrin. 1). The influence of current French and English work can be discerned in the foliage and occasional drolleries (though not in the example illustrated), but the stylistic dominant is the continuing Byzantinism of the draperies and the facial formula. This last is the familiar arrangement of con-

Fig. 164.
Baltimore, Walters Art Gallery, Ms. 37, f.83v. Book of Hours, Deposition from the Cross.

centric circles, centered between the brows, the radius of the first being the length of the nose, that of the second being twice the module and establishing the outline of the hair and beard, and so on. The massive drapery folds fall in angular shapes with deeply notched edges, exaggerating the relatively restrained manner of the early thirteenth-century miniatures in the Weingarten and Thuringian manuscripts. There is but little suggestion of form beneath these draperies with their almost baroque vehemence, but it is a highly individual and powerfully expressive manner even if lacking the sense of organic consistency that is found in contemporary French and English work.[73]

Interestingly enough, it is in the illustrated texts of the early and mid-thirteenth-century German epic poems that there is the greatest awareness of the expressive possibilities of such an organic style. Examples are an *Aeneid of Heinrich von Veldeke* in Berlin (SB, germ. fol. 282), and three manuscripts in Munich, a *Carmina Burana* of 1225 from Benediktbeuren (SB. Clm. 4660), a *Parzifal* of *c.* 1235 (SB, Cod. germ. 19), and a *Tristan* of *c.* 1240 (SB, Cod. germ. 51).[74] Although there is still much that is Romanesque in the miniatures of these books, particularly the rather thick and opaque pigments and the simple borders of colored bands, they are the ancestors of the fourteenth-century collections of such secular texts, which are of more than usual interest. Illumination in German religious texts as late as *c.* 1300 still tends to be somewhat conservative, not to say archaic. In a Lectionary of the Gospels (Washington, D.C., Library of Congress, Ms. acc. 558564) probably

from the lower Rhineland region near Flanders, an initial I has been elaborated with a representation of Christ in Judgment with the four Evangelists and their symbols (Fig. 167). They are enveloped in dense foliage, and leaves and tendrils sprout from the sides and ends of the letter, more or less after the manner of current usage in the Lowlands. But the effect as a whole is rather heavy and unaccented, with neither the drama of the Cistercian Missal miniature (Fig. 166, Plate XXVI) nor the liveliness and gaiety of contemporary Flemish style.[75]

In the many regional styles of the Dugento (thirteenth century) in Italy,[76] Byzantine influences continued to be strong, especially in those areas where they were most powerful in earlier periods. A case in point is provided by the miniatures in a treatise on the medical

n illo tpr Sedm Johan.
Cum subleuasset o
culos dñs ihc et uidis
set quia multitudo ma
rima uenit ad eum :
dicit ad philippum Vn
de ememus panes ut
manducent hi ." Hoc
autem dicebat temp
tans eum · ipse enim
sciebat quid esset fa
cturus · Respondit
ei philippus Ducen
torum denariorum
panes non sufficiunt e
is · ut unusquisq; modi
cum quid accipiat · Dr
cit ei unus ex discipl̃is
eius · andreas frater sy
monis petri · Est puer
unus hic · qui habet quin
q; panes ordeaceos et

Fig. 167.
Washington, D.C., Library of Congress, Ms. acc. 558564.
Gospel Lectionary, Initial I with Christ in Judgment and
the Four Evangelists.

Fig. 165.
Brussels, Bibliothèque Royale, Ms. 1175, f.156v. Le Vieil
Rentier d'Audenarde, Farming Scenes.

Fig. 168.
Rome Biblioteca Angelica, Ms. 1474, f.7. Pietro da Eboli,
De balneis Puteolani, *The Calatura Spring.*

bathed in, or poured over the head, and are particularly effective, the text states, in curing gout and stomach disorders, a point to which the banqueting scene in the room above the bath directly refers. The miniatures are heavily painted in opaque pigments, predominantly red, blue, and gray-green. The grounds are burnished gold, usually laid over a rose-colored priming coat that is visible where the gold has flaked off, as in the upper angles of the Calatura miniature. This technique is Byzantine, as are also the architectural forms and the modeling of the figures by strong white highlights on the brownish flesh tints and the heavy black contours. But these figures, for all their conventionalized anatomy, move with considerable litheness, are reasonably well proportioned, and are remarkably expressive in their movements and varied poses and gestures. In these characteristics they are Gothic, though in another idiom than those of France and England.

In northern Italy, Bologna was an outstanding center of manuscript production in the thirteenth century, a concomitant, no doubt, of its importance as the seat of a great university. Oderisi da Gubbio, the illuminator with whom Dante spoke in Purgatory is named in Bolognese documents of 1269 and 1271, and a certain Franco Bolognese is also referred to in the same passage of the *Divine Comedy* as standing in a relationship to Oderisi much like Giotto's to Cimabue. The city was noted for its production of legal texts and Bibles. A volume of Justinianus's *Infortiatum* (Turin, Biblioteca Nazionale, Ms. E. I. 8) may contain miniatures by Oderisi himself. Typical of the Bibles produced in or near Bologna is a two-volume copy in the William S. Glazier Collection (N. Y., Pierpont Morgan Library, Glazier Ms. 38) with which at least two others can be associated (Baltimore, Walters Art Gallery, Ms. 151: Madrid, Biblioteca Nacionale, Ms. A. 25).[79] The Madrid Bible is signed *Johannes filius Jacobini* and dated 1272, which must be about the time of the Glazier volume.

The illumination of the Glazier Bible consists of historiated and decorated initials and developed borders like the one on f.1 (Fig. 169) with the text of St. Jerome's Prologue. The foliage and stems of the framing border are free adaptations of motives from the classical decorative repertory, as would be expected, but non-Italian elements figure in other respects. This is particularly so of the page design as a whole, which should be compared with English work like William of Devon's Bible (Fig. 152) or the Picardy Psalter (Fig. 158). The drawing of the marginal border drolleries is under-

properties of the mineral baths at Pozzuoli, *De balneis Puteolanis,* near Naples (Rome, Biblioteca Angelica, Ms. 1474).[77] The text was composed, it is generally believed, by the early thirteenth-century south Italian poet Pietro da Eboli for Frederick II. The Angelica manuscript was probably written and illuminated in a south Italian scriptorium (possibly Sicilian) shortly after mid-century. Its eighteen miniatures illustrate in stylized patterns the distinctive characteristics of as many different springs, the ways in which the waters could be used, and even refer to their chemical properties in the different colors used to paint them. The spring called *Calatura* (Fig. 168) is shown on f.7; its waters may be drunk,

Fig. 169.
New York, Pierpont Morgan Library, Ms. Glazier 38, f.1.
Bible, St. Jerome's Prologue.

standably unlike that of their English and French counterparts, but the idea undoubtedly originated in them. Moreover, as is also the case of the miniatures attributed to Oderisi da Gubbio, the forms consist of linear patterns rather than modeled surfaces, and the color scheme of grays and blues with tan and gold, heightened by accents of light green and orange-red, is very much like that of contemporary French work.

Thirteenth-century illumination presents an overall picture of great variety that seems comparable in some ways to that of the twelfth, with its largely independent

and self-directing centers in the monastic scriptoria. But the vast increase in production during the thirteenth century, and the growing importance of secular and commercial factors brought about many changes in style and taste. These ultimately served to reinforce the primacy of those centers in which imagination and innovation were encouraged—Paris, northern France and Flanders, and England. And it is in those regions that the most creative investigations took place in the continuing efforts to achieve an expressive unity of text and illustration during the fourteenth century.

NOTES

1. M. Meiss, *French Painting in the time of Jean de Berry. The late xivth century and the Patronage of the Duke,* 2 vols. (London-New York: Phaidon, 1968).

2. *La librairie de Charles V* (Paris: Bibliothèque Nationale, 1968).

3. A. Cabrol, *The Books of the Latin Liturgy* (London: Sands & Co., 1932), pp. 43–45, 136.

4. Cf. C. J. Liebmann, "Arts and Letters in the reign of Philip II Augustus of France: The Political Background," *The Year 1200,* vol. 2, pp. 1–6.

5. H. Martin, *Les miniaturistes français* (Paris: H. Leclerc, 1906). Ross, Introd., n. 23.

6. Reproduced in color in *MFM,* pl. xlii.

7. H. Martin and P. Lauer, *Les principaux manuscrits à peintures de la Bibliothèque de l'Arsenal* (Paris: Société française pour la reproduction de manuscrits à peintures, 1929), pl. vii.

8. A. de Laborde, *Étude sur la Bible moralisée illustré,* 5 vols. (Paris: Soc. fr. de reprod. de mss. à peintures, 1911–25).

9. Reproduced in color in *MFM,* pl. xl.

10. H. Hahnloser, *Villard de Honnecourt, Kritische Gesamtausgabe des Bauhüttenbuches* (Vienna: A. Schroll, 1935).

11. E. Wolf, II, *A Descriptive Catalogue of the John Frederick Lewis Lewis Collection of European Manuscripts* (Philadelphia: Free Library, 1937), pp. 200–204. *IBMAR,* no. 52, pp. 21–22.

12. S. C. Cockerell, and M. R. James, *A Book of Old Testament Illustrations . . . in the Pierpont Morgan Library* (Cambridge: Roxburghe, 1927); reprinted as *Old Testament Miniatures,* preface by J. Plummer, with facsimile illustrations in color (New York: Braziller, 1970).

13. Cf. f. 3 of the Bibliothèque Nationale portion; *ibid.,* p. 199.

14. B. G. v. Vitzthum von Eckstädt, *Die Pariser Miniaturmalerei von der Zeit des hl. Ludwig bis zu Philipp von Valois und ihr Verhältnis zur Malerei in Nordwesteuropa* (Leipzig: Quelle & Meyer, 1907). Cf. also, Millar, chap. 5, n. 4.

15. Cf. Rickert, *PiBMA,* pp. 105–9, fig. 92.

16. M. R. James, *The Trinity College Apocalypse* (London: Roxburghe, 1909). *The Trinity College Apocalypse:* Introd. and descrip. by Peter H. Brieger, 2 vols. (London: Eugrammia Press, 1967).

17. M. R. James, *The Apocalypse in Art,* The Schweich Lectures of the British Academy, 1927 (London, 1931).

18. Cf. Millar, chap. 5, n. 4; p. 47.

19. "Das Naumburger Lettnerkreuz im Kaiser-Friedrich-Museum in Berlin," *Jahrbuch der Königlich Preussischen Kunstsammlungen* (Berlin) 36 (1915):137–52.

20. H. Omont, *Psautier de Saint-Louis, Ms. lat. 10525 de la Bibliothèque Nationale* (reproduction intégrale) (Paris: Bibliothèque Nationale, 1902). Abbé V. Leroquais, *Les psautiers manuscrits latins des bibliothèques publiques de France,* 3 vols. (Mâcon: Protat, 1940–41), 2:101, pls. 82–85.

21. Reproduced in color in *MFM,* pl. xlii.

22. Cf. Morgan Ms. 638.

23. Cf. E. Panofsky, *Gothic Architecture and Scholasticism* (New York: Meridian Book, 1958).

24. P. Frankl, *Gothisc Architecture* (Baltimore: Penguin, 1962), pp. 102–5.

25. Cf. *MFM,* p. 46.

26. But cf. R. Branner, "Note on Pierre de Montreuil and Saint-Denis," *AB,* 34 (1963):355–57.

27. A folio of BM Add. Ms. 17341, a Ste.-Chapelle manuscript related to Arsenal 1186, is reproduced in color in *BM Process Reproductions from Illuminated Manuscripts,* pl. 22.

28. Cf. Wormald, chap. 5, n. 20.

29. Millar, chap. 5, n. 4; pl. 77.

30. L. M. C. Randall, *Images in the Margins of Gothic Manuscripts* (Berkeley-Los Angeles: University of California Press, 1966).

31. A cruciform design on the disk being nibbled by the mice would seem to identify it as a eucharistic wafer, and the whole might be a reference to the admonition of St. Hippolytus of Rome, *c.*

A.D. 215 in his treatise on the apostolic tradition: 32, 2. "And let all take care that no unbaptized person taste of the Eucharist, or a mouse or other animal, and that none of it at all fall and be lost." Cf. *The Apostolic Tradition of Hippolytus,* trans. Burton Scott Easton (Cambridge: Cambridge University Press, 1934; reprint Archon Press, 1962), p. 60. I am indebted to Father John O'Malley of Wayne State University, Detroit, for this reference.

32. Rickert, *PiBMA,* pl. 100.

33. *Ibid.,* pp. 112–13, pl. 94a.

34. E. Millar, *The Rutland Psalter* (Oxford: Roxburghe, 1937). Cf. Randall, p. 36 and figs. *passim.*

35. *Ibid.,* p. 37 and fig. 143; others *passim.*

36. *Ibid.,* p. 9, n. 38.

37. Formerly Malvern, Dyson Perrins Coll. no. 4; cf. S. C. Cockerell, *The Work of W. de Brailes* (Cambridge: Roxburghe, 1930).

38. H. Swarzenski, "Unknown Bible Pictures by W. de Brailes," *Journal of the Walters Art Gallery,* 1 (1938):55–69. E. Millar, "Additional Miniatures by W. de Brailes," *Journal of the Walters Art Gallery,* 2 (1939):106–9.

39. M. R. James, "The Drawings of Matthew Paris," *Walpole Society* 14 (1925–26).

40. *Gesta Abbatorum Mon. S. Albani.* Rolls ser., 1, pp. 394 ff.

41. Cf. Rickert, *PiBMA,* p. 119.

42. M. R. James, *The Life of St. Alban* (complete reproduction) (Oxford: Clarendon, 1924). Millar, chap. 5, n. 4; p. 56.

43. L. Delisle, and P. Meyer, *L'Apocalypse en français au xiiie siècle* (Paris: Société des anciens textes français, 1901).

44. Cf. James, n. 17; Rickert, *PiBMA,* p. 236, for additional bibliography.

45. Paris, BN. Ms. fr. 403; Oxford, Bodleian Ms. Auct. D. 4. 17; N.Y., Morgan Ms. 524; London, BM, Add. Ms. 35166; Malvern, Dyson Perrins Ms. 10.

46. Cf. Rickert, *PiBMA,* pl. 113b.

47. M. R. James, *The Apocalypse in Latin and French,* Bodleian Ms. Douce 180 (Oxford: Roxburghe, 1922). A. G. and W. O. Hassall, *The Douce Apocalypse* (New York: Yoseloff, 1961).

48. Millar, chap. 5, n. 4; pp. 62–63.

49. Hassall, pls. 13–14.

50. *Ibid.,* pp. 9–10.

51. Cf. Gaspar and Lyna, chap. 4, n. 33; no. 95, pp. 219–28. Delaissé, chap. 6, n. 13; pp. 50–53. Randall, pp. 29–30.

52. *MFM,* fig. 52.

53. Cf. Randall, p. 34.

54. Cf. Wixom, chap. 5, n. 61; p. 168 ff.

55. Panofsky, *ENP,* pp. 140–41.

56. Cf. Wixom, p. 169; other miniatures, *ibid.,* p. 171.

57. *IBMAR,* no. 59, pl. xxvii.

58. H. Martin, *Les miniaturistes français* (Paris: H. Leclerc, 1906). Idem, *La miniature française du xiiie au xve siècle* (Paris-Brussels: van Oest, 1923). E. G. Millar, *The Parisian Miniaturist Honoré* (New York: Yoseloff, 1959).

59. *The Decretals of Gratian,* Tours, Bibliothèque Municipale, Ms. 558; cf. Millar, *Honoré,* pl. 1.

60. Panofsky, *ENP,* 1:15–16.

61. Cf. David M. Robb, and J. J. Garrison, *Art in the Western World* (New York: Harper & Row, 1963), fig. 304.

62. M. R. James, *Catalogue of the Manuscripts and Printed Books . . . forming Portion of the Library of J. Pierpont Morgan,* 4 vols. (London: Chriswick Press, 1906–7), no. 19; cf. Randall, p. 34.

63. F. McCulloch, "The Funeral of Renart the Fox," *Journal of the Walters Art Gallery,* 25–26 (1962–63):9–27.

64. Gaspar & Lyna, n. 51; no. 43, p. 114. J. Van den Gheyn, *Le psautier de Peterborough* (Haarlem: Musée des Enluminures, 1905).

65. Delaissé, chap. 6, n. 13; p. 57.

66. Cf. *La librairie de Charles V* (Paris: Bibliothèque Nationale, 1968), pl. iv.

67. S. C. Cockerell, *The Gorleston Psalter* (London: Chiswick Press, 1907).

68. Reproduced in color in Delaissé, p. 55.

69. J. Herbert, *Illuminated Manuscripts* (London: Methuen, 1911), p. 204, pl. xxix.

70. Randall, p. 37.

71. Gaspar and Lyna, n. 51; 1:192–96. L. Verriest, *Le Vieil Rentier d'Audenarde* (Brussels: Duculot, 1950).

72. Cf. Randall, figs. 375, 465, 622, 727.

73. Reproduced in color in Swarzenski, *Early Medieval Illumination,* pl. xxi.

74. F. Jacobi, *Die deutsche Buchmalerei in ihren stilistischen Entwicklungsphasen* (Munich: Bruckmann, 1923), figs. 14–16.

75. Cf. *IBMAR,* no. 138.

76. Salmi, chap. 5, n. 50; pp. 15–46. *Mostra storica nazionale della miniatura—Roma 1954* (Florence: Sansoni, 1954), pp. 115–275.

77. C. M. Kauffman, *The Baths of Pozzuoli* (Oxford: B. Cassiter, 1959). Petrus de Ebulo, *De balneis Puteolorum et Baiarum. Cod. Angelico 1474;* introd. A. D. Lattanzi (Rome: Libreria dello Stato, 1962).

78. Salmi, pp. 17–18, pl. VIIa.

79. *Manuscripts from the William S. Glazier Collection,* ed. J. Plummer (New York: Pierpont Morgan Library, 1959), no. 124, p. 18.

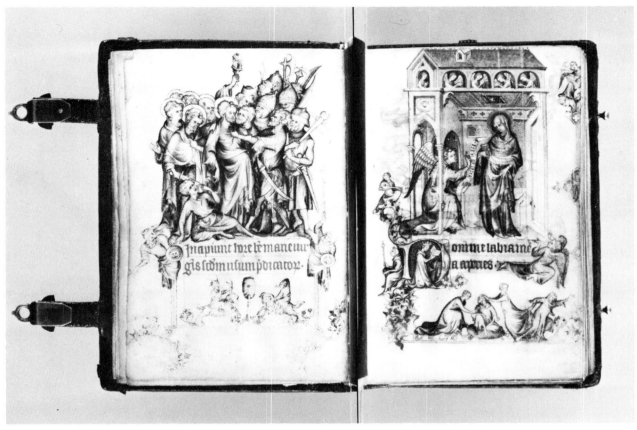

Fig. 170.
New York, Metropolitan Museum of Art, The Cloisters,
Ms. 54. 1. 2, Purchase 1954, ff.15v–16. Jean Pucelle, Hours
of Jeanne d'Évreux, Betrayal of Christ: The Annuncia-
tion.

8

Manuscript Illumination
in the Early Fourteenth Century

In the opening years of the fourteenth century, there was a marked reaction in Parisian illumination against the realistic innovations of form and space that distinguished the work of Maître Honoré. His son-in-law, Richard de Verdun, succeeded him as director of the atelier, and while no specific manuscripts can be identified with him, there are a number of very early fourteenth-century books illuminated in a somewhat flattened and linear style best characterized as a decorative simplification of Honoré's manner. One of the most engaging of these is a *Vie-de-Saint-Denis* (Paris, BN, Ms. fr. 2090–2092) made in 1317 for Philip the Tall. It is noteworthy for the lively vignettes of the Parisian scene in the architectural settings of the various episodes, which often include specific buildings, recognizable even though portrayed in flat patterns suggesting tapestry work.[1] Its elongated figures and rather garrulous narrative seem to reflect slightly earlier English taste.

The marginal drolleries in the Book of Hours of Jeanne d'Évreux (N.Y., The Cloisters, Ms. 54. 1. 2)[2] may also be regarded as reflecting English usage, whether directly or through northern French or Franco-Flemish intermediaries, but in nearly every other respect, the miniatures of this tiny book (93 x 60 mm: 3⅝ x 2⁵⁄₁₆″) represent even greater innovations in manuscript illumination than Maître Honoré's (Fig. 166, Plate XXVI). It was made at the order of Charles IV of France for his second wife, Jeanne d'Évreux, according to the will in which she left it to Charles V on her death in 1371; the manuscript can thus be dated between 1325 when Jeanne d'Évreux was married to Charles IV and 1328 when he died. The entry in the will also states that the manuscript had been illuminated by an artist named Pucelle—*un bien petit livret d'oroisons . . . que pucelle enlumina.*[3] He has been identified as the Jean Pucelle who designed the great seal of the Parisian Confraternity of Saint-Jacques-aux-Pèlerins between 1319 and 1324; his name also appears in two other manuscripts of about the same general period, the Breviary of Jeanne de Belleville (Paris, BN, Ms. lat. 10483–10484) and the Bible of Robert de Billyng (Paris, BN, Ms. lat. 11935).

Jeanne d'Évreux's Book of Hours follows Dominican usage and comprises the Offices of the Virgin and of St. Louis, the Seven Penitential Psalms, and the Litanies, as well as the usual calendar of saints' days and feasts preceding the text. The reading for each of the canonical hours in the Office of the Virgin is introduced by a pair of facing miniatures of scenes from the lives of Christ and the Virgin. Thus, on ff.15v-16, Matins of the Hours of the Virgin begins with the Betrayal of Christ confronting the Annunciation (Fig. 170). Both miniatures are in grisaille, i.e., monochrome washes of black and gray, occasionally touched with color—flesh tones, blue roof, and angel's wing in the Annunciation, red for the Virgin's nimbus and book, around the angels above, and in the background of the kneeling queen, presumably Jeanne d'Évreux, in the initial D at the beginning of the prayer.

Pucelle's choice of grisaille for the miniatures in Jeanne d'Évreux's Book of Hours may have been dictated by the same taste that is observed in contemporary window designs, as in the church of Saint-Ouen at Rouen, where occasional colors in the figures only partially offset the general cameo effect. But it is also clear that, by using grisaille, he was able to create forms of plastic character exceeding even that of Honoré's figures (Fig. 160, Plate XXV). Employing a wide range of subtly differentiated nuances of tone and value, not only is the three-dimensional bulk of a figure suggested, but one figure can be placed before another in depth, so that the apostles and soldiers in Christ's Betrayal become a homogeneous group of mass volumes, merging in space. Contours are subordinated to surfaces delicately modeled by variations of gray that are quite unlike the sharp edges and sculpturesque planes that make Honoré's figures quite as plastic but also make them appear to be forms that happen to overlap instead of being elements of a unified and integrated group.

Plastic forms must be placed in three-dimensional settings to be most effectively expressive, and Pucelle's innovations in creating such environments for his figures were also significant. The figures in Christ's Betrayal seem to stand before the neutral plane of the folio parchment like those of a sculptured bas-relief. Many of the miniatures in Jeanne d'Évreux's Hours have architectural frames (ff.34v, 35) like those of the St. Louis Psalter miniatures (Fig. 149, Plate XXIV) and foliated or diapered backgrounds similar to those used by Honoré (Fig. 160, Plate XXV). In these, thanks to the modeling of the forms and their placement on ground *planes* instead of ground *lines,* there is the same analogy with a sculptured relief. Yet a different spatial formula is seen in the Annunciation of f.16. The Virgin is in a room from which the front wall has been removed, and receives the salutation of Gabriel kneeling in an adjoining space like a small anteroom. Above, in the gabled attic, angels look down through windows, and the dove of the Holy Spirit descends through an opening in the ceiling of the Virgin's chamber. Like the grouped figures of the Betrayal, the building seems to

float in front of the plane of the parchment folio, an impression heightened by the little flying angel supporting the lower right corner.

There have been architectural elements in miniatures from very early times (Figs. 53–55, 62 and 66 [Plate VIII]), and they assumed considerable importance in the thirteenth century (Figs. 146 and 149 [Plate XXIV]), but always as accessories to the figures or as frames around them. In Pucelle's Annunciation, the figures stand *in* a building for the first time in a miniature. This effect is created in part by details like one anteroom column being in front of Gabriel while his wing and robe overlap the other, although these are persuasive touches. It is rather the foreshortened paneling of the right side wall, the converging lines of the ceiling, and the attempted perspective of the arch framing Gabriel in the left wall that suggest the volume of space enveloping the figures. Variations in light also contribute. The consoles marking the front plane are strongly accented. The beveled moldings on the right wall are distinguished from each other by the shading, and the brightness of the whole wall is contrasted with the darker values of the other two and the ceiling. By such means, Pucelle created a coherent space in which his figures could persuasively exist. It was not the mathematically rationalized space that the concept of true perspective was to make available to artists of the later fifteenth century, but a realization of it that is no less acceptable because the process was intuitive rather than rational.

There is no precedent in northern mediaeval art for Pucelle's innovations in creating convincing forms and surrounding them with viable space, but there is in early fourteenth-century Italian art. One of the few analogues to his grisailles on neutral backgrounds is the series of Giotto's monochrome Vices and Virtues in the Arena Chapel at Padua of *c.* 1305. But the ideas which inspired Pucelle most creatively came from Siena. Whether he actually went to Italy or not,[4] his familiarity with Sienese painting cannot be doubted, specifically the great altarpiece by Duccio of the Virgin and Child Enthroned with Saints known as the Maestà. It was painted by 1311, and a series of narrative scenes from the lives of Christ and the Virgin were added before the painter's death in 1318. It was from these latter that Pucelle drew some of his most inspired conceptions, particularly in the realization of pictorial space.

Italo-Byzantine art of the earlier Middle Ages had subordinated the concern with plastic form of the classical tradition to other interests, yet, at the same time, it retained the formulas of earlier spatial devices even though employing them in a somewhat unsystematic way. These were consequently available to Duccio for use in landscape settings of subjects like the Holy Women at the Tomb and the interiors of others like the Annunciation.[5] In Pucelle's Annunciation, the Virgin stands as she does in Duccio's, but the angel kneels; in earlier versions he is usually standing (Fig. 130), as he does in the panel from the Siena *Maestà,* which is now in the National Gallery in London. However, he does kneel in another of the *Maestà* narratives, which is related in concept to the Annunciation but differs in emotional overtones: the Annunciation of the Virgin's Death. From this last Ducciesque composition, Pucelle also took the architectural scheme of chamber and anteroom, to which he added the attic and gabled roof, thus maintaining the graphic integrity of the page and at the same time presenting a coherent image of the three-dimensional form of the building as a whole.

In drawing ideas from Italy, a Parisian illuminator like Pucelle might seem to have compromised the prestige of his city in the art for which it was famous, as attested in the often-quoted passage in Dante's *Divine Comedy.* Yet the circumstance exemplifies a principle as valid in art as in physics—that a vacuum is abhorrent. The vigorously imaginative style developed during the thirteenth century in Paris culminated in Honoré's work and then lapsed into decorative and uninspired mannerism in the early fourteenth, precisely the time when Italian painting was in one of its most creative phases. It is one of the seeming paradoxes in the history of mediaeval art that, whereas in sculpture French Gothic ideas long continued to dominate Italian style, French Gothic painting should have been so profoundly influenced by Italian concepts in its later phases. The overall principle obtains in both media. French sculpture was still vital in the fourteenth century and influenced that of Italy. French illumination had begun to lose the lively inventiveness of its thirteenth-century exemplars, and came inevitably under the spell of Italian innovations.

In leaving her Book of Hours to Charles V, Jeanne d'Évreux made the specific point that it had been illuminated by Jean Pucelle. This is borne out by the consistent style of the twenty-five full-page miniatures, the numerous historiated initials, and the drolleries in the line endings, all of which are clearly the work of one artist. In this respect, the case is different with the other two

manuscripts mentioned above, which are known from inscriptions in them to have been produced in Pucelle's workshop. The colophon of the Bible of Robert de Billyng[6] states that it was the work of Pucelle and two assistants, Anciau de Cens and Jaquet Maci, and that it was completed on 30 April, 1327. Yet another assistant named J. Chevrier worked with them on Jeanne de Belleville's two-volume breviary, in which a number of marginal notations record payments to the assistants for work done. From these it can be concluded that Pucelle had a workshop in which various duties were carried out by different helpers, sometimes with separate gatherings allotted to one worker or another, but sometimes with more than one artist working on a given folio or even on a given miniature. Several different hands can be identified in both manuscripts, but the enterprises were directed by Pucelle himself.

Internal evidence suggests that the Belleville Breviary was being made in the Pucelle atelier between 1323 and 1326 at about the same time as Jeanne d'Évreux's Book of Hours. As in the latter, more than a few features reveal a knowledge of Italian and specifically Sienese art. On f.24v (Fig. 171) of the first volume (Ms. lat. 10423), the reading begins with a miniature of Saul about to hurl a spear at David (1 Samuel 18:10–11). He is seated in a vaulted room and David stands in a smaller adjoining one, a little like the arrangement of anteroom and chamber in the Évreux Annunciation (Fig. 170). Both rooms are foreshortened, and the vaults are coffered, an architectural feature unknown in northern Europe during the Middle Ages but employed continuously in Italy since antiquity. Efforts to foreshorten the heads and other parts of the bodies are not always completely successful, but the fact that they were made is significant. This is particularly the case in the figures and structures at the bottom of the page. Color plays an important part in the Belleville Breviary miniatures,[8] but some details, like the two altars in the *bas-de-page,* are in grisaille. Throughout, the forms are modeled in varying tones of gray and color, and are as plastic as those in the Évreux Hours. In general, there are few Italianisms in the Breviary miniatures, but this is not surprising in view of their multiple authorship; they are understandably more apparent in those presumably by Purcelle himself and less so in those of his assistants.

No less important than the adaptation of ideas from Italy in the Belleville illuminations is the development of northern elements in the marginal decoration. The

Fig. 171.
Paris, Bibliothèque Nationale, Ms. lat. 10483, f.24v. Jean Pucelle, Breviary of Jeanne de Belleville, Saul and David: Allegorical Scenes.

ivy tendrils and leaves that began to sprout from initials (Fig. 151) and architectural frames (Fig. 150) in the thirteenth century have now crept all around the text and even between the columns. They form a leafy trellis inhabited by figures like the lute player in the upper left corner and the grotesque hybrid with a flute dangling from the foliage above. There is a darting dragonfly a little lower in the left margin, and a bagpiper sits atop the tendril between the text columns. These last have been thought to be canting puns on the artists' names: a dragonfly is *pucelle* in mediaeval French, and the bagpiper a *chevrier*. While it may be true that these motives do not appear in all manuscripts that can be associated with Pucelle, and are found in others having no connection with him,[9] it is equally true that the marginal decoration of the Belleville Breviary plays a more considerable role than the entertainment that conceivably was its original purpose, though it is not without humor also, *vide* the monkey clutching at a butterfly in the lower left corner.

In the latter part of the thirteenth century, marginal drolleries commenting satirically on human foibles and frailty became very popular.[10] Occasionally there may be a sequence through a number of folios, and they are often irrelevant to the text, but they sometimes furnish a serious parallel or comment, as in the Tenison Psalter, an English manuscript of *c.* 1284 (London, BM, Add. Ms. 24686).[11] In the Belleville Breviary, the figures in the *bas-de-page* are an integral part of the textual content. The Breviary is a service book based on the Psalms, with the Offices for the Canonical Hours, but containing readings in addition to those in a Book of Hours. The reading on f.24v of the Belleville Breviary is from Psalm 38 (39), which begins "I said I will take heed unto my ways, that I sin not with my tongue." The theme of the *bas-de-page* is a parallel drawn by Thomas Aquinas in *De sacramentis* between the psalm and the sacrament of the Eucharist, the latter illustrated by the priest in the Gothic chapel door receiving the wafer of the Host from an angel. In the flanking groups, the Deadly Sin of Hardness of Heart as exemplified by Cain murdering Abel is contrasted with its opposite Christian Virtue of Charity in giving alms to the poor.

In addition to the *bas-de-page* commentary on the Psalms,[12] the calendar of the Belleville Breviary was illuminated with miniatures illustrating the Articles of Faith and the concordance of the Old Testament Prophets with the Apostles of the New. Only the folio with November and December remains of the Belleville

calendar, and it has been mutilated, but the full scheme is known from later copies.[13] Moreover, on f.2 of the first volume, there is a detailed explanation of the psalter and calendar iconography entitled "Exposition des ymages des figures qui sunt au kalendier et ou sautier," in which the frequently obscure symbolism is explained.[14] Panofsky has commented on the unusual nature of such a commentary in a liturgical volume on its pictorial content,[15] and suggests that it may have been written by a Dominican theologian, although the point has been disputed.[16] It is clear, however, that by introducing new elements of content in the marginal and *bas-de-page* illustrations, and by embodying them in forms beginning to assume something of the substance and tangibility of actuality, Pucelle created a new conception of the relationship between text and illustration, making the latter something capable of existence as a self-sufficient and independent entity.

No single personality like Jean Pucelle appears in early fourteenth-century English illumination, but many distinguished manuscripts can be identified with the East Anglian region, where a number of fine books had been made earlier. One of these is Queen Mary's Psalter (London, BM, Royal Ms. 2. B. vii),[17] so named from having once been presented to her. It is not certainly dated but appears to be from the first quarter of the fourteenth century. It is elaborately illuminated with a great variety of subject matter, ranging from monumental full-page miniatures of Old and New Testament themes and scenes from the lives of the saints to marginal drolleries drawn from the Bestiary. The Adoration of the Magi (Fig. 172) on f.112v precedes Psalm 26 (27), which begins *Dominus illuminatio mea et salus mea,* "The Lord is my light and my salvation." The large miniature and the initial with David praying are painted in full color on a burnished-gold ground for the former and a diaper pattern for the latter. There is but little modeling, the forms constructed by strong contours with vigorous inner lines for draperies and other details. The architectural setting of elliptical arches and niches along the sides with images of saints is somewhat reminiscent of French usage (cf. Fig. 149), an impression that is strengthened by the tinted grisaille technique of the *bas-de-page* drollery of the habits of the weasel as described in the Bestiary. Line had always been favored in Anglo-Saxon and English illumination, and the style of the painted miniatures in Queen Mary's Psalter continues the tradition. At the same time, the artist of the Psalter would appear to have appreciated

Fig. 172.
London, British Museum, Ms. Royal 2. B. VII, f.112v.
Queen Mary's Psalter, The Adoration of the Magi.

the grisaille technique to which Jean Pucelle had given so much distinction at about the same time in Paris: the animals in his bestiary scenes have much in common with the drolleries in Jeanne d'Évreux's Book of Hours (Fig. 170).

Many of the miniatures in the Psalter of Robert de Lisle (London, BM, Arundel Ms. 83) are composed in linear patterns enhanced with color like those of Queen Mary's Psalter. The book contains two psalters, though neither text is complete. The first has a calendar and the usual added hymns, as well as the Office of the Dead and the Hours of the Passion. There is a calendar in the second part also, but most of its illustration consists of allegorical subjects and scenes from the life of Christ. A coat of arms in the first part allows the inference that it was made for a certain Sir William Howard from near Norfolk before 1308. A note in the calendar of the second part states that it was given to Robert de Lisle's daughter in 1339. The style of the Illustrations in this part of the book can thus be dated c. 1325–1330, and it is seen in the miniature on f.127 of the Three Living and the Three Dead (Fig. 173). Three kings confront their dead counterparts, who warn them in the dialogue of the text below that their present grandeur will end in death and to conduct themselves accordingly. The theme first appears in late thirteenth-century French literature,[19] and became very popular in the fourteenth, one of its most monumental pictorial versions being the frescoed Triumph of Death in the Campo Santo at Pisa.[20] The Robert de Lisle miniature is one of its earliest portrayals in art,[21] and although the dramatic and macabre elements are not stressed as they are in later versions, the contrasting emotions of living and dead are well suggested. As in the Queen Mary Psalter, the flesh surfaces are untinted, though there is some modeling in the draperies and light color washes in the background.[22] Like the theme itself, the style of the miniature seems to derive from French practice in the simple yet monumental design and the elegantly stylish drawing. Another group of miniatures also in the second part of Robert de Lisle's Psalter is in a more vigorously modeled and strongly colored style, influenced in all probability by the Italianate elements in Pucelle's contemporary work in Paris.[23]

In striking contrast to the simple compositions and delicate color harmonies of the miniatures in the Queen Mary and Robert de Lisle Psalters is the style of illumination in a group of manuscripts more or less contemporary with them, including a Psalter made c. 1330

for the Saint-Omer family of Mulbarton in East Anglia, not far from Norfolk (London, BM Add. ms. 39810).[24] The text begins on f.7 with an elaborate initial B (Fig. 174) enclosing the Tree of Jesse. Scenes from Genesis in the vine border begin at the lower left with the Creation sequence and continue up the right side to Noah's Drunkenness at the top. The tendrils sprouting from the vine stem are inhabited by figures and animals that are a commentary on the adjacent subjects—animals and birds beside the Creation scenes, and men chopping trees and dressing the timber logs to build Noah's Ark in the middle of the right border. Below, on either side and above the Fall of Adam and Eve, are kneeling figures of two members of the Saint-Omer family.

Just as the transparent linear designs of the Queen Mary and Robert de Lisle Psalters carry on the earlier tradition of Matthew Paris (Fig. 156), so the brilliant coloring and dense patterns of the Saint-Omer Psalter miniatures hark back to the Windmill and Peterborough books (Figs. 161, 163). The popularity of this manner in early fourteenth-century England is proven by many existing manuscripts illuminated in comparable if not necessarily related styles, among them the Ormesby Psalter (Oxford, Bodleian Ms. Douce 366),[25] the Gorleston Psalter (London, BM Add. Ms. 49622),[26] a Book of Hours in Cambridge (Fitzwilliam Museum, Ms. 242),[27] and the Tickhill Psalter (N.Y. Public Library, Spencer Coll., Ms. 26).[28] The last-named book takes its title from a note that it was written and gilded about 1310 by Brother John Tickhill, prior of the monastery at Worksop near Nottingham. But Egbert's comprehensive study makes it clear that its miniatures and those in a number of related books were the work of an itinerant group of lay artists who undertook such commissions, inserting appropriate portraits and coats of arms. The manuscripts are frequently illuminated in several styles of different periods. Some of the miniatures in the Tickhill Psalter are unfinished (ff.107–112),[29] allowing interesting insights into the artists' working methods. Alterations of the original miniatures in the Ormesby Psalter included the insertion of a portrait of Robert of Ormesby, the monk for whom it was named, and the Saint-Omer Psalter did not receive its latest decoration until the second quarter of the fifteenth century.

Around the middle of the fourteenth century, there is a noticeable decline in both the quantity and quality of English illumination. The beginning of the Hundred

Years' War with France (1337) may have contributed to waning patronage and changing taste. It was also a time of devastating epidemics like the Black Death of 1348–1349, the dreaded sicknesses that made the macabre warning of the Three Living and the Three Dead (Fig. 173) so timely, and may well have taken its toll of patrons and artists alike to leave many manuscripts unfinished. Such books as the Luttrell Psalter (London, BM Add. Ms. 42130),[30] the Taymouth Book of Hours (London, Yates Thompson Ms. 13),[31] and the Smithfield *Decretals* (London, BM Roy. Ms. 10 E. iv)[32] continue the tradition of lively marginal illustration with scenes full of charming humor in a style that is expressive enough, but often rough in drawing and slipshod in execution. Not until the last quarter of the fourteenth century did new influences bring new life into English illumination.

Flemish illumination in the early fourteenth century shares many characteristics with the French and English examples considered, yet is distinguished from them by something of the earthy quality seen in the drawings of the earlier *Vieil Rentier d'Audenarde* (Fig. 165). An instance to the point is the decoration of a Bible (Brussels, Bibl. Roy. Ms. 9157)[33] dating from about 1330–1340, particularly in the numerous marginal drolleries. It was in the collection of the dukes of Burgundy in the time of Philip the Bold in the later fourteenth century; his coat of arms at the bottom of f.1 (Fig. 175) replaces another that cannot be identified. The manuscript is undoubtedly Flemish, although no precise place of origin can be determined.[34] The text on folio 1 is St. Jerome's Letter to Brother Ambrosius, who kneels to the Virgin and Child in the initial F with which it begins. But the most interesting feature of the illumination is the marginal ornament. The supporting trellis of tendrils and leaves is not so dense as in the Saint-Omer Psalter (Fig. 174), but its grotesque population is even more so. Part of it is human, in the hunting scenes at the top and the young people amusing themselves around the coats of arms below. But under the bar on which they stand is an animal ballet of rabbits, hares, and dogs, dancing to the music of goats and donkeys. Beside the large initial F, a monkey holds up a flask to examine its content like a mediaeval doctor with his uroscope. In the right margin is a mounted knight properly accoutered with shield and banner, and immediately above are two jousting rabbits mounted on dogs below an ass singing from a book before a goat holding a crucifix between his front hoofs. Many of the drolleries

that appear all through the four hundred and seventy-six folios of the book are of similar satirical intent, the quality that most significantly distinguishes these fourteenth-century grotesques from the comparatively innocent types of earlier times.

The illumination of religious texts in Germany during the fourteenth century continued the traditions established in the preceding century, for the most part, but the Byzantinisms still quite pronounced then tend to disappear. There is also a noticeable softening of the drapery conventions of harsh surfaces, angular folds, and notched edges that characterize so much earlier German illumination (cf. Fig. 166, Plate XXVI). These changes are seemingly a consequence of influences from France and Flanders, and are understandably most apparent in work from the Rhineland region near those countries. An example is a Lectionary of Bible readings with selections from the writings of the Church Fathers in the Walters Art Gallery of Baltimore (Ms. 148).[35] No date or place of origin is given, but on stylistic grounds it has been assigned to the Rhineland region and dated around 1320. The miniature on f.45v (Fig. 176) shows Christ and the two disciples on the Way to Emmaus (Luke 24:13–32) and His meeting with the disciples and the Incredulity of Thomas (John 21:26–29). The vermilion of the simple border is also used in the draperies of the figures, along with gray, lavender, pink, olive green, and blue. The figures are drawn with considerable vigor against plain, burnished-gold grounds. Their swaying poses and the heavy drapery folds show the influence of contemporary French style, but with the slight exaggeration that bespeaks their Rhineland origin. The same thing is to be said of the small heads and attenuated bodies, and the emphatic characterization of the gestures.

In manuscript illumination of the early fourteenth century in the upper Rhineland and Switzerland, a style developed that was more indigenous to the region than that of the lower Rhine country, where the Walters Lectionary probably originated. There is not much indication of external influences, and the manuscripts show little of the decorative exuberance and sophisticated elegance following French example that is found in lower Rhenish style. But there is attractive illumination and more than a little interest in the texts of secular poems and love songs, categories of subject matter that began to be popular in the thirteenth century and continued in the fourteenth. A particularly distinguished book identified with Rüdiger II Manesse (Heidelberg,

Fig. 173.
London, British Museum, Ms. Arundel 83, f.127. Psalter
of Robert de Lisle, The Three Living and Three Dead.

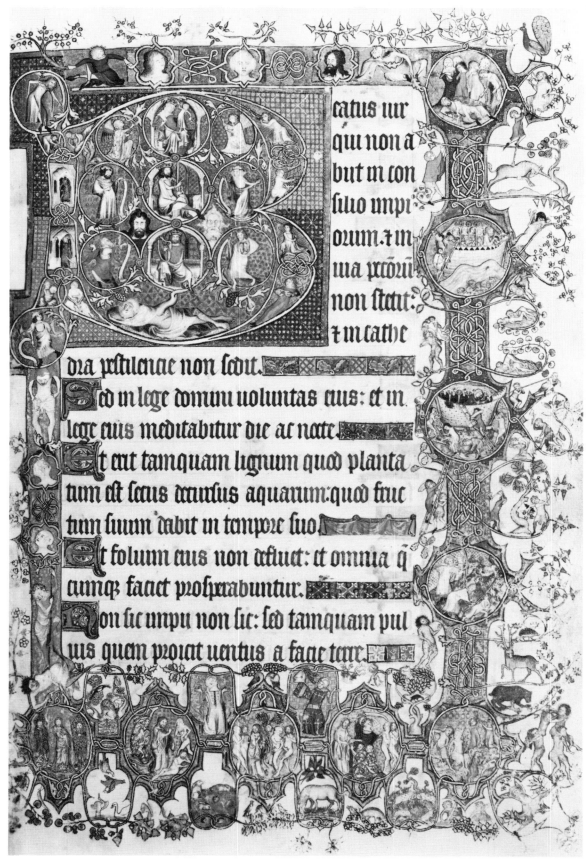

Fig. 174.
London, British Museum, Ms. Add. 39810, f.7. The Saint-
Omer Psalter, Initial B of Psalm I.

Fig. 175.
Brussels, Bibliothèque Royale, Ms. 9157, f.1. Bible, Letter to Brother Ambrosius.

Universitätsbibliothek Ms. pal. germ. 848)[36] was made in the early fourteenth century, probably in Zürich. The love songs of its text are illustrated with one hundred and thirty-seven full-page miniatures of the *minnesingers* or troubadours who composed them, in hawking and hunting scenes, tournaments, sports, and the like. On f.249v, Konrad von Altstetten indulges in a moment of dalliance while hawking (Fig. 177). Above is his coat of arms, and similar devices identify most of the persons represented in the book. A border of colored bands frames the figures, which are painted on the plain vellum in reds, blues, and greens. The contours are rather heavy and the figures are compact, with little suggestion of French contemporary mannered elegance. But the designs are very decorative, well suited to the flat plane of the unadorned parchment, and the characterization of the scenes and the individuals is spirited. In addition to their distinctive formal character, the Manesse Codex miniatures are an invaluable source of cultural history, at least of the aristocratic classes.

When a courtly style as distinguished from courtly subject matter appears in German illumination, it is drawn from other sources. The outstanding instance of this is in manuscripts made for Johann von Neumarkt,[37] chancellor of Charles IV, king of Bohemia from 1347 until 1378. Charles was an avid patron of the arts, who summoned artisans from many countries to decorate his capital city of Prague. He is not known to have been a bibliophile, but his chancellor was. The *Liber Viaticus* of Johann von Neumarkt (Prague, Landesmuseum Ms. XIII. A .12), a travel book made for him about 1354, is sumptuously illustrated with miniatures and historiated initials like the C with the Annunciation (Fig. 178).

The Virgin is seated and Gabriel kneels to her as he does in Jean Pucelle's version (Fig. 170). God the Father appears above, but instead of sending the Holy Spirit, He holds the Christ Child, so identified by the cross-nimbus. This iconographic peculiarity originated in Italy, where it can be traced back to early fourteenth-century Florentine painting.[38] The figure style is also Florentine, the well-modeled forms and rounded faces based on Giottesque types rather than the Ducciesque formulas preferred by Jean Pucelle. Also Italian is the design of the foliage sprays in the tooled gold spandrels between the initial proper and its frame. Final confirmation of the Italian sources for the style developed by Johann von Neumarkt's illuminators is seen in the foliage sprouting from the initial. Its leaves are those of the acanthus, unknown in northern illumination, where French ivy and other indigenous flora were preferred, but widely used in Italy.

In Italy itself, manuscript illumination in the early fourteenth century tended to follow the monumental pictorial arts of mural and panel painting rather than pioneering along new lines as it did in France. The point is illustrated in the miniatures of a manuscript of the *Speculum Humanae Salvationis*—The Mirror of Human Salvation—in the Biblioteca Corsiniana in Rome (Ms. 55. K. 2), dated from internal evidence about 1335.[39] The Mirror of Human Salvation was compiled about 1324 by Ludolph of Saxony, a Dominican monk in a house of the order at Strasbourg.[40] It contains forty-eight chapters, of which most present a Biblical theme or subject with three parallel or contrasting episodes from biblical or secular history, with each of the four illustrated by a minature at the top of the folio. Thus the text of chapter eight in the *Speculum* (Fig. 179) on f.9v is illustrated by the Nativity of Christ, and the parallel or typological scenes are Pharaoh's cup-bearer dreaming of the vine (Genesis 40:9–13), Aaron's flowering rod, and the Tiburtine Sibyl foretelling Christ's birth to the Roman emperor Octavian, the last two on f.10.

These subjects illustrate chapter eight of the *Speculum* in all the more than three hundred known manuscripts of the text and also in the numerous printed editions of the later fifteenth century. The Corsini manuscript is unique, however, in adding a miniature of an incident in the life of St. Francis of Assisi to the typological illustrations; it is usually placed in the lower left corner of the folio verso under the text of the first subject in the group of four. The subjects of the Francis-can miniatures either parallel one of the major themes of a given chapter or are related to them by association. Thus the Franciscan miniature on f.9v is of the incident described in chapter ten of St. Bonaventura's *Life of St. Francis,* when the image of the Christ Child in the Christmas *Presepio* came to life in the saint's arms.

Internal evidence suggests that the Corsini *Speculum* was written and illuminated at Assisi itself, yet the style of the miniatures has little in common with contemporary Italian work. On the contrary, the rather slender figures with bushy hair and expressively gesturing hands are much closer to late thirteenth-century French types, even if lacking the stylish elegance of the best of such work. There are comparable French overtones in Bolognese miniatures of the late thirteenth century (Fig. 169), an implicit acknowledgment of the distinction of French and particularly Parisian illumination recognized in the often-quoted passage in Dante's *Purgatorio.* More-

Fig. 177.
Heidelberg, Universitätsbibliothek, Ms. pal. germ. 848, f.249v. The Manesse Codex, Konrad von Altstetten.

Fig. 176.
Baltimore, Walters Art Gallery, Ms. 148, f.45v. Lectionary, The Way to Emmaus and the Incredulity of Thomas.

Fig. 178.
Prague, Landesmuseum, Ms. XIII. A. 12. Liber Viaticus of
Johann von Neumarkt. Initial C with the Annunciation.

over, at the time when the Corsini *Speculum* was presumably made, there were direct relations between Assisi and Avignon, where the Papacy had its seat from 1309 until 1377. It is reasonable to assume that there might well have been scribes and illuminators in the Assisi scriptorium who were conversant with French style and practice, if they were not, indeed, Frenchmen themselves.

The converse was also true. The frontispiece of a manuscript of Vergil's poems (Milan, Biblioteca Ambrosiana, Ms. S. P. F. 1') that once belonged to the poet Petrarch is signed by Simone Martini, who is better known as one of the outstanding mural and panel painters of Siena in the first half of the fourteenth century. But he is known to have painted a miniature of Laura, Petrarch's inamorata, and the Vergil miniature (Fig. 180) probably dates from around 1340 when both men were at the papal court in Avignon. Vergil, reclining under a tree, is being inspired to write. Standing near him is Servius, who composed a commentary on the poems, with Aeneas, and protagonists of the *Eclogues* and the *Bucolics* are engaged in appropriate activities in the foreground. The poses of Servius and Aeneas show the influence of French style, as does also the drapery pattern of the poet's robes. But unlike even the most imaginative figures in contemporary French illumination (Fig. 170), the bodies are tangible forms under the covering robes, and the turf and trees and sky are parts of a landscape such as no French illuminator of the time had as yet imagined. Also unprecedented is the transparent curtain through which the tree trunks are visible, and the subtly varied values of blue in the sky and green in the grass seen through its filmy veil. The two sonnets written by Petrarch to his friend the painter[41] are an appropriate appreciation of the sensitive imagination that restored to illumination something of the lyric realism of its earliest known exemplars (Fig. 4).

Simone Martini was not the only Sienese artist to find inspiration in French illumination; the response of artists like Jean Pucelle to Sienese ideas earlier in the century was apparently evidence of a natural affinity between the two. A Missal known as the St. George Codex (Vatican, Archivio Capitolare di S. Pietro, Ms. C. 129) contains miniatures in a style so close to Simone's in the Ambrosian Vergil frontispiece that they were long thought to be by him. They are now considered the work of an associate of Simone in the Papal Court at Avignon, and are assigned with some others[43] to the anonymous Master of the St. George Codex. The manuscript was commissioned by Cardinal Jacobus de Stephanescis of San Giorgio in Velabro in Rome, and can be dated around 1320. It contains offices for the Feast of the Annunciation and others, as well as an account of the life and miracles of St. George, which begins on f.85 (Fig. 181). In the lower part of the folio, St. George rescues the princess of Cappadocia from the dragon at the foot of a hill surmounted by a castle, from which a crowd of spectators looks on. He appears again in the initial D of *Deus,* with Cardinal de Stephanescis kneeling in prayer beside it in the left margin.

It has been observed that the composition of the St. George Codex miniature repeats that of a fresco by Simone Martini in the north porch of Notre-Dame-des-Doms at Avignon commissioned by the same Jacobus de Stephanescis for whom the manuscript was made.[43] As in the Vergil miniature, there are overtones of French style, particularly the facial types and the movement of the figures. But the draperies are disposed in broad and simple planes instead of the French fall-and-cascade formula, and the figures they clothe are more monumental as a result. In this, as in the freely designed foliage of the marginal borders, the most notable contrast between contemporary Italian and French illumination in the early fourteenth century is seen. At the same time, the St. George Master did not lose sight of the fact that his miniature was to decorate the page of a book. Cardinal Jacobus kneels outside and away from the initial D enclosing his patron saint, but he kneels on a spray of foliage whose formal purpose, along with other comparable motives, is to contribute to the decorative unity of the page by joining the letters of the text and the pictorial forms in an elegant harmony.

Bologna was the most important center of Italian illumination in the late thirteenth century, and its illuminators continued to be productive in the early fourteenth. Their work, unlike that of their Sienese counterparts, shows but little influence of the French ideas so skillfully adapted by Simone Martini and the St. George Master to their own ends. The miniatures in a volume of *Decretals* (Paris, BN Ms. lat. 3988),[44] written and illuminated in Bologna in the first half of the fourteenth century, are typical. The *Decretals* are the second part of the body of canon law drawn up originally in the twelfth century by Gratian, a Bolognese monk, which were subsequently enlarged by the addition of decrees laid down by later popes. The text is thus a typical expression of the legalistic interests for which

Fig. 179.
Rome, Biblioteca Corsiniana, Ms. 55. K. 2, f.9v. Speculum
Humanae Salvationis, *The Nativity: Pharaoh's Cupbearer:*
The Miracle of the Presepio at Greccio.

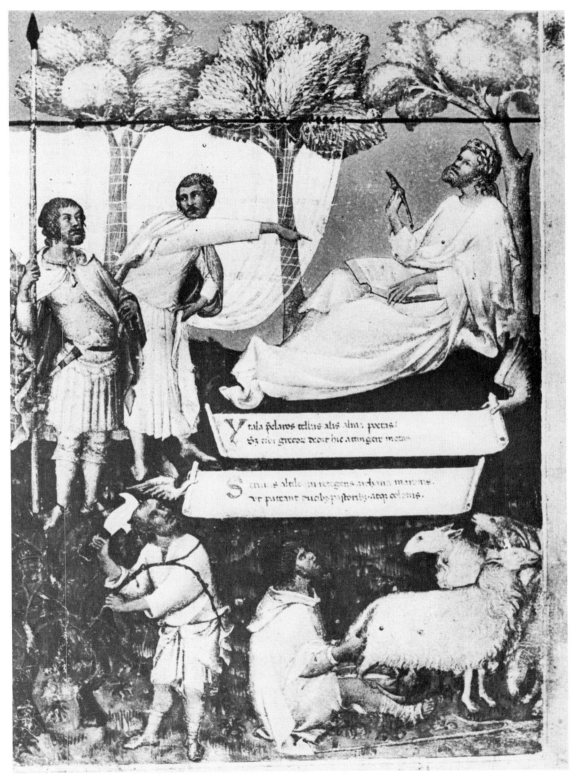

Fig. 180.
Milan, Biblioteca Ambrosiana, Ms. S. P. F. 1', f.1. Poems
of Vergil, Author Portrait by Simone Martini.

the University of Bologna was noted. The miniature of the Pope presiding over a discussion between bishops and lay scholars (Fig. 182) is on f.69. The setting is a galleried courtyard with crenelated battlements and traceried windows, but it is only in such details that Gothic style is suggested. There is a remarkable feeling of space, created by linear perspective and the foreshortening of the massive walls, solid enclosures of figures equally solid in their robes, which fall in large and well-articulated planes. The sense of reality thus conveyed is something new in Italian illumination, having little to do with either the Byzantinism of previous periods or French Gothicism. It is indicative, rather, of the revolution brought about in Italian painting by the Florentine artist Giotto.

In Florence itself, the outstanding illumination of the early fourteenth century came from the atelier of Pacino da Buonaguida,[45] a contemporary of Giotto. He was primarily a painter of panel pictures, but a number of manuscripts have been assigned to his studio on stylistic grounds, including a volume with scenes from the Life of Christ in the Pierpont Morgan Library in New York (Ms. 643). The miniature of Christ appearing to Mary Magdalene (Fig. 183) on f.27 is an illustration of John 20:14–17. The composition is freely adapted from Giotto's fresco of the same subject in the Arena Chapel at Padua, the nearly square design of the mural painting made more vertical to accommodate it to the book page format. In other respects, the miniature is a paradigm of Giottesque influence in early fourteenth-century Florentine art. The fall-and-cascade drapery formula was derived from northern Gothic usage, but the folds are filled with forms of classic bulk, and their expressive gestures are combined with well-characterized emotion in the faces. At the same time, the sharply profiled hills of the landscape refer back to the traditional Byzantine formula (Fig. 25), which had been handed down in Italy as well as through the later phases of east Christian art (Fig. 32). In all these respects, the Florentine miniature stands in contrast to the French Gothicism of the Corsini *Speculum* style (Fig. 179) with which it is nearly contemporary. In its own way, however, the Florentine miniature is equally effective as a design for a book page. The dark blues, greens, and pinks are set in relief against the azure sky and foiled by delicate gold arabesques inside the upper margins.

Quite different from the Giottesque monumentality of Pacino da Buonaguida's Scenes from the life of Christ

is the lively narration of the miniatures in a book known as *Il Biadajolo,* in the Laurentian Library in Florence (Ms. Tempi 3).[46] The text is a detailed record of grain prices and market conditions in Florence between 1320 and 1335, prosperous in the early years, a famine in 1328–1329, and relative plenty toward the end. The author was a grain merchant (*Il Biadajolo*) named Domenico Lenzi, who wrote the book to provide a record of the time so that all who read it might fully appreciate God's generosity and be aware of the consequences of forgetting it. This moralistic intention is made clear in a number of ways. The actual title of the book is *Specchio Umano,* or Mirror of Mankind, a term used from earliest mediaeval times for didactic or morally instructive treatises like Vincent of Beauvais's *Speculum Maius* (Great Mirror)[47] or the *Speculum Humanae Salvationis.* The statistics making up the greater part of the text are occasionally interrupted by verses and narratives exhorting the reader to reflect on the moral implications of what he has read. And, finally, many of the miniatures contain angels and demons taking part in the scenes to make it clear that human actions are directed and controlled by supernatural powers.

The open-air grain market in the Piazza Or San Michele in Florence (Fig. 184) during the famine of 1328–1329 is on f.79. The circumstances are also described by the Florentine historian Giovanni Vilani (*c.* 1275–1348), thus the miniature is a contemporary record of a current event. The artist treated his subject with as much interest in topical detail as the chronicler. Soldiers attempt to keep order as the frantic populace battle to obtain food. In the foreground, some are eating what they have been able to get. On the left side, a woman reaches for a bag of grain as she guards another, and, a little higher up in the margin, another woman with a child on her lap bewails the unsuccessful effort of a man to find anything for her. On the lower right, a representative of the Compagnia della Madonna di Or San Michele is seated behind a bench, directing the giving out of the food. Above him is a Gothic shrine with a painting of the Madonna and Child. It is probably the one painted by Ugolino da Siena between 1315 and 1330 to replace an earlier one destroyed by fire in 1304,[48] itself to be succeeded by Bernardo Daddi's version of 1347, which is now enshrined in the tabernacle designed by Andrea Orcagna between 1352 and 1359.

Elsewhere in the book (f.58), another full-page miniature shows Florence welcoming the poor people

Fig. 181.
Vatican, Archivio Capitolare di San Pietro, Ms. C. 129,
f.85. The Saint George Codex, St. George Slaying the
Dragon.

Explicit liber primus deo gratias.

Fig. 183.
New York, Pierpont Morgan Library, Ms. 643, f.27.
Pacino da Buonaguida, Scenes from the Life of Christ,
Christ appearing to Mary Magdalene.

Fig. 182.
Paris, Bibliothèque Nationale, Ms. lat. 3988, f.69. The
Decretals of Gratian, The Pope presiding over a council.

Fig. 184.
Florence, Biblioteca Laurenziana, Ms. Tempi 3, f.79.
Il Biadajolo, The Market of Or San Michele. (Photo
Pineider)

expelled from Siena during the same famine of 1328–1329. Three buildings in it can be identified, the Baptistery and the towers of the Bargello and Palazzo Vecchio. They were probably introduced as symbols, the Baptistery standing for the city itself as the shrine of its patron saint, the Bargello representing the traditional government order of earlier days, and the Palazzo Vecchio the "Nuovo Popolo" or new government that had done much to build up the city in the thirteenth century. There are symbolic elements in the Or San Michele miniature also (Fig. 184). A black, bat-winged demon hovers over the struggling people in the plaza and receives a sword and scourge from God, Who instructs him in the inscriptions to deal with sinners as they deserve. An angel ascends to heaven in the upper left as he lets fall two broken gold trumpets, similar to those in an earlier miniature, with which he had promised to bring peace and happiness to those who live rightly. Such ideas were central to Domenico Lenzi's purpose in writing his *Specchio Umano,* but even more significant for the future was the spirit of civic pride expressed in the portrayal of specific buildings in what is probably the earliest surviving portrayal of his native city, a harbinger of the realism that most significantly distinguishes the art of the Renaissance from that of the Middle Ages. It was not in Florence, however, or indeed in Italy, that the most consistent steps to this end were taken in the art of manuscript illumination, but in the Franco-Flemish world of northern France and the Low Countries.

NOTES

1. Cf. *MFM,* pl. L.

2. *The Hours of Jeanne d'Evreux,* introd. J. J. Rorimer (New York: Metropolitan Museum, 1957).

3. K. Morand, *Jean Pucelle* (Oxford: Clarendon, 1962), p. 31, ii.

4. Morand, pp. 6–8; but cf. C. Nordenfalk, "Maitre Honoré and Maitre Pucelle," *Apollo* 79 (1964):359.

5. David M. Robb, "The Iconography of the Annunciation in the Fourteenth and Fifteenth Centuries," *AB* 18 (1936):480 ff. Panofsky, *ENP* 1:30.

6. Morand, no. 11, p. 31; 5:45–47.

7. *Ibid.,* no. 10, p. 31; 4:43–45.

8. Reproduced in color in J. Dupont & C. Gnudi, *Gothic Painting* (Geneva: Skira, 1954), p. 38.

9 Morand, p. 44.

10. Cf. Randall, chap. 7, n. 30. Idem, "Exempla as a Source of Gothic Marginal Illumination," *AB* 39 (1957):97–107. Idem, "The Snail in Gothic Marginal Warfare," *Speculum* 37 (1962): 358–67.

11. D. D. Egbert, *The Tickhill Psalter and Related Manuscripts* (New York: New York Public Library, 1940), p. 15.

12. V. Leroquais, *Les bréviaires manuscrits des bibliothèques publiques de France,* 5 vols. (Macon: Protat, 1934–39), 3:198 ff, pls. xxvii–xxxvi.

13. Morand, p. 44.

14. W. H. Weale, et al., *A Descriptive Catalogue of the Second Series of Fifty Manuscripts in the Collection of Henry Yates Thompson* (Cambridge: Cambridge University Press, 1902), pp. 365–68; reprinted in E. G. Holt, *A Documentary History of Art* (Garden City: Doubleday-Anchor, 1957), 1:129–34.

15. *ENP,* p. 33 and n. 1.

16. Morand, p. 11.

17. Sir G. Warner, *Queen Mary's Psalter* (London: H. Hart, 1912).

18. Cf. T. H. White, chap. 6, n. 8; pp. 91–93.

19. S. Glixelli, *Cinq poèmes des trois morts et des trois vifs* (Paris, 1914)

20. M. Meiss, *Painting in Florence and Siena after the Black Death* (Princeton: Princeton University Press, 1951).

21. Male, É., *L'art religieux de la fin du Moyen Âge en France* (Paris: Colin, 1931), pp. 355–58.

22. Reproduced in color in W. Oakeshott, *The Sequence of English Medieval Art* (London: Faber & Faber, 1950), opp. pl. 35.

23. Cf. Rickert, *PiBMA,* p. 163, n. 46. It should be observed that Pucelle also used the Three Living and Three Dead theme; cf. Morand, pl. xix, c.

24. Cf. Weale, n. 14; pp. 74–82.

25. S. C. Cockerell and M. R. James, *Two East Anglian Psalters at the Bodleian Library* (Oxford: Roxburghe, 1926).

26. Cockerell, chap. 7, n. 67.

27. F. Wormald and P. M. Giles, "A Handlist of the Additional Manuscripts in the Fitzwilliam Museum," *Transactions of the Cambridge Bibliographical Society* 3 (1951), pp. 197–207.

28. Cf. Egbert, n. 11.

29. *Ibid.,* pp. 77–78, pls. lxxxiv–lxxxvi.

30. E. G. Millar, *The Luttrell Psalter* (London: British Museum, 1932).

31. Weale, n. 14; no. 57, pp. 50 ff.

32. Randall, p. 36.

33. Gaspar and Lyna, chap. 7, n. 51; no. 126, p. 312.

34. But cf. *La Librairie de Philippe le Bon,* no. 1 (Brussels: Bibliothèque Royale, 1967), pp. 9–10.

35. Cf. *IBMAR,* no. 137, p. 50.

36. R. Sillib, *Zur Geschichte der grossen Heidelberger Manessischen Liederhandschrift* (Heidelberg: C. Winter, 1921).

37. M. Dvorák, "Die Illuminatoren des Johann von Neumarkt," *Jahrb. der Kunsthist. Slgen. des Allerh. Kaiserhauses* 22 (1901): 35–126; reprinted in *Gesammelten Aufsätze zur Kunstgeschichte* (Munich: R. Piper, 1929), pp. 74–207.

38. Cf. Robb. n. 5; *AB* 523–26.

39. A. Alessandrini, "Un prezioso codice Corsiniano di origine francescane (*Speculum humanae salvationis,* ca. 1324–1330)," *Miscellanea Francescana* 58 (1958):420–83.

40. J. Lutz and P. Perdrizet, *Speculum humanae salvationis. Texte critique. Les sources et l'influence iconographique,* 4 vols. (Mulhouse: E. Meininger, 1907–9).

41. Petrarch, *The Sonnets,* trans. J. Auslander, nos. 57, 58 (London: Longmans, Green, 1931), pp. 57–58.

42. Paris, BN, Ms. lat. 15619: N.Y., Pierpont Morgan Library, Ms. 713.

43. R. Van Marle, *Simone Martini et les peintres de son école* (Strasbourg: Heitz, 1920), p. 65.

44. P. d'Ancona, *La miniature italienne du xe au xvie siècle* (Paris: Van Oest, 1925).

45. R. Offner, *A Critical and Historical Corpus of Florentine Painting* (New York: New York University Institute of Fine Art, 1930–47), sec. 3, vol. 2, pt. 1, p. 20, pls. viii, 1–22. P. d'Ancona, *La miniatura fiorentina,* 2 vols. (Florence: Olschki, 1914).

46. Offner, sec. iii, vol. 2, pt. 2, pp. 43–44, pls. xviii, 1–9a; sec. iii, vol. 7, pp. 3–6.

47. É. Male, *The Gothic Image* (New York: Harper Torch Books, 1958), pp. 23–26.

48. G. Coor-Achenbach, "Contributions to the study of Ugolino di Nerio's Art," *AB* 37 (1955):160, n. 32.

9

Franco-Flemish Manuscript Illumination
in the Later Fourteenth Century

Jean Pucelle was the outstanding personality in Parisian illumination in the first half of the fourteenth century, and his style dominates it until well past mid-century. In this respect, his place in the history of manuscript illumination is comparable to Giotto's in contemporary Italian painting. Both were innovators, so far ahead of their time that at least a generation of successors passed before there was any significant enlargement of their ideas. In Parisian illumination of around mid-century, the overall impression is of an elegant refinement of earlier ideas but little that goes beyond them. What innovations there are appear to be in consequence of influences from non-Parisian ateliers.

A case in point is provided by the miniatures in a collection of the poems of Guillaume de Machaut (*c.* 1300–1377), written and illuminated about 1370 (Paris, BN Ms. fr. 1584). On folio D (Fig. 185), the poet receives a visit from *Amour,* who presents to him a stylishly dressed young man named *Doux-Penser* and two equally elegant young ladies, *Plaisance* and *Espérance.* This copy of Guillaume de Machaut's writings was made during his lifetime, and the miniature is an illustration of the prologue in which the poet describes the sources of his inspiration in allegorical terms. Machaut's poetry and music (he was a composer as well) mark a significant point in the history of French literature, for he established new poetic forms like the ballade

and rondelai, and brought a personal and lyric element to their content that was quite different from the abstraction of earlier love poetry like the *Roman de la Rose.* His accomplishment was thus comparable to Pucelle's, enhancing the expressive forms of his art in both style and content.

Much the same thing can be said of the miniature illustrating the prologue of his book. The architectural forms of the poet's pavilion and the little building in the right foreground are shown in a semi-perspective scheme very much like that of the Virgin's house in Pucelle's Annunciation (Fig. 170). The miniature is largely in grisaille, i.e., grayish monochrome, with relatively thin washes of color in the sky and buildings, and this too is in the Pucelle tradition. However, the contours of the figures are not so emphatically linear as they are in the *bas-de-page* of Pucelle's Belleville Breviary (Fig. 171), nor are the drapery folds so deeply furrowed. Instead, the forms are modeled in broad and simple planes and there is a more pronounced sense of mass. Also different is the treatment of the setting, a developed landscape of rising terraces with trees and shrubs, a pond with ducks, a man driving a horse, rabbits darting in and out of their holes, and a castle and windmill outlined against the distant sky. The likeness of the seated poet leaning forward to receive his guests is no less realistic. Their features are more or less conventional, but the sharp

Fig. 185.
Paris, Bibliothèque Nationale, Ms. fr. 1584, f. D. Works
of Guillaume de Machaut, The Poet receives Amour and
his children.

forms of his drawn face, with its prominent nose and chin, were in all probability a portrait from the life of the author, who was still alive when the miniature was painted.

Living persons had been represented in miniatures before this, but the concept was entirely different from the very personal and human presentation seen here. Charles the Bald is in the dedication miniature of the Vivian Bible (Fig. 67). Egbert, archbishop of Trier, receives his Psalter from Ruodprecht the scribe (Fig. 76) on f.17 of the book at Cividale. And an Ottonian emperor accepts the homage of his provinces in the miniature from the volume of Gregory the Great's *Epistles* now in the Musée Condé at Chantilly (Fig 79). However, in every instance, the person is identified by an inscription or attribute like Charles the Bald's crown and the fact that he is enthroned, not by any recognizable resemblance to the man himself, a point made clear by the uncertainty as to whether the emperor in the Chantilly miniature is Otto II or Otto III. By contrast, the figure of Guillaume de Machaut has the specific traits mentioned in descriptions of his appearance, even to the peering glance of one whose eyes are failing, as the poet's did shortly after the work was composed.

Portraiture in this sense—a visual account of the physical characteristics of an individual and recognizable as such—appears in mediaeval art in the latter part of the fourteenth century. A panel painting of John the Good of France in the Louvre in Paris,[1] traditionally attributed to Girard d'Orléans and painted in all probability between 1360 and 1364, is generally thought to be the earliest portrait of this sort in French art. A few years later, statues of John's son, Charles V, and his queen, Jeanne de Bourbon, made for the chapel of the Quinze-Vingts in Paris, are among the first efforts of the same kind in monumental sculpture.[2] In manuscript illumination, Charles V appears in a miniature on f.2 of a Bible made for him (The Hague, Meermanno-Westreenianum Museum, Ms. 10 B 23) in 1371, according to a dedicatory inscription facing it on f.1v (Fig. 186).[3] In the same inscription, the artist is identified as John of Bruges, and it is also stated that the miniature was painted by his own hand—*propria sua manu*. A note at the end of the manuscript states that it was commissioned by Jean de Vaudetar, Charles V's chancellor, who is shown giving it to his monarch in the miniature on f.2.

Charles is seated in an armchair placed at an angle to the picture plane. It is on a checkered floor, whose paving lines converge in perspective as it rises toward the blue background hanging spangled with gold fleurs-de-lys. There are touches of color in the chair and the miniature of Christ Enthroned in the Book held by Vaudetar, but the figures are rendered *en grisaille,* most subtly modeled to suggest the texture of materials like wood and wool and flesh, as well as the plastic bulk of the forms represented.[4] They are thus directly related to the spatial volume created by the perspective rendering of the floor and chair, a concept of space undoubtedly derived from Jean Pucelle's practice (cf. Fig. 170). That John of Bruges (also known as Jean Bondol) knew Pucelle's work is certain; a Book of Hours being made in the older master's atelier for Blanche of Burgundy but unfinished when she died in 1348 was completed a little more than twenty years later under Bondol's supervision.[5] But where Pucelle and those artists who succeeded him thought of space as a volume limited on all sides, from which one enclosing plane is removed to allow the interior to be seen (Figs. 170, 171, 185), Bondol implies that the space in his dedication miniature is only the visible portion of a larger volume that is limitless, at least so far as his design is concerned. The likeness of Charles V is a notable study of visual reality and character. His appearance is well known, from other miniatures, from statues like the one made for the Chapel of the Quinze-Vingts and another on the north tower of Amiens Cathedral, and the portrait in grisaille on silk that is part of the so-called *Parement de Narbonne* in the Louvre,[6] all dating between 1370 and 1380. The beak-like nose in the miniature by Bondol appears in all of them, the most striking feature in the countenance of one of the few effective rulers of France during a period almost unmatched in turbulence in its entire history.

From the foregoing, it is clear that the qualities distinguishing the Guillaume de Machaut miniature (Fig. 185) from the rank and file of Parisian illumination in the immediate succession to Jean Pucelle are the qualities found in Jean Bondol's work. He was not a Parisian or a Frenchman, but, as his sobriquet—of Bruges—indicates, came from Flanders in the Netherlands. The direct characterization and down-to-earth realism of his manner thus appear to be in the direct line of inheritance from the earthiness of the late thirteenth-century *Rentier d'Audenarde* (Fig. 165) and the lively naturalism of the early fourteenth-century Flemish Bible (Fig. 175). This tradition was carried on in Flemish illumination through the later fourteenth century, as can be seen in two manuscripts associated with Louis de Male, Count of Flanders, and his wife Marguerite de Brabant, a Missal and a Breviary (Brussels, Bibl. Roy. Mss. 9217, 1427).[7] In the Crucifixion (Fig. 187) on f.115v of the Missal, the man and woman kneeling at the foot of the cross are probably Louis and his countess, whom he married in 1357; a reasonable date for the manuscript would be *c.* 1360. Identification of the couple would no doubt be certain if coats of arms once visible in the side borders had not been over-painted with the blue bands of rosettes that now connect the Evangelist symbols in the angles;[8] their shields can still be discerned on the folio recto. No reason is at hand for this and similar alterations in other parts of the book, but the armorial devices must have added considerably to the decorative structure of the page in the original design. The variegated diaper backgrounds, in red, blue, and gold indicate continuing English influence, but other characteristics are more in the Flemish tradition—the realistic details of figures in the windows of the architecture at the top of the miniature, and the rather harsh characterization of the Virgin and St. John towering above the kneeling figures at the foot of the cross. These too are distinctly individualized, even if not precisely identified.

It was from this background that Jean Bondol came to Paris about 1368 for a career that lasted until around 1381,[9] and where the greater part of work identified with him was for French patrons. His style has been recognized in some of the finished miniatures and preliminary sketches for many uncompleted ones in the Bible in French known as that of Jean de Sy (Paris, BN, Ms. fr. 15397),[10] from the name of the man who translated it into French at the request of King John II. Bondol is also known as the designer of the cartoons from which the series of tapestries known as the "Angers Apocalypse" was woven by Nicholas Bataille in Paris.[11] They were commissioned by Louis, duc d'Anjou, the younger brother of Charles V, who loaned him not only his painter but also an illuminated English thirteenth-century Apocalypse manuscript for a model (Paris, BN Ms. fr. 403),[12] as is indicated by a marginal note in an inventory of Charles V's library in 1380: "le roi l'a bailée à Mons. d'Anjou pour faire son beau tappis.''

Charles V of France, Louis, duke of Anjou, and their brothers, Philip the Bold, duke of Burgundy, and John, duke of Berry, were of the Valois family, collateral to the House of Capet, which had succeeded to the French throne when Philip VI followed the last Capetian, Charles IV, in 1328. Philip's son and successor, John II,

was succeeded in turn by Charles V, who held the sceptre from 1364 until 1380. As has already been remarked, France was not a peaceful country in the fourteenth century. It was the time of the Hundred Years' War with England, and of ceaseless internal strife within the country itself, a state of affairs that did not change until the fifteenth century, when a treaty of peace was finally signed with England in 1453. Of the four brothers, only Charles V was an effective ruler. Louis of Anjou was notable for his avarice and cruelty in a time when such traits were more common than not, and John of Berry was an object of hatred during much of his life.[13]

But all were generous patrons of the arts, as has been noted of Charles V and Louis of Anjou. Philip the Bold of Burgundy engaged the outstanding late fourteenth-century sculptors in the Franco-Flemish world, Jean de Marville and Claus Sluter, to embellish the Carthusian monastery at Champmol, near Dijon. And John of Berry was an impassioned collector of fine books, commissioning them from some of the leading illuminators of the day and caring for his treasures in a fashion that a twentieth-century bibliophile could only envy. Three inventories[14] of his collection, from 1401 until 1416, describe many of the scores of books he owned in terms that still identify them today: "a very rich Book of Hours . . . a very beautiful Book of Hours." Sometimes there is a clue to authorship, as in the case of Jeanne d'Évreux's Book of Hours (Fig. 170), left in her will to Charles V and later acquired by John; all three inventories list "Item unes petites heures de Nostre Dame, nommées Heures de Pucelle, enluminée de blanc et de noir . . . a little Book of Hours of Our Lady, called the Hours of Pucelle, illuminated in black and white. . . ."

It would be a mistake to assume that John of Berry's interest in fine books was from sincere religious conviction. All Books of Hours of a given usage are much the same, and one is no different from another if used only in worship or meditation. The many different copies he owned and commissioned were regarded by him much as a modern collector would feel about a complete collection of books illustrated by William Blake, which he enjoys and treasures but does not read. For him, they were works of art, as rare and costly as the paintings, sculptures, jewelry, and enamels that he also collected, and desirable for the same reason. All the more interest then attaches to the fact that the most distinguished manuscripts so far identified as commissioned by him were nearly all illuminated by Franco-

Fig. 186.
The Hague, Museum Meermanno-Westreenianum, Ms. 10. B 23, ff.1v-2. Bible of Charles V, Charles V and Jean de Vaudetar by Jean Bondol.

Flemish artists rather than Parisians. This could not have been because there were no distinguished French or Parisian illuminators at that time, for there were, as will be seen. But his preference was clearly for the work done by artists who came from the Low Countries to work in France,[15] properly designated by the term Franco-Flemish, as Jean Bondol had come from Bruges to work for Charles V.

A Psalter made for Duke John (Paris, BN Ms. fr. 13091)[16] probably between 1380 and 1385, was illuminated in part by another Franco-Flemish artist, André Beauneveu, according to the 1402 inventory of the Duke's collections. More is known of Beauneveu than is usual about artists of this period. Born at Valenciennes in Flanders between about 1330 and 1340, he was an architect and sculptor as well as a painter, and is first recorded in the service of Countess Yolande of Flanders in 1360. In 1364 he was painter to Charles V —*imagier du roi*—and was also working on the royal tombs at Saint-Denis.[17] The statue of Charles V on a buttress of the chapel added by Cardinal de la Grange to the cathedral at Amiens is by him,[18] executed between 1373 and 1375, and between 1393 and 1397, he was *Maître des oeuvres de taille et de peinture* to the Duke of Berry. That he was held in high regard by his contemporaries is indicated by the words of praise written by his fellow Fleming, Jean Froissart (1337?–1410?) in the *Chroniques de France* (Book IV, chap. 14). He

presumably died between 1402 and 1412, since his death is referred to in the later inventory.

The miniatures of the Berry Psalter mentioned in the inventory as by the hand of Beauneveu[19] are of twenty-four full-page Prophets and Apostles who face each other in the opening folios; Isaiah (Fig. 188) is on f.11v. The text of his prophecy of Christ's birth (7:14) at the bottom in Latin and French is enclosed by the lower marginal border, which rises on both sides and ends in the upper margin in a spray of foliage and a dragon. Isaiah is seated on an elaborate throne, holding an opened scroll in his left hand and pointing to it with his right. The throne stands on a checkered floor against a reticulated background. This background is deep blue with gray checks, the floor tiles are red and green, and the throne is white with lavender shading, but the figure is in grisaille except for points of color in the eyes.[20] The same formula is used for the other twenty-three miniatures, with some minor variations such as occasional foliated backgrounds instead of the reticulated type, and slightly different poses.[21]

Beauneveu's miniatures are clearly the work of one who thinks in sculptural rather than pictorial or graphic terms .With all but the smallest touches of color eliminated from the grisaille figures, they approach the effect of forms carved in stone. The thrones are elaborations of the architectural shrines housing the figures in the jambs of a cathedral portal, and only enough space is

Fig. 187.
Brussels, Bibliothèque Royale, Ms. 9217, f.115v. The
"Missal of Louis de Male," The Crucifixion.

Fig. 189.
Paris, Bibliothèque Nationale, Ms. lat. 18014, f.22. Petites
Heures de Jean de Berry, The Annunciation with other
figures. (Photo courtesy Millard Meiss)

indicated to provide for the masses of figures and accessories. In the Isaiah miniature, the receding lines of the checkered floor converge slightly, and in others of the series they are parallel, but the thrones are so placed that intersection is not visible. In this respect, Beauneveu and Bondol (Fig. 186) work toward different ends in employing generally comparable devices. Charles V's chair is placed well in front of the fleur-de-lys hanging; Isaiah's throne stands directly against the blue checked background plane. Therefore, for all the seeming relationship of Beauneveu's style in the 1380s to Pucelle's of the 1330s and Bondol's of his own time—the grisaille figures and the free patterns of spiky ivy foliage in the borders—Beauneveu appears to have attempted

no more in his miniatures than an imitation of three-dimensional statuary on a two-dimensional plane, whereas Pucelle and Bondol sought to enlarge the pictorial vocabulary of their art with plastic values. The rather coarse brushwork of Beauneveu's figures admittedly models their sculpturesque surfaces with considerable effectiveness, but it is quite different from the subtly graphic touches by which Pucelle and Bondol established their plastically realized forms.

It has already been observed that the formal and iconographic innovations that are so noteworthy in Pucelle's early fourteenth-century style were derived from slightly earlier Italian painting, specifically Sienese. From Pucelle, Bondol learned what he needed to

place his figures in viable space, while Beauneveu re-acted only very slightly to both Pucellian and Italian stimuli. In the closing years of the fourteenth century, another illuminator of major stature in the service of the Duc de Berry was to find inspiration in Italian art—Jacquemart de Hesdin.[22] Like Bondol and Beauneveu, he was a Franco-Fleming, and is first noted as in Duke John's service in 1384. There is no precise notice of his death, but it can be inferred that he was still alive in 1413 from a reference in the duke's inventory of that year to a book finished in Jacquemart's atelier in 1409. That book was the *Grandes-Heures* (Paris, BN Ms. lat. 919), so called for its considerable dimensions (39.7 x 29.5 cm: *c.* 15¾ x 11¾"). One other book, the *Très Belles Heures* (Brussels, Bibl. Roy. Ms. 11060–11061) is described in the 1402 inventory as "by the hand of Jacquemart de Hesdin," and two others have been attributed to the Jacquemart atelier from stylistic affin-ities with the two documented manuscripts. They are the *Petites Heures* (Paris, BN Ms. lat. 18014) and part of another called the *Très Riches Heures* (Paris, BN. Ms. n.a. lat. 3093). All these books were once in Duke

John's library, although it is not documented that he commissioned the *Petites Heures.* On stylistic grounds, it appears to be the earliest of the four, with a probable date in the mid-1380s and no later than 1388.[23]

It will be recalled that whereas the psalter had been the book most used in private devotions earlier in the Middle Ages, the Book of Hours had assumed that role by the middle of the fourteenth century. The psalter in which Beauneveu had a hand (Fig. 188, Plate XXVII) was somewhat old-fashioned in its illustrative scheme of a group of miniatures at the beginning not directly related to the text, like the Psalters of Blanche of Cas-tille (Fig. 142) and St. Louis (Fig. 149, Plate XXIV). All four of the Jacquemart Books of Hours are quite elaborate, with many different orders of service or offices for various times in the liturgical calendar. The one hundred and twenty-six folios of the *Grandes Heures,* for instance, have the texts of seven offices following the opening calendar pages—the Hours of the Virgin (ff.8–42v), the Seven Penitential Psalms and Litanies of the Saints (ff.45–52), the Little Hours of the Cross (ff.53–55v), the Little Hours of the Holy

Fig. 191.
Brussels, Bibliothèque Royale, Ms. 11060–11061, p. 54.
Très Belles Heures de Jean de Berry, *The Visitation by*
Jacquemart de Hesdin.

Fig. 190.
Brussels, Bibliothèque Royale, Ms. 11060–11061, pp.
10–11. Très Belles Heures de Jean de Berry, *John of*
Berry presented to the Virgin and Child.

Spirit (ff.56–58), the Large Hours of the Passion (ff.61–85v), the Large Hours of the Holy Spirit (ff.86–101), and the Office of the Dead (ff.106–123v). In a luxury manuscript like the *Grandes Heures,* each office would have a full-page miniature as frontispiece and smaller ones at the beginning of each section, with illuminated initial letters for the sentences and elaborate marginal borders.

It can be readily understood that no one illuminator could do all the work involved in an undertaking like the *Grandes Heures* in a reasonable length of time,[24] and the 1413 inventory states that the book was the product of "Jaquemart de Hodin et autres ouvriers—Jacquemart de Hesdin and other artists of the Duke." It states further, however, that forty-five *grans histoires* in the manuscript were by Jacquemart himself. These are now lost, with the possible exception of a painting on parchment in the Louvre[25] of Christ Carrying the Cross,[26] and none of the hands in the miniatures and initials in the book can be identified with it.[27] But it goes without saying that the enterprise was supervised by Jacquemart de Hesdin as the *chef d'atelier,* and his was the guiding spirit. It is because many of the same compositions appear in the miniatures of the *Petites Heures* that it is now unquestionably accepted as a Jacquemart atelier product about twenty years earlier.

The *Petites Heures du Duc de Berry,* so named from its relatively small size (21.5 x 14.5 cm: *c.* 8½ x 5¾"), is almost certainly the "très belles Heures, contenant pluseurs heures et commémoraciones de Dieu et de ses sains" listed in the inventories of 1402 and 1413. It is further described as beginning with a calendar illustrated from the Epistles of St. Paul and the Old and New Testaments, and that there is an Annunciation with several apostles around it at the beginning of the Hours of Our Lady. Such is the miniature on f.22 (Fig. 189) of the *Petites Heures.* It is more than probable that it is by Jacquemart himself, because the *chef d'atelier* usually executed the most prominent miniature in a book like this, the frontispiece of the office of Matins in the Hours of the Virgin. His indebtedness to Jean Pucelle is apparent in a number of respects. The calendar, with its illustrated concordance of Old and New Testament themes, follows the idea invented for the Belleville Breviary.[28] The border foliage is of the freely flowing spiky type seen in the same book (Fig. 171), and the Annunciation itself is an augmented variation of the scheme created by Pucelle in the Hours of Jeanne d'Évreux (Fig. 170).[29]

It will be recalled that the features distinguishing Pucelle's Annunciation in the Évreux Hours from more traditional northern conceptions were largely derived from Italian and specifically Sienese usage. Jacquemart de Hesdin continued along those lines and provided the central theme with a frame of individual figures in small Gothic niches—five full-length standing apostles on each side, two others kneeling on either side of Jeremiah below, and half-length figures of the Virgin and St. John with the Man of Sorrows at the top. Panofsky has pointed out the general affinity of this scheme with a type of cult image current in earlier fourteenth-century Italy, like Duccio's Rucellai Madonna or the even more monumental *Maestà* in the cathedral at Siena; the conceptual parallel is strengthened by the portrait of John of Berry in the initial D below, kneeling as if before a polyptych above an altar. In the Annunciation scene itself, there are comparable enrichments of the Pucelle formula. It takes place in a vaulted Gothic structure, with a foreshortened tile floor creating a volume of space in which the angel directly approaches the Virgin with a gesture at once commanding and respectful, heightening the dramatic unity of the theme to complement the augmented formal unity of the developed spatial patterns in the setting.

In the *Très Belles Heures de Jean de Berry* (Brussels, Bibl. Roy. Ms. 11060–11061),[30] the changing conceptions of space within the miniature and the structural relationship of its design to the page on which it lies are carried further. The manuscript is identified with Jacquemart d'Hesdin in the 1402 inventory—"Item, unes très belles heures, richement enluminées et ystoriés de la main Jaquemart de Odin, et par les quarrefors des feuillez en pluseurs lieux faictes des armes et devises de Monseigneur. . . ."—and is generally thought to have been illuminated for the most part in the middle 1390s. It contains the Office of the Virgin, the Penitential Psalms and Litanies of the Saints, the Hours of the Cross, and the Office of the Dead. There are eighteen full-page miniatures in the text proper, each on the verso of its folio,[31] and historiated initials introduce the principal divisions of the text. In addition, a double miniature on pp. 11–12 has been inserted as a frontispiece (Fig. 190), where a calendar is usually found. It represents John of Berry being presented by SS. Andrew and John the Baptist to the Virgin and Child;[32] the same subject appears on p. 14 but in a single composition.[33] The double miniature is on folios originally a little larger than the rest of the book, which have been cropped to fit, mutilating the margin borders.

The authorship of the diptych frontispiece in the Brussels *Très Belles Heures* has been much disputed, the only agreement being that it cannot be by the same artist who did the other eighteen full-page miniatures, or at least not at the same time.[34] The figures are *en grisaille,* which, along with the Virgin's elaborate throne, has suggested André Beauneveu as the author (Fig. 188, Plate XXVII). To others, the delicate modeling of the figures and the foreshortened checkered floor of the Duc de Berry group seem in the manner of Jean Bondol (Fig. 186). The strikingly Sienese facial types of all the figures, and particularly John the Baptist, are unlike any in Bondol's work, and no specific attribution seems possible other than to an anonymous master of considerable talent, or perhaps to Jacquemart himself at a stage of his career even before the *Petites Heures,* in which his style might have been a synthesis of those developed by the Duke's older artists. For all the mystery of its authorship, the diptych frontispiece of the Brussels Hours is a work of the highest quality, and great historic importance for two iconographic features. One is a new interpretation of the traditional theme of the Madonna suckling the Child on her lap as the *Sedes Sapientiae*—the Seat of Wisdom—to which the motive of her Son writing His response to the praying suppliant has been added, in this case the kneeling Duke on the facing page. The same humanizing sentiment gives the mortal equal size and importance in the composition with the sacred personages, a relatively early instance of a concept that frequently appears in Netherlandish painting of the fifteenth century. Before, in compositions like the Crucifixion in the eleventh-century Gospel-book of Judith of Flanders (Fig. 95), or the Missal of Louis de Male (Fig. 187), human figures were much smaller in scale than biblical characters. Here John of Berry has been elevated from the subordinate place he occupied in the initial of the *Petites Heures* Annunciation folio (Fig. 189) to equality with the scriptural protagonists.

In the eighteen miniatures, such as the Visitation (Fig. 191) on p. 54 of the Brussels Hours, painted by Jacquemart himself according to the 1402 inventory, there are a number of innovations. One is a more developed feeling for pictorial space than has hitherto been seen, and the problem thereby posed of the relationship between the pictorial design as a whole and the book page. The other is the evidence seen in them

of a new and possibly direct infusion of Italian ideas. The miniature of Christ Carrying His Cross on page 186 of the Brussels Hours is an adaptation with but few variations of Simone Martini's panel painting of the subject in the Louvre.[35] Others, like the Presentation in the Temple on page 98 and Christ's Betrayal on page 164, can be related to Giottesque compositions.[36] It is important to note that it is to Italian compositions as aesthetic unities and wholes that these miniatures in the *Très Belles Heures* are to be compared, rather than isolated stylistic and iconographic details such as Pucelle had abstracted from Sienese models and as Jacquemart himself had also done in the earlier *Petites Heures.*

It is significant that Jacquemart's Italian models were panel paintings and mural designs, not miniatures in manuscripts save possibly as intermediaries. In conceiving them as substantive and self-sufficient aesthetic unities, the problem of establishing the reality of individual details within the whole inevitably arose, no less than the creation of viable space in which they could exist. Thus, in the second dedication page of the *Très Belles Heures,*[37] in which the iconographic elements of the diptych frontispiece (Fig. 190) are combined, the Virgin's throne is placed at an angle to the picture plane and is paralleled by the diagonal lines of the tessellated floor leading back in space to the kneeling duke and his patron saints. In the Visitation (Fig. 191), the little building from which St. Elizabeth emerges is also diagonal to the picture plane, and the ground slopes up in a series of hills and ridges that carry the eye to the distant castle standing out against the blue sky. The ancestry of these intersecting shapes may be found in Italian work, perhaps (cf. Fig. 183), but there they are only backdrops. Here they play a major role in creating the visual impression of three dimensions in space.

Comparison of the Brussels Hours landscape with that in the Guillaume de Machaut miniature (Fig. 185) is also instructive. Many details are similar, even to the small building in the right foreground. But the curving ridges of the poet's garden rise in parallel lines on a steeply tilted ground plane of unmodulated surfaces patterned with trees and animals, in an effect more like a tapestry than the rolling surfaces that fill the space in Jacquemart's Visitation. And where the distant sky in the Machaut miniature is no more than a surface against which the decorative shapes are silhouetted, the flat blue of the later landscape connotes infinite space lying beyond. There is even an effort on Jacquemart's part to indicate the season of the year. The foliage of the trees is that of late spring or early summer in contrast to the wintry bareness of the Annunciation to the Shepherds and the Flight into Egypt.[38]

The scene of the Annunciation on f.22 of the *Petites Heures* (Fig. 189) is enclosed within bands of little Gothic shrines housing the Apostles and other figures, as described above, with the opening lines of Matins of the Office of the Virgin in the space below the miniature proper. Out of the narrow strips that are the edges of these bands emerge tendrils of foliage filling the lower and right margins with the ivy leaves commonly used for such purposes in French illumination since the late thirteenth century. Their aesthetic function is to contribute to the decorative relationship between the pictorial design, the script of the text, and the flat plane of the manuscript folio.[39] In the full-page miniatures of the *Très Belles Heures,* including the inserted diptych frontispiece (Figs. 190, 191), the marginal ornament is organized in a quite different way. The wayward rinceaux have been replaced by straight stems, the ivy leaves by a variety of red and blue flowers (the columbine and poppy can be identified) placed symmetrically on either side of the central stems, and these foliate bands are punctuated by regularly spaced quatrefoil medallions decorated with monograms and armorial devices. The monogram—a U or V interlaced with an E—is of uncertain meaning. The heraldic devices are a white swan, a bear, and the gold *fleurs-de-lys* of France on a blue ground, all of which appear in other manuscripts made for the Duc de Berry. They are the "quarrefors . . . faictes des armes et de devises de Monseigneur" mentioned in the 1402 inventory as part of Jacquemart's decoration of the manuscript—a significant point, for it indicates that they were somewhat unusual.

Coats of arms are frequently found in the marginal decoration of earlier manuscripts, it is true. They were much favored by East Anglian illuminators of volumes like a Book of Hours in the Fitzwilliam Museum at Cambridge (Ms. 242)[40] or the Tickhill Psalter,[41] both of the early fourteenth century. Nor is it surprising to find them in early fourteenth-century Flemish books like the Bible in the Brussels Bibliothèque Royale (Ms. 9157; Fig. 175), in view of the demonstrable relationships between English and Flemish illumination at the time. It will also be recalled that originally there were coats of arms in the marginal borders of the Crucifixion

in the so-called Missal of Louis de Male (Fig. 187); and in a stylistically related volume, the Breviary of Louis de Male (Brussels, Bibl. Roy. Ms. 9427), the family arms appear no less than five times throughout the book. Italian examples of the same general period include those on ff.17 and 41 in the St. George Codex of about 1320 made for Cardinal Jacobus de Stephanescis, and on many of the illuminated folios in an unfinished three-volume Bible (Vatican, Bibl. Apost. Ms. lat. 3550) made about the same time in Rome for Abbot Matthew of the Celestines.[42]

The armorial devices in the examples just cited are motives in the marginal borders, along with birds and animals and drolleries, in decorative schemes in which the rinceaux are the controlling element. In the full-page miniatures of the *Très Riches Heures,* it is the quatrefoils that dominate the marginal ornament, organized in a rigid trellis or frame by the connecting stems and symmetrically disposed flowers interspersed with birds and butterflies. The difference between this and the older French and Franco-Flemish marginal schemes has been put by Panofsky with his accustomed clarity when he speaks of the Brussels Hours miniatures as "framed rather than bordered."[43] Even in so elaborate a scheme as that of the Jesse Tree folio of the Saint-Omer Psalter (Fig. 174), the function of the border is to relate the text with its developed initial and the narrative medallions to the two-dimensional plane of the folio. In the *Très Belles Heures* miniatures, the "frame" of flowering stems, birds and butterflies, and quatrefoil medallions insulates or isolates the three-dimensional scene from the folio plane and imposes the principle that its reality must be accepted on its own terms, not by formal integration with other elements. Stated differently, it is only by accident, so to speak, that these miniatures are in a book; they could just as well be panel paintings, existing in their own right and independent of formal relationship to anything else.

The germ of this idea was already present in the scheme of the Annunciation on f.22 of the *Petites Heures* (Fig. 189). It probably originated in the characteristic forms of Italian cult pictures, as has been pointed out,[44] though it should also be observed that there are schemes something like it in early fourteenth-century Italian illumination; the opening verses of Genesis in the Vatican Bible (Ms. lat. 3550) referred to above are "framed" by panels of scenes from the Creation of the Universe through the Expulsion from the Garden of Eden. On the *Petites Heures* Annunciation folio, free rinceaux still relate the simulacrum of an altarpiece with collateral images, and the few lines of text to the parchment plane in the traditional way, a way which was continued by the majority of Jacquemart de Hesdin's contemporaries and illuminators of the early fifteenth century in the north. Only in atelier products like the *Grandes Heures du Duc de Berry* (Paris, BN Ms. lat. 919), which now lacks Jacquemart's *grans histoires* and is largely the work of assistants, was his formula continued and there in an overelaborated and ostentatious way.[45] The significance of Jacquemart's innovation is very great, none the less. By conceiving the illuminated miniature as a substantive entity, independent of the written text and to be evaluated only in its own terms, he returned to the conception of pictorial art found in such an early stage of Occidental book decoration as is seen in the Vatican Vergil (Fig. 4). In so doing, he also took a step along the way to be followed in Western manuscript illumination in ensuing decades, to its ultimate loss of imaginative creativity as an independent and self-sufficient art by becoming either imitative of panel painting or literally illustrative.

NOTES

1. Cf. Panofsky, *ENP* 1: 36, fig. 28.
2. H. Karlinger, *Die Kunst der Gotik* (Berlin: Propyläen, 1926), p. 410.
3. *ENP*, 2, pl. 8: Meiss, chap. 7, n. 1; pp. 21, 100, 113, 204.
4. Cf. *La librairie de Charles V*, pl. v, for a reproduction in color.
5. Panofsky, *ENP* 1:35.
6. *Ibid.* 2, fig. 29.
7. Gaspar and Lyna, chap. 7, n. 51; nos. 143, 144. *La Librairie de Philippe le Bon* (Brussels: Bibliothèque Royale, 1967), nos. 12, 18.
8. Reproduced in color in Delaissé, *Miniatures médiévales*, p. 67.
9. U. Thieme and F. Becker, *Allgemeines Lexikon der bildenden Künstler* (Leipzig: W. Engelmann, 1910–50), 4:279. Meiss, pp. 19–23.
10. H. Martin, *La miniature française du xiiie au xve siècle* (Paris-Brussels: Van Oest, 1923), figs. lix–lxiv.
11. A. Lejard, *Les tapisseries de l'Apocalypse de la Cathédrale d'Angers* (Paris: A. Michel, 1942).
12. *Librairie . . . Charles V*, no. 123.
13. Cf. Meiss, pp. 30–35.
14. *Ibid.*, pp. 352–53.
15. *Ibid.*, pp. 247–53, 298–308.
16. *Ibid.*, pp. 135–54.
17. P. Vitry and G. Brière, *L'Église abbatiale de Saint-Denis et ses tombeaux* (Paris: Longuet, 1925), pp. 153–55.
18. Cf. Karlinger, n. 2; p. 408.
19. Meiss, p. 7.
20. Reproduced in color in *MFM*, pl. lxiii.
21. Meiss, figs. 51–74.
22. Thieme-Becker, n. 9; xvi, p. 571. Meiss, pp. 226–27.
23. Meiss, pp. 155–93, 334–35.
24. Cf. *AB* 38 (1956):189–91.
25. Cf. Wixom, chap. 5, n. 61; p. 267.
26. O. Pächt, "Un tableau de Jacquemart d'Hesdin?," *Revue des Arts* 6 (1956):149–60.
27. Meiss, pp. 332–34.
28. *Ibid.*, figs. 83–85.
29. *Ibid.*, fig. 94, for a reproduction in color.
30. *Ibid.*, pp. 198–255, 321–23.
31. The Brussels Book of Hours is paginated rather than foliated.
32. Reproduced in color in Delaissé, *Miniatures médiévales*, pp. 92–93.
33. Cf. R. M. Tovell, *Flemish Artists of the Valois Courts* (Toronto: University of Toronto Press, 1950), pl. 2 for a reproduction in color.
34. Cf. Panofsky, *ENP* 1: 46–47; Meiss, pp. 200–208.
35. *ENP* 2, pl. 20.
36. Meiss, figs. 187, 191.
37. *Ibid.*, fig. 181.
38. *Ibid.*, figs. 185, 188.
39. For a more extended and excellent discussion of this point, cf. Meiss, pp. 203–4.
40. Cf. Rickert, *PiBMA*, pl. 128.
41. Cf. Egbert, *The Tickhill Psalter*, pls. v, xxxviii, L.
42. S. Beissel, *Vatikanische Miniaturen* (Frieburg i. B., St. Louis: Herder, 1893), no. 22.
43. *ENP* 1:49.
44. *ENP* 1:43.
45. Cf. Meiss, figs. 216–32.

Fig. 192.
Chantilly, Musée Condé, Ms. 1284, f.51v. The Limbourg
Brothers, The Très Riches Heures de Jean de Berry, *The*
Meeting of the Three Magi. (Photo Giraudon)

Manuscript Illumination in the Late Middle Ages

In the inventory of John of Berry's collections drawn up after his death in 1416, one item is *en une layette pluseurs cahers d'une Très riches heures que faisoient Pol et ses frères, très richement historiés et enluminés,* "in a portfolio, several gatherings of a very rich Book of Hours made by Paul and his brothers, very richly historiated and illuminated." This has been identified as the manuscript known as the *Très Riches Heures de Jean de France, duc de Berry* (Chantilly, Musée Condé, Ms. 1284),[1] and its creators as Paul, Herman, and John Malouel, usually called the Limbourg brothers[2] from their presumed origin in the Netherlandish district of that name.[3] The manuscript contains the Hours of the Virgin, the Penitential Psalms and Litany of the Saints, the Hours of the Cross and of the Holy Spirit, the Office of the Dead, the Hours of the Passion, and masses and offices for various special feasts, as well as the calendar and readings from the Gospels with which it opens. The script is by one hand throughout, with the exception of a few minor passages. This is not true, however, of the one hundred and thirty-one miniatures, of which sixty-six are full page and sixty-five about one-fourth that size. Of these, forty-four large and twenty-seven small are of the early fifteenth century and by the Limbourg brothers. The remaining twenty-two full-page miniatures and thirty-eight smaller ones are in a late fifteenth-century style associated with Jean Colombe, who worked for the Dukes of Savoie to whom the book, unfinished when the Duke of Berry died in 1416, presumably passed by inheritance.[4]

The Limbourg brothers are first noted as manuscript illuminators for Philip the Bold, John of Berry's brother, in 1402, but by 1410 they were in the duke's service. A Book of Hours at the Cloisters of the Metropolitan Museum in New York (Ms. 54. 1. 1.)[5] is also known as the Hours of Ailly. It is believed to be the one listed in the Berry inventories of 1413 and 1416 as "Unes belles Heures, très bien et richement historiées . . . lesquelles heures monseigneur a fait faire par ses ouvriers"; it is thought to be among the first commissions of the brothers for the Duke of Berry and to date between 1410 and 1413. Its extensive illumination shows thorough familiarity with Jacquemart de Hesdin's innovations, not least among them the foliage-frame enclosure of the scenes, which the Limbourgs enlarged upon in their own way.[6] Furthermore, in one of the books from the Jacquemart atelier, the *Petites Heures,* an inserted miniature on f.288v,[7] at the beginning of a prayer to be said for one going on a voyage, is certainly a Limbourg product,[8] proof of the close relationship between the Limbourg atelier and that of the older master.

The Chantilly *Très Riches Heures* were begun in 1413 and remained unfinished, as has been noted, when the Duke of Berry died in 1416. Careful analysis of the seventy-one early fifteenth-century miniatures has identified three different hands, possibly, but not certainly, the three brothers, since the enterprise was one of those described elsewhere in which several illuminators may have worked on a single miniature. There is also a

Fig. 193.
Chantilly, Musée Condé, Ms. 1284, f.2v. The Limbourg
Brothers, The Très Riches Heures de Jean de Berry,
February. (Photo Giraudon)

Plate XXIV. Paris, Bibliothèque Nationale, Ms. lat. 10525, f. 11v. The Psalter of St. Louis, Abraham, Eliezer and Rebekah.

Plate XXV. Paris, Bibliothèque Nationale, Ms. lat. 1023, f. 7v. Breviary of Philippe le Bel, Scenes from the Life of David by Maître Honoré.

Plate XXVI. Hamburg, Staats- und Universitätsbibliothek,
Ms. in scrin. 1ʳ, f. 1. Cistercian Missal, Initial M with
the Resurrection of Christ.

general threefold aspect of style and corresponding differences of content of more than usual interest. One group of miniatures is even more directly dependent on Italian models than Jacquemart's *oeuvre* was. A second is notable for its elegant and decorative figures dressed in ultra-stylish costumes of the day. In the third, there is even greater naturalism of form, space, and subject matter than anything hitherto encountered. In all three categories, the relationship to Jacquemart de Hesdin's innovations in the preceding decades is clear, but the Limbourgs carry their concepts even further.

All three categories are represented in varying degrees in the Meeting of the Three Magi near Mount Golgotha (Fig. 192) on f.51v. No such meeting is mentioned in the Scriptures, but it was apparently suggested in a popular history of the Three Wise Men written in the late fourteenth century.[9] In the elaborate panoply of the Magi and their attendants, one of the three categories mentioned is immediately apparent. Gold is used lavishly in the costumes, banners, horse trappings, and the like, even on the sculptures in the little building or *Montjoie* marking a spot from which the city of Jerusalem could be seen. The costumes are brightly colored—predominantly blue, red, and yellow—and there are consciously exotic notes in the Negroid and Oriental types among the followers.

The Italian element is not so obvious in the miniatures of the Three Magi Meeting as in some others in the manuscript, but it is present none the less in an unusual and interesting way. In the 1402 inventory, two gold medals of Roman emperors are listed with a note that they were bought from a Florentine merchant in Paris.[10] The originals are no longer known, but copies made for the duke still exist, and the design of one representing Constantine reappears almost line for line in the Magus on the left side of the miniature.[11] Moreover, the one in the right foreground probably reproduces the design of another and similar medallion, for, as Panofsky points out, he and his horse are precisely circumscribed by a circle centered at the point on the left thigh from which the folds of his tunic fan out. The miniature of the Purification of the Virgin on f.54v is even more Italianate for it faithfully follows in all compositional details the frescoed Presentation of the Virgin by Taddeo Gaddi in the Baroncelli Chapel of Santa Croce at Florence.[12] In thus taking over an Italian design as a whole, the Limbourgs followed Jacquemart de Hesdin's example, but they widened the range of their models and drew upon earlier fourteenth-century

Giottesque and Pisan and north Italian sources as well as the Sienese exemplars to which the older master had limited himself, for the most part. And throughout the *Très Riches Heures,* typically Italianate acanthus foliage replaces the traditionally northern ivy and grape vine *rinceaux* that the Limbourg brothers themselves had used for marginal ornament in earlier books.

Decorative elegance is the most obvious characteristic of the Meeting of the Magi miniature, but it also contains naturalistic elements of more than passing interest. The distant sky, for example, shades from light blue at the horizon to a darker value at the zenith, an optical subtlety that Jacquemart de Hesdin did not observe in the miniatures of the *Très Belles Heures* (Fig. 191). Moreover, the little Gothic shrine or *Montjoie* where the Wise Men meet is the likeness of a monument that stood on the road from Saint-Denis to Paris, which had been erected by Charles V, suggesting that the way to Bethlehem was through the environs of Paris itself. This is confirmed by the buildings in the background, some of which still stand. At the extreme left are the Sainte-Chapelle and the façade of Notre-Dame, with a tower of the episcopal palace at the right and the more distant spire of Sainte-Geneviève-des-Ardents in between. On the hills are the Tour de Montlhéry and the abbey of Montmartre. Nor are these recognizably specific buildings seen as isolated forms, for they are shown as they would have appeared from the Hotel de Nesle, Jean de Berry's town house when he was in Paris. In like fashion, the backgrounds of most of the calendar miniatures in the *Très Riches Heures* (ff.2–12v) have likenesses of châteaux owned by the duke, or, as in the June picture on f.6v, scenes of recognizable buildings observed from an identifiable viewing point, for it is the same as in the Meeting of the Magi. There are no earlier examples in the history of manuscript illumination or of painting in general of such exact reproductions of specific optical experiences, in which both the characteristics of individual forms and their relationship to each other are taken into account.

Such "portraits" of specific buildings appear in many miniatures throughout the manuscript. The Temptation of Christ on f.161v takes place on a rocky crag towering above the Duc de Berry's château at Mehun-sur-Yèvre where most of his books were kept.[13] On f.195, St. Michael battles a dragon in the sky above the shrine dedicated to him at Mont-Saint-Michel. In many of the Calendar illustrations, the artists' naturalistic sense went even beyond such literal descriptions and created landscapes communicating the mood and character of the season. July (f.7v) is of a rustic scene of harvesting and sheep-shearing in the fields near the duke's Château du Clain in Poitiers, peopled by figures brightly colored and precisely outlined as they would appear in the dry heat of summer. In February on f.2v (Fig. 193), white profiles of snowy hills are outlined against a bluish-gray sky that shades to a cold and steely hue above, the first rendering of a snow scene in the history of painting.[14]

There is a long tradition in mediaeval art of such association of symbols of the months with scenes of activities appropriate to them.[15] They appear in sculpture on the façades of Gothic cathedrals, and on the pages of the calendars that were part of every devotional volume like the Book of Hours. In earlier occupation sequences, the month is symbolized by a sign of the zodiac and the activity is in a separate design. Jean Pucelle had changed this in the calendar he compiled for the Belleville Breviary[16] in which the scenes of human activities were replaced by tiny vignettes of unpeopled landscapes that vary from month to month. This notion of calendar illustration is found in many of the major French manuscripts of the later fourteenth and early fifteenth centuries, particularly those from Jacquemart de Hesdin's atelier.[17] In the *Très Riches Heures,* the two complementary ideas are combined in a single composition. Below is a scene portraying the typical activity or mood of the month. Above, concentric semicircular bands carry the name of the month, indicate its division into *kalends, ides,* and so on, and identify the zodiacal signs of the two constellations that are the astrological "houses" of the sun for the month in question, Aquarius and Pisces for February. In the lunette, a figure with a golden disk riding in a chariot is the sun. None of the duke's châteaux appear in the February miniature, as they do in most of the calendar illustrations, but the mood of the month is directly communicated in the contrast between the world of nature with its chilled denizens and the redolent domesticity within the little hut in the left foreground.

The miniatures of the *Très Riches Heures* are a milestone in the history of painting. Their creators developed their style on the foundation of Jacquemart de Hesdin's innovations, extending and refining the Italianisms and naturalism of his manner to the point that these miniature scenes of life in the Franco-Flemish world of the early fifteenth century are significantly in advance of anything contemporary with them in the Western world

as visual interpretations of experience. But they are also a summation of a way of interpreting experience, and mark its end at the same time. It is significant that throughout the part of the book identifiable with the Limbourg brothers, marginal borders consist of occasional sprays of Italianate acanthus foliage, or, on the calendar pages, are omitted entirely. On them, only the decorative arcs of the astronomical designs suggest that the compositions have anything to do with the illumination of a book folio. If they are blocked out (as they often are when the miniatures are cited as illustrations of painting in the general sense) there is nothing to indicate that they are not substantive panel paintings of any dimension. As such, they well deserve the admiration they have been accorded and the popularity they enjoy. But as manuscript illuminations, they were an irrevocable step in the direction already implied in Jaquemart de Hesdin's art toward its ultimate demise. In this connection, it is significant that the Limbourg brothers' work influenced their contemporaries in France and the Netherlands only in relatively superficial ways. Some of the *Très Riches Heures* miniatures were copied in the Grimani Breviary (Venice, Biblioteca di San Marco, Ms. unnumbered),[18] but almost exactly a century later.

The case is different of three distinguished manuscript illuminators who were active in Paris in the early fifteenth century, all anonymous, but creators of quite individual styles. They are known as the Boucicaut, Bedford, and Rohan Masters, from the patrons who commissioned or owned their most distinctive works. The three appear to have been associated at one time or another, for there are some points of similarity in their styles in what seem to be their earlier products, but all of their mature works bear the stamp of individuality that makes them worthy contemporaries of the Limbourg brothers.

The Boucicaut Master is so designated from his authorship of a Book of Hours (Paris, Musée Jacquemart-André, Ms. 2)[19] made for one of Charles VI's most distinguished soldiers and statesmen, Jean II le Meingre, the Maréchal de Boucicaut, whose likeness appears in several of the miniatures (Fig. 195), sometimes alone and sometimes with his wife, Antoinette de Turenne. The date of their marriage, 1393, is a *terminus post quem* for the book, which must have been finished before 1415 when the Marshal was captured by the English at Agincourt; circumstantial and internal evidence suggests that it was begun about 1400 and fin-

Fig. 194.
Paris, Musée Jacquemart-André, Ms. 2, f.65v. The Bou-
cicaut Master, The Hours of the Maréchal de Boucicaut,
The Visitation. (Photo Bulloz)

ished by 1410 or 1411, with a possibility that it may have been completed between 1405 and 1408.[20] It is a book of considerable size, measuring 27.4 x 19.0 cm (10⅞ x 7½″), of two hundred and forty-two folios with forty-two full-page miniatures (exclusive of two added on ff.241–242 by a later owner) and numerous decorated initials. The calendar is not illustrated, but the various offices are introduced by biblical and other scenes appropriate to their texts (Fig. 194), and the suffrages of the saints are illustrated, with their images, like the one of St. Catherine, being venerated by the Marshal on f.38v (Fig. 195).

A number of other manuscripts have been attributed to the Boucicaut Master and his atelier, as well as miniatures in books associated with other artists; several in the *Grandes Heures du Duc de Berry* have been identified with him or his associates.[21] But even without such evidence that the Boucicaut Master knew the expressive forms and vocabulary of Jacquemart de Hesdin, this would be clear in a composition like the Visitation (Fig. 194) on f.65v of the Boucicaut Hours. The setting, a deep landscape of hills dotted with trees and outlined against the distant sky, bears on this point, no less than the affectionate gestures of the protagonists. The systematized tendrils of leaves and flowers in the marginal border are anchored, so to speak, by the large acanthus-like sprays in the angles and the left side, and perform the same function as the Berry coats-of-arms in the Visitation of the Brussels Hours (Fig. 191), creating a frame through which the scene is observed. The foreground hills in the Boucicaut composition are a series of overlapping planes as they are in the Brussels miniature, and both share a common disregard for scale and mathematically constructed linear perspective.

But the differences between the two miniatures in form and content are even more striking than the similarities, and mark the Boucicaut Master as one of the great progressive artists of his generation. Thus, instead of the flat and unmodulated blue sky of Jacquemart's Visitation, there is a subtle shading of values from light at the horizon to dark at the zenith, the intervening levels marked by clouds of varying shapes of white and gray touched with spots of crimson and yellow. In the landscape on the far side of the lake, with its rustic details of peasants and animals, nearer forms are stronger in color and more distinct in shape while more distant ones lose substance and outline in an all-pervasive gray-blue haze. This is an effect the

Limbourg brothers were to employ very effectively a few years later; that the Boucicaut Master was the source of the idea is not open to question, for such an effect of atmospheric perspective was not to be achieved for nearly two decades elsewhere, even in Italy. And, finally, the place of the humble Joseph attending Mary in the Brussels Visitation has been taken by two angels, one carrying her prayer book and the other the train of her mantle.

Differences in style such as those noted between the Visitations of Jacquemart de Hesdin and the Boucicaut Master imply differences in technique. It is obvious that the Boucicaut Master's luminous sky was created by a different pigment structure and method of application from those that produced the opaque matte surfaces of Jacquemart's. There are a number of treatises on fourteenth-century methods of painting in general known to exist, and one specifically on manuscript illumination in a unique copy (Naples, Biblioteca Nazionale, Ms. XII. E. 27).[22] In all, the illuminator is given detailed instruction on how to make his colors more brilliant and transparent, usually by combining the traditional binding medium of beaten egg-white or "glare" with gum arabic, a substance that had become much more generally available to Western artists in the fourteenth century that previously.[23] Such a combination of glare and gum arabic is particularly recommended for blue pigments like those used for the sky and distant landscape in the Boucicaut Visitation.

The treatises referred to above are all Italian, but it is known that similar ones were available in Paris in the early fifteenth century. A manuscript compiled by Jean Lebègue (Paris, BN, Ms. lat. 6741), registrar of the *Chambre des comptes,* in 1431 was based on information gleaned from a north Italian named Giovanni Alchiero, who was interested in the techniques of painting. Alchiero had been in Paris at least as early as 1398, when he wrote one of the treatises included in Lebègue's compilation after the dictation of a certain Jacques Coene, a Flemish painter then living in Paris.[24] Alchiero also obtained information from a certain Brother Dionysius of Santa Maria del Sacco in Milan in 1409, from a Flemish textile worker named Theodore in Bologna in 1410, and, in the same year, from the Italian painter Michelino de Besozzo in Venice.[25] Neither Alchiero nor Lebègue seems to have been an artist; they were primarily interested in bringing together all the information they could get on various artistic techniques, including manuscript illumination.

Fig. 195.
Paris, Musée Jacquemart-André, Ms. 2, f.38v. The Bou-
cicaut Master, The Hours of the Maréchal de Boucicaut,
St. Catherine venerated by the Maréchal de Boucicaut.
(Photo Bulloz)

What can be inferred from the texts in their compilations of the international aspect of the art around 1400 is confirmed by the list of illuminators in Paris recorded in the book of the Masters of the King's Mint for 1391 (Paris, BN, Ms. fr. 22119).

Although they were contemporaries, the Limbourg brothers and the Boucicaut Master differed significantly in approaching the key problem of naturalistic painting around 1400, the rendering of space. For all the touches of realism in the *Très Riches Heures* Meeting of the Magi and February scenes (Figs. 192–193), the miniatures are primarily decorative in their organization. Conversely, for all the decorative pattern of light rays in the Boucicaut Visitation, it is only superimposed on a scheme of forms and colors intended to create an impression of objects enveloped in three-dimensional depth. The difference in point of view is even more pronounced in interior scenes. The peasants in the Limbourg February picture warm themselves in a cottage from which one side has been removed, a formula set nearly a century earlier by Jean Pucelle (Fig. 170). And even in full-fledged interiors, like the hall where Jean de Berry celebrates the January feast in the *Très Riches Heures* (f.2) or the Gothic nave designed by the Limbourgs for the Funeral of Raymond Diocrès (f.86v, completed by Jean Colombe), there is but scant sense of environment in the tapestry-like patterns of gold and color. By contrast, the Maréchal de Boucicaut venerates St. Catherine (Fig. 195) in a vaulted space that recedes to the right, curtained off from the kneeling marshal and the saint by a hanging with the silver and green chevrons of his coat of arms. Following upon and refining Jean Bondol's method of *implying* space (Fig. 186), the Boucicaut Master frames the scene in an opening between two slender piers spanned by an architrave, cutting off the tapestried wall behind St. Catherine on the left and the vaulted bays on the right above the marshal and the angel holding the shield. Yet these very devices that might seem to amputate space imply its extension and amplify its expressive effect, introducing at the same time two-dimensional patterns affirming the consubstantiality of the picture plane and the parchment folio. Thus the many decorative elements—the chevroned hanging, the spangled red tapestry with Boucicaut's motto, *Ce que vous voudres,* on the canopy and behind the saint, the heraldic shields (repainted with the device of a later owner), and the windows in which silver foil represents the glass[26]—contribute to the impression of an actual room in which the protagonists move with dignity and grace.

Differing though they did in method and expressive aims, the Limbourg brothers and the Boucicaut Master were alike in serving aristocratic patrons and embodying their tastes and interests in the commissions executed for them. In so doing, both represent in manuscript illumination the phenomenon known in the history of art as the "International Style," manifest in all aspects of European culture around the year 1400.[27] A point noted above is pertinent, the replacing of Joseph carrying his carpenter's tools, who accompanies the Virgin in Jacquemart's version of the Visitation (Fig. 191) by angels carrying her prayer book and train in the Boucicaut Master's (Fig. 194). They follow her like pages attending a great lady in a ceremonial pageant, quite unlike the humble peasant in the same scene of the Brussels Hours. In so doing, they strike a note that echoes throughout the Boucicaut Hours miniatures, in which no opportunity was overlooked to set the personages of biblical and sacred history in the milieu of contemporary nobility, specifically that of the Maréchal de Boucicaut. Thus the Coronation of the Virgin takes place in a pavilion of Boucicaut silver and green against a background spangled with the marshal's armorial device, to cite but one of many instances.[28] In the same spirit, the Limbourg brothers made gorgeously attired Oriental potentates of the Three Wise Men (Fig. 192), and peopled the grounds of the Duc de Berry's château at Dourdan with modishly pirouetting young men and women enjoying the pleasures of a day in April.[29]

The decorative stylization of both forms and compositions in the Limbourg and Boucicaut miniatures is the pictorial equivalent of a precisely similar process of stylization in contemporary culture. This process was an international phenomenon in western Europe, best understood as a consequence of changing social and economic circumstances of which the kaleidoscopically changing political scene was also a part. During the fourteenth century, the values that had been the foundation of earlier mediaeval culture were more and more critically questioned. The authority of both the Church on the one hand and feudal social order on the other was challenged, one by the spirit of free inquiry stimulated by the rise of the universities, the other by the concomitant emergence of a new social class of men of affairs and merchants. In such circumstances, not without parallel in other historical periods, such as the eighteenth century, it is the natural tendency of the class whose prerogatives are challenged to stress those concepts and institutions peculiar to it and to emphasize the characteristics that distinguish it from the chal-

Fig. 196.
Paris, Bibliothèque Nationale, Ms. lat. 17294, f.106. The
Bedford Master, The Breviary of the Duke of Bedford.
The Epiphany.

lenging class or group. So about the middle of the fourteenth century began the institution of chivalric orders like that of the Garter in England (c. 1348), the Annunziata in Italy (1362), the Seraphim in Sweden (1336), and, a little later, the Golden Fleece in Flanders (1429). Earlier mediaeval orders like the Knights of St. John of Jerusalem (c. 1048), the Knights Templars (c. 1118), and the Teutonic Knights (1190) were primarily military, made up of men who had fought to free the Holy Land or were vowed to some such purpose. By contrast, the orders like those of the Garter and the Golden Fleece were social, limited to persons of noble birth and organized to maintain the privileges to which they were exclusively entitled. To a man like the Duc de Berry or the Maréchal de Boucicaut, it was only proper that his Book of Hours should reflect this, for such luxury volumes were symbols of his social position, quite as much as was his coat of arms.[30]

This is all the more meaningful when it becomes a demonstrable element of content, as it can be seen to be in the calendar miniatures of the *Très Riches Heures*. In the illustrations where the activities are gay and agreeable—feasting in January, enjoying a spring day in April, hunting in August—the mannered aristocracy are the protagonists. For the months that are disagreeable, like the cold of February, or when hard toil is the keynote—plowing in March, harvesting in June, planting the fields in October—the tasks are carried out by people of the soil. The distinction is a matter of style as well as descriptive detail. In the "aristocratic" scenes, the figures are tall and lithe with small heads, and their elaborately attired forms are shown by preference in the profile views that lend themselves best to decorative treatment. In the "laboring" group, the forms are short and stocky, with rounded heads on bodies often seen in foreshortened poses and portrayed as three-dimensional bulks. Such self-conscious interest in a totally different mode of life can best be understood as born from desire or need to confirm the stability of a cultural system no longer adequate to the thought of its time. The same preoccupation with the charms of a supposedly simple way of life made the pastoral poetry of late antiquity popular in Alexandria and Rome, and Marie-Antoinette and her maids-in-waiting played at being shepherdesses in the *Hameau* of the Petit-Trianon with much the same feeling that gave the Duc de Berry vicarious pleasure in viewing chilled peasants baring themselves to the fire in their little cottage.

Contemporary with the Master of the Boucicaut Hours and an occasional collaborator with him was the anonymous Bedford Master,[31] so called from his authorship of two manuscripts for John of Lancaster, Duke of Bedford, the Englishman who was regent of France after the death of Charles VI in 1423 until 1435. The manuscripts are a Book of Hours (London, BM Add. Ms. 18850)[32] and a Breviary according to the use of Salisbury (Paris, BN Ms. lat. 17294).[33] A number of other books attributed to the Bedford Master atelier on stylistic grounds are probably earlier than the Bedford manuscripts, which are thought to date between about 1424 and 1435; the "Hours of Charles VI" (Vienna, NB Ms. 1855) is from around 1420.[34] However, the Bedford Master's hand has been identified in even earlier works, notably some of the miniatures in the *Grandes Heures du Duc de Berry*,[35] from which it can be concluded that he was one of the "autres ouvriers de Monseigneur" in Jacquemart de Hesdin's workshop and a contemporary there of the Boucicaut Master. In any event, in early Bedford works, which also include a Breviary of Paris usage (Châteauroux, Bibl. Mun. Ms. 2),[36] a close affinity with the Boucicaut Master is apparent, and also some relationship to the Limbourg brothers.

The miniature of the Epiphany or Adoration of the Magi (Fig. 196) of the Bedford Breviary is characteristic. The shelter of the Holy Family is a combination of the frontal and side views of the structure shown in the Nativity and Epiphany in the Boucicaut Hours,[37] and the Virgin's throne is a bed, a simplified version of the elaborately tapestried *Lit de Justice* with canopy and cloth of honor in the same Boucicaut miniatures. But the solemn ceremony of the Boucicaut Epiphany has become a narrative in the Bedford Master's. Borrowing the background of the *Très Riches Heures* Meeting of the Three Magi (Fig. 192), he peopled it with the wise men's retinue, guided by the star, which is a half-length figure of the Virgin and Child in a glory. One Magus takes a chalice from his servant. The eldest kneels to present a coffer for which the Child reaches, His gestures echoed by Joseph seated on the left. Such genre touches abound in the Bedford oeuvre: it is as if he sought to synthesize the courtly and rustic components of International Style content.

The marginal decoration has also become more elaborate. The rinceaux of carefully modeled fruits, flowers, and leaves enclose little scenes related to the theme of the principal miniature. Below, at the left, the Magi

Fig. 199.
Paris, Bibliothèque Nationale, Ms. lat. 5888, f.8. Miche-
lino da Besozzo, Eulogy of Gian Galeazzo Visconti, The
Virgin and Child receiving the Duke.

ask Herod where they will find the Child. Right and above, Herod consults the priests and scribes and bids the wise men farewell in the center, and they open their caskets of gifts below on the right. The Boucicaut Master developed a somewhat similar idea in a Book of Hours of *c.* 1415 (Paris, Bibl. Mazarine, Ms. 469),[38] but without compromising the decorative integrity of the page design. In the Bedford Master's little annotating vignettes, there are the same naturalistic tendencies seen in the larger miniatures, perspective foreshortening of landscapes and buildings, skies shading from light to dark, and the like. They approach, in fact, like the larger compositions, the effect of individual and self-sufficient pictorial entities or small, independent panel paintings. Only in the armorial device of John of Lancaster and his duchess Jeanne of Luxembourg in the lower margin is there any reference to the now-outmoded tradition that the embellishment of a book page could be a design in which pictures and words make up a formal unity. For the rest, it is to contemporary panel painting in Flanders like that of the Master of Flémalle, or Robert Campin, as he is now generally thought to be, that one must look for the source of the Bedford Master's small realisms of natural appearance and his touches of genre characterization.

John of Lancaster, an Englishman, was one of the Bedford Master's outstanding patrons, and the fact is symbolic of the circumstances in France and Paris toward the end of the first quarter of the fifteenth century. Charles VI, nephew of the Duc de Berry, and his brothers, who had been patrons of the great early fifteenth-century illuminators, had seen the realm he inherited from his father yield its sovereignty to England's Henry V. In 1422, the Dauphin he had once sought to disown had attempted to dethrone him, but the effective power remained in the English hands of the Duke of Bedford as regent of France for young Henry VI, and what was left of the French court sat at Bourges. It is more than historic coincidence that declining traditional patronage of manuscript illumination and the reorientation of its artistic aims and expressive ideals came at the same time. Yet it was precisely during the grim years after French chivalry yielded to the English bowmen at Agincourt in 1415 that one of the great masterpieces of late mediaeval illumination was created, the Book of Hours called that of the Duc de Rohan (Paris, BN Ms. lat. 9471) by the anonymous master designated by his authorship of the book.[39]

The Rohan Hours are so named after the numerous armorial bearings of that family in the book, but there is conclusive evidence that they were later additions.[40] It was originally made for Yolande of Aragon, wife of Louis II, King of Sicily and Duke of Anjou, who was a nephew of the Duc de Berry and an executor of his will. From the Berry estate, Yolande had purchased the Book of Hours by the Limbourg brothers known as the *Belles Heures de Jean de France* or the *Heures d'Ailly*, now in the Cloisters of the Metropolitan Museum in New York and it was presumably in her possession by 1418, the generally accepted date for the Rohan Hours. In any event, there is good evidence in some of the Rohan miniatures that the illuminator knew the Limbourg brothers' work and also that of the Bedford Master with whom he seems to have been associated earlier.[41] From this, it seems probable that the Rohan Master may also have been among the "autres ouvriers de Monseigneur" in the production of the *Grandes Heures.* His temperament was quite different from his contemporaries', however, for his innovations were expressive rather than technical, concerned as he was with content rather than the problems of realism with which they were involved.

There are eleven full-page miniatures in the Rohan Hours and fifty-four of lesser dimensions, as well as four hundred and sixty-nine marginal scenes. On f.159 at the beginning of the Office of the Dead, the miniature represents the Dying Man before his Judge (Fig. 197, Plate XXVIII). From his mouth come the Latin words of Psalm 30:6 (King James 31:5), "Into thine hand I commit my spirit; thou hast redeemed me, O Lord God of Truth." From heaven, the Almighty speaks in French the words of Christ's promise to the repentant thief (Luke 23:43), "Today shalt thou be with me in Paradise." Above the dying man, his soul is rescued from a demon by the archangel Michael. The setting is a charnel hill, strewn with bones, rising steeply to a blue sky gleaming with golden-winged cherubs. There is no space or perspective, but the flat plane of the background gives relief to the solidly modeled figures, the Eternal Father regarding with infinite pity the ultimate agony of the emaciated body as the soul departs. There are neither the myriad details of form and narrative so engaging in the Bedford Master's oeuvre, nor the formal elegance of the Boucicaut Master, nor the picturesque panoramas unfolded in the Limbourg brothers' miniatures. When an architectural setting is called for, as in the

Fig. 200.
Florence, Biblioteca Laurenziana, Ms. corale 3, f.41v.
Camaldolese Gradual, Initial C with choristers. (Photo
Pineider)

Annunciation and the Purification of the Virgin,[42] a nominal combination of colonettes and vaults, almost *à la* Pucelle, suffices. But the sentiment and emotions of the protagonists could not be more powerfully communicated. The yearning grief in the face of the Eternal is no less clearly expressed in the tense coils of the scroll bearing His words of comfort. The final statement of mortal faith in the assurance of spiritual life to come is echoed in the long and slow curve of the band with the dying man's last prayer.

It was customary to introduce the Office of the Dead in Books of Hours with an appropriate theme.[43] A miniature on f.212 of an early Boucicaut manuscript (Paris, BN Ms. lat. 1161)[44] shows a burial in a galleried graveyard much like the one in contemporary descriptions of the Cemetery of the Innocents in Paris. In other books, including the Boucicaut Hours, the illustration is of a *chapelle ardente*,[45] with the coffin in a church choir under a catafalque covered with burning candles.[46] This motif also appears in the Bedford Master's manuscripts,[47] and in those of the Limbourg brothers, including the early *Belles Heures de Jean de France*,[48] from which the Rohan Master probably took the idea, since it appears in a miniature on f.176 of the Rohan Hours. It is not alone there, however, but is one of eight half-page illustrations of successive moments in the dying man's last hours interspersed through the Office of the Dead.

Such preoccupation, not to say obsession, with Death is not surprising in view of the general character of the times.[49] Nor is it unique in the Rohan Master's work. A Dance of the Dead was painted in 1424 on the walls of the Cemetery of the Innocents in Paris, in which people from all walks of life performed macabre *pas-de-deux* with their skeletal counterparts. The theme also appears at about the same time in the Office of the Dead in two Bedford manuscripts (Paris, BN Ms. Rothschild 2535; N.Y., Morgan Ms. 359). But it was the Rohan Master's achievement to state the late mediaeval conception of Death in a single, monumental design, of such dignity and profound poignance that it could well be said of it, as did Dio Chrysostom of the Pheidian Zeus, that once seen, it could not be otherwise conceived. At the same time, it is stated in a way characteristic of the mediaeval point of view in its most significant and distinctive quality. Disregarding the steps of his contemporaries in their attempted conquest of pictorial space, oblivious to the visual charm of narrative and

Fig. 201.
London, British Museum, Ms. Egerton 3277, f.123. The Bohun Psalter, Initial D with the story of Lazarus.

genre that enlivens their folios, he expresses in two-dimensional patterns of line and color, and in the telling characterization of his forms, the same desire his predecessors of decades and centuries earlier had had: to transform the written text into the Word of God.

The precise identity and origin of the Rohan Master has not been determined, but it has been observed[50] that his characteristic figure type of a rather heavy body and chalky faces with almond-shaped eyes and straining poses is not without parallel in contemporary north Spanish work. Something of the emotional expressionism of the Rohan Master's work, so unlike anything in the oeuvre of other Parisian ateliers, can also be found there and in illumination from nearby Languedoc.[51] In view of Yolande's origin in Aragon, it is reasonable to assume that a Spanish illuminator might have been in her entourage. A similar circumstance is indicated for the miniatures in illuminated copies of the poetry of Christine de Pisan, who was much in favor in the court of Charles VI. They are by a north Italian artist who apparently worked for no one else.[52] Such interchanges must have been even more extensive around the year 1400, the period of the International Style, than is indicated so far by documentary evidence.

Italian ideas were important in shaping the International Style as it developed in Parisian and Franco-Flemish illumination, particularly from Lombardy. The awakening interest in nature apparent in the Limbourg, Boucicaut, and Bedford manuscripts could hardly have taken the form it did without the example of such late fourteenth-century north Italian treatises as the *Tacuinum* or *Theatrum Sanitatis*. The text is based on an Arabian twelfth-century work, in which hygienic advice is given on all kinds of food and drink, health problems in differing climatic conditions and seasons of the year, suggestions about when certain activities are most suitable, and the like. The miniature illustrating the finding of the mandragora root (Fig. 198, Plate XXIX) is on p. 73 of a late fourteenth-century copy (Rome, Biblioteca Casanatense, Ms. 4182) of north Italian provenance.[53] The subject is the same as that of the early sixth-century illustration in the Viennese Dioscurides manuscript (Fig. 7); the much desired mandrake herb is pulled from the ground by a dog, a necessary procedure to avoid the death which came to anyone or anything hearing the cries of the human-shaped root when drawn from the earth. In this, as in most of the late fourteenth-century copies of the *Theatrum Sanitatis*,

the text is brief, for the burden of its meaning is carried by the illustration. This is lively and naturalistic to a degree, presenting in the aggregate a picturesque and engaging description of the living habits and customs of the day that has a charm all its own. The style has been related to that of the outstanding Lombard artist in the later fourteenth century, Giovannini dei Grassi,[54] a point of particular interest in the International Style context, since Giovannini's work was demonstrably known to both the Limbourg brothers[55] and the Boucicaut Master.[56]

The "courtly" component of the International Style also figures in Lombard illumination around the year 1400, notably in the work of Michelino da Besozzo.[57] First mentioned about 1388, and living at least until 1442, he was also a panel painter, one highly esteemed in his day; some of the notes compiled by Giovanni Alchiero and later assembled by Jean Lebègue originated with him. He was primarily an illuminator, however, and in that capacity he decorated the text of the funeral oration written for the obsequies of Gian Galeazzo Visconti, duke of Milan, in 1402. The manuscript (Paris, BN Ms. lat. 5888) can be dated around 1403. In the principal miniature on f.1 (Fig. 199), the duke is being received in heaven by the Madonna and Child attended by the Twelve Virtues. The diadem of immortality is placed on his head by the Child, and eight angels carry banners with the Visconti emblems. In the smaller miniature, Pietro da Casteletto, the author of the eulogy, addresses a group of mourners. In the marginal border, quatrefoils with the Visconti devices alternate with prophets whose scrolls are inscribed with praises of the duke; they are connected by a delicate rinceau of gold and blue leaves.

Many characteristics of Michelino's illuminated apotheosis of the Milanese duke are reminiscent of the International Style found in the manuscripts made for the Parisian and Flemish courts.[58] Iconographically, the theme of a mortal being received in heaven by the Virgin and Child is also seen in both the dedication miniatures of the Brussels Hours.[59] Stylistically, there are the same lightly swaying figures in robes of pink and green and blue that move as if in the measures of a pavane. The gold diaper pattern on blue of the background implies no more space than does the host of crimson angels under the blue arch surmounting the central group. Such similarities are not surprising. Gian Galeazzo Visconti was the Duc de Berry's brother-in-law and there were close relations between the two courts at all times. There is no conclusive evidence that the obvious artistic interrelationship between them was the result of predominant influences originating in one or the other, but this was usually the case in the time of the International Style. All the same, Michelino's design could not be taken as anything but Italian. The rather dense composition of both miniatures on f.1 of the Visconti eulogy and the transparent rinceau and quatrefoil pattern of the border have no counterparts in contemporary illumination north of the Alps.

In Florence another aspect of Italian International Style illumination is seen in a group of manuscripts identified with Lorenzo Monaco.[60] Born in Siena about 1370 as Piero di Giovanni, he took the name Lorenzo when he became a monk in the Florentine community of Santa Maria degli Angeli in 1391. He was also a panel painter, executing the Coronation of the Virgin of 1414, now in the Uffizi Gallery, for his monastery, and also decorating or supervising the illumination of a number of manuscripts during his long career, which ended about 1423/1424. The characteristic products of this, one of the latest of monastic scriptoria, were the large service books called *corale* in Italian. They were large volumes, in order that the words and musical notes could be read by a group of choristers as they are shown in the initial C (Fig. 200) on f.41v of one, a Gradual of the Camaldolese Order from Santa Maria degli Angeli (Florence, Bibl. Laurenziana, Corale 3). It is a volume of some size, measuring 67.1 x 48.3 cm (*c.* 26½ x 19″).

There are no full-page miniatures in the book, but the folios at the beginning of each textual division are ornamented with large initial letters, some enclosing scenes like the one illustrated, others with figures of prophets. A date of 1409 on f.9 probably refers to the musical text and possibly the elaborate foliate ornament, but not necessarily to the scenes or figures, although an early fifteenth-century date would not be inconsistent with their style.[61] There is some disagreement about the precise authorship of the individual miniatures, which may have been by Lorenzo or designed by him and executed by assistants. In either case, they are attractive examples of late Gothic illumination in Florence. The intricate border leafage is worked out in blue and green, with touches of white, red, and gold. In the miniature, the white-robed Camaldolese monks are solidly modeled and the lectern supporting the choir-book is shown in perspective, but these three-dimensional ele-

ments are not emphasized in the admirably decorative unity of visual and literal elements of the folio.

It will be recalled that the flourishing tradition of English manuscript illumination in the early fourteenth-century declined in both quantity and quality around 1350; in the last quarter of the century, a more productive phase began, as can be seen in a group of manuscripts identified with Humphrey de Bohun, seventh Earl of Hereford, either by inscription or association.[62] His death in 1372–73 establishes the general period of their execution. A Psalter that contains both his armorial devices and the royal arms of England (London, BM Egerton Ms. 3277) may also have belonged to his daughter Mary, who married Henry of Lancaster, subsequently Henry IV, in 1380. The large initial D on f.123 is elaborated with marginal foliage, and the gold ground of the story of Lazarus in the lower one and the saturated colors of the figures are reminiscent of earlier East Anglian work like the Saint-Omer Psalter (Fig. 174). But the bulky figures, and their heads with unmodeled features, staring eyes, and dark hair and beards, are without English precedent. They can be found, however, in northern Italian Trecento painting. Their appearance here can hardly have been the result of direct influence, like the Italianisms of Pucelle's style in Paris, but doubtless came indirectly, possibly from Bohemia, where East Anglian illumination was known in the fourteenth century and from which a reciprocal influence could be reasonably assumed.[63] The style is particularly well represented in the standing figure of the Virgin to the left of the initial. Also characteristic of the Bohun group of manuscripts is the comparatively restrained use of marginal scenes. On f.123 of Egerton 3277, they are limited to two medallions, above and below the Virgin, of episodes in a story from the *Golden Legend,* in which she came to the aid of a faithless nun.

The English aspect of the International Style around 1400 is seen in panel paintings like the well-known Wilton Diptych in the National Gallery in London,[64] and in such manuscripts as the Lytlington Missal and the *Liber Regalis,* which are both in the library of Westminster Abbey in London.[65] The latter contains the order of coronation of a king and queen and may have been made for Richard II at the time either of his marriage to Anne of Bohemia in 1382 or of his second marriage in 1396 to Isabella of France. In either case, it indicates well-established international relationships in both the political and artistic circles of the time.

Two names of illuminators stand out around the year

1400 in English illumination, John Siferwas and Herman Scheerre. Siferwas was probably an Englishman; at least he has been identified as the F. John Cyfrewas who was ordained acolyte by the bishop of Winchester in 1380,[66] and a Dominican monk named "Johannes Sifirwas" referred to in a document of 1420 may also be the same person. His signature appears in two manuscripts, the Sherborne Missal made between 1396 and 1407 (Alnwick Castle, Library of the Duke of Northumberland), and a Lectionary commissioned for Salisbury Cathedral by John, 5th Lord Lovell of Tichmarsh (London, BM, Harley Ms. 7026). Both client and artist appear in the dedicatory miniature on f.4v of the Lectionary (Fig. 202), which must be dated before 1408, the year of Lovell's death, at the latest. The spiral inscription on the left identifies the patron, and the artist's signature—Frater Johannes Siferwas—is below the presentation scene.

Dedicatory miniatures are not unusual in late mediaeval manuscripts (cf. Fig. 186), but Siferwas treated the theme in a rather unusual way. Both the figures are shown half-length and in profile. There are strong reds and blues in the architectural features and the inscribed scroll, but the portraits are grisaille studies in line, their three-dimensional masses created by the curvilinear patterns of the strong contours. In so constructing his figures, Siferwas continued a traditionally English stylistic practice. He remains faithful to tradition also in the lively and naturalistic birds and animals enlivening the marginal borders of other folios in the Lectionary and the Sherborne Missal.[67] Yet, at the same time, Siferwas was not immune to continental influences, particularly iconographic.[68] To these he might well have been introduced by the anonymous Netherlandish master who was the dominant personality in the scriptorium that produced a monumental Missal of the Carmelite Order shortly before 1398, probably in the house at Whitefriars in London.[69]

If Siferwas was an English representative of the International Style in illumination, Herman Scheerre, undoubtedly from the Netherlands, was among the first of many artists from that region who exercised their talents in England and for English patrons,[70] including John of Lancaster, Duke of Bedford, for whom Scheerre illuminated a Psalter and Book of Hours (London, BM, Add. Ms. 42131) some time after 1414. Another Book of Hours made for John Beaufort, Earl of Somerset (London, BM, Roy. Ms. 2. A. xviii), has an Annunciation with two devotional figures (Fig. 203) on f.23v, an insertion in the volume. The adorants are assumed to be the Earl of Somerset and his wife, Margaret de Holand, whom he married about 1399; it seems probable, however, that the book was not made until about 1408 or 1409.

The overall effect of the miniature is established by the gray-shaded white of the architectural setting, foiled by the green and gold of the background, canopy draperies, and *prie-dieu,* and also the delicate pink of the angel's robe and the Virgin's deep blue garment. The golden sprays of the aedicula were apparently a later addition to the original design. All surfaces are most softly modeled with touches of color, a method quite unlike Siferwas's emphasis on contours. In all these respects, Scheerre is revealed as an artist of pictorial rather than graphic instincts, and the sources of his style would be most reasonably sought in the continental milieu of his origin, that is, the Low Countries. The closest parallel to his Annunciation, in characterization of the protagonists, the involved arabesque of the angel's scroll, and the architectural setting with its sculptured prophets in niches, is the one painted by Melchior Broederlam of Ypres on the shutters for the altarpiece in the Chartreuse de Champmol at Dijon, for which he was paid in 1394.[71] Broederlam's version of the theme established a scheme that was widely copied or adapted in Netherlandish art at the turn of the century[72] and that recurs in nearly all the known Scheerre manuscripts.[73] These last can be identified by his signature in some cases, and in others by his personal motto that appears in the diagonal inscriptions on the textile covering the *prie-dieu* in the Beaufort Annunciation. It reads *Omnia levia sunt amanti; qui amat non laborat,* "All is easy for one who loves; he who loves toils not." This is followed in the Beaufort miniature by two words, *de daer,* which were long thought to have some cryptic meaning but are actually a Netherlandish term for "the author," as Panofsky points out.[74]

Herman Scheerre's Netherlandish affiliation was with Flanders, which was politically allied with Burgundy in the early fifteenth century, and was artistically influenced by the International Style of France. Had he gone to Paris instead of England, his skillfully developed art might well have won him a place beside the Limbourg brothers and the Boucicaut Master. In the Dutch part of the Low Countries, the cultural picture was somewhat different.[75] Society there was not organized in such an elaborately mannered structure, and book purchasers were well-to-do bourgeoisie or clergy rather

Fig. 202.
London, British Museum, Ms. Harley 7026, f.4v. John
Siferwas, The Lovell Lectionary, Lord Lovell and John
Siferwas.

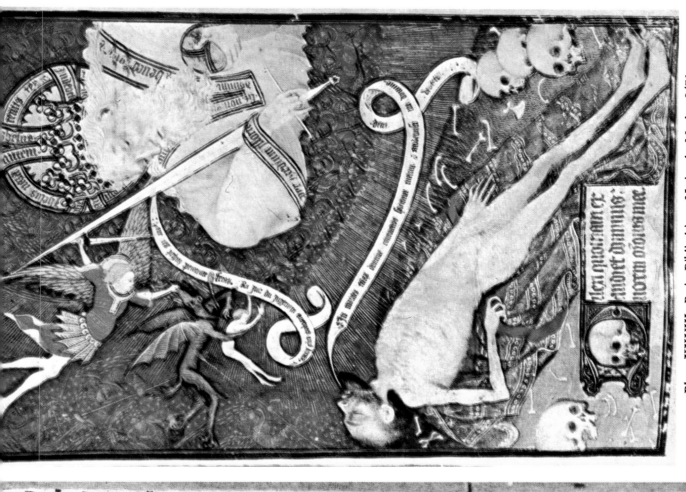

Plate XXVIII. Paris, Bibliothèque Nationale, Ms. lat. 9471, f. 159. The Rohan Master, The Rohan (Yolande of Aragon) Hours, The Dying Man and his Judge.

Plate XXVII. Paris, Bibliothèque Nationale, Ms. fr. 13091, f. 11v. André Beauneveu, Psalter of John of Berry, Isaiah.

Plate **XXIX.** Rome, Biblioteca Casanatense, Ms. 4182, p. 73.
Theatrum Sanitatis, The Mandragora. (Photo author)

Plate **XXX.** Rome, Biblioteca Angelica, Inc. 530, f. 6. Pliny the Elder, *Historia Naturale* (printed by N. Jenson, Venice, 1476), Preface. (Photo author)

Fig. 203.
London, British Museum, Ms. Royal 2. A. XVIII, f.23v.
Herman Scheerre, The Beaufort Hours, The Annuncia-
tion with devotional figures.

Fig. 204.
Baltimore, Walters Art Gallery, Ms. 174, f.152. The
Zweder van Culemborg Master, Carthusian Missal, The
Crucifixion.

than the aristocratic bibliophiles who patronized the Limbourg brothers and the Boucicaut and Bedford Masters. Dutch manuscripts of the late Middle Ages are often dismissed as provincial by comparison with the sophisticated products of the Parisian scriptoria, but many of them have miniatures of considerable individuality of style and the highest quality.

One of the leading Dutch illuminators in the first half of the fifteenth century is known as the Master of Zweder van Culemborg, the bishop of Utrecht in 1425, for whom the anonymous artist made a Missal (Brixen, Episcopal Seminary, Ms. C 20 [no. 62]), which is his best-known work. In another Missal for Carthusian use (Baltimore, Walters Art Gallery, Ms. 174), his style is seen in a number of miniatures, including the full-page Crucifixion (Fig. 204) on f.152. In some respects, the Zweder Master seems to represent an older tradition than his Parisian contemporaries like the Bedford Master. The landscape of the Crucifixion miniature is only a barren slope leading to the gold background, the finely tooled all-over pattern of foliage of which sets off the figures. The simple color scheme is organized around the blue and lavender robes of the Virgin, contrasted with red and green in the other figures. The whole is framed in bands of blue foliage with heraldic devices in the angles, bordered by a rinceau of stems, blossoms, and acanthus-like leaves around the entire folio. In this and in some of the individual figure motives and the curling scroll of the centurion's inscription, the Zweder Master reveals his knowledge of some of the Boucicaut Master's innovations. But he simplifies the composition and stresses the pathetic in his expressive characterization of the theme. In this more than anything else, his work is representative of the Dutch version of the International Style in the early fifteenth century.

The Crucifixion by the Master of Zweder van Culemborg is in the best tradition of manuscript illumination in that its pattern of forms and colors is so organized as to respect the two-dimensional plane of the folio it ornaments. It is achieved by a sensitive balance between the abstraction of the gold background, the delicate linear touches that model the figures, particularly the nudes, and the precise yet spirited patterns of the enclosing borders. At the same time, in framing the composition, the Zweder Master subscribed to the idea that had begun to take form in the work of Jacquemart de Hesdin, that the miniature was a self-sufficient pictorial entity, comparable to a panel painting. As has

been noted, this was a concept that could be fully realized only by investigating the problems of pictorial space with its attendant complications of portraying three-dimensional forms and their interrelationships on the picture plane. It is not a historical accident that efforts to solve these problems began to be made in manuscript illumination at precisely the time when they were first being explored by the great pioneers of realism in late mediaeval painting, Robert Campin and the van Eyck brothers. The Zweder Master himself was directly influenced by them in some of his later commissions in the early 1430s.[76] But this circumstance is much more clearly defined in miniatures like the Birth of John the Baptist (Fig. 205) on f.93v of a manuscript in the Museo Civico of Turin known as the "Milan Hours."

The "Milan Hours" is part of the manuscript referred to as "unes très belles Heures de Nostre-Dame" in the Duc de Berry's inventory of 1413. It was unfinished at that time, although it had been begun apparently before 1382 in the workshop of an artist who has been thought to be Jacquemart de Hesdin or the anonymous painter of the *Parement de Narbonne,* a silk hanging with designs in grisaille in the Louvre in Paris.[77] The manuscript had been given by the Duc de Berry to his keeper, Robinet d'Estampes, who divided it into two parts, keeping the portion that had been illuminated.[78] What happened to the rest at the time is not known, but from heraldic devices it has been surmised that it was acquired by a member of the house of Holland and Bavaria, probably Duke William VI. At some time, possibly but not certainly before William's death in 1417, some of the unfinished folios in this part of the *Très-Belles Heures de Notre-Dame* were decorated by several fifteenth-century Netherlandish artists, among them the painter of the Birth of John the Baptist miniature. Once again, at some indeterminable time, this portion of the manuscript was divided, one part finding its way into the Biblioteca Reale at Turin, where it was destroyed by fire in 1904, the other into the Trivulzio Collection in Milan; this last part, usually referred to now as the "Hours of Milan" or *Heures de Milan,* was subsequently acquired by the Italian state and deposited in the Turin Museo Civico. The part destroyed in the Turin fire of 1904 (*Heures de Turin*) had been published[79] with reproductions of its miniatures, some of which were in the same style, or close to it, as the Birth of John the Baptist. There were eleven of these, not all by the same artist.

The identity of the artist who painted the Birth of John miniature and the date of its execution have been much debated.[80] Evidence in the manuscript seems to indicate that the miniatures in a style comparable to that of early fifteenth-century panel painting were done when the book was owned by the House of Holland-Bavaria and Hainaut, whose coat of arms appears in some. Since it is known that John of Holland-Bavaria, brother of William VI and his successor in 1417, employed the painter Jan van Eyck in one capacity or another from 1422 until 1424, it has seemed possible that van Eyck was the artist and that the miniatures in question could be of the early 1420s. However, regardless of differences of opinion about their authorship, the miniatures of the Birth of John group in the "Milan Hours" clearly exemplify the status of manuscript illumination at a moment when its technical development as a branch of painting was very advanced, but also when its continued existence as an independent and creative art was no longer certain.

The large miniature of the Birth of John the Baptist shows a well-furnished bedroom with servants bustling about as they take care of the new-born child and the household. Behind it, in a smaller room, Zacharias writes the name of his son on a tablet (Luke 1:57–63). God the Father appears in the initial D with which the text of the office begins, sending the dove of the Holy Spirit down to the *bas-de-page,* where the Baptism of Christ is portrayed in a deep river landscape. The ivy-leaf rinceau in the marginal border is of the type current in the Franco-Flemish ateliers of the late fourteenth century. As was often the case, these borders had been executed in advance through the entire volume, with spaces left for the miniatures, initials, and *bas-de-pages;* these last were executed in the late fourteenth century only in the part kept by Robinet d'Estampes, which is now in the Bibliothèque Nationale. On one page in the destroyed "Heures de Turin" portion, the original rinceau was replaced by a border of thick stems and acanthus-like leaves in a later fifteenth-century style,[81] but apart from it, the original type appears throughout.

Whoever the creator of the Eyckian miniatures in the *Très Belles Heures de Notre-Dame* may have been, he was conversant with the methods and style of the most advanced illuminators of the early fifteenth century. His way of rendering space in the interior scene of the birth room enlarges on the method employed by the Boucicaut Master in the miniature of the Marshal ador-

ing St. Catherine (Fig. 195). The rather steeply tilted floor level is intersected laterally by several planes—the servants and table end in the foreground, the end of the bed in the middle distance, the farther wall beyond that, and, still further, the room where Zacharias sits—articulating the depth and creating the impression of recession in the pictured space. The table with its still-life of plates and jugs is incorrectly foreshortened, but the parallel lines of the ceiling beams and the top of the tester bed converge near the right margin of the miniature in the rear room, directly connecting it visually with the principal chamber. The maid servant seen from the back is very like a girl in the July miniature in the Limbourg *Très-Riches Heures.* The landscape of the Baptism in the *bas-de-page* is carried back in depth by a series of loosely brushed overlapping planes, which differ only in the heightened delicacy of color nuances from the rendering of a somewhat similar effect in the Boucicaut Visitation (Fig. 194).[82] Even in one technical point, the rendering of the window glass by silver foil, the Birth of John miniature stems from the tradition of the Boucicaut Master.

Yet, for all his indebtedness to the great illuminators preceding him, the John the Baptist Master (or Jan van Eyck) lifts their ideas and methods to an expressive level only suggested in their work. In so doing, his treatment of light is a key factor. This is not to say that light is not an important element in the Boucicaut and Limbourg miniatures. It is the golden glory of the former's Visitation that brings the subtly delineated shapes of its distant landscape into focus. It is the grayed light of the February miniature in the *Très-Riches Heures* that sharpens the outlines of its snowy landscape. But the essential function of the light in these examples is decorative or descriptive, pervading the scenes in an overall and unaccented illumination that seeks little more than to make the shapes visible. In the Birth of John miniature, it is a vital and expressive element. Reflected in gleaming highlights from the brass and pewter vessels, it glows warmly on the polished table and chest, makes the window a luminous opening in the birth room, and brings the brightness of day into Zacharias's little chamber in the rear. From these differing qualities of light comes the feeling that the room is not just an empty cubic volume but is filled with atmosphere, which transforms its space into a warm and comfortable milieu. In the same way, the varied qualities and intensities of light in the Baptism scene

Fig. 205.
Turin, Museo Civico, unnumbered ms., f.93v. The "Milan
Hours," The Birth of John the Baptist.

open its landscape into infinity. The glinting tips of waves reflecting the cloud-filled sky, the touches of rose from the lowering sun, and the incredibly subtle modulation of the blues lightening to the neutral sky at the zenith make this, for all its minute dimensions, one of the first true landscapes in the modern sense, in which the material reality of the world around us has become one with the no less real infinity of limitless space.

Significantly, it is in precisely the extraordinarily expressive quality of this tiny landscape and the means of its attainment that the end of manuscript illumination as the art of making the written word splendid and meaningful is signaled. The principal miniature of the folio is framed in a narrow red and gold molding that seems only by chance to touch the ivy-leaf rinceaux in the margins. The *bas-de-page* scene is overlapped at the ends by this leafy border, but it could seemingly be extended laterally without limitation. What this means in the concept of the decorated book page can be seen in comparing it with earlier *bas-de-pages.* In one of the first, the mid-thirteenth-century Bible of William of Devon (Fig. 152), the *bas-de-page* is a scaffold for the sportive drolleries, and there is no difference in principle in early fourteenth-century English manuscripts like the Peterborough Psalter (Fig. 163). In the Belleville Breviary (Fig. 171), Jean Pucelle makes the stem below the *bas-de-page* the front of a narrow strip or shelf instead of a standing line and is thus able to realize his interest in plastic volume by giving his forms

some relief or projection from the neutral plane of the vellum. But this remains the dominant and controlling factor in the harmoniously decorative organization of the page as a whole. For all the spatial potential of the plastically realized forms and the intimations of perspective depth in the architecture, these are only incidental to the arrangement of script and illustration and ornament in a two-dimensionally unified design.

In the Baptism, in the *bas-de-page* below the Birth of John, the low horizon line is the distant edge of an uninterrupted and continuous surface, but the subtly changing tints of blue beyond it do not die away but merge with the tone above, so that the vellum is no longer a neutral plane but becomes the sky, opening to infinity. In consequence, the written script hangs in emptiness, formally related only by its spiky shapes to the pointed ivy leaves of the rinceau border, itself an unavoidable physical inheritance from the past. This is not to say that the irresistible charm and almost unbelievable beauty of the miniature paintings is uninspired. For the man of Jan van Eyck's day, nature was beautiful because it was both manifestation and proof of the presence of God in all things, but the communication of this concept in pictorial terms was by now the function of the painter, not the illuminator. He, by tradition and definition, was committed to the mediaeval conviction that first truth is found in the written word because it is the Word of God.

NOTES

1. P. Durrieu, *Les Très Riches Heures de Jean de France, duc de Berry* (Paris: Plon, 1904).

2. Cf. Thieme-Becker, 23:227 ff.

3. F. Gorissen, "Jan Maelwael und die Bruder Limburg," *Gelre* 14 (1954):153–221. M. Rickert, *AB* 39 (1957):73–77.

4. The miniatures and some text folios are reproduced in color in *The Très Riches Heures of Jean, Duke of Berry:* preface by M. Meiss; introd. and legends by J. Lognon and R. Cazelles (New York: Braziller, 1969).

5. J. Porcher, *Les Belles Heures de Jean de France, Duc de Berry* (Paris: Bibliothèque Nationale, 1953). Cf. also *The Belles Heures of Jean, Duke of Berry, Prince of France:* introd. by J. J. Rorimer; n. by M. B. Freeman (New York: Metropolitan Museum, 1958), with color reproductions of some of the miniatures.

6. Cf. Porcher, *MFM,* pl. lxviii.

7. *Ibid.,* pl. lxx.

8. Meiss, *14th cent.,* p. 71.

9. Panofsky, *ENP* 1:64.

10. Meiss, *14th cent.,* pp. 53–54, figs. 462–65.

11. Panofsky, *ENP* 1:64; 2, fig. 86. R. Weiss, "The Medieval Medallions of Constantine and Heraclius," *The Numismatic Chronicle,* 7th ser., 3 (1963):128–44.

12. Cf. Karlinger, *Kunst der Gotik,* p. 570.

13. Meiss, *14th cent.,* p. 291.

14. Panofsky, *ENP* 1:65.

15. J. C. Webster, *The Labors of the Months* (Princeton: Princeton University Press, 1938).

16. Morand, *Pucelle,* pl. v.

17. Meiss, *14th cent.,* figs. 83–85, 217–18.

18. Scato de Vries and S. Morpurgo, *Il breviario Grimani della Biblioteca di San Marco in Venezia* (Leyden: Sijthoff, 1904–10).

19. Meiss, M., *French Painting in the time of Jean de Berry. The Boucicaut Master* (London: Phaidon, 1968). Panofsky, *ENP* 1:53–61.

20. Meiss, *French Painting* . . . , pp. 132–33; *ENP*, 1:55.

21. Meiss, *14th cent.*, p. 332.

22. M. P. Merrifield, *Original Treatises on the Arts of Painting*, 2 vols. (London: J. Murray, 1849). D. V. Thompson, Introd., n. 19.

23. Merrifield, 1:294; 2:408–10. Thompson, pp. 21, 53 ff, n. 120.

24. P. Durrieu, "Jacques Coene," *Arts anciens de Flandre"* 2 (1905):5–22; "Le maitre des Heures du Maréchal de Boucicaut," *Revue de l'art ancien et moderne* 19 (1906):401–15; 20 (1906): 21–35, identified the Boucicaut Master with Jacques Coene, followed by J. Porcher (*Jean Lebègue; les histoires que l'on peut raisonnablement faire sur les livres de Salluste*. Paris, 1962) and Meiss, *BM*, pp. 60–62; but cf. Panofsky, *ENP* 1:54.

25. Merrifield, 1:1–15; J. Porcher, Note in *Mélanges Franz Calot* (Paris: Librairie d'Agences, 1960).

26. S. M. Alexander, "Medieval Recipes Describing the Use of Metal in Manuscripts," *Marsyas* 12 (1964–65):34–51. The St. Catherine miniature is reproduced in color in J. Lassaigne, *Flemish Painting—The Century of Van Eyck* (New York: Skira, 1957), p. 20.

27. *L'art européen vers 1400* (Vienna: Kunsthistorisches Museum, 1962). *The International Style*, ed. D. Miner and P. Verdier (Baltimore: Walters Art Gallery, 1962).

28. Meiss, *BM*, fig. 36.

29. *Très Riches Heures*, n. 5; pl. 5.

30. Cf. Meiss, *BM*, pp. 8–9.

31. Thieme-Becker, *Allg. Lex. Kstler* 37:211 ff.

32. Cf. B. Martens, *Meister Francke* (Hamburg: Friederichsen, de Gruyter, 1929). E. P. Spencer, "Master of the Duke of Bedford; the Bedford Hours," *Burlington Magazine* 107 (1965): 495–502. Idem, "Master of the Duke of Bedford: the Salisbury Breviary," *Burlington Magazine* 108 (1966):606–12.

33. V. Leroquais, *Les bréviaires* . . . 3:271, pls. lv-lxv.

34. E. Trenkler, *Livre d'Heures, Handschrift 1855 der Österreichischen Nationalbibliothek* (Vienna: Kunstverlag Wulfrum, 1948).

35. Cf. n. 21 above.

36. V. Leroquais, *Les bréviaires* . . . 1:315, pls. lxvi-lxxiv.

37. Ff. 73v, 83v; cf. Panofsky, *ENP*, figs. 66–67.

38. Meiss, *BM*, pp. 113–14, pls. 258–69.

39. A. Heimann, "Der Meister der 'Grandes Heures de Rohan' und seine Werkstatt," *Städel-Jahrbuch*, 7/8 (1932):1–61. J. Porcher, *The Rohan Book of Hours* (New York: Yoseloff, 1959).

40. Porcher, pp. 5–6.

41. *Ibid.*, pp. 8–10.

42. *Ibid.*, pls. 2, 5.

43. For a detailed discussion, cf. Meiss, *BM*, pp. 30–33, figs. 135–74.

44. *BM*, fig. 153.

45. Panofsky, *ENP*, figs. 62, 70.

46. W. H. Forsythe, "A Head from a Royal Effigy," *The Metropolitan Museum of Art Bulletin*, n.s. 3 (1945), pp. 214 ff.

47. Cf. Trenkler, n. 34; pl. 15.

48. Meiss, fig. 145.

49. Cf. fig. 173; Panofsky, *ENP*, pp. 71 ff. J. Huizinga, *The Waning of the Middle Ages* (Garden City: Doubleday Anchor, 1956), pp. 138–51.

50. Porcher, pp. 7–8; but cf. L. M. J. Delaissé, *A Century of Dutch Illuminated Manuscripts* (Berkeley: University of California Press, 1968), p. 84, n. 7.

51. Cf. Wixom, chap. 5, n. 61; no. vi, 5, p. 224.

52. Porcher, *MFM*, p. 59; *Mss . . . xiiie au xvie siècle*, nos. 149–52.

53. B. Toesca, *Theatrum Sanitatis, Cod. 4182 della R. Biblioteca Casanatense* (Rome: Libreria dello Stato, 1940).

54. P. d' Ancona, *La miniature italienne*, pp. 22–23.

55. Panofsky, *ENP*, p. 64.

56. Meiss, *BM*, p. 67 f.

57. P. Toesca, "Michelino da Besozzo e Giovannino dei Grassi," *L'Arte* 8 (1905):321–29.

58. P. Durrieu, "Michelino da Besozzo et les relations entre l'art français à l'époque du regne de Charles VI," *Mémoires de l'Academie des Inscriptions et Belles-lettres*, 38, pt. 2 (1911):365–93.

59. Fig. 190 and *ENP*, fig. 41.

60. M. L. d' Ancona, "Some new attributions to Lorenzo Monaco," *AB*, 40 (1958):175–191.

61. A companion volume, Laurenziana Corale 4, is dated 1410, but the minatures were not painted until c. 1505. Cf. Ancona, p. 180, n. 3.

62. M. R. James, and E. G. Millar, *The Bohun Manuscripts* (Oxford: Roxburghe, 1936).

63. O. Pächt, "A Giottesque Episode in English Medieval Art," *Journal of the Warburg and Courtauld Institutes*, 6 (1943).

64. Cf. Panofsky, *ENP*, 1:118; 2, fig. 181.

65. Cf. Rickert, *PiBMA*, pls. 154, 155.

66. J. Herbert, *The Sherborne Missal* (Oxford: Roxburghe, 1920).

67. Rickert, *PiBMA*, pl. 165.

68. Cf. Panofsky, *ENP*, 1:404, n. 1184.

69. M. Rickert, *The Reconstructed English Carmelite Missal* (Chicago: University of Chicago Press, 1952).

70. C. Kuhn, "Herman Scheere and English Illumination of the Early Fifteenth Century," *AB*, 22 (1940):138 ff.

71. Lassaigne, *Flemish Painting*, pp. 18–19.

72. Cf. e.g., Panofsky, *ENP*, 2, figs. 108b, 142, 156, 161, 165.

73. *Ibid.*, figs. 175, 176, 179.

74. Rickert, *PiBMA*, p. 82; Panofsky, *ENP*, pp. 116–17.

75. A. W. Byvanck, *La miniature dans les Pays-Bas septentrionaux* (Paris: Van Oest, 1937). Idem, *De middeleeuwsche Boekillustratie in de noordelijke Nederlanden* (Antwerp: De Sikkel, 1943). Delaissé, n. 50. Panofsky, *ENP*, pp. 98–129. D. Miner, "Dutch Illuminated Manuscripts in the Walters Art Gallery," *The Connoisseur Yearbook* (1955), pp. 66–77.

76. Panofsky, *ENP*, 1:103.

77. For scholarly opinion on this point, cf. Meiss, *14th Cent.*, pp. 107–18.

78. Now Ms. n.a. lat. 3093 in the Bibliothèque Nationale, Paris.

79. P. Durrieu, *Heures de Turin* (Paris, 1902).

80. Panofsky, *ENP*, 1:232–46; Lassaigne, *Flemish Painting*, pp. 62–69.

81. Panofsky, *ENP*, 2, fig. 294.

82. Reproduced in color in Lassaigne, p. 65.

Fig. 206.
Manchester, *The John Rylands Library, Ms. lat. 27, ff.10v–
11. Speculum Humanae Salvationis,* The Nativity, Pharaoh's Cupbearer, Aaron's Rod, The Tiburtine Sibyl.

Epilogue·
Manuscript Illumination in the Fifteenth Century

During the latter part of the fourteenth century, the outstanding developments in north European manuscript illumination were stimulated by a twofold interest—the representation of space, and the portrayal of individualized or specific forms. By the end of the first quarter of the fifteenth century, a miniature like the Birth of John the Baptist or the Baptism of Christ in its *bas-de-page* (Fig. 205) is a composition on a two-dimensional plane of objects identifiable as household furnishings, buildings, clouds in the sky, and the like, all of which exist in space even if the artist has not created an optical effect that is consistent throughout. From what remains of panel painting from the same period, it is seen to share the same interests with illumination. This trend toward consistent realism continues in the second quarter of the fifteenth century in northern panel painting and manuscript illumination alike. It is, indeed, a dominant consideration in the pictorial embellishment of hand-written books from this time on. This phenomenon is historically contemporary with the awakening in Italy of a renewed interest in the antique past, and even though the classical component of Renaissance culture south of the Alps does not become a major consideration in the north until late in the fifteenth century, there is none the less a clear reversion there to the antique conception of page design, with its clear distinction between script and illustration. For all the Gothic and northern realistic detail in

Simon Marmion's account of episodes in the life of Charles V (Fig. 212), it is more comparable as a book page design to an illustration in the Vatican Vergil (Fig. 4) than it is to the Epiphany in Queen Mary's Psalter (Fig. 172).

An equally significant factor in the history of manuscript illumination in the fifteenth century was the development of the printed book and the related graphic pictorial arts of woodcut and metal engraving. However obscure the precise facts may be of when and where books were first made by printing letters cast in metal instead of writing them by hand, the technique of producing volumes that way and in multiple copies was well developed in Germany around the middle of the fifteenth century.[1] Pictorial designs of lines carved in relief on wood blocks that could be inked and stamped on textile, parchment, or paper can be dated as early as the closing years of the fourteenth century.[2] The idea of combining such a stamped woodcut design with words to produce something like the miniature and hand-written text of an illuminated folio appears as early as 1423 in the St. Christopher in the John Rylands Library at Manchester (Schreiber, 1349),[3] probably in direct imitation, indeed, of contemporary manuscript illumination.[4] The so-called block-books of the fifteenth century were printed from such woodcut designs, often reproducing as well as the woodcutter could the illuminated pages that were his models.[5] The

resiouissant esperant veoir la iournee de ses
amours voir ioyr Mais auant ce que gerart
ait son chant fine laloette quil auoit oy chanter
vey ioindre les eylles et soy asseoir deuat luy

Coment gerart a tout son esprenier ala
toler auy champs ou Il prist laloette a son
col lancelet de sampye Cuydant quil retoynen
auy coy Il delaissa airsletine et ala grer sampye

Hors gerars sery le destrier de
lesperon osta les longes de lesprnier
sy les bailla a son hoste, lesprenier
quy vey de loing laloette se debaty dessus
le poinct Gerars lacha les iecz sy laissa
lesprenier aler laloette monta en hault Mais
lesprenier se hasta desirant a prendre la

Fig. 207.
Brussels, Bibliothèque Royale, Ms. 9631, f.77. The Wavrin
Master, Roman de Girart de Nevers, *Girart hunting.*

Fig. 208.
Vatican, Biblioteca Apostolica, Ms. Ottob. lat. 501, f.38.
Pontifical, Consecration of a bishop.

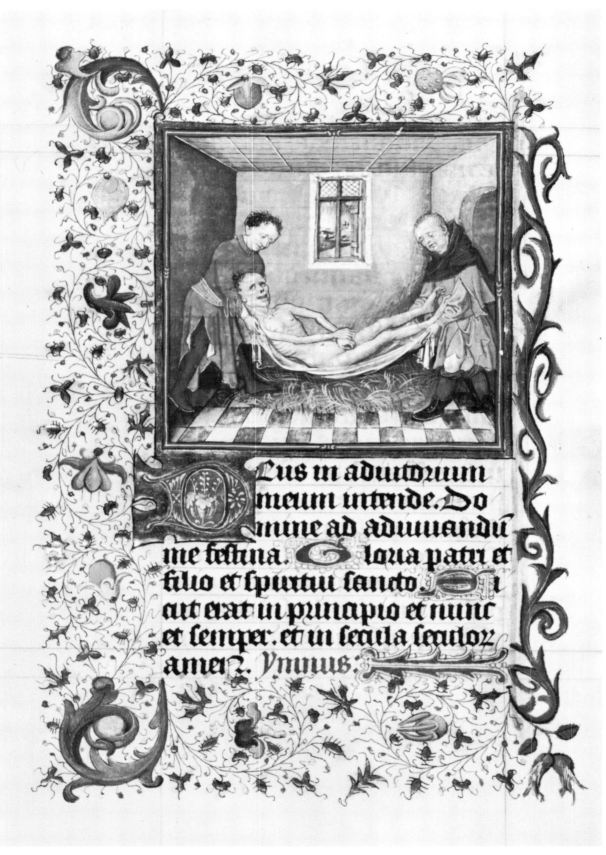

Fig. 209.
New York, Pierpont Morgan Library, Ms. 945, f.99v.
The Catherine of Cleves Master, Hours of Catherine of
Cleves, A corpse being prepared for burial.

Fig. 210.
New York, Pierpont Morgan Library, Ms. 917, p. 266.
The Catherine of Cleves Master, Hours of Catherine of
Cleves, St. Lawrence.

block-books cannot be precisely dated, but illustrated books with the text printed from movable type were published by Albrecht Pfister at Bamberg in 1461 and 1462. By the end of the fifteenth century, typographic books (to distinguish them from block-books) with woodcut illustrations and occasionally metal engravings were being printed in all major European countries.

It is often said that the art of the illuminated manuscript was killed by the invention and development of printing and its cognate graphic arts of woodcut and metal engraving, if for no other reasons than that multiple identical copies of a given text could be produced, instead of the unique volume with its equally unique miniatures that is an illuminated manuscript, and that the printed book would generally cost less—to say nothing of the benefits assumed to result from wider circulation of its ideas. None of these considerations seems to have carried a great deal of weight in the fifteenth century. There are numerous instances of printed books being copied by hand, including the colophon giving the publisher's name and the date when the printing was completed. The reason for such copying of printed books can only be guessed, but since time was of the essence, it may have been thought that it was less expensive to have a text copied by hand than to buy the printed version.[6] Nor was the invention of printing considered an unqualified blessing by everyone; as early as 1485, the archbishop of Mainz urged that steps should be taken to "protect the purity of our divine books" from errors of incorrect and vulgar German[7] made in mass producing them.

Another reason offered for the changing nature of manuscript illumination in the fifteenth century is that illuminators began then to concern themselves with the same problems of portraying realistic form and space in which panel painters were involved; in so doing, they were distracted from the decorative aim that was the traditional expressive purpose of their art, and it was reduced to a subordinate role, having "died of an overdose of perspective."[8] This came about in ways that have been touched on elsewhere, and the point has some justification, yet it may legitimately be asked whether the development so characterized was the malady itself or only a symptom. It has been pointed out[9] that the woodcutters and metal engravers whose graphic processes replaced illumination as the art of book decoration were as indefatigable as their painter contemporaries in attempting to solve the problems of pictorial realism without losing creative originality. In

the final analysis, manuscript illumination yielded up its distinctive character as an art because it could no longer give expressive form to the changing concepts and ideals of the time.

This is not to say that there was no continuing demand for the hand-written illuminated book during the fifteenth century and later. Federigo da Montefeltro, duke of Urbino from 1444 until 1482, assembled a notable library of over a thousand such volumes, some of which are now in the Urbino section of the Vatican Biblioteca Apostolica.[10] Many of them were bought from or made to the duke's order by Vespasiano da Bisticci, one of the outstanding book purveyors of the day. He was also a writer,[11] compiling a series of biographies of his contemporaries (*Vite de uomini illustri del secolo XV* [Florence, 1859]), including Federigo. Of the Urbino library, Vespasiano said that all the volumes were written on parchment by skilled scribes, many of them decorated with miniatures, and that it contained not a single printed book, since the duke would have been ashamed to have one in his library. Yet a no less distinguished bibliophile, King Matthias Corvinus of Hungary bought printed and manuscript books with equal enthusiasm,[12] some of the latter being hand-written copies of printed texts.[13] From available evidence, it is clear that printed and manuscript books were both being produced in the latter part of the fifteenth century, sometimes almost literally side by side in the same establishment.

An equally catholic taste is evident in the decoration and illustration of fifteenth-century books,[14] with both miniatures and woodcuts appearing sometimes in the same volume. None the less, for reasons that range from economic to technical to aesthetic, the lines of development followed in the two methods of book illustration took different courses. By the close of the century, the mechanical and reproductive woodcut process could produce designs rivaling the hand-painted miniature in naturalistic realism,[15] achieving the effect, moreover, in patterns of graphic character that make them decorative complements of the black-and-white printed script even when they were colored, as was frequently the case, by tinted washes that permitted the printed lines to show through clearly. The result is an aesthetic unity comparable in its way to that of the illuminated manuscripts of the earlier Middle Ages.

For the illuminator, such a decorative unity was no longer possible. Concerned as he had become with the solution of pictorial problems involving combinations

Fig. 211.
Brussels, Bibliothèque Royale, Ms. 9242, f.1. Jean Wau-
quelin, Chroniques de Hainaut, *Philip the Good receiv-*
ing the book, by Roger Van der Weyden(?)

of realistic forms placed in realistic space, the possibility of harmonizing his designs with the planar abstraction of the text patterns simply did not exist. Changing patronage and taste also contributed to the increasing popularity of the printed illustrated book as against the illuminated manuscript. The latter were usually commissioned by or intended for wealthy individuals, whereas the former appealed to a larger and broader group in which the bourgeoisie were the essential consumers. This change of market could not but have had its effect upon the methods of book decoration as well as production, an effect anticipated in the preference for colored line drawings over painted illuminations in certain types of books of popular appeal, whether manuscript or printed, as will be seen.

By and large, then, miniatures in fine books of the fifteenth century could be the work of painters like Simon Marmion (Fig. 212) in northern France or Flanders, or Jean Fouquet (Fig. 213) in central France, or they could be designed by a Roger van der Weyden perhaps for execution by another (Fig. 211), or they could frankly imitate currently popular modes in painting, as is the case with much Italian illumination of the later fifteenth century (Fig. 208). Only in the category of books referred to above does anything approaching the decorative consistency of earlier illuminated volumes appear, moralistic treatises and popular romances being illustrated in a loose and sketchy technique like that of a drawing, as if deliberately avoiding the heavy pigments and dense patterns of the miniatures in the luxury volumes of the day.

An example of the religious tracts so illustrated can be seen in an early fifteenth-century German *Speculum Humanae Salvationis* (Manchester, John Rylands Library, Ms. 27), one of the literally hundreds of copies made of this popular moralizing treatise.[16] The illustration of chapter 8 (Fig. 206) is on ff.10v–11 and shows, like that of the same text in the Corsini *Speculum* (Fig. 179), the Nativity of Christ, Pharaoh's cupbearer dreaming of the vine, Aaron's flowering rod, and Christ's birth foretold by the Tiburtine Sibyl, the usual themes for this text. The designs are executed in outline with watercolor washes of red, green, and greenish-blue. Although the manuscript is probably to be dated in the early fifteenth century, the style of the illustrations is more in the vein of the preceding century than in that of contemporary work. The figures are long and slender and there is but little suggestion of bulk or mass, or of perspective space. It is a naïve style, but the

simply indicated forms have a distinctively individual character, in the manner of folk art, which this is. The clear, almost transparent patterns of the miniatures are in complete harmony with the script of the text they illustrate, written in brownish ink and accented with rubricated initials.

The technique of an illustration in the prose tale of Girart de Nevers (Fig. 207) in the Bibliothèque Royale at Brussels (Ms. 9631) is much like that of the *Speculum* miniatures, but the content is very different. Originally composed around 1227–29 as a poem, this story of chivalrous romance was retold in prose in the fifteenth century for Charles I, count of Nevers and Réthel, and this copy was probably made for Jean de Wavrin, a writer and impassioned bibliophile, around 1460, possibly in Lille in Flanders. This is suggested by the watermark in the paper of which the book is made. The anonymous artist has been called the Wavrin Master since he appears to have executed a number of commissions for him.[17] The illustration on f.77 is of the scene when the hero of the romance is reminded of his momentarily forgotten inamorata by the discovery of her ring magically worn by a lark that his falcon has brought to him. Unlike the crowded narratives of many contemporaries (Fig. 210), the Wavrin Master has reduced his composition to essentials of setting and protagonists. His graphic method is equally terse, a flexible line to establish the contours, and a few washes of brown and green, yet the simply defined forms are vividly characterized. The parts played in the narrative by the attentive dog and the contrast between the alert falcon and the lark are unmistakable. And, as in the fifteenth-century *Speculum* miniatures, the formal unity of the miniature, with its strong linear patterns and the no-less-vigorous chirographic rhythms of the script, is immediately apparent.[18]

There are many equally realistic, even genre touches in the miniature of the consecration of a bishop (Fig. 208) on f.38 of a service book called a Pontifical (Vatican, Bibl. Apost. Ms. Ottob. lat. 501) containing the text of rites performed by the pope or archbishops.[19] The book was made for Vitéz János the Younger, in 1489. He was subsequently bishop of Veszprém in Hungary and of Vienna, and the book may have been made in Hungary for use in the coronation rite of a king; Matthew Corvinus of Hungary is named, and his emblems appear throughout the decoration of the book. The central figure in the scene of a bishop's consecration is Vitéz himself, and most of the others are recognizably portraits. Some of the realistic details are called for in the directions for the conduct of the ceremony written in red in the lower part of the miniature, like the two bottles "of the best wine" the bishop receives, and the acolyte in the right foreground warming the water to be used in the lustration. But the dwarf and monkey on the left and the little white dog in the center can hardly be anything but amusing and picturesque intrusions in the thoroughly naturalistic representation of a solemn ritual, framed in an elaborate shrine that casts a shadow around the edges, as if the whole were a painting hanging on a wall. The artist's style has more than a little in common with that of the Florentine naturalist Domenico Ghirlandaio, and the basic concept of the miniature is in no way different from that of contemporary panel painting.[20]

Realism is the keynote of the illuminated ornament of the Hours of Catherine of Cleves (N.Y., Morgan Library, Ms. 917), a Dutch manuscript of about 1440, but quite a different kind of realism than that of the Vatican Pontifical.[21] The book was made for her by an anonymous artist, probably in Utrecht, whose style has some characteristics in common with the Master of Zweder van Culemborg's in its earlier stages, but who explored new and pioneering ideas before the volume was completed. Catherine of Cleves's Book of Hours is unusual in a number of ways. The text, for instance, contains a series of offices in addition to the usual ones of the Hours of the Virgin or the Little Office of the Blessed Virgin Mary, the Penitential Psalms, the Litany, and the Office of the Dead. There is such a special office for each day of the week, the one for Monday being the Hours of the Dead, which is in addition to the canonical Office of the Dead. The latter is illustrated with two miniatures,[22] but the added cycle has no less than ten, including two of the Mass of the Dead that follows the Hours. The augmented content of the basic theme required the invention of new motives, one of which is the illustration of the reading for Prime in the Hours of the Dead, showing the body of the dead man being prepared for burial (Fig. 209); it is f.99v of the portion of the book that once belonged to the Duke of Arenberg (now Morgan Ms. 945).[23]

Both the Boucicaut and Rohan Masters had enlarged the iconography of Death in various ways,[24] but with none of the grim horror of the Cleves Master's miniature, in which the rigid shrunken corpse is being carried from the bed upon which the man is shown dying in a previous miniature. The unsparing naturalism of the figure is the more expressive in the simple yet beautifully portrayed room, with its accurate perspective and foreshortening, and the sensitive differentiations between the lighted and shadowed walls of the interior that focus on the landscape seen through the window. Only in the border decoration of the folio is there much to suggest earlier traditions of illuminated page designs. The delicate rinceaux of ivy leaves with heavier accents in the angle motives is somewhat reminiscent of the Boucicaut Master (Fig. 194), and, a little closer in time and space, the Master of Zweder van Culemborg (Fig. 204). But other and more immediately available motives also appear, like the strawberry in the upper right border, and this concept was developed in the borders of other folios in the Cleves Hours.

The miniatures and borders are remarkably consistent in style throughout the book,[25] and there is reason to believe that they were generally executed by one artist in sequence from the beginning to the end. The majority of the earlier miniatures have borders like the one just described, but many of the later ones are framed with such extraordinarily naturalistic forms as the fish and eels enclosing St. Lawrence, and the words of his suffrage (Fig. 210), on page 266 of the Morgan section of the book. It does not need to be pointed out that naturalistic details had frequently appeared in the borders and *bas-de-pages* of late fourteenth- and fifteenth-century manuscripts, and that collateral scenes had been introduced in them by the Boucicaut and Bedford Masters (Fig. 196). Such ideas were also used effectively by the Cleves Master and his Dutch contemporaries in the first half of the fifteenth century. The fish eating eels and themselves in the border of the St. Lawrence miniature are not without symbolic overtones;[26] the saint was traditionally the protector of the poor, and the large fish swallowing smaller ones was a popular allegory of the oppression by the rich of those less fortunate.

Several miniatures in the Cleves Hours give some indication that their creator was familiar with the innovations of the great early fifteenth-century masters of realism in Flemish painting,[27] and it has been suggested[28] that in giving the large-scale and tangible objects in the borders their extraordinary realism, the Cleves Master was attempting to explore the world of nature in ways beyond the capabilities of the minute vignettes of the miniatures themselves. Judged in this way, these borders of coins, weapons, bird and animal cages, mussels, and crabs constitute another stage in the variations of the idea initiated in the Gothic marginal

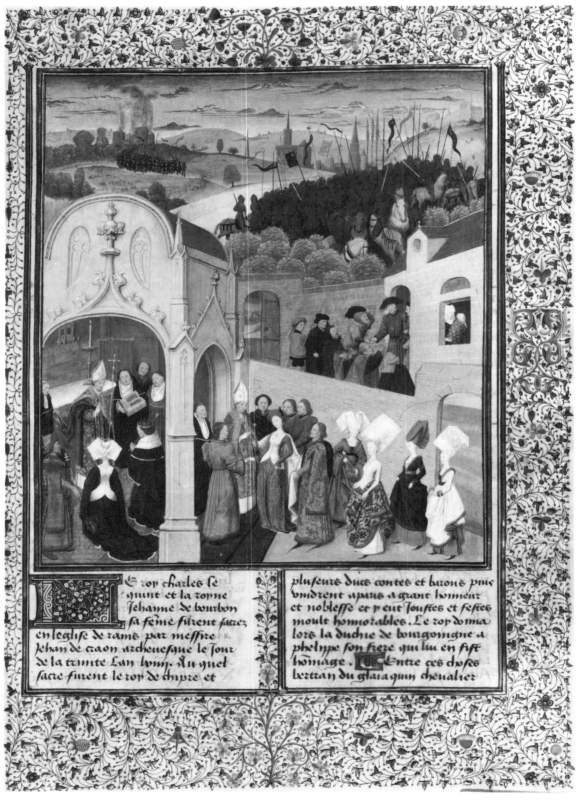

Fig. 212.
Brussels, Bibliothèque Royale, Ms. 9232, f.423. Jean
Mansel, La Fleur des Histoires, *Episodes in the life of*
Charles V of France, by Simon Marmion.

drollery and its introduction of a new element in the text-and-miniature equation of the illuminated folio. By now, the border has attained to a degree of reality more immediately apparent than that of the miniature it encloses, so that "one almost has the impression of seeing the borders through a magnifying glass while looking at the miniatures with binoculars."[29] The idea was to be further exploited in the later fifteenth century, but its first creative statement was in the Book of Hours of Catherine of Cleves.

So far as is known, the Catherine of Cleves Master was a manuscript illuminator and did not engage in panel painting. In Flanders, Jan van Eyck had been employed as an illuminator in his early years, one of the considerations in attributing some of the miniatures in the Milan Hours (Fig. 205) to him, although he was primarily active as a panel painter. There is no reference to his younger contemporary, Roger Van der Weyden, as an illuminator, but he has been credited with the composition and design, if not the actual execution[30] of the miniature showing Philip the Good, Duke of Burgundy, receiving the volume of which it is the frontispiece (Fig. 211), part one of the *Chroniques de Hainaut* as translated by Jean Wauquelin (Brussels, Bibl. Roy., Ms. 9242, f.1); the book was written and illustrated at Mons in 1448. The association of the miniature with Roger Van der Weyden rests largely on the similarity between some of the portraits and likenesses of the same individuals painted by him as substantive works. Precedence for such presentation miniatures goes back as far as the Carolingian Bible of Charles the Bald (Fig. 67), but the mid-fifteenth century conception is understandably conveyed in different terms. There are no allegorical figures, or angels, though this might be thought to be because the book is not of the Scriptures but is a secular history. But the exact likenesses of the participants and the beautifully recorded effects of light and texture in the interior scene convey the impression that it is being observed through an open window. The heraldic devices of the Duke's counsellors punctuate the fine rinceaux of the marginal borders, a decorative complement of the bastard Gothic script of the text. But the miniature itself is enclosed in a double molding of gold, the inner one seemingly shaded by the outer, so that the final effect is of a painting hanging on a wall.[31]

By comparison with the relatively restrained color scheme and the rational space and light patterns of the miniature representing Philip the Good and his court-iers, the gay hues and patterned landscape in the miniature of episodes in the life of Charles V of France (Fig. 212) may seem archaic. It is taken from another of the secular histories that were popular in the Flemish Lowlands in the fifteenth century called *La Fleur des Histoires* by Jean Mansel (Brussels, Bibl. Roy., Ms. 9232), the miniature is on f.423 in the second part of a four-volume work. A dense foliate border around the entire folio encloses the miniature and the text, which are separated from each other by thin framing bands of blue and gold, which function in much the same way as the more elaborate moldings of the Philip the Good presentation illustration. But where that dealt with a single episode, the *Fleur des Histoires* miniature presents a number, beginning with the marriage of Charles V and Jeanne de Bourbon in 1350, shown in the right foreground. Inside a Gothic aediculae, they next appear being crowned in the Cathedral at Reims, an event in 1364, followed by the birth of the dauphin, who was to be Charles VI in 1368, celebrated by the giving of alms as the newborn prince is shown by his nurse through a window. In the background are battle scenes referring to the Hundred Years' War with the English. Continuous pictorial narrative such as this is somewhat anachronistic at the time this miniature was executed, probably between 1455 and 1460. But it was painted by Simon Marmion, who was active in both Flanders and northern France as a panel painter and illuminator, and his manner might well be termed the ultimate phase of the International Style of the early fifteenth century. The lively colors and flattened planes of the landscape[32] could easily be transferred directly to a woven tapestry from this design in which Marmion characteristically achieves a synthesis of French and Flemish styles.

Jean Fouquet of Tours[33] was a contemporary of Simon Marmion, and like him was renowned as both an illuminator and painter of panels, most of his career having been in the service of the French kings Charles VII and Louis XI, and their courts. For Étienne Chevalier, royal treasurer of Charles VII, he illuminated a Book of Hours of which most of the miniatures are in the Musée Condé at Chantilly, where they have been detached and separately framed.[34] The miniature of Christ Carrying His Cross (Fig. 213) presumably once illustrated the Hours of the Passion. Above, against a background that includes the Sainte-Chapelle of Paris and a portion of the royal palace, the Saviour carries the cross with the assistance of Simon of Cyrene, passing in front of Judas hanged from a tree. Below, a black-smith and his wife forge the nails with which He will be fastened to the cross. Between the two levels, St. Veronica with the handkerchief is in a decorated letter D on the left of a panel balanced on the right by a composition of flowers; this last was painted over the opening lines of the prayer in the eighteenth century.

Fouquet is believed to have painted the Étienne Chevalier miniatures around 1450–55, and although the landscape setting of the Carrying of the Cross has some of the same buildings of the Parisian scene as the Limbourg brothers miniature of the Meeting of the Three Magi of about forty years before, there are significant stylistic differences. Fouquet is known to have been in Rome in the late 1440s, and there he must have learned the accurate perspective system that so clearly differentiates the spatial relationships of the several levels of his composition. The interest in reality thus suggested is also evident in the factual details of the forms, and even the incident of the blacksmith and his wife that dominates the foreground. This *mise-en-scène* is believed to have been suggested by the action in a religious play or mystery of the Passion, in which the main theme would be enacted on a raised stage, with other related but subordinate motives performed concurrently on a lower level. In another miniature from the Chevalier Hours of Christ before Pilate, carpenters make the cross in the same "fore-stage," as it might be called.[35] These themes are known to have figured in mystery plays from the late fourteenth century on,[36] and it is well established that much of the iconography of late mediaeval art was suggested by the religious dramas of the day.

In the one manuscript documented as a work of Jean Fouquet, (Paris, BN, Ms. fr. 247, *Antiquités judaiques*), the folios painted by him or in his atelier have light foliate marginal borders of the kind current in Parisian work in the early fifteenth century. It is known, however, that the book had been begun for John of Berry, and the borders are of that period. In the Étienne Chevalier Hours, there are none. The miniatures are edged with thin gold bands, and although those in the Musée Condé are exhibited in narrow gilt frames that make it almost impossible to distinguish them from small panel paintings, several others[37] have not been trimmed. In all, the formal conception is that of a substantive pictorial design, self-sufficient and unaffected in any way by its role as the decoration of a book page. One detail that appears in most of the Étienne Chevalier miniatures makes the difference in content between the illuminated volume of the earlier Middle Ages and those of the eve of the Renaissance abundantly clear—the way in which the initial letter and, originally, the following text are incorporated in the pictorial design. In the thirteenth century (Fig. 152) and even as late as the latter part of the fourteenth (Fig. 188), script and illustration have their own identity or reality, and the miniature painter's problem was to harmonize them in a formally unified design. In the Chevalier miniature of Christ Carrying His Cross, the letter D and the words that once followed it are on a panel resting on a rock in the foreground; in others in the series, similar panels are supported by angels or animals. The inference is clear. The written symbol, once thought to be real because it was the Word of God, is now stated to be real because it is a part of something that can be held up or cast a shadow. It is real because it can be painted like any other object that is seen, not created because it is a reality in its own right.

Yet another attempted resolution of the aesthetic contradiction between the two-dimensional book page and script, and its three-dimensional pictorial embellishment is seen in the work of the Master of the Hours of Mary of Burgundy.[38] He was an anonymous Flemish illuminator, active apparently about 1475 to 1490 in Ghent or Brussels, who served the Burgundian court. He made two Books of Hours for Mary of Burgundy,[39] daughter of Charles the Bold and Isabella of Bourbon, and wife of Maximilian I, whom she married in 1477, whence his designation. His style has also been found in other books, chiefly executed for aristocratic patrons like Engelbert of Nassau, who was Lieutenant of the Realm under Philip the Fair, Mary of Burgundy's son, for whom he made, *c.* 1485–90, the Book of Hours that bears his name (Oxford, Bodleian Library, Ms. Douce 219–220).[40] The miniature of St. Barbara (Fig. 214) on f.41 illustrates her suffrage in the prayers to various saints contained in the book, in addition to the usual Hours of the Virgin, Hours of the Cross, the Office of the Dead, and so on. She is shown seated on the floor of a portico, through whose columns masons are seen constructing the tower in which her father intended to imprison her. The sides of the arch above her are continued down to frame the opening lines of her suffrage written on the parchment folio. Miniature and text are completely surrounded by gold leaf, on which are painted daisies and other flowers in pink and white and red, with a butterfly on one and a great dragonfly on another.

In strewing the folio margins with objects, the Mary

Fig. 213.
Chantilly, Musée Condé. Jean Fouquet, Hours of Étienne
Chevalier, Christ carrying the Cross. (Photo Bulloz)

of Burgundy Master follows the example of his Dutch predecessor, the Catherine of Cleves painter (Fig. 211), and even earlier illuminators who introduced naturalistic forms in the borders of their miniatures.[41] But he carries the idea still farther by enlarging the relative scale of the flowers and insects, approximately life-size on the tiny page of the book, which measures 13.8 x 9.7 cm (5⅜ x 3⅞"), and by skillful touches of shading to suggest that they are actual objects resting on the gold surface. Behind this plane from which the forms project, the script occupies an intermediate area from which the still-more-distant forms of the masons and the tower are seen. This has been referred to as a "window aspect,"[42] since it presents the objects portrayed as if seen through an opening within the picture itself, an idea the illuminator had previously developed in the miniatures he painted in the Vienna Book of Hours.[43] He thus goes even farther than Jean Fouquet in creating the illusion of reality, for in painting the flowers and insects in the margin with utmost clarity and precision as those things nearest the observer, and at the same time rendering the forms in the miniature more impressionistically, he recreated the effect of normal optical experience, that when objects near at hand appear sharp, more distant ones are blurred—a pictorial achievement unsurpassed even by Velásquez. Between the planes thus optically defined as near and far, the script occupies a neutral place, part of neither one, yet coexistent with both.

By the time the Mary of Burgundy Master was creating his masterpieces of illumination, books with text printed from movable type and illustrated with woodcuts were already in production.[44] The earliest such book of which the date is certain was published in Bamberg in Germany by Albrecht Pfister on 14 February 1461, a collection of fables called *Der Edelstein*, compiled by Ulrich Boner. Six years later, in 1467, the first printed and illustrated book produced in Italy was the *Meditationes* of Johannis de Turrecremata, abbot of the Benedictine monastery of Santa Scholastica at Subiaco near Rome. Its inspirational texts were illustrated with woodcuts based on a series of frescoes in the Roman church of Santa Maria sopra Minerva, no longer existent, but the book was printed in Rome by a German, Ulrich Han, and the woodcuts appear to have been the work of a German artisan.[45] In Italy as in Germany, the earliest illustrated printed books were copied from manuscripts and the woodcut designs were intended to be colored to resemble miniatures,[46] and some of the

books produced in Venice as early as 1470 by migrant German printers incorporated outline woodcut designs of rubrics and borders obviously intended for coloring by hand.[47] Many of them originated in the workshop of Nicolaus Jenson, a Frenchman sent to Mainz by Louis XI to learn methods of printing, according to tradition. One of his most successful ventures was the publication in both Latin and Italian of Pliny the Elder's *Historia Naturalis*. It was available printed on either paper or parchment;[48] the copy of which the beginning text is illustrated (Fig. 215, Plate XXX) is on paper (Rome, Biblioteca Angelica, Inc. 530), and was printed in 1476.[49] An elaborate border of foliage, interlaces, armorial emblems, and other decorative motives has been painted in the wide margins by a Ferrarese artist of the late fifteenth century, who also illuminated the initial letters for which blank spaces were left by the printer at the beginning of each chapter or heading. In the D of the preface on f.6, the figure is Pliny, the

Fig. 214.
Oxford, Bodleian Library, Ms. Douce 219–220, f.41. The Mary of Burgundy Master, Hours of Engelbert of Nassau, St. Barbara.

Fig. 216.
Munich, Bayerischesstaatsbibliothek. Prayer-Book of Maximilian I, f.37v. "Knight, Death and Devil," by Albrecht Dürer.

gnouerunt vias meas: qui
b^9 iuraui in ira mea: si introi
bunt in requiem meam Aue.
Gloria patri et filio: ⁊ spiritui
sancto. Sicut erat inprincipio
et nunc et semper: et in secula
seculorum amen. Dominus
tecum. Aue maria gratia ple
na dominus tecū. Hymnus.
Dem terra pontus ethe
ra: colunt adorant pre
dicant: trinā regentem machi
nam: claustrū Marie baiulat
Cui luna sol et omnia deserui

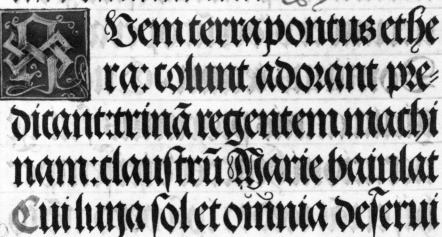

author. There is some disagreement among scholars of typography and bibliography as to whether or not the handwritten books that continued to be produced until well into the sixteenth century in Italy were influenced in their designs by printed books like this, or the opposite.[50] Suffice it to note that by the end of the fifteenth century, an illuminated folio in an Italian manuscript[51] differs in no important respect from a decorated page in a printed book, down to the humanistic script of the text in each, whether written by hand or stamped by a metal cast.

The drawings by Albrecht Dürer for the Prayer Book of Maximilian I[52] might seem to represent the same idea as the painted decorations of the Jenson Pliny, but the actual case was quite different. The general scheme is seen in the decoration of f.37v (Fig. 216) in the portion of the Prayer-Book in the Munich Staatsbibliothek. The text is of a prayer "to be remembered in the agony of death," and the drawing in the *bas-de-page* and left margin deals with the theme of one of Dürer's most famous engravings, Knight, Death and Devil. It is executed in violet ink, though others are in red or olive-green. The printed text is black, with rubricated initials for some phrases, and the word *hymnus* at the end of line nine is also in red. The large initial with which the hymn begins is painted blue and gold. Pen flourishes and interlaces are interspersed with a crane, a griffon, and an involved mass of foliage with a grotesque mask in the upper and right margins, all in the same violet ink. Light pink rulings separate the text lines and surround the printed area, the latter continued to the edges of the folio.

The Prayer Book, of which part is in Munich (the rest is in the museum at Besançon), is one of five copies, each differing somewhat from the others. The volume divided between Munich and Besançon is the one that belonged to Maximilian himself. Although the decoration was never completed (other artists including Lucas Cranach, Hans Burgkmair, and Hans Baldung Grien also worked on it), it might appear that the project was intended to be no more than the embellishment of a printed text with hand-executed ornament for an individual patron. The text, with its red rubrics and occasional decorative flourishes like the one of the letter M in the bottom line, had been composed by 30 December 1513 in the printing shop of Johannes Schönsperger of Augsburg, but most of Dürer's drawings are dated in 1514 or 1515. Several facts argue against the conclusion that the Dürer designs were an end in themselves

and that Maximilian's copy of the book was to be unique. The type face, apparently designed especially for the book, is archaic for its time and imitates the script found in liturgical manuscripts of a century earlier. The printed flourishes of some of the letters also contribute to the impression that the text is handwritten. Moreover, the pink rulings, unnecessary in a printed book but essential in a handwritten one, heighten still more the resemblance to a manuscript page. Had the project been completed, each printed text page to be decorated would have been overprinted twice, once from a woodcut with the figural and ornamental design in the appropriate color, and a second time with another block to print the pink rulings. Reproducing the fluent calligraphy of Dürer's designs in woodcut would have been no problem for his well-trained and skillful cutters.

Dürer's drawings for Maximilian I's Prayer Book are testimony to his incomparable graphic skill and to his inheritance as a northerner of the centuries-old tradition of the potential harmony between words and pictures, between text and illustration. Books had been among his continuing interests from the time of his early apprenticeship and training in Wolgemuth's workshop, where woodcuts were prepared for the volumes produced by Anton Koberger of Nuremberg, probably the most successful German publisher of the day. His woodcut illustrations for the Apocalypse were one of his first major projects and a landmark in the iconography of the theme. No less important were his series of woodcut illustrations for the Large and Small Passions of Our Lord and for the Life of the Virgin. In all of these, he worked in the idiom of the day, training both himself and his woodblock cutters to an unprecedented achievement of decorative and realistic designs of utmost originality, in books that rank among the finest examples of their kind.

In the Prayer Book drawings, Dürer could not develop the full-page compositions of the woodcut books and returned instead to the marginal type of decoration. In so doing, he reverted to the concept if not the forms of his Gothic predecessors. A slender tree trunk marks the left margin of the text column, with a branch encircled by the Devil's tail and spreading above to become a leafy perch for a crane. An ornamental flourish at the top becomes a griffon, changes again into variations of the flourish, and descends on the right side of the folio. The two-dimensional patterns that predominate in this essentially decorative part of the design give way to a three-dimensional scheme in the landscape of the *bas-de-page* into which the Devil plunges on the left. The colored lines of this design are incredibly light, appearing at times to vanish like wisps of smoke, yet they hold their own against the massive blacks and reds of the script, an aesthetic unity that coexists with that of the textual design.

Dürer's association with Maximilian I[53] began in 1512 and a number of commissions resulted, like the Triumphal Arch and the Triumphal Procession, both suffused with the mixture of antiquarianism and contemporary ideas that was characteristic of the emperor's extraordinary tastes and interests. But of all the projects for Maximilian, none was more personal, perhaps, than the Prayer Book. The idea has been lucidly put by Panofsky:[54] "Each copy, printed on vellum, would have simulated a hand-written manuscript, written in what would have looked like liturgical Gothic script in black and cinnabar, provided with what would have looked like the rulings required by medieval scribes, and decorated with what would have looked like pen drawings in colored inks. This must have been precisely what Maximilian wanted. A printed book creating the illusion of a hand-written and hand-decorated *Livre d'Heures,* or, to put it the other way, an apparently hand-written and hand-decorated *Livre d'Heures* produced by the printing press, would have symbolized to perfection the tastes and aspirations of a prince engrossed in the past, yet keenly interested in every invention and device of modern technics: of a collector of manuscripts enamored of typography."

A little more than twenty years before Dürer and Maximilian I conceived the idea of the Prayer Book, a few lines written in 1491 by Bernardino di Michelangelo Cingnoni, a miniaturist in Siena, gave a mournful prophecy of the future of illumination as an art: "Pell' arte mia non si fa più niente—Pell' arte mia è finitá per l'amore de' libri, che si fanno in forma che non si miniano più."[55] Translated freely, this reads: "For my art there is no longer any need. My art is finished by the love for books so made that they cannot be illuminated." It is the epitaph of the art to which Dürer's Prayer Book is one of the finest monuments.

NOTES

1. For a succinct and reasonable account, cf. R. Hirsch, *Printing, Selling and Reading 1450-1550* (Wiesbaden: Harrassowitz, 1967), pp. 13–26.

2. A. M. Hind, *An Introduction to a History of Woodcut,* 2 vols. (Boston: Houghton, Mifflin, 1935; reprint New York: Dover, 1963).

3. Hind, 1, fig. 44.

4. Panofsky, *ENP,* 1:123.

5. Cf. *Printed Book Illustrations of the Fifteenth Century* (Manchester: The John Rylands Library, 1933), p. 10, pls. 6–7.

6. C. F. Bühler, *The Fifteenth Century Book* (Philadelphia: University of Pennsylvania Press, 1960), pp. 34–39.

7. Cf. Hirsch, pp. 88–89, and also pp. 1–2 for a comment by Rabelais.

8. Panofsky, *ENP,* 1:28.

9. J. Held, *AB,* 37 (1955):208.

10. J. W. Thompson, *The Medieval Library* (Chicago: University of Chicago Press, 1939), pp. 536–44.

11. E. P. Goldschmidt, "Preserved for Posterity, Some Remarks on Medieval Manuscripts," *The New Colophon,* 2 (1950):330–32.

12. G. Fraknoi, et al., *Biblioteca Corvina: La Biblioteca di Mattia Corvino, Re d'Ungheria* (Budapest, 1927). J. Fitz, "König Mathias Corvinus und der Buchdruck," *Gutenberg Jahrbuch,* 14 (1939):128–37.

13. Bühler, p. 62.

14. *Ibid.,* p. 68.

15. E.g., Dürer's woodcut Apocalypse; cf. E. Panofsky, *Albrecht Dürer,* 2 vols. (Princeton: Princeton University Press, 1943; 3d. ed. 1948, pp. 51–59, nos. 281–95, figs. 76–81.

16. Cf. chap. 8, n. 40.

17. Cf. Delaissé, *Miniatures médiévales,* no. 43 with a reproduction in color on p. 185; also *Librairie . . . Philippe le Bon,* no. 158.

18. For further examples by the Wavrin Master and related works, the majority in paper books, cf. *Mss. à peintures . . . xiiie au xvie siècle,* nos. 301–10.

19. *Le Miniature del Pontificale Ottoboniano (Cod. Vat. Ottob. 501),* Codices e Vaticanis Selecti, 3 (Rome: Luigi Moretti, 1903).

20. For a well-phrased general account of manuscript illumination of the period in Italy, see *The Miniatures of the Renaissance;* introd. by A. M. Albareda (Vatican City: Apostolic Library, 1950).

21. J. Plummer, *The Hours of Catherine of Cleves* (New York: Braziller, 1966). Cf. also Delaissé, chap. 10, n .75; pp. 37–39, 81–86.

22. On ff. 168v–169 of the Guennol part of the book; cf. Plummer, nos. 99–100.

23. For an account of the reconstitution of the manuscript, cf. Plummer, pp. 10–13.

24. Cf. chap. 10, n. 43.

25. Plummer, p. 22.

26. *Ibid.,* no. 128.

27. Panofsky, *ENP,* 1:103–4; Delaissé, p. 38.

28. Panofsky, in *The Book of Hours of Catherine of Cleves,* ed.

J. Plummer, (New York: Pierpont Morgan Library, 1964), p. 10.

29. Meiss, p. 9.

30. Panofsky, *ENP*, 1:268 and n. 3; but cf. Delaissé, *Miniatures médiévales*, p. 123; a reproduction in color on p. 121.

31. Cf. also L. M. J. Delaissé, *La miniature flamande. Le mécénat de Philippe le Bon* (Brussels: Bibliothèque Royale, 1959). *La librairie de Philippe le Bon* (Brussels: Bibliothèque Royale, 1967).

32. Reproduced in color in Delaissé, *Miniatures médiévales*, p. 149.

33. T. Cox, *Jehan Fouquet, native of Tours* (London: Faber & Faber, 1931). K. G. Perls, *Jean Fouquet* (Paris: Hyperion, 1940). P. Wescher, *Jean Fouquet and his Times* (New York: Reynal & Hitchcock, 1947).

34. J. Van Moé, "Les Fouquet de Chantilly," *Verve*, 2 (1942): 5-6.; 3 (1945):11-12. J. Porcher, *MFM*, pp. 71-77.

35. Cf. *MFM*, fig. 80.

36. E. Roy, "Le mystère de la Passion en France," *Revue Bourguignonne de l'enseignement supèrieure*," 13-14. É Male, *L'art religieux de la fin du Moyen-Age*, 4th ed. (Paris: Colin, 1931), pp. 60-62.

37. E.g. no. 194 in the collection of Robert Lehman, N.Y.; cf. *IBMAR*, pl. lxv.

38. O. Pächt, *The Master of Mary of Burgundy* (London: Faber & Faber, 1948).

39. Vienna, NB., Cod. 1857: Berlin, Print Room, Ms. 78 B 12.

40. J. J. G. Alexander, *The Master of Mary of Burgundy: A Book of Hours for Engelbert of Nassau* (New York: Braziller, 1970), with facsimile reproductions in color.

41. Cf. *The Hours of Margeurite d'Orléans* of c. 1426-30. Paris, BN. Ms. lat. 1156 B, f. 135, reproduced in color in *MFM*, pl. lxxviii.

42. Cf. Pächt, pp. 25-28. Only some of the incidental conclusions reached in this perceptive study need be modified in the light of what has been learned of the Catherine of Cleves Master.

43. Cf. *ibid.*, pls. 12-13; Alexander, pl. 1.

44. Cf. Hind, n. 2; 1:273-394.

45. L. Donati, "A Manuscript of 'Meditationes Johannis de Turrecremata' (1496)," *The Literary Chronicle*—University of Pennsylvania, 21 (1955):51-60.

46. Cf. Bühler, pp. 66-93; Hind, 2:398 ff.

47. A. W. Pollard, "Woodcut Designs for Illuminators in Venetian Books," *Bibliographica*, 3 (1897):122 ff.

48. D. Fava, "Libri membranacei stampati in Italia nel Quattrocento," *Gutenberg-Jahrbuch*, 12 (1937):55-84.

49. Cf. *Catologo* . . . , chap. 7, n. 76; p. 365, no. 576.

50. S. Morison, *The Art of Printing*. (New York: Diament Typographic Service, 1945), p. 35. Bühler, p. 46.

51. *E.g.*, a Pliny *Historia Naturalis* of 1481 (Venice, Bibl. Marciana, Ms. lat. VI, 245 [2976]), reproduced in color in Salmi, *Miniatura Italiana*, pl. lxviii.

52. K. Giehlow, *Kaiser Maximilians I Gebetbuch* (Vienna: Selbstverlag, 1907). G. Leidinger, *Albrecht Dürers und Lukas Cranachs Randzeichnungen zum Gebetbuche Kaiser Maximilians I* (Munich: Kunstverlag Riehn & Reusch, 1922). Panofsky, *Albrecht Dürer*, 1:182-94.

53. L. Baldass, *Der Künstlerkreis Maximilians* (Vienna: A. Schroll, 1923).

54. *Albrecht Dürer*, 1: p. 184; quoted by permission of the Princeton University Press.

55. G. Goye, *Carteggio inedito d'artisti dei secoli xiv. xv. xvi.* (Florence, 1839-1840), 1:267; cited by Bühler, pp. 92-93.

Appendix

In the early years of Christianity, the Bible was the service book for all religious ceremonies, but as the Offices or prescribed forms for the various rites were developed, the need for selected readings appropriate to the several types of gathering led to the compilation of the different kinds of service books now known. An eleventh-century liturgist named John of Garland lists twelve separate volumes as necessary in conducting the church services, including the missal, gradual, breviary, psalter, and others for more specialized rituals. In all cases, whether the books are of the Mass, the Office, or the Sacraments, the texts are from the Scriptures, selected and arranged as appropriate to the ceremony, augmented by special prayers or musical interpolations.

The BENEDICTIONAL is a special service book of blessings to be pronounced over the congregation during the Mass, sometimes by the priest but more usually by a bishop,[2] such as Aethelwold of Winchester. Though not a part of the Roman ritual in the Middle Ages, the practice of giving such blessings or benedictions was widespread in mediaeval times.

The BOOK OF HOURS[3] is a devotional book intended for private rather than liturgical use. It is so named from its inclusion of prayers to be said at certain times of day, an idea suggested by the term used to designate it in all languages, *Livre d'Heures* in French, *Stundenbuch* in German, *Libro d'oro* in Italian, *Libro de Horas* in Spanish. The times of day are the Canonical Hours when special prayers or "offices" were to be offered, a practice instituted by the Benedictine Order in the sixth century. Initially there were three such special hours, each one identified with a particularly significant event in Christian history: nine o'clock in the morning, when the Holy Spirit descended on the disciples at Pentecost; noon, which was the hour of the Crucifixion; and three in the afternoon, when Christ died. Other times were subsequently appointed for these special prayers or offices, the entire sequence being *matins* at midnight, *lauds* at three A.M. or daybreak, *prime* at six A.M., *tierce* or *terce* at nine A.M., *sext* at noon, *nones* at three P.M., *vespers* at six P.M. or sunset, and *compline* at nine P.M.

Originally, these special prayers, along with a calendar listing the principal church feasts and saints' days, were added to the Psalter, which was the book mostly used for private devotions until the thirteenth century. At first, the added prayers were the Little Office of the Virgin Mary, the Penitential Psalms, the Litanies of the Saints, the Suffrages, and the Office or Vigils of the Dead. But as others were added to answer a growing need for a more emotional component in private contemplation and prayer, the combined Psalter and Book of Hours became too large for convenient use and they were separated, the Book of Hours becoming the prayer book of the laity as the Breviary was of the priesthood or those in holy orders.[4] Other additions to the Book of Hours included selected Gospel readings pertaining to four of the major church feasts, Christmas, the Annunciation, Epiphany, and Pentecost; two special intercessory prayers addressed to the Virgin—*Obsecro te* and *O intemerata;* the Hours of the Holy Cross; the Hours of the Holy Spirit; the Fifteen Joys of the Virgin; and the Seven Petitions to the Savior.

All of these do not necessarily appear in every Book of Hours, but by the end of the fourteenth century, a French example could consist of the following:

The Calendar, almost invariably in French, although the offices would be in Latin.
    Four Gospel Lessons—*cursus evangelii.*
    Prayers to the Virgin—*Obsecro te* and *O intemerata.*
    Hours or Office of the Virgin:
        Matins—*Domine labia mea aperies.*
        Other hours—*Deus in adjutorium meum intende.*
        Compline—*Converte nos Deus salutaris noster.*
    Hours of the Passion.
    Hours of the Holy Spirit.
    Hours of the Cross (not invariable).
    The Penitential Psalms, seven in all, the most emotional part of the Psalter.
    The Litany, the most emotional part of the liturgical office.

Memorials or Suffrages of the Saints (not invariable).
    Office of the Dead or Vigils, also with great emotional content, in two parts—Vespers (*Placebo*), and Matins (*Dirige*).

Some idea of the textual complexities of a Book of Hours is suggested by the content of Catherine of Cleves's Hours, and the *Grandes Heures* of the Duc de Berry. Since a Book of Hours was intended for personal use, it could include offices that had special significance for the individual it was made for. Thus the Hours of Jeanne d'Évreux include the Office of Saint Louis of France, who was held in particular veneration by the ladies of the French court in the fourteenth century.

Individual tastes and interests could also find expression in the illustration of the Book of Hours. Only seldom are any two exactly alike, but over a period of time certain subjects came more and more to be associated with certain prayers. The following table lists some of the iconographic cycles of the three offices:

Time	Hours of the Virgin	Hours of the Passion	Hours of the Holy Spirit
Matins	Annunciation	Betrayal	Baptism
Lauds	Visitation	Caiphas	Pentecost
Prime	Nativity	Pilate	The Holy Trinity
Tierce	Annunciation to the Shepherds	Flagellation	Peter Preaching
Sext	Adoration of the Magi	Way to Calvary	Peter and the Faithful
Nones	Presentation in the Temple	Crucifixion	Peter and Paul Baptizing
Vespers	Flight into Egypt	Descent into Limbo	Peter Celebrating Mass
Compline	Coronation of the Virgin	Entombment	Gregory Inspired by the Holy Spirit

The Penitential Psalms are usually illustrated with a miniature of David, the Office of the Dead with the *chambre ardente,* a burial scene, or some related theme (Fig. 209), and the Memorials or Suffrages of the Saints by figures representing them (Figs. 195, 210, 214) or episodes in their lives.

The BREVIARY[5] is a devotional book for use by the clergy, primarily, although some, like those of Philippe le Bel and Jeanne de Belleville, were made for laity. The basic textual element is the Psalter, and the form of the book evolved from the practice in early monastic times of reading all the Psalms every day, modified rather soon to provide for their reading through the

week instead. They were to be read at the Canonical Hours (cf. description of the Book of Hours), and, in time, various further readings and prayers were added. The form of the Breviary was established by the end of the thirteenth century and is essentially in five parts and provides prayers and readings for every Sunday and weekday through the ecclesiastical year, usually grouped to correspond to the four seasons.

The five parts found in each section of the Breviary are the Psalter, the Proper of the Seasons, i.e., the prayers and readings proper to the indicated days; the Proper of the Saints, of readings appropriate to the saint of a given day; the Common of the Saints, with offices for the feasts of various categories or groups of saints and also including some special occasions such as the dedication of churches; and, finally, a section with offices like those of the Virgin Mary, the Office of the Dead, and the like. Being a devotional book, the Breviary does not include the ritual services of the Eucharist, Baptism, and Marriage. The Breviary was for the clergy what the Book of Hours was for the laity, but unlike the latter was only seldom elaborately illustrated and then, as a rule, for an individual commission like the one made for the Duke of Bedford (Fig. 196).

CHORALE is a term loosely applied to any volume containing the words and musical notations for any service in which a choir or group of musicians takes part, though these are more specifically designated as *graduals, tropers* (*q.v.*) and the like. In Italy (sp. *corale*), it refers to the large service books from which a choral group could read the words and music of the offices (Fig. 200).

The EVANGELIARY or EVANGELISTARY consists of Gospel texts selected or arranged for reading as a part of the Mass, rather than the compilation by author that is found in a GOSPEL-BOOK.

The GRADUAL (sometimes GRAIL) is a musical service book with the variable and fixed portions of the Mass sung by the choir or soloist. The former include the *introit* for the beginning of the office, the *gradual* in response to the reading of the Epistle, the *Alleluia* or anthem, the *offertory*, and the *antiphon* of the Communion with its psalm. The fixed part of the Gradual consists of the *Kyrie, Gloria, Credo, Sanctus,* and *Agnus Dei* and is known as the Proper of the Mass. They are sometimes collected in a separate volume known as a KYRIALE.

The term LECTIONARY means literally a selection of texts to be read. In a sense, every office or service book is a lectionary of a kind, but the practice of making such selections for specific occasions or purposes seems to have begun very early (Fig. 36). Bibles and Psalters were sometimes used as liturgical books, with marks or rubrics indicating passages to be read on certain days, but the inconvenience of the procedure undoubtedly suggested the idea of excerpting and assembling the individual readings. A technical term for such extracts is *pericope* (*q.v.*)

The word MISSAL[6] is derived from the Latin *missa* meaning the Mass, and the books so designated contain the texts of the Divine Office, both recited and chanted. The modern Roman Missal is basically that approved by Pius V in 1570 and contains many elements also found in the Breviary—the Propers of the Seasons and of the Saints, the Common of the Saints, and so on. But it also contains the Ordinary of the Mass, the *Ordo Missae,* in which the Eucharist is celebrated, and also the Mass of the Dead, neither of which is found in the Breviary. These were taken from the Sacramentary (*q.v.*). Musical chants may also appear in the Missal, in which case it has some of the functions of the Gradual. The importance of the Ordinary of the Mass in both the Missal and the Sacramentary is indicated in many manuscripts by the special emphasis given some parts of its text by illuminated decoration. Thus the Preface beginning *Per omnia saecula saeculorum* frequently has an elaborated initial. And the central rite called the Canon of the Mass, in which the eucharistic elements are blessed, begins *Te igitur* and is often accompanied by a representation of the Crucifixion (Fig. 40), even when no other illumination occurs.

An OCTATEUCH is a volume containing the first eight books of the Old Testament (Fig. 16), a bibliographic unit used primarily in the Eastern Church.

The PENTATEUCH, like the Octateuch, is a unit of the Old Testament, the first five books, in this case comprising those of the Mosaic Law. The Ashburnham Pentateuch (Paris, BN, Ms. n.a. lat. 2334) is a notable example (Fig. 35).

PERICOPE is from a Greek word meaning a cutting or fragment. As applied to a service book (Fig. 82), it refers to a compilation of extracts or selections from the Biblical text to be read in churches or used as sermon texts.

The PONTIFICAL[7] contains the texts of services proper to the pope or a bishop in rituals of ordination, consecration, and blessing.[8] It is a sacramental book, since the Mass is a part of the several individual ceremonies. Previous to the twelfth and thirteenth centuries, the rites here provided for would have been included in the Sacramentary, the individual volume of the Pontifical having come into existence as the ceremonies became more developed in the later Middle Ages (Fig. 208).

The PSALTER[9] was one of the basic liturgical and service books of the Middle Ages, with the Sacramentary and the Gospel-book. Its reading in entirety, daily at first and then weekly, was a fundamental part of the Benedictine Rule that ultimately gave rise to the procedures of worship at the Canonical Hours, which became the basis of both communal and private devotions. Its role in the latter category made it the principal if not the only book for personal religious practice until the end of the thirteenth century, when it was gradually supplanted by the Book of Hours. It usually contained other hymns than the Psalms themselves, the songs from both Old and New Testaments called the Canticles, as well as texts spoken in concert, like the Apostles' Creed.

There is considerable variety in the decoration and illustration of Psalter texts,[10] an indication of its role as a private devotional book. They may range from the marginal commentaries of the Anglo-Saxon Psalter from Bury St. Edmunds (Fig. 94), to the compositions for each psalm in the Utrecht Psalter and its related books, to the pairing of prophets and apostles introducing the Psalter of the Duc de Berry (Fig. 188). The liturgical division of the Psalter sometimes determines the character of its decoration. An organization in eight sections is the usual one for Psalters containing the Gallican version of the text[11] made by St. Jerome in 392. This is marked by making the initial letters at the beginning of each section larger or more elaborate than the others. In the same way, the structure of a Psalter in the Vatican Biblioteca Apostolica (Ms. lat. 83), designed for the Ambrosian liturgy followed in Milan instead of the Gallican, is in sections of ten psalms each, with more ornate initial letters at the beginning of each division.

The SACRAMENTARY,[12] a liturgical book, is the collection of ritual texts that became the *Missale plenarium* in the later Middle Ages and is thus a remote ancestor of the modern Roman Missal (*q.v.*). Unlike the Missal, its content is limited to those portions of the Mass actually spoken by the celebrant, whether pope, bishop, or priest. The Canon of the Mass (cf. the discussion of the Missal) is its principle element, accompanied by the Proper of the Seasons, the Proper and Common of the Saints, Masses for Occasional Offices, and various benedictions and blessings for ceremonies in which the leader of the congregation would be required to take part.

The Sacramentary is among the oldest of liturgical texts, since its function was essential to the forms of Christian worship as they were established in its early history. A variety of usages were known in the early Middle Ages, named, among others, the Leonine, Gelasian, and Gregorian from their identification with popes of those names, although the associations are more legendary than historical.[13] In time, the usage developed in Rome from the fourth to the eighth centuries took precedence. It was the form that served as model for the Carolingian reforms, and it was in almost general use from that time on, save for some individual exceptions; the Mozarabic use is still observed in Toledo, for instance, and the Ambrosian in Milan.

No two Sacramentaries are exactly alike, and this is true of their decoration as well as the texts. However, the structural organization of the book could provide a scheme for its ornament, as can be seen in the Gelasian Sacramentary in the Biblioteca Apostolica of the Vatican (Ms. Reg. lat. 316), which, for all its name, is based on Roman liturgical usage of the mid-seventh century.[14] It is in three parts, each beginning with a decorated cross page and an elaborated *Incipit* and introduction facing it (Fig. 37). Ff.3v–4 in the Gelasian Sacramentary are at the beginning of a section with the Proper of the Seasons from Christmas to Pentecost and also including a number of special prayers and Masses for ordinations, baptisms, dedications, and the like. The second section begins with a similar cross page and decorated text design, on ff.131v–132. It contains the Proper and Common of the Saints, and the texts of five Masses for the season of Advent. Part three also has a cross page and developed text patterns on ff.172v–173,[15] preceding the Canon of the Mass, which is followed by a number of prayers and Masses for special occasions. The textual recension of Vatican Ms. Reg. lat. 316 is important, because it is one of the earliest instances (*c.* 750) of the Canon of the Mass appearing in the text; its omission from older Sacramentaries may have been because the Canon was committed to memory during the first centuries of Christianity.

The TROPER is a musical service book in which are collected words by "uninspired authors," i.e., nonscriptural, which were set to music and inserted or "farsed" at certain points in the order of the Mass. These interpolations, known as tropes, were chosen for their appropriateness to the season or the feast being celebrated, in the nature of a commentary or elucidation. There was some parallel to this practice in the Eastern Church, but it was infrequent in the West until about the ninth century. It may have been one of the many contributions to the musical liturgy of the abbey at St. Gall, notable from the seventh to the twelfth centuries as a center of activity in that field.

NOTES

1. For a concise and authoritative discussion of the history of various types of liturgical and devotional books and their frequently complicated interrelationships, cf. A. Cabrol, *The Books of the Latin Liturgy* (London: Sands & Co., 1932). E. J. Thiel, "Die liturgischen Bücher des Mittelalters," *Aus dem Antiquariat X, Börsenblatt für den Deutschen Buchhandel 83,* 17 October, 1967, pp. 2379–95. C. Wordsworth, and H. Littlehales, *The Old Service Books of the English Church* (London: Methuen, 1904), is a detailed account of English manuscript and printed service books.

2. A. Franz, *Die kirchliche Benediktionen im Mittelalters* (Freiburg i. B. - St. Louis: Herder, 1909).

3. V. Leroquais, *Les livres d'heures manuscrits de la Bibliothèque Nationale,* 2 vols. (Paris: Mâcon, Protat, 1927).

4. .*Ibid.,* 1:vi.

5. V. Leroquais, *Les Bréviaires manuscrits des bibliothèques publiques de France,* 5 vols. (Paris: Mâcon, Protat, 1939).

6. *Ibid., Les Sacramentaires et les missels manuscrits des bibliothèques publiques de France,* 4 vols. (Paris: Mâcon, Protat, 1924).

7. *Ibid., Les Pontificaux manuscrits des bibliothèques publiques de France,* 4 vols (Paris: Mâcon, Protat, 1937).

8. Cabrol, pp. 49–58.

9. V. Leroquais, *Les Psautiers manuscrits des bibliothèques publiques de France,* 3 vols. (Paris: Mâcon, Protat, 1940–41).

10. J. J. Tikkanen, *Die Psalter-Illustration im Mittelalters* (Helsingfors-Leipzig: Drückerei der Finnischen Literatur-Gesellschaft, 1895–1900).

11. Cf. Wordsworth & Littlehales, p. 110.

12. Cf. Leroquais, n. 6.

13. Cf. Cabrol, pp. 69–112

14. L. Duchesne, *Christian Worship: Its Origin and Evolution,* 5th ed. (New York: Macmillan, 1919). *Enciclopedia Cattolica,* Città del Vaticano, 1948, x, cols. 1564 ff.

15. Cf. Grabar-Nordenfalk, *EMP,* p. 128.

Frequently used bibliographical abbreviations:
AB—*Art Bulletin*
ABI—Weitzmann, K. *Ancient Book Illumination*
AM—Boeckler, A. *Abendländische Miniaturen*
BM—Meiss, M. *Painting in the Time of Jean de Berry; The Boucicaut Master.*
BP—Grabar, A. *Byzantine Painting*
CR—Hubert, J., Porcher, J. and Volbach, W. F. *The Carolingian Renaissance*
ECA—Morey, C. R. *Early Christian Art*
"ECM"—Morey, C. R. "Notes on East Christian Miniatures"
EDA—Hubert, J., Porcher, J. and Volbach, W. F. *Europe in the Dark Ages*
EMP—Grabar, A. and Nordenfalk, C. *Early Medieval Painting*
ENP—Panofsky, E. *Early Netherlandish Painting*
14th cent.—Meiss, M. *French Painting in the time of Jean de Berry; The Late XIVth Century and the Patronage of the Duke.*
GLP—Thompson, E. M. *An Introduction to Greek and Latin Palaeography*
IAECP—Henry, F. *Irish Art in the Early Christian Period*
IAVI—Henry, F. *Irish Art during the Viking Invasions*
IBMAR—Miner, D. *Illuminated Books of the Middle Ages and Renaissance*
IRC—Weitzmann, K. *Illustrations in Roll and Codex*
MA—Morey, C. R. *Mediaeval Art*
MFM—Porcher, J. *Medieval French Miniatures*
MRA—Swarzenski, H. *Monuments of Romanesque Art*
PiBMA—Rickert, M. *Painting in Britain; The Middle Ages*
RP—Grabar, A. and Nordenfalk, C. *Romanesque Painting*
SIM—Wattenbach, W. *Das Schriftwesen im Mittelalter*

Bibliography

Albareda, A. M. Introduction to *Miniatures of the Renaissance.* Vatican City: Apostolic Library, 1950.

Alessandrini, A. "Un prezioso codice Corsiniano di origine francescana (*Speculum humanae salvationis,* ca. 1324–1330)," *Miscellanea Francescana* 57 (1958):420–83.

Alexander, S. M. "Medieval Recipes Describing the use of Metal in Manuscripts," *Marsyas* 12 (1964–1965):34–51.

Allen, T. G. *The Egyptian Book of the Dead, Documents in the Oriental Institute Museum.* Chicago: Oriental Institute, 1960.

Alton, E. H., Meyer, P., and Simms, G. O. *Evangeliorum Quattuor Codex Cenannensis: The Book of Kells.* 3 vols. Olten-Lausanne: Urs Graf Verlag, 1950.

Anderson, A. O. and M. O. *Adomnan's Life of Columba.* Camden: Nelson, 1961.

Avery, M., "The Alexandrian Style at Santa Maria Antiqua," *AB* 7 (1925):131 ff.

———. *The Exultet Rolls of South Italy* (plates only). Princeton: Princeton University Press, 1936.

Battifol, P. *The Amiatinus Codex,* Paris, 1895.

Bauer, A. and Strzygowski, J. *Eine Alexandrinische Weltchronik* (Denkschriften der K. Akademie d. Wissenschaften, Phil.-hist. Kl., li, Abh. 2). Vienna. 1906, pp. 169 ff.

Baumstark, A. "Bild und Liturgie in antiochenischen Evangelienbuchschmuck des 6. Jahrhunderts." *Ehrengabe deutscher Wissenschaft, Johann Georg Herzog von Sachsen gewidmet,* edited by E. Fessler. Freiburg i/B., 1920, pp. 233 ff.

Beissel, S. *Vatikanische Miniaturen.* Freiburg i/B.-St. Louis, Mo.: Herder, 1893.

Bertaux, É. *L'art dans l'Italie méridionale.* Paris: Fontemoing, 1904.

Bethe, E. *Buch und Bild im Altertum.* Leipzig: Harrassowitz, 1945.

Biagi, G. *Reproductions from Illuminated Manuscripts: Fifty Plates from the Laurentiana.* London: Quaritch, 1914.

Bianchi-Bandinelli, R. *Hellenistic-Byzantine Miniatures of the Iliad* (Ilias Ambrosiana). Olten: Urs Graf Verlag, 1955.

Bischoff, B. *Literarisches und Kunstlerisches Leben in St. Emmeram während des frühen und hohen Mittelalters.* Studien und Mitt. zur Geschichte des Benediktiner-Ordens 51 (1933):102–42.

Bloch, H. "Monte Cassino, Byzantium and the West in the Earlier Middle Ages." *Dumbarton Oaks Papers* 3 (1946): 178–87.

Bloch, P. *Die ottonische Kölner Malerschule.* Düsseldorf: Schwann, 1967.

Boeckler, A. *Abendländische Miniaturen bis zum Ausgang der romanische Zeit.* Berlin-Leipzig: Leitzmann, 1950.

———. "Beiträge zur romanischen Kölner Buchmalerei, Mittelalterliche Hss." *Festgabe für H. Degering.* Leipzig: Hiersemann, 1926, pp. 15–28.

———. *Der Codex Wittekindeus.* Leipzig: Harrassowitz, 1938.

———. *Kölner ottonische Buchmalerei.* Beiträge zur Kunst des Mittelalters. Berlin, 1950.

———. "Die Reichenauer Buchmalerei—Die Kultur der Abtei Reichenau." *Erinnerungschrift zur 1200. Wiederkehr des Grundungs-jahres des Inselklosters.* Munich, 1925, pp. 956–98.

——— and Schmid, A. A. "Die Buchmalerei." *Handbuch der Bibliothekswissenschaft* 1:249–387. Stuttgart: K. F. Koehler Verlag, 1950.

Bognetti, G. P., de Capitani d'Arzago, A. and Chierici, G. *Santa Maria di Castelseprio.* Milan: Fondazione Treccani, 1948.

Boissonade, J. F., ed. *Choricii Gazaei orationes,* etc. Paris, 1846.

Boutemy, A. "La miniature (viiie-xiie)." *L'Histoire de l'Église en Belgique* 2. Brussels, 1946.

———. "Le style franco-saxon, style de Saint-Amand." *Scriptorium* 3 (1949):260–64.

———. "Un grand enlumineur du xme siècle: l'abbé Odbert

de Saint-Bertin." *Annales de la Federation archéologique et historique de la Belgique* 37 (1947):247 ff.

Boyle, L. E. "The Emergence of Gothic Handwriting." *The Year 1200* 2 New York: Metropolitan Museum, 1970, pp. 175–183.

Byvanck, A. W. *De middeleeuwsche Boekillustratie in de noordlijke Nederlanden.* Antwerp: De Sikkel, 1943.

————. *La miniature dans les Pays-Bas septentrionaux.* Paris: Van Oest, 1937.

Buberl, P. "Die romanische Malereien im Kloster Nonnberg." *Kunstgeschicht. Jahrb. der K. K. Zentralkommission* 3 (1909):25–40.

Buchtal, H. *The Miniatures of the Paris Psalter: A Study in Middle Byzantine Painting.* London: Warburg Institute, 1938.

Bühler, C. F. *The Fifteenth-Century Book.* Philadelphia: University of Pennsylvania Press, 1960.

Burnam, J. M. *A Classic Technology Edited from Codex Lucensis 490.* Boston: R. G. Badger, 1920.

Cabrol, A. *The Books of the Latin Liturgy.* London: Sands & Co., 1932.

Cockerell, S. C. *The Gorleston Psalter.* London: Chiswick Press, 1907.

————. *The Work of W. de Brailes.* Cambridge: Roxburghe, 1930.

———— and James, M. R. *A Book of Old Testament Illustrations . . . in the Pierpont Morgan Library.* Cambridge: Roxburghe, 1927; reprinted with a foreword by J. Plummer, in color facsimile. New York: Braziller, 1970.

————. *Two East Anglian Psalters at the Bodleian Library.* Oxford: Roxburghe, 1926.

Codices e Vaticanis selecti 1. *Fragmenta et picturae Vergiliana Codicis Vatic. lat. 3225.* 2nd ed. Rome: Vatican, 1930.

———— 2. *Picturae Ornamentate complure scripturae specimina. Cod. Vat. lat. 3867.* Rome: Vatican, 1902.

———— 3. *Le miniature del Pontificale Ottoboniano. Cod. Vat. Ottob. 501.* Rome: Luigi Moretti, 1903.

———— 5. *Il Rotulo di Giosuè.* Rome: Vatican, 1905.

———— 8. *Il Menologio di Basilio II.* Turin, 1907.

———— 15. *Codicis Vergiliani qui Augusteus apellatur reliquiae quam simillime expressae . . . prefatus est.* Turin, 1926.

Collezione paleografica Vaticana 1. *Le Miniature della Bibbia Cod. Vat. Palat. gr. 1 e del Salterio Cod. Vat. Palat. gr. 381.* Rome, 1905.

Coor-Achenbach, G. "Contributions to the Study of Ugolino di Nerio's Art. *AB* 37 (1955):153–65.

Coppier, A.-C. "Le rôle artistique et social des orfèvres-graveurs français au Moyen-Age." *Gazette des Beaux-Arts* 79 (1937):270–71.

Cox, T. *Jehan Fouquet, Native of Tours.* London: Faber & Faber, 1931.

Curtius, E. R. *European Literature and the Latin Middle Ages.* New York: Harper Torchbooks, 1963.

D'Ancona, M. L. "Some new attributions to Lorenzo Monaco." *AB* 40 (1958):175–91.

D'Ancona, P. *La miniatura fiorentina.* 2 vols. Florence: Olschki, 1914.

————. *La miniature italienne du xᵉ au xviᵉ siècle.* Paris: Van Oest, 1925.

———— and Aeschlimann, E. *Dictionnaire des miniaturistes du Moyenáge et de la Renaissance.* 2nd ed. Milan: Hoepli, 1949.

Degering, H. and Boeckler, A. *Die Quedlinburger Itala-fragmente.* Berlin: Cassiodor-Gesellschaft 1, 1932.

Delaissé, L. M. J. *A Century of Dutch Illuminated Manuscripts.* Berkeley: University of California Press, 1968.

————. *La miniature flamande. Le mécénat de Philippe le Bon.* Brussels: Bibliothèque Royale, 1959.

————. *Miniatures médiévales.* Geneva: Deux-Mondes, 1959.

Delisle, L. and Meyer, P. *L'Apocalypse en français au xiiiᵉ siècle.* Paris: Société des anciens textes français, 1901.

Deuchler, F. *Der Ingeborgpsalter.* Berlin: Walter de Gruyter, 1967.

DeWald, E. T. *The Illustrations of the Utrecht Psalter.* Princeton: Princeton University Press, 1933.

Dodwell, C. R. *The Canterbury School of Illumination.* Cambridge: Cambridge University Press, 1954.

————. *The Great Lambeth Bible.* London: Faber & Faber, 1959.

———— and Turner, D. H. *Reichenau Reconsidered.* London: Warburg Institute Survey 2, 1965.

Dominguez Bordona, J. *Spanish Illumination.* 2 vols. Florence: Pantheon, 1930.

————. *Exposiçion de codices miniados españoles.* Madrid: Sociedad española de amigos del arte, 1929.

Donati, L. "A Manuscript of 'Meditationes Johannis de Turrecremata (1469)." *The Library Chronicle* 21. University of Pennsylvania (1955):51–60.

Du Cange, D. *Glossarium medie et infimae latinitatis.* Paris: Firmin Didot, 1845.

Duchesne, L. *Christian Worship: Its Origin and Evolution.* 5th ed. New York: Macmillan, 1919.

Dufrenne, S. "Les copies anglaises du Psautier d'Utrecht." *Scriptorium* 18 (1964):185–97.

Durrieu, P. *Heures de Turin.* Paris, 1902.

————. "Jacques Coene." *Arts anciens de Flandre* 2 (1905): 5 ff.

————. "Les Heures du Maréchal de Boucicaut du Musée Jacquemart-André." *Revue de l'Art Chrétien* 63 (1913): 73 ff., 145 ff., 300 ff.; 64 (1914):28 ff.

————. "Le Maître des Heures du Maréchal de Boucicaut." *Revue de l'art ancien et moderne* 19 (1906):401–15; 20 (1906):21–35.

————. "Michelino da Besozzo et les relations entre l'art français à l'époque du regne de Charles VI." *Mémoires de l'Academie des Inscriptions et Belles-lettres* 38, pt. 2 (1911):365–93.

Durrow, Book of. Cf. Luce, Meyer et al. *Evangeliorum Quattuor Codex Durmachensis.*

Dvořák, M. "Die Illuminatoren des Johann von Neumarkt." *Jahrb. der Kunsthist. Slgen. des Allerh. Kaiserhauses* 22 (1901):35–126.

Egbert, D. D. *The Tickhill Psalter and Related Manuscripts.* New York: New York Public Library, 1940.

Engelbregt, J. *Het Utrechts Psalterium, een Eeuw Wettenschappelijke Bestudering (1860–1960).* Utrecht: Haentjens Dekker & Gumbert, 1964.

Ehl, H. *Die ottonische Kölner Buchmalerei.* Forschungen zur Kunstgeschichte Westeuropas iv. Bonn-Leipzig: Schröder, 1922.

Enciclopedia Cattolica. Città del Vaticano 10 (1948), cols. 1564 ff.

English Romanesque Illumination. Oxford: Bodleian Library, 1951.

Fava, D. "Libri membranacei stampati in Italia nel Quattrocento." *Gutenberg-Jahrbuch* 12 (1937):55–84.

Formaggio, D. and Basso, C. *La Miniatura.* Novara: Istituto Geografica de Agostini, 1960.

Forsythe, W. H. "A Head from a Royal Effigy." *The Metropolitan Museum of Art Bulletin,* n.s. 3 (1945):214 ff.

Fox, C. *Pattern and Purpose—A Survey of Early Celtic Art in Britain.* Cardiff: National Museum of Wales, 1958.

Frankl, P. *Gothic Architecture.* Baltimore: Penguin, 1962.

Frantz, M. A. "Byzantine Illuminated Ornament." *AB* 16 (1934):73–95.

Franz, A. *Die Kirchliche Benediktionen im Mittelalters.* Freiburg i/B-St. Louis, Mo.: Herder, 1909.

Friend, A. M., Jr. "The Canon Tables of the Book of Kells." *Mediaeval Studies in memory of Arthur Kingsley Porter* 2. Cambridge, Mass.: Harvard University Press, 1939, pp. 611–66.

————. "Carolingian Art in the Abbey of Saint-Denis." *Art Studies* 1 (1923):678 ff.

————. "Notes on two pre-Carolingian ivories." *American Journal of Archaeology,* 2nd ser. 27 (1923):59.

————. "The Portraits of the Evangelists in Greek and Latin Manuscripts" 1. *Art Studies* 5 (1927):115–47; 2. *Art Studies* 7 (1929):3–29.

Garrison, E. B. *Studies in the History of Mediaeval Italian Painting* 1, Florence, 1953.

Gaspar, C. and Lyna, F. *Les principaux manuscrits à peintures de la Bibliothèque Royale de Belgique.* 2 vols. Paris: S.F.R.M.P., 1937–45.

Gaye, G. *Carteggio inedito d'artisti dei secoli xiv, xv, xvi.* vol. 1. Florence, 1839–40.

Gebhardt, O. von. *The Miniatures of the Ashburnham Pentateuch.* London: Asher & Co., 1883.

Gerstinger, H. *Die Wiener Genesis.* Vienna: Dr. B. Filser, 1931.

Giehlow, K. *Kaiser Maximilians I Gebetbuch.* Vienna: Selbstverlag, 1907.

Ginot, M. E. *Le manuscrit de Sainte-Radegonde de Poitiers et ses peintures.* Paris: S.F.R.M.P., 1914–20.

Glixelli, S. *Cinq poèmes des trois morts et des trois vifs.* Paris, 1914.

Goldschmidt, A. *Der Albani Psalter in Hildesheim.* Berlin: G. Siemens, 1895.

————. *Die Elfenbeinskulpturen aus der Zeit der karolingischen und sächsischen Zeit; aus der romanischen Zeit.* 4 vols. Berlin: B. Cassirer, 1914–26.

————. *German Illumination.* 2 vols. Paris-Florence: Pantheon, 1928.

————. "Das Naumburger Lettnerkreuz im Kaiser-Friedrich Museum in Berlin." *Jahrb. der Kghlich. Preussische Kunstslgen* 36 (1915):137–52.

Goldschmidt, E. P. "Preserved for Posterity, Some Remarks on Mediaeval Manuscripts." *The New Colophon* 2 (1950): 330–32.

————. *The Printed Book of the Renaissance.* Cambridge: Cambridge University Press, 1950.

Gorissen, F. "Jan Maelwael und die Bruder Limburg." *Gelre* 54 (1954):153–221.

Grabar, A. *Byzantine Painting.* New York: Skira, 1953.

————. *Les miniatures du Grégoire de Nazianze de l'Ambrosienne.* Paris: Van Oest, 1943.

———— and Nordenfalk, C. *Early Medieval Painting.* New York: Skira, 1957.

————. *Romanesque Painting.* New York: Skira, 1958.

Greene, B. da C. and Harrsen, M. *Exhibition of Illuminated Manuscripts held at the New York Public Library.* Introduction by C. R. Morey. New York: The Pierpont Morgan Library, 1934.

Grodecki, L. et al. *Le vitrail français.* Paris: Deux-Mondes, 1958.

Guignard, J. "La miniature gothique; le Psautier d'Ingeburge." *Art de France* 1 (1960):278–80.

Hahnloser, H. R. *Villard de Honnecourt; Kritische Gesamtausgabe des Bauhüttenbuches,* Vienna: A. Schroll, 1935.

———— and Rücker, F. *Das Müsterbuch von Wolfenbüttel.* Vienna: Wiener Gesellschaft für vervielfältigende Kunst, 1929.

Harrsen, M. "The Countess Judith and the Library of Weingarten." *Papers of the Bibliographical Society of America* 24 (1930):1–13.

Hartel, W. von and Wickhoff, F. "Die Wiener Genesis." *Beilage z. xv u. xvi B. d. Kunsthist. Sammlungen d. A. H. Kaiserhauses.* Vienna, 1895.

Haseloff, A. *Eine thüringische-sächsische Malerschule des 13. Jahrhunderts.* Studien zur deutschen Kunstgeschichte 9. Strasbourg: Heitz, 1897.

———— and Sauerland, H. V. *Der Psalter Erzbischof Egberts von Trier.* Festschrift der Gesellschaft f. nützliche Forschungen. Trier, 1901.

Haskins, C. H. "England and Sicily in the Twelfth Century." *English Historical Review* 26 (1911):43–73.

————. *The Renaissance of the Twelfth Century*. Cambridge, Mass.: Harvard University Press, 1933.

Hassall, A. G. and W. O. *The Douce Apocalypse*. New York: Yoseloff, 1961.

Hawthorne, G. H. and Smith, C. S. *On Divers Arts: The Treatise of Theophilus*. Chicago: University of Chicago Press, 1963.

Hedfors, H., ed. and trans. *Compositiones ad tingenda musiva. . . .* Uppsala, 1932.

Heimann, A. "Der Meister der 'Grandes Heures de Rohan' und seine Werkstatt," *Städel-Jahrbuch* 7/8 (1932):1–61.

Heinemann, F. von. *Die Handschriften der Hzgl. Bibliothek zu Wolfenbüttel* 6, no. 2403, p. 124.

Henry, F. *Irish Art during the Viking Invasions (800–1020 A.D.)*. Ithaca: Cornell University Press, 1967.

————. *Irish Art in the Early Christian Period (to 800 A.D.)*. Ithaca: Cornell University Press, 1965.

Herbert, J. A. *Illuminated Manuscripts*. London: Methuen, 1911.

————. *The Sherburne Missal*. Oxford: Roxburghe Club, 1920.

Hirsch, R. *Printing, Selling and Reading, 1450–1550*. Wiesbaden: Harrassowitz, 1967.

Homburger, O. *Die Anfänge der Malerschule von Winchester im 10. Jahrhundert*. Studien über christliche Denkmäler 12. Leipzig, 1912.

Hubert, J. Porcher, J. and Volbach, W. F. *The Carolingian Renaissance*. New York: Braziller, 1970.

————. *Europe in the Dark Ages*. London: Thames & Hudson, 1969. Also published as *Europe of the Invasions*. New York: Braziller, 1969.

Huizinga, J. *The Waning of the Middle Ages*. Garden City: Doubleday Anchor, 1956.

Inguanez, M. and Avery, M. *Miniature Cassinesi del secolo xi illustranti la vita di S. Benedetto* (dal Cod. lat. 1202). Monte Cassino, 1934.

Jacobi, F. *Die deutsche Buchmalerei in ihren stilistischen Entwicklungsphäsen*. Munich: Brückmann, 1923.

James, M. R. *The Apocalypse in Art*. The Schweich Lectures of the British Academy, 1927. London, 1931.

————. *The Apocalypse in Latin and French* (Bodleian Ms. Douce 180). Oxford: Roxburghe, 1922.

————. *The Bestiary*. Oxford: Roxburghe, 1928.

————. *The Canterbury Psalter*. London: Percy Lund, Humphries & Co., 1934.

————. *Catalogue of Manuscripts and Printed Books . . . forming Portion of the Library of J. Pierpont Morgan*. London: Chiswick Press, 1906–7.

————. "The Drawings of Matthew Paris." *Walpole Society* 14 (1925–26).

————. *The Trinity College Apocalypse*. Introduction and description by P. H. Brieger. 2 vols. London: Eugrammia Press, 1967.

————. and Millar, E. G. *The Bohun Manuscripts*. Oxford: Roxburghe, 1936.

Jantzen, H. *Ottonische Kunst*. Munich: Münchener Verlag, 1946.

Jones, L. W. and Morey, C. R. *The Miniatures of the Manuscripts of Terence*. 2 vols. Princeton: Princeton University Press, 1930–31.

Kantorowicz, E. H. "The Carolingian King in the Bible of San Paolo fuori le Mura." *Late Classical and Mediaeval Studies in honor of A. M. Friend*. Princeton: Princeton University Press, 1955, pp. 287–300.

Karlinger, H. *Die Kunst der Gotik*. Berlin: Propyläen Verlag, 1926.

Katterbach, B. *Le miniature dell' Evangeliario di Padova*. Rome: Danesi, 1931.

Kauffman, C. M. *The Baths of Pozzuoli*. Oxford: B. Cassirer, 1959.

————. "The Bury Bible." *Journal of the Warburg and Courtauld Institutes* 29 (1966):60–81.

Keck, A. S. "Observations on the Iconography of Joshua." *AB* 32 (1950):267–74.

Kells, Book of. Cf. Alton, Meyer and Simms. *Evangeliorum Quattuor Codex Cennanensis*.

Kendrick, T. D., Brown, T. V., Bruce-Mitford, R. L. S., Roosen-Runge, H., Ross, A. S. C., Stanley, E. G. and Warner, A. E. A. *Evangeliorum Quattuor Codex Lindisfarnensis*. *The Book of Lindisfarne*. 2 vols. Olten-Lausanne: Urs Graf, 1956–60.

Koehler, W. "Byzantine Art in the West." *Dumbarton Oaks Papers* 1 (1941):63–87.

————. *Die Karolingischen Miniaturen* 1, *Die Schule von Tours*. 3 vols. Berlin: Deutscher Verein für Kunstwissenschaft, 1930–33; 2, *Die Hofschule Karls des Grossen*. 2 vols. Berlin (*ibid.*), 1958: 3, *Die Gruppe des Wiener Krönungsevangeliars. Metzer Handschriften*. 2 vols. Berlin (*idem.*), 1960.

————. "Die Tradition der Ada-Gruppe und die Anfänge des ottonischen Stils in der Buchmalerei." *Festschrift zu 60. Geburtstage von Paul Clemen*. Bonn, 1926, pp. 255–72.

Kühn, C. "Herman Scheerre and English Illumination of the Early Fifteenth Century." *AB* 22 (1940):138 ff.

Kunst des frühen Mittelalters. Berne: Kunstmuseum, 1949.

Laborde, A. de. *Étude sur la Bible moralisée*. 5 vols. Paris: S.F.R.M.P., 1911–25.

Lassaigne, J. *Flemish Painting—The Century of Van Eyck*. New York: Skira, 1957.

Latil, A. M. *Le miniature nei rotoli dell' Exultet: Documenti per la storia della miniatura in Italia* 3. Monte Cassino, 1899–1901.

Lawlor, H. J. and Lindsay, W. M. "The Cathach of St. Columba." *Proceedings of the Royal Irish Academy*, 1916, pp. 241 ff.

Lehane, B. *The Quest of Three Abbots*. New York: Viking, 1968.

Lehman-Haupt, H. and Ives, S. A. *An English Thirteenth-Century Breviary.* New York: H. P. Kraus, 1942.

Leroquais, Abbé V. *Les bréviaires manuscrits des bibliothèques publiques de France.* 5 vols. Paris: Mâcon Protat, 1939.

————. *Les livres d'heures manuscrits de la bibliothèque nationale.* 2 vols., Mâcon (Protat), 1927.

————. *Les pontificaux manuscrits des bibliothèques publiques de France.* 4 vols., Paris (Mâcon Protat), 1937.

————. *Les psautiers manuscrits latins des bibliothèques publiques de France.* 3 vols., Mâcon (Protat), 1940–1941.

————. *Les sacramentaires et les missels manuscrits des bibliothèques de France.* 4 vols., Paris (Mâcon Protat), 1924.

Leidinger, G., *Albrecht Dürers und Lukas Cranachs Randzeichnungen zum Gebetbuch Kaiser Maximilians I.* Munich (Riehn & Reusch), 1922.

————. *Der Codex Aureus der Bayerischen Staatsbibliothek in München.* 6 vols., Munich (Hugo Schmidt), 1921–1925.

————. *Das sog. Evangeliarum Kaiser Ottos III* (Miniaturen aus Handschriften der Kgl. Hof-und Staatsbibliothek i). Munich (Riehn & Tietze), 1912.

————. *Das Perikopenbuch Kaiser Heinrichs II* (Miniaturen aus Handschriften der Kgl. Hof-und Staatsbibliothek v). Munich (Riehn & Tietze), n.d.

Lejard, A. *Les tapisseries de l'Apocalypse de la Cathédrale d'Angers.* Paris: A. Michel, 1942.

Lethaby, W. R. "The Painted Book of Genesis in the British Museum." *Archaeological Journal* 69 (1912):88 ff.; 70 (1913):162 ff.

Levi, D. "Allegories of the Months in Classical Art." *AB* 23 (1941):251–91.

————. *Antioch Mosaic Pavements.* Princeton: Princeton University Press, 1947.

La librairie de Charles V. Edited by M. Thomas. Paris: Bibliothèque Nationale, 1968.

La librairie de Philippe le Bon. Edited by G. Dogaer and M. Debae. Brussels: Bibliothèque Royale, 1967.

Liebmann, C. J. "Arts and Letters in the reign of Philip Augustus of France: The Political Background." *The Year 1200* 2:1–6.

Lindisfarne, Book of. Cf. Kendrick et al. *Evangeliorum Quatuor Codex Lindisfarnensis.*

Loerke, W. "The Miniatures of the Trial in the Rossano Gospels." *AB* 42 (1961):171–95.

Löffler, K. *Der Landgrafenpsalter.* Leipzig: Hiersemann, 1925.

Lowe, E. A. *The Beneventan Script.* Oxford: Clarendon, 1914.

————. "The 'Script of Luxeuil'—A Title Vindicated." *Revue Benedictine* (1953), pp. 132–42.

Luce, A. A., Simms, O., Meyer, P. and Bieler, C. *Evangeliorum Quattuor Codex Durmachensis. The Book of Durrow.* 2 vols. Olten-Lausanne: Urs Graf, 1960.

Lutz, J. and Perdrizet, P. *Speculum humanae salvationis. Texte critique—les sources et l'influence iconographique.* 4 vols. Mulhouse: E. Meininger, 1907–9.

Magnani, L. *Le miniature del Sacramentario d'Ivrea.* Vatican City: Biblioteca Apostolica, 1934.

Mâle, É. *L'art religieux de la fin du Moyen-âge en France.* Paris: Colin, 1931.

————. *The Gothic Image.* New York: Harper Torchbooks, 1958.

Manitius, M. *Handschriften antiken Autoren in mittelalterlichen Bibliothekskatalogen.* Edited by Karl Manitius. Leipzig: Harrassowitz, 1935.

Mansi, G. D. *Sacrorum conciliorum nova,* xix, *Concilium Lemovicensis* 2, 1031, col. 521, D-E.

Les manuscrits à peintures du viie au xiie siècle. Paris: Bibliothèque Nationale, 1954.

Les manuscrits à peintures du xiiie au xvie siècle. Paris: Bibliothèque Nationale, 1955.

Martin, H. *La miniature française du xiiie au xve siècle.* Paris-Brussels: Van Oest, 1923.

————. *Les miniaturistes français.* Paris: H. Leclerq, 1906.

McCulloch, F. "The Funeral of Renart the Fox." *Journal of the Walters Art Gallery* 25–26 (1962–63):9–27.

MsGurk, P. "The Irish Pocket Gospel Books." *Sacris Erudiri* 8 (1956):249 ff.

————. *Latin Gospel-books from* A.D. *400 to* A.D. *800.* Paris-Brussels-Antwerp-Amsterdam: Érasme, 1961.

Meiss, M. *French Painting in the time of Jean de Berry: The Late XIV Century and the Patronage of the Duke.* 2 vols. London-New York: Phaidon, 1968.

————. *French Painting in the time of Jean de Berry; The Boucicaut Master.* London-New York: Phaidon, 1968.

————. *Painting in Florence and Siena after the Black Death.* Princeton: Princeton University Press, 1951.

————. (Preface); Lognon, J., Cazelles, R. (Introduction and legends). *The Très Riches Heures of Jean, Duke of Berry.* New York: Braziller, 1969.

Merrifield, M. P. *Original Treatises on the Arts of Painting.* 2 vols. London: J. Murray, 1849.

Merton, A. *Die Buchmalerei in St. Gallen.* 2nd ed. Leipzig: Hiersemann, 1923.

Metz, P. *The Golden Gospels of Echternach.* London: Thames & Hudson, 1957.

Micheli, G. L. *L'enluminure du haute Moyen-âge et les influences irlandaises.* Brussels: Editions de la Connaissance, 1939.

Millar, E. G. "Additional Miniatures by W. de Brailes." *Journal of the Walters Art Gallery* 2 (1939):106–9.

————. *English Illuminated Manuscripts from the Xth to the XIIIth Century.* Paris-Brussels: Van Oest, 1926.

————. *English Illuminated Manuscripts of the XIVth and XVth Centuries.* Paris-Brussels: Van Oest, 1928.

————. *The Luttrell Psalter.* London: British Museum, 1932.

————. *The Parisian Miniaturist Honoré.* New York: Yoseloff, 1959.

————. *The Rutland Psalter.* Oxford: Roxburghe, 1937.

Miner, D. "Dutch Illuminated Manuscripts in the Walters Gallery." *The Connoisseur Yearbook* (1955), pp. 66–77.

————. *Illuminated Books of the Middle Ages and Renaissance.* Baltimore: Walters Art Gallery, 1949.

———— and Verdier, P., eds. *The International Style.* Baltimore: Walters Art Gallery, 1962.

Mitchell, S. *Medieval Manuscript Painting.* New York: Viking, 1965.

Morand, K. *Jean Pucelle.* Oxford: Clarendon, 1962.

Morey, C. R. "The 'Byzantine Renaissance'." *Speculum* 14 (1939):139–59.

————. "Castelseprio and the Byzantine 'Renaissance.'" *AB* 34 (1952):173–201.

————. *Early Christian Art.* 3rd ed. Princeton: Princeton University Press, 1953.

————. *Mediaeval Art.* New York: Norton, 1942.

————. *The Mosaics of Antioch.* London, New York and Toronto: Longmans, Green, 1938.

————. "Notes on East Christian Miniatures." *AB* 11 (1929): 4–103.

————. "The Sources of Mediaeval Styles." *AB* 7 (1924):35–50.

Morison, S. *The Art of Printing.* New York: Diament Typographic Service, 1945.

Mostra storica nazionale della miniatura. Florence: Sansoni, 1954.

Muñoz, A. *Il codice purpureo di Rossano ed il frammento Sinopense.* Rome: Danesi, 1907.

Naville, E. H. *Das Aegyptische Todtenbuch der xviii-xx Dynastie.* 3 vols. Berlin: A. Asher, 1886.

Neuss, W. *Die Apokalypse des hl. Johannes in der altspanischen und altchristlichen Bibel-Illustration.* Spanische Forschungen der Görresgesellschaft 2–3. Münster i. W., 1931.

————. *Die katalanische Bibelillustration um die Wende des ersten Jahrtausends und die altspanische Buchmalerei.* Veröffentl. d. roman. Auslands-Instituts d. Rhein, Bonn iii. Bonn-Leipzig: Schröder, 1922.

Niver, C. "The Psalter in the British Museum, Harley 2904." *Mediaeval Studies in Memory of A. Kingsley Porter* 2. Cambrdige, Mass.: Harvard University Press, 1939, pp. 681–87.

Nordenfalk, C. "An Illustrated Diatesseron." *AB* 50 (1968): 119–140.

————. "Before the Book of Durrow." *Acta Archaeologica* 18 (1947):141–74.

————. "Eastern Style Elements in the Book of Lindisfarne." *Acta Archaeologica* 13 (1942):157–69.

————. "En senantik initialhandskrift." *Konsthistorisk Tidskrift* 6 (1957):117–27.

————. "Insulare und kontinentale Psalter-Illustrationen aus dem xiii. Jahrhundert." *Acta Archaeologica* 10 (1939): 107–20.

————. "Maître Honoré and Maître Pucelle." *Apollo* 79 (1964):359 ff.

————. "Der Meister des Registrum Gregorii." *Münchener Jahrbuch der Bildenden Kunst,* 3d ser. 1 (1950):61–77.

————. "A Note on the Stockholm *Codex Aureus,*" *Nordisk Tidskrift för Bok-och Biblioteksväsen* 38 (1951):145–56.

————. *Die spätantiken Kanontafeln.* Göteborg: O. Isacsons, 1938.

Oakeshott, W. *The Artists of the Winchester Bible.* London: Faber & Faber, 1945.

————. *The Sequence of English Medieval Art.* London: Faber & Faber, 1950.

O'Connor, R. B. "The Mediaeval History of the Double-Axe Motif." *American Journal of Archaeology,* 2d ser. 24 (1920):151–70.

Omont, H. *Évangiles avec peintures byzantines du xie siècle.* 2 vols. Paris: Berthaud, 1908.

————. "Miniatures des homilies sur la Vierge du moine Jacques." *Bulletin de la S. F. R. M. P.* 11, 1927.

————. *Psautier de Saint-Louis, Ms. lat. 10525 de la Bibliothèque Nationale* (reproduction intégrale). Paris: Bibliothèque Nationale, 1902.

Oursel, C. *La miniature du xiie siècle à l'abbaye de Cîteaux.* Dijon: L. Venot, 1926.

Pächt, O. "A Giottesque Episode in English Mediaeval Art." *Journal of the Warburg and Courtauld Institutes* 6 (1943):51 ff.

————. *The Master of Mary of Burgundy.* London: Faber & Faber, 1948.

————. "Un tableau de Jacquemart de Hesdin?" *Revue des Arts* 6 (1956):149–60.

Pächt, O., Dodwell, C. R. and Wormald, F. *The St. Albans Psalter.* London: Warburg Institute, 1960.

Panofsky, D. "The Textual Basis of the Utrecht Psalter." *AB* 25 (1943):50–58.

Panofsky, E. *Albrecht Dürer.* 2 vols. Princeton: Princeton University Press, 1943: 3d ed. 1948.

————. *Early Netherlandish Painting.* 2 vols. Cambridge, Mass.: Harvard University Press, 1953.

————. *Gothic Architecture and Scholasticism.* New York: Meridian, 1958.

Perls, K. *Jean Fouquet.* Paris: Hyperion, 1940.

Plummer, J. *The Hours of Catherine of Cleves.* New York: Braziller, 1966.

————. *Manuscripts from the William S. Glazier Collection.* New York: The Pierpont Morgan Library, 1959.

Plummer, J. et al. *The Book of Hours of Catherine of Cleves.* New York: The Pierpont Morgan Library, 1964.

Pollard, A. W. "Woodcut Designs for Illuminators in Venetian Books, 1469–1473." *Bibliographica* 3 (1897):122 ff.

Porcher, J. *Les Belles Heures de Jean de France, Duc de Berry.* Paris: Bibliothèque Nationale, 1953.

————. *L'enluminure française,* Paris: Arts et Métiers graphiques, 1959.

————. *Jean Lebègue, les histoires que l'on peut raisonnablement faire sur les livres de Salluste.* Paris, 1962.

————. *Medieval French Miniatures.* New York: Abrams, 1959.

————. *The Rohan Book of Hours.* New York: Yoseloff, 1959.

————. *Le sacramentaire de Saint-Étienne de Limoges.* Paris: Nomis, 1953.

Premerstein, A. v., Wessely, K. and Montuani, J. *Dioscurides, Codex Aniciae Julianae picturis illustratis, nunc Vindob. Med. gr. I.* Codices Graeci et Latini photogr. depicti, 10. Leipzig, 1906.

Prochno, J. *Das Schreiber-und Dedikationsbild in der deutschen Buchmalerei bis zum Ende des 11. Jahrhunderts.* Berlin, 1929.

Rand, E. K. *A Survey of the Manuscripts of Tours.* 2 vols. Cambridge, Mass.: Mediaeval Academy of America, 1929.

———— and Jones, L. W. *The Earliest Book of Tours.* Cambridge, Mass.: Mediaeval Academy of America, 1934.

Randall, L. M. C. "Exempla as a source of Gothic Marginal Illumination." *AB* 39 (1957):97–107.

————. *Images in the Margins of Gothic Manuscripts.* Berkeley-Los Angeles: University of California Press, 1966.

————. "The Snail in Gothic Marginal Warfare." *Speculum* 37 (1962):358–67.

Rickert, M. *Painting in Britain: The Middle Ages.* Baltimore: Penguin, 1954.

————. *The Reconstructed English Carmelite Missal.* Chicago: University of Chicago Press, 1952.

————. Review of Friederich Gorissen. "Jan Maelwael und die Brüder Limburg." *AB* 39 (1957):73–77.

Robb, D. M. "The Iconography of the Annunciation in the Fourteenth and Fifteenth Centuries." *AB* 18 (1936): 480–526.

———— and Garrison, J. J. *Art in the Western World.* 4th ed. New York: Harper & Row, 1963.

Roberts, C. H. "The Codex." *Proceedings of the British Academy* 40 (1954):169–204.

Roosen-Runge, H. *Farbgebung und Technik frühmittelalterliche Buchmalerei.* 2 vols. Munich-Berlin: Deutscher Kunstverl. 4, Kunstwissenschaftliche Studien, bd. 38. 1967.

Rorimer, J. J. Introduction *The Hours of Jeanne d'Evreux.* New York: Metropolitan Museum, 1957.

Ross, J. D. A. "Methods of Book Production in a xivth Century French Miscellany (London, B.M., Ms. Royal 19. D. 1.)," *Scriptorium* 6 (1952):63–75.

Roy, E. "Le mystère de la Passion en France." *Revue Bourguignonne de l'enseignement supérieure* 13–14.

Salmi, M. *La miniatura italiana.* Milan: Electa Editrice, 1956.

Saxl, F. and Meier, H. *Verzeichnis astrologischer und mythologischer illustrierter Handschriften des lateinischen Mittelalters 3. Handschriften in englischen Bibliotheken.* Edited by H. Bober. Heidelberg: C. Winter, 1953.

———— and Wittkower, R. *British Art and the Mediterranean.* London: Oxford University Press, 1948.

Sethe, K. *Die Totenliteratur der alten Ägypter; Die Geschichte einer Sitte.* Sitzungsber. Preuss. Akad. Phil.-hist. Kl. Berlin, 1931, pp. 520 ff.

Scato de Vries and Morpurgo, S. *Il breviario Grimani della Biblioteca di San Marco in Venezia.* Leyden: Sijthoff, 1904–10.

Schapiro, M. "The Image of the Disappearing Christ; The Ascension in English Art around the year 1000." *Gazette des Beaux-Arts* 23 (1943):135–52.

————. *The Parma Ildefonsus.* New York: New York University Press, 1964.

Schramm, P. E. *Die deutschen Kaiser und Könige in Bildern ihrer Zeit.* Leipzig: W. Götz, 1928–29.

Sillib, R. *Zur Geschichte der grossen Heidelberger Manessischen Liederhandschrift.* Heidelberg: C. Winter, 1921.

Smith, E. B. *Early Christian Iconography and the School of Provence.* Princeton: Princeton University Press, 1918.

Stern, H. *Le Calendrier de 354: étude sur son texte et sur ses illustrations.* Paris: Institut français d'archéologie de Beyrouth, Bibliothèque archéologique et historique 14, 1953.

Stettiner, R. *Die illustrierten Prudentiushandschriften.* 2 vols. Berlin: Preuse, 1895–1905.

Stornaiolo, C. *Le miniature della Topografia Cristiana di Cosma Indicopleuste: codice Vaticano greco 699.* Milan: Hoepli, 1908.

————. *Miniature delle Omilie di Giacomo Monaco.* Codices e Vaticanis selecti, serie minore 1. Rome, 1910.

Strzygowski, J. *Die Calendarbilder des Chronographen vom Jahre 354.* Jahrb. d. Kais. Deutschen Archäolog. Instituts, Erganzungsheft i. Berlin, 1888.

Sudhoff, K. *Beiträge zur Geschichte der Chirurgie im Mittelalter.* 2 vols. Leipzig: J. Barth, 1914–18.

Swarzenski, G. *Die Regensburger Buchmalerei des 10. und 11. Jahrhunderts.* Leipzig: Hiersemann, 1901.

————. *Die Salzburger Malerei von den ersten Anfängen bis zur Blütezeit des romanischen Stils.* Denkmäler der suddeutschen Malerei des frühen Mittelalters 2. Leipzig: Hiersemann, 1913.

Swarzenski, H. *The Berthold Missal and the Scriptorium of Weingarten Abbey.* New York: The Pierpont Morgan Library, 1943.

————. *Early Medieval Illumination.* New York-Toronto: Oxford, Irish Books, 1951.

————. *Monuments of Romanesque Art.* Chicago: University of Chicago Press, 1954.

————. "Unknown Bible Pictures by W. de Brailes." *Journal of the Walters Art Gallery* 1 (1938), pp. 55–69.

————. "The Xanten Purple Leaf and the Carolingian Renaissance." *AB* 22, 1940, pp. 7–24.

Teyssèdre, B. *Le Sacramentaire de Gellone et la figure humaine dans les manuscrits francs du viiie siècle.* Toulouse: E. Privat, 1959.

Thiel, E. J. "Die liturgischen Bücher des Mittelalters," *Aus dem Antiquariat X, Börsenblatt für den Deutschen Buchhandel* 83. 17 October, 1967, pp. 2379–95.

Thiele, G. *Antike Himmelsbilder.* Berlin, 1898.

Thieme, U. and Becker, F. *Allgemeines Lexikon der bildenden Künstler.* Leipzig: W. Engelmann, 1910–50.

Thomas, G. W. C. *The Circle and the Cross.* New York: Abingdon Press, 1964.

Thompson, D. V. *The Materials of Medieval Painting.* London: Allen & Unwin, 1936; reprinted as *The Materials and Techniques of Medieval Painting,* N. Y. (Dover), 1956.

———— and Hamilton, G. H. *De Arte Illuminandi.* New Haven: Yale University Press, 1933.

Thompson, E. M. *An Introduction to Greek and Latin Palaeography.* London: Oxford University Press, 1912.

Thompson, J. W. *The Mediaeval Library.* Chicago (University of Chicago Press), 1939.

Thulin, C. *Die Handschriften des corpus Agrimensorium Romanorum.* 2 vols. Berlin: Teubner, 1913.

Tikkanen, J. J. *Die Genesismosaiken von S. Marco in Venedig und ihr Verhältnis zu den Miniaturen der Cottonbibel.* Acta Societatis Scientiarum Fennicae 17, 1889.

————. *Die Psalterillustrationen im Mittelalter.* Acta Societatis Scientiarum Fennicae 21, no. 5, 1903.

Toesca, B. *Theatrum Sanitatis. Cod. 4182 della R. Bibl. Casanatense.* 2 vols. Rome: Libreria dello Stato, 1940.

Toesca, P. "Michelino da Besozzo e Giovannino dei Grassi." *L'Arte* 8 (1905):321–29.

————. "Miniature romane dei secoli xi e xii; Bibbie miniate." *Rivista del R. Istituto d'Archeologia e Storia dell' Arte* 1 (1929):69–76.

————. *La pittura e la miniatura nella Lombardia.* Milan: Hoepli, 1912; reprint (Einaudi), 1966.

Tovell, R. M. *Flemish Artists of the Valois Courts.* Toronto: University of Toronto Press, 1950.

Trenkler, E. *Livre d'Heures, Handschrift 1855 der Österreichischen Nationalbibliothek.* Vienna: Kunstverlag Wulfrum, 1948.

Tselos, D. "A Greco-Italian School of Illuminators and Fresco Painters." *AB* 38 (1956):1–30.

————. *The Sources of the Utrecht Psalter Miniatures.* Minneapolis, 1955.

Turner, D. H. "Manuscript Illumination." *The Year 1200* 2: 133–70.

Ullman, B. L. *Ancient Writing.* New York: Longmans, Green, 1932.

Underwood, P. "The Fountain of Life in Manuscripts of the Gospels." *Dumbarton Oaks Papers* 5 (1950):43–138.

Valentine, L. N. *Ornament in Medieval Manuscripts.* London: Faber & Faber, 1965.

Van den Gheyn, J. *Le psautier de Peterborough.* Haarlem: Musée des Enluminures, 1905.

Van Marle, R. *Simone Martini et les peintres de son école.* Strasbourg: Heitz, 1920.

Van Moé, E. A. *L'Apocalypse de Saint-Sever.* Paris: Editions de Cluny, 1942.

Van Moé, J. "Les Fouquet de Chantilly." *Verve* 2 (1942):5–6; 3 (1945):11, 12.

Vita Caroli Magni (Life of Charlemagne). Foreword by S. Painter. Ann Arbor: University of Michigan Press Paperback, 1960.

Vitry, P. and Brière, G. *L'eglise abbatiale de Saint-Denis et ses tombeaux.* Paris: Longuet, 1925.

Vitzthum von Eckstädt, B. G. v. *Die Pariser Miniaturmalerei von der Zeit des hl. Ludwig bis zu Philippe von Valois und ihr Verhältnis zur Malerei in Nordwesteuropa.* Leipzig: Quelle & Meyer, 1907.

Volbach, W. F. *Early Christian Art.* London: Thames & Hudson, 1961.

Warner, G. F. *The Gospels of Mathilda, Countess of Tuscany.* New York: Roxburghe, 1917.

————. *Queen Mary's Psalter.* London: H. Hart, 1912.

———— and Wilson, H. A. *The Benedictional of Aethelwold.* Oxford: Roxburghe, 1910.

Wattenbach, W. *Das Schriftwesen im Mittelalter.* 4th ed. Graz: Akad. Druck-u. Verlagsanstalt, 1958.

Weale, W. H. et al. "Exposition of Images—the Belleville Breviary." *A Descriptive Catalogue of the Second Series of Fifty Manuscripts in the Collection of Henry Yates Thompson.* Cambridge: Cambridge University Press, 1902, pp. 365–68; reprinted in Holt, E. G. *A Documentary History of Art* 1. Garden City: Doubleday Anchor, 1957, pp. 129–34.

Webster, J. C. *The Labors of the Months in Antique and Mediaeval Art.* Princeton: Princeton University Press, 1938.

Weitzmann, K. *Ancient Book Illumination.* Cambridge: Harvard University Press, 1959.

————. *Die byzantinischen Buchmalerei des 9. und 10. Jahrhunderts.* Berlin: Mann, 1935.

————. *The Fresco Cycle of Santa Maria di Castelseprio.* Princeton: Princeton University Press, 1951.

————. "Die Illustrationen d. Septuaginta." *Münchener Jahrb. d. bildenden Kunst.* 3d Ser. 3/4, 1952–53.

————. *Illustrations in Roll and Codex.* Princeton: Princeton University Press, 2nd ed., 1970.

————. *The Joshua Roll: A Work of the Macedonian Renaissance.* Princeton: Princeton University Press, 1948.

————. *Studies in Classical and Byzantine Manuscript Illumination.* Edited by H. L. Kessler, ed., Chicago: University of Chicago Press, 1971.

Wellesz, E. *The Vienna Genesis*. New York: Yoseloff, 1960.

Werkmeister, O.-K. *Irisch-northumbrische Buchmalerei des 8. Jahrhunderts und monastische Spiritualität*. Berlin: Walter de Gruyter, 1967.

Wescher, P. *Jean Fouquet and his Times*. New York: Reynal & Hitchcock, 1947.

White, H. J. "The Codex Amiatinus and its Birthplace." *Studio Biblica* 2 (1890):283 ff.

White, T. H. *The Bestiary—A Book of Beasts*. New York: Capricorn Books—Putnam, 1960.

Wilmart, A. "Les livres de l'abbé Odbert," *Bulletin de la Société des Antiquaires de la Morinie* 14 (1924), pp. 169–80.

de Wit, J. *Die Miniaturen des Vergilius Vaticanus*. Amsterdam: Swets-Zeitlinger, 1959.

———. "Vergilius Vaticanus und nordafrikanische Mosaiken." *Mnemosyne* 3a, ser. 3 (1933–1934):217 ff.

Wixom, W. D. *Treasures from Medieval France*. Cleveland: Cleveland Museum of Art, 1967.

Wolfe, E. II. *A Descriptive Catalogue of the John Frederick Lewis Collection of European Manuscripts*. Philadelphia: Philadelphia Free Public Library, 1937.

Woodruff, H. "The Illustrated Manuscripts of Prudentius." *Art Studies* 7 (1929), pp. 33 ff.

Wordsworth, C. and Littlehales, H. *The Old Service Books of the English Church*. London: Methuen, 1904.

Wormald, F. *The Benedictional of St. Ethelwold*. New York: Yoseloff, 1959.

———. "Decorated Initials in English Manuscripts from A.D. 900 to 1100." *Archaeologia* 91 (1945):107–35.

———. *English Drawings of the 10th and 11th Centuries*. London: Faber & Faber, 1952.

———. *The Miniatures in the Gospels of St. Augustine. Corpus Christi College, Ms. 286*. Cambridge: Cambridge University Press, 1954.

———. "The Monastic Library." *The Year 1200* 2 (1970): 169–74.

———. "Some illustrated manuscripts of the Lives of the Saints." *Bulletin of the John Rylands Library* (Manchester, 1952), pp. 248 ff.

———. "The Survival of Anglo-Saxon Illumination after the Norman Conquest." *Proceedings of the British Academy* 30 (1944):127–45.

——— and Giles, P. M. "A Handlist of the Additional Manuscripts in the Fitzwilliam Museum." *Transactions of the Cambridge Bibliographical Society* 3 (1951):197–207.

Wright, D. H. and Campbell, A. Introduction to *The Vespasian Psalter*. Copenhagen: Rosenkilde & Begger, 1967.

The Year 1200. 1, *The Exhibition*. Edited by K. Hoffmann; 2, *A Background Survey*. Edited by F. Deuchler. New York: Metropolitan Museum, 1970.

Zimmerman, E. H. *Vorkarolingische Miniaturen*. 5 vols. Berlin: Deutschen Vereins für Kunstwissenschaft, 1916–18.

———. *Die Fuldaer Buchmalerei in karolingischer und ottonischer Zeit*. Kunstgeschichtliches Jahrbuch der K. K. Zentralkommission 4. Vienna, 1910.

Index